Switched Networks
Companion Guide

Cisco Networking Academy

Cisco Press

800 East 96th Street

Indianapolis, Indiana 46240 USA

Switched Networks Companion Guide

Published by:
Cisco Press
800 East 96th Street
Indianapolis, IN 46240 USA

Printed in the United States of America

First Printing May 2014

Library of Congress Control Number: 2014935305

ISBN-13: 978-1-58713-329-9

ISBN-10: 1-58713-329-6

Warning and Disclaimer

This book is part of the Cisco Networking Academy® series from Cisco Press. The products in this series support and complement the Cisco Networking Academy curriculum. If you are using this book outside the Networking Academy, then you are not preparing with a Cisco trained and authorized Networking Academy provider.

For more information on the Cisco Networking Academy or to locate a Networking Academy, Please visit www.cisco.com/edu.

ıı|ııı|ıı
CISCO.

Publisher
Paul Boger

Associate Publisher
Dave Dusthimer

Business Operation Manager, Cisco Press
Jan Cornelssen

Executive Editor
Mary Beth Ray

Managing Editor
Sandra Schroeder

Development Editor
Ellie C. Bru

Project Editor
Mandie Frank

Copy Editor
John Edwards

Technical Editor
Rick McDonald

Editorial Assistant
Vanessa Evans

Designer
Mark Shirar

Composition
Tricia Bronkella

Indexer
Ken Johnson

Proofreader
Debbie Williams

Trademark Acknowledgments

All terms mentioned in this book that are known to be trademarks or service marks have been appropriately capitalized. Cisco Press or Cisco Systems, Inc., cannot attest to the accuracy of this information. Use of a term in this book should not be regarded as affecting the validity of any trademark or service mark.

Special Sales

For information about buying this title in bulk quantities, or for special sales opportunities (which may include electronic versions; custom cover designs; and content particular to your business, training goals, marketing focus, or branding interests), please contact our corporate sales department at corpsales@pearsoned.com or (800) 382-3419.

For government sales inquiries, please contact governmentsales@pearsoned.com.

For questions about sales outside the U.S., please contact international@pearsoned.com.

Feedback Information

At Cisco Press, our goal is to create in-depth technical books of the highest quality and value. Each book is crafted with care and precision, undergoing rigorous development that involves the unique expertise of members from the professional technical community.

Readers' feedback is a natural continuation of this process. If you have any comments regarding how we could improve the quality of this book, or otherwise alter it to better suit your needs, you can contact us through email at feedback@ciscopress.com. Please make sure to include the book title and ISBN in your message.

We greatly appreciate your assistance.

About the Contributing Authors

Erich Spengler is the Director for the Center for System Security and Information Assurance, based at Moraine Valley CC. Erich is a Professor of Computer Integrated Technologies at Moraine Valley and has been teaching Cisco Academy courses for over 15 years. Erich is an ITQ-certified instructor for Cisco Academy. Erich is an active CISSP and has helped dozens of others earn the CISSP designation.

Erich has over 25 years of professional experience in IT systems and security. Erich's Center has trained over 1000 faculty since 2003 in VMware, CyberSecurity, Cisco, EMC, and Linux.

In his downtime, Erich enjoys spending time with his wife and two daughters.

Wayne Lewis wears three hats: Cisco Academy Manager for the Pacific Center for Advanced Technology Training, NetAcad Contact for the Central Pacific Academy Support and Instructor Training Center, and Professor at Honolulu Community College. Okay . . . four hats: Wayne teaches calculus, linear algebra, and differential equations at the University of Hawaii at Manoa.

Honolulu CC has been an instructor training center for Cisco Academy since 1998, and its instructors are responsible for training many of the initial cohorts of Cisco Academy instructors in countries throughout Asia, Europe, and the Americas. Wayne has been involved in curriculum development and assessment for Cisco Academy since 1999.

Wayne spends his free time doing math (representation theory, algebraic geometry, and several complex variables) and watching marathon sessions of TV series with his family (their favorites to rewatch are South Park, The Office, Monty Python, and Lost).

Dedications

From Erich:

To my wife, Kristi, and daughters, Emily and Lauren, for all your love and support . . . for always doing your best and making me the proudest husband and father in the world.

From Wayne:

To my wife, Leslie, and daughters, Christina and Lenora, for making it all worthwhile.

Contents at a Glance

Contents

Syntax Conventions

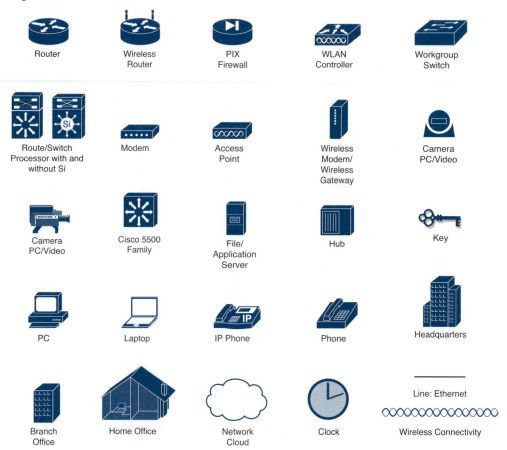

The conventions used to present command syntax in this book are the same conventions used in the IOS Command Reference. The Command Reference describes these conventions as follows:

- **Boldface** indicates commands and keywords that are entered literally as shown. In actual configuration examples and output (not general command syntax), boldface indicates commands that are manually input by the user (such as a **show** command).

- *Italics* indicate arguments for which you supply actual values.

- Vertical bars (|) separate alternative, mutually exclusive elements.

- Square brackets ([ ]) indicate an optional element.

- Braces ({ }) indicate a required choice.

- Braces within brackets ([{ }]) indicate a required choice within an optional element.

Introduction

Switched Networks Companion Guide is the official supplemental textbook for the Cisco Networking Academy Switched Networks course. Cisco Networking Academy is a comprehensive program that delivers information technology skills to students around the world. The curriculum emphasizes real-world practical application, while providing opportunities for you to gain the skills and hands-on experience needed to design, install, operate, and maintain networks in small- to medium-sized businesses, as well as enterprise and service provider environments.

As a textbook, this book provides a ready reference to explain the same networking concepts, technologies, protocols, and devices as the online curriculum. This book emphasizes key topics, terms, and activities and provides some alternate explanations and examples as compared with the course. You can use the online curriculum as directed by your instructor and then use this Companion Guide's study tools to help solidify your understanding of all the topics.

Who Should Read This Book

This book is intended for students enrolled in the Cisco Networking Academy Switched Networks course. The book, as well as the course, is designed as an introduction to data network technology for those pursuing careers as network professionals as well as for those who need only an introduction to network technology for professional growth. Topics are presented concisely, starting with the most fundamental concepts and progressing to a comprehensive understanding of network communication. The content of this text provides the foundation for additional Cisco Academy courses, and preparation for the CCNA Routing and Switching certifications.

Book Features

The educational features of this book focus on supporting topic coverage, readability, and practice of the course material to facilitate your full understanding of the course material.

Topic Coverage

The following features give you a thorough overview of the topics covered in each chapter so that you can make constructive use of your study time:

- **Objectives:** Listed at the beginning of each chapter, the objectives reference the core concepts covered in the chapter. The objectives match the objectives stated in the corresponding chapters of the online curriculum; however, the question format in the Companion Guide encourages you to think about finding the answers as you read the chapter.

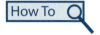

- **"How-to" feature:** When this book covers a set of steps that you need to perform for certain tasks, the text lists the steps as a how-to list. When you are studying, the icon helps you easily refer to this feature as you skim through the book.

- **Notes:** These are short sidebars that point out interesting facts, timesaving methods, and important safety issues.

- **Chapter summaries:** At the end of each chapter is a summary of the chapter's key concepts. It provides a synopsis of the chapter and serves as a study aid.

- **Practice:** At the end of chapter there is a full list of all the Labs, Class Activities, and Packet Tracer Activities to refer back to for study time.

Readability

The following features have been updated to assist your understanding of the networking vocabulary:

- **Key terms:** Each chapter begins with a list of key terms, along with a page-number reference from inside the chapter. The terms are listed in the order in which they are explained in the chapter. This handy reference allows you to find a term, flip to the page where the term appears, and see the term used in context. The Glossary defines all the key terms.

- **Glossary:** This book contains an all-new Glossary with more than 300 terms.

Practice

Practice makes perfect. This new Companion Guide offers you ample opportunities to put what you learn into practice. You will find the following features valuable and effective in reinforcing the instruction that you receive:

- **Check Your Understanding questions and answer key:** Updated review questions are presented at the end of each chapter as a self-assessment tool. These questions match the style of questions that you see in the online course. Appendix A, "Answers to 'Check Your Understanding' Questions," provides an answer key to all the questions and includes an explanation of each answer.

- **Labs and activities:** Throughout each chapter, you will be directed back to the online course to take advantage of the activities created to reinforce concepts. In addition, at the end of each chapter, there is a "Practice" section that collects a list of all the labs and activities to provide practice with the topics introduced in the chapter. The labs and class activities are available in the companion *Switched Networks Lab Manual* (ISBN 978-1-58713-3275). The Packet Tracer Activities PKA files are found in the online course.

- **Page references to online course:** After headings, you will see, for example, (1.1.2.3). This number refers to the page number in the online course so that you can easily jump to that spot online to view a video, practice an activity, perform a lab, or review a topic.

Lab Manual

The supplementary book *Switched Networks Lab Manual*, by Cisco Press (ISBN 978-1-58713-327-5), contains all the labs and class activities from the course.

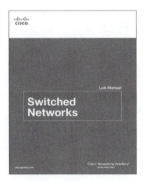

Practice and Study Guide

Additional Study Guide exercises, activities, and scenarios are available in *CCNA Routing and Switching Practice and Study Guide* (ISBN 978-158713-344-2), by Allan Johnson. The Practice and Study Guide coordinates with the recommended curriculum sequence. The CCNA edition follows the course outlines for *Scaling Networks* and *Connecting Networks*.

About Packet Tracer Software and Activities

Interspersed throughout the chapters you'll find many activities to work with the Cisco Packet Tracer tool. Packet Tracer allows you to create networks, visualize how packets flow in the network, and use basic testing tools to determine whether the network would work. When you see this icon, you can use Packet Tracer with the listed file to perform a task suggested in this book. The activity files are available in the course. Packet Tracer software is available only through the Cisco Networking Academy website. Ask your instructor for access to Packet Tracer.

How This Book Is Organized

This book corresponds closely to the Cisco Networking Academy Connecting Networks course and is divided into eight chapters, one appendix, and a glossary of key terms:

- Chapter 1, "Introduction to Switched Networks": The role of switched networks in computer networking is examined. LAN design principles are introduced, emphasizing converged networks and features that differentiate switches. Frame-forwarding methods, MAC address table theory, and types of switching domains are explored.

- Chapter 2, "Basic Switching Concepts and Configuration": Navigating configuration modes on Cisco switches and performing switch system administration are explored. Port configuration and basic switch security options are introduced.

- Chapter 3, "VLANs": VLANs differentiate switches from other networking devices. The various types of VLANs are defined. VLAN trunking theory and configuration are carefully introduced. Security solutions specific to VLANs are explored.

- Chapter 4, "LAN Redundancy": Examines the benefits and implementations of Spanning Tree Protocols and First Hop Redundancy Protocols.

- Chapter 5, "Link Aggregation": Describes the characteristics, benefits, and implementations of EtherChannel, with PAgP and LACP.

- Chapter 6, "Inter-VLAN Routing": Introduces the three major types of inter-VLAN routing: legacy, router-on-a-stick, and multilayer switching. Some new features of Cisco Layer 2 switches related to Layer 3 behavior are explored.

- Chapter 7, "DHCP": Describes DHCPv4 and DHCPv6 in great detail. The DHCPv6 content is new to CCNA.

- **Chapter 8, "Wireless LANs":** This chapter goes into considerable detail introducing and analyzing wireless LAN solutions. Topics include wireless LAN operation, wireless LAN security, and wireless LAN configuration.

- **Appendix A, "Answers to 'Check Your Understanding' Questions":** This appendix lists the answers to the "Check Your Understanding" review questions that are included at the end of each chapter.

- **Glossary:** The glossary provides you with definitions for all the key terms identified in each chapter.

CHAPTER 1

Introduction to Switched Networks

Objectives

Upon completion of this chapter, you will be able to answer the following questions:

- How do you describe the convergence of data, voice, and video in the context of switched networks?

- How do you describe a switched network in a small- to medium-sized business?

- How do you explain the process of frame forwarding in a switched network?

- How do you compare a collision domain to a broadcast domain?

Key Terms

This chapter uses the following key terms. You can find the definitions in the Glossary.

Introduction (1.0.1.1)

Modern networks continue to evolve to keep pace with the changing way that organizations carry out their daily business. Users now expect instant access to company resources from anywhere and at any time. These resources not only include traditional data but also video and voice. There is also an increasing need for collaboration technologies that allow real-time sharing of resources between multiple remote individuals as though they were at the same physical location.

Different devices must seamlessly work together to provide a fast, secure, and reliable connection between hosts. LAN switches provide the connection point for end users into the enterprise network and are also primarily responsible for the control of information within the LAN environment. Routers facilitate the movement of information between LANs and are generally unaware of individual hosts. All advanced services depend on the availability of a robust routing and switching infrastructure on which they can build. This infrastructure must be carefully designed, deployed, and managed to provide a necessary stable platform.

This chapter begins an examination of the flow of traffic in a modern network. It examines some of the current network design models and the way that LAN switches build forwarding tables and use the MAC address information to efficiently switch data between hosts.

Class Activity 1.0.1.2: Sent or Received Instructions

Individually, or in groups (per the instructor's decision), discuss various ways that hosts send and receive data, voice, and streaming video.

Develop a matrix (table) listing network data types that can be sent and received. Provide five examples.

Note

For an example of the matrix, see the document prepared for this modeling activity.

Save your work in either hard- or soft-copy format. Be prepared to discuss your matrix and statements in a class discussion.

LAN Design (1.1)

In this section, you will explore the design of local-area networks. The Cisco Borderless Network architecture for delivery of services and applications provides a setting for the exploration of switched network design. And you will learn how the fundamental core-distribution-access model applies to switched networks.

Converged Networks (1.1.1)

Converged networks were cutting edge ten years ago, but now they are standard fare for switched environments. The integration of voice, video, and data on a switched infrastructure provides a seamless experience for users. IP phones and video devices are fully integrated into the data network.

Growing Complexity of Networks (1.1.1.1)

Our digital world is changing. The ability to access the Internet and the corporate network is no longer confined to physical offices, geographical locations, or time zones. In today's globalized workplace, employees can access resources from anywhere in the world, and information must be available at any time and on any device. These requirements drive the need to build next-generation networks that are secure, reliable, and highly available.

Data networks originally served the purpose of transporting data between workstations and servers. As networks became more reliable, voice and video traffic was integrated with data traffic, creating a converged network. A converged network is one where data, voice, and video are integrated. Next-generation converged networks must not only support current expectations and equipment but must also be able to integrate legacy platforms.

Legacy Equipment

Legacy equipment can hinder convergence. Figure 1-1 illustrates legacy telephone equipment. A business site can contain equipment that supports both legacy PBX telephone systems and IP-based phones. This sort of equipment is rapidly migrating toward IP-based phone switches.

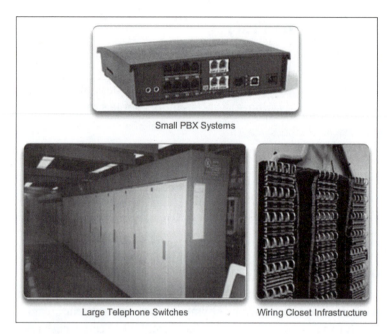

Figure 1-1 Legacy Components

Advanced Technology

Although converged networks have existed for some time now, they were initially only feasible in large enterprise organizations because of the network infrastructure and complex management requirements. There were high network costs associated with convergence because more expensive switch hardware was required to support the additional bandwidth. Converged networks also required extensive management in relation to QoS, because voice and video data traffic needed to be classified and prioritized on the network. Few individuals had the expertise in voice, video, and data networks to make convergence feasible and functional.

Over time, convergence has become easier to implement and manage, and less expensive to purchase. Figure 1-2 illustrates some of the newer platforms for converged networks that help to provide access to the network anytime, anywhere, and on any device.

Unified Communication - Media
Convergence Server

Cisco Catalyst 2960 LAN Switches

Cisco Unified IP Phones

Figure 1-2   Converged Network Components

Elements of a Converged Network (1.1.1.2)

To support collaboration, business networks employ converged solutions using voice systems, IP phones, voice gateways, video support, and videoconferencing, as illustrated in Figure 1-3.

Figure 1-3   Many Types of Traffic on One Network

Including data services, a converged network with collaboration support can include features such as the following:

- *Call control*: Telephone call processing, caller ID, call transfer, hold, and conference

- *Voice messaging*: Voicemail

- *Mobility*: Receive important calls wherever you are

- *Automated attendant*: Serve customers faster by routing calls directly to the right department or individual

One of the primary benefits of transitioning to the converged network is that there is just one physical network to install and manage. This results in substantial savings over the installation and management of separate voice, video, and data networks. Such a converged network solution integrates IT management so that any moves, additions, and changes are completed with an intuitive management interface. A converged network solution also provides PC softphone application support, as well as point-to-point video, so that users can enjoy personal communications with the same ease of administration and use as a voice call.

The convergence of services onto the network has resulted in an evolution in networks from a traditional data transport role to a superhighway for data, voice, and video communication. This one physical network must be properly designed and implemented to allow the reliable handling of the various types of information that it must carry. A structured design is required to allow management of this complex environment.

Video

Video 1.1.1.2: Observing Spanning Tree Protocol Operation

Go to the online course and play the video in the second graphic to view a few of the collaboration services in action.

Cisco Borderless Network (1.1.1.3)

With the increasing demands of the converged network, the network must be developed with an architectural approach that embeds intelligence, simplifies operations, and is scalable to meet future demands. One of the more recent developments in network design is the *Cisco Borderless Network*.

The Cisco Borderless Network is a network architecture combining innovation and design that allows organizations to support a borderless network that can connect anyone, anywhere, anytime, on any device—securely, reliably, and seamlessly. This architecture is designed to address IT and business challenges, such as supporting the converged network and changing work patterns.

The Cisco Borderless Network provides the framework to unify wired and wireless access, including policy, access control, and performance management across many different device types. Using this architecture, the borderless network is built on a hierarchical infrastructure of hardware that is scalable and resilient, as shown in Figure 1-4. By combining this hardware infrastructure with policy-based software solutions, the Cisco Borderless Network provides two primary sets of services: network services and user and endpoint services, all managed by an integrated management solution. It enables different network elements to work together and allows users to access resources from any place at any time, while providing optimization, scalability, and security.

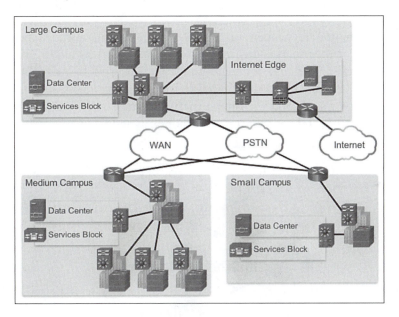

Figure 1-4   Cisco Borderless Network

Video 1.1.1.3: Observing Spanning Tree Protocol Operation

Go to the online course and play the video in the second graphic to learn more about the evolution of the borderless network.

Hierarchy in the Borderless Switched Network (1.1.1.4)

Creating a borderless switched network requires that sound network design principles are used to ensure maximum availability, flexibility, security, and manageability. The borderless switched network must deliver on current requirements and future required services and technologies. Borderless switched network design guidelines are built upon the following principles:

- *Hierarchical*: Facilitates understanding the role of each device at every tier; simplifies deployment, operation, and management; and reduces fault domains at every tier

- *Modularity*: Allows seamless network expansion and integrated service enablement on an on-demand basis

- *Resiliency*: Satisfies user expectations for keeping the network always on

- *Flexibility*: Allows intelligent traffic load sharing by using all network resources

These are not independent principles. Understanding how each principle fits in the context of the others is critical. Designing a borderless switched network in a hierarchical fashion creates a foundation that allows network designers to overlay security, mobility, and unified communication features. Two time-tested and proven hierarchical design frameworks for campus networks are the three-tier layer model, as shown in Figure 1-5, and the two-tier layer model, as shown in Figure 1-6.

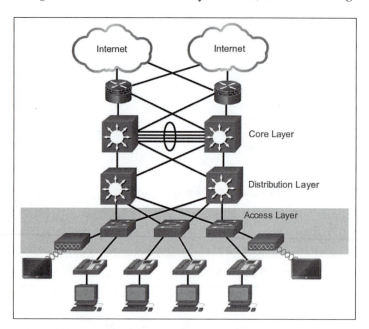

Figure 1-5   Access Layer

The three critical layers within these tiered designs are the *access*, *distribution*, and *core* layers. Each layer can be seen as a well-defined, structured module with specific roles and functions in the campus network. Introducing modularity into the campus hierarchical design further ensures that the campus network remains resilient and flexible enough to provide critical network services. Modularity also helps to allow for growth and changes that occur over time.

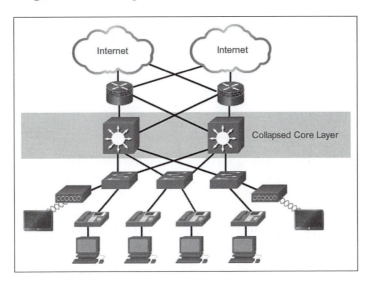

Figure 1-6   Collapsed Core

Access, Distribution, and Core Layers (1.1.1.5)

The access-distribution-core hierarchical network model is the most referenced network model in computer networking. It is simple, but it carries the rudimentary information necessary to convey networking concepts in context.

Access Layer

The access layer represents the network edge, where traffic enters or exits the campus network. Traditionally, the primary function of an access layer switch is to provide network access to the user. Access layer switches connect to distribution layer switches, which implement network foundation technologies such as routing, quality of service, and security.

To meet network application and end-user demand, the next-generation switching platforms now provide more converged, integrated, and intelligent services to various types of endpoints at the network edge. Building intelligence into access layer switches allows applications to operate on the network more efficiently and securely.

Distribution Layer

The distribution layer interfaces between the access layer and the core layer to provide many important functions, including

- Aggregating large-scale wiring closet networks

- Aggregating Layer 2 broadcast domains and Layer 3 routing boundaries

- Providing intelligent switching, routing, and network access policy functions to access the rest of the network

- Providing high availability through redundant distribution layer switches to the end user and equal-cost paths to the core

- Providing differentiated services to various classes of service applications at the edge of the network

Core Layer

The core layer is the network backbone. It connects several layers of the campus network. The core layer serves as the aggregator for all the other campus blocks and ties the campus together with the rest of the network. The primary purpose of the core layer is to provide fault isolation and high-speed backbone connectivity.

Figure 1-7 shows a three-tier campus network design for organizations where the access, distribution, and core are each separate layers. To build a simplified, scalable, cost-effective, and efficient physical cable layout design, the recommendation is to build an extended-star physical network topology from a centralized building location to all other buildings on the same campus.

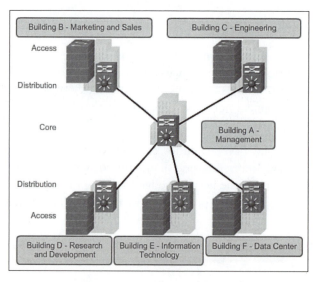

Figure 1-7   Three-Tier Campus Network Design

In some cases where extensive physical or network scalability does not exist, maintaining separate distribution and core layers is not required. In smaller campus locations where there are fewer users accessing the network or in campus sites consisting of a single building, separate core and distribution layers might not be needed. In this scenario, the recommendation is the alternate two-tier campus network design, also known as the collapsed core network design.

Figure 1-8 shows a two-tier campus network design example for an enterprise campus where the distribution and core layers are collapsed into a single layer.

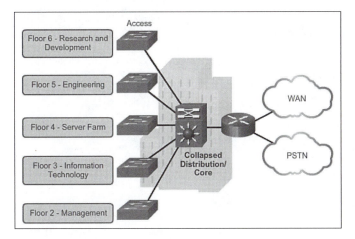

Figure 1-8   Two-Tier Campus Network Design

Activity 1.1.1.6: Identify Switched Network Terminology

Go to the online course to perform this practice activity.

Switched Networks (1.1.2)

In this topic, you will learn about the various types of switches and their *form factors*. A discussion of multilayer switching will put in context our exploration of access layer switches, which are the focus of this course.

Role of Switched Networks (1.1.2.1)

The role of switched networks has evolved dramatically in the last two decades. It was not long ago that flat Layer 2 switched networks were the norm. Flat Layer 2 data networks relied on the basic properties of Ethernet and the widespread use of hub repeaters to propagate LAN traffic throughout an organization. As shown in Figure 1-9, networks have fundamentally changed to switched LANs in a hierarchical network.

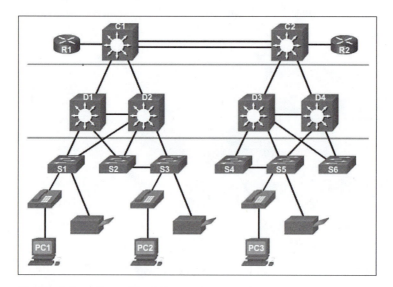

Figure 1-9   Hierarchical Networks

A switched LAN allows more flexibility, traffic management, and additional features, such as

- Quality of service
- Additional security
- Support for wireless networking and connectivity
- Support for new technologies, such as IP telephony and mobility services
- Layer 3 functionality

Figure 1-10 shows the hierarchical design used in the borderless switched network.

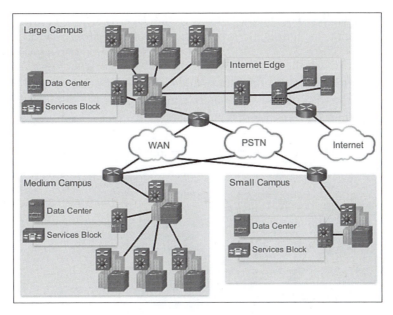

Figure 1-10   Borderless Switched Network

Form Factors (1.1.2.2)

There are various types of switches used in business networks. It is important to deploy the appropriate types of switches based on network requirements. Here are some common business considerations when selecting switch equipment:

- **Cost:** The cost of a switch will depend on the number and speed of the interfaces, supported features, and expansion capability.

- **Port Density:** Network switches must support the appropriate number of devices on the network.

- **Power:** It is now common to power access points, IP phones, and even compact switches using Power over Ethernet (PoE). In addition to PoE considerations, some chassis-based switches support redundant power supplies. PoE will be explored in Section 1.1.3.3.

- **Reliability:** The switch should provide continuous access to the network.

- **Port Speed:** The speed of the network connection is of primary concern to end users.

- **Frame Buffers:** The ability of the switch to store frames is important in a network where there might be congested ports to servers or other areas of the network.

■ **Scalability:** The number of users on a network typically grows over time; therefore, the switch should provide the opportunity for growth.

When selecting the type of switch, the network designer must choose between a fixed or a modular configuration, and stackable or nonstackable. Another consideration is the thickness of the switch, which is expressed in number of rack units. This is important for switches that are mounted in a rack. For example, the *fixed configuration switches* shown in Figure 1-11 are all 1 rack unit (1U). These options are sometimes referred to as switch form factors.

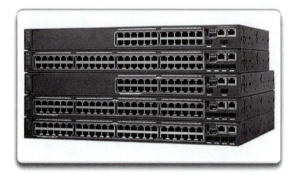

Figure 1-11   Fixed Configuration Switches

Fixed Configuration Switches

Fixed configuration switches do not support features or options beyond those that originally came with the switch. The particular model determines the features and options available; features and options are limited to those that originally come with the switch. For example, a 24-port gigabit fixed switch cannot support additional ports. There are typically different configuration choices that vary in how many and what types of ports are included with a fixed configuration switch.

Modular Configuration Switches

Modular configuration switches offer more flexibility in their configuration. Modular configuration switches typically come with different-sized chassis that allow for the installation of different numbers of modular line cards, as shown in Figure 1-12. The line cards actually contain the ports. The line card fits into the switch chassis the way that expansion cards fit into a PC. The larger the chassis, the more modules it can support. There can be many different chassis sizes to choose from. A modular switch with a single 24-port line card could have an additional 24-port line card added to bring the total number of ports up to 48.

Figure 1-12   Modular Switches

Stackable Configuration Switches

Stackable configuration switches can be interconnected using a special cable that provides high-bandwidth throughput between the switches, as shown in Figure 1-13. Cisco StackWise technology allows the interconnection of up to nine switches. Switches can be stacked one on top of the other with cables connecting the switches in a daisy-chain fashion. The stacked switches effectively operate as a single larger switch. Stackable switches are desirable where fault tolerance and bandwidth avail-ability are critical and a modular switch is too costly to implement. Using cross-con-nected connections, the network can recover quickly if a single switch fails. Stackable switches use a special port for interconnections. Many Cisco stackable switches also support StackPower technology, which enables power sharing among stack members.

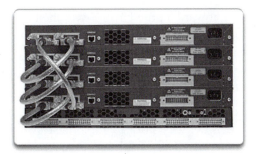

Figure 1-13   Stackable Switches

Traffic Flow (1.1.2.3)

To select the appropriate switch for a network, you need to have specifications that detail the target traffic flows. Companies need a network that can meet evolving requirements. A business might start with a few PCs interconnected so that they can share data. As the business adds more employees, devices—such as PCs, printers, and servers—are added to the network. Accompanying the new devices is an increase in network traffic. Some companies also rely on converged VoIP phone systems, which add more traffic.

To select the appropriate switches, it is important to perform and record traffic flow analyses regularly. *Traffic flow analysis* is the process of measuring the bandwidth usage on a network and then analyzing the data for performance tuning, capacity planning, and making hardware improvement decisions. Analyzing the various traffic sources and their impact on the network allows you to more accurately tune and upgrade the network to achieve the best possible performance.

There are many ways to monitor traffic flow on a network. Individual switch ports can be manually monitored to record bandwidth utilization over time. Traffic flow analysis tools can automatically record traffic flow data in a database and perform an associated trend analysis. While the software is collecting data, you can see how every interface is performing at any given point in time on the network. This gives the network administrator a visual means of identifying traffic flow patterns.

Multilayer Switching (1.1.2.4)

Multilayer switches are typically deployed in the core and distribution layers of an organization's switched network. Multilayer switches are characterized by their ability to build a routing table, support a few routing protocols, and forward IP packets at a rate close to that of Layer 2 forwarding. Multilayer switches often support specialized hardware, such as application-specific integrated circuits (ASIC). ASICs, along with dedicated software data structures, can streamline the forwarding of IP packets independent of the CPU.

There is a trend in networking toward a pure Layer 3 switched environment. When switches were first used in networks, none of them supported routing; now, almost all switches support routing. It is likely that soon all switches will incorporate a route processor because the cost of doing so is decreasing relative to other constraints. Eventually the term *multilayer switch* will be redundant.

The Catalyst 2960 switches shown in Figure 1-14 illustrate the migration to a pure Layer 3 environment. With IOS Releases prior to 15.x, these switches supported only one active switched virtual interface (SVI). With IOS Release 15.x, these switches now support multiple active SVIs, as well as support for static routes! This means that the switch can be remotely accessed through multiple IP addresses on distinct networks.

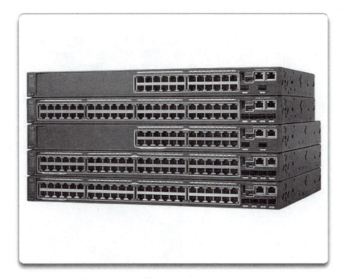

Figure 1-14   Cisco Catalyst 2960 Series Switches

Packet Tracer Activity 1.1.2.5: Comparing 2960 and 3560 Switches

In this activity, you will use various commands to examine three different switching topologies and compare the similarities and differences between the 2960 and 3560 switches. You will also compare the routing table of a 1941 router with a 3560 switch.

Switch Features (1.1.3)

Relative to routers, the features associated with a switch or a product line of switches vary dramatically. It is important for a switch administrator to understand the features available so that well-informed switch-purchasing decisions are made for an organization.

Port Density (1.1.3.1)

The *port density* of a switch refers to the number of ports available on a single switch. Figure 1-15 shows the port density of three different switches.

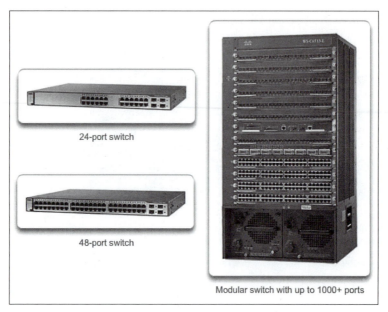

24-port switch

48-port switch

Modular switch with up to 1000+ ports

Figure 1-15   Port Densities

Fixed configuration switches typically support up to 48 ports on a single device. They have options for up to four additional ports for *small form-factor pluggable (SFP)* devices. High port densities allow for better use of limited space and power. If there are two switches that each contain 24 ports, they would be able to support up to 46 devices, because at least one port per switch is lost with the connection of each switch to the rest of the network. In addition, two power outlets are required. Alternatively, if there is a single 48-port switch, 47 devices can be supported, with only one port used to connect the switch to the rest of the network and only one power outlet needed to accommodate the single switch.

Modular switches can support very high port densities through the addition of multiple switch port line cards. For example, some Catalyst 6500 switches can support in excess of 1000 switch ports.

Large enterprise networks that support many thousands of network devices require high-density, modular switches to make the best use of space and power. Without using a high-density modular switch, the network would need many fixed configuration switches to accommodate the number of devices that need network access. This approach can consume many power outlets and a lot of closet space.

The network designer must also consider the issue of uplink bottlenecks. For example, to achieve target performance, a series of fixed configuration switches might require many ports for bandwidth aggregation between switches. With a single modular switch, bandwidth aggregation is less of an issue, because the backplane of the chassis can provide the necessary bandwidth to accommodate the devices connected to the switch port line cards.

Forwarding Rates (1.1.3.2)

Forwarding rates define the processing capabilities of a switch by rating how much data the switch can process per second. Switch product lines are classified by forwarding rates, as shown in Figure 1-16. Entry-level switches have lower forwarding rates than enterprise-level switches. Forwarding rates are important to consider when selecting a switch. If the switch forwarding rate is too low, it cannot accommodate full wire-speed communication across all of its switch ports. Wire speed is the data rate that each Ethernet port on the switch is capable of attaining. Data rates can be 100 Mb/s, 1 Gb/s, 10 Gb/s, or 100 Gb/s.

For example, a typical 48-port Gigabit Ethernet switch operating at full wire speed generates 48 Gb/s of traffic. If the switch only supports a forwarding rate of 32 Gb/s, it cannot run at full wire speed across all ports simultaneously. Fortunately, access layer switches typically do not need to operate at full wire speed, because they are physically limited by their uplinks to the distribution layer. This means that less expensive, lower-performing switches can be used at the access layer, and more expensive, higher-performing switches can be used at the distribution and core layers, where the forwarding rate has a greater impact on network performance.

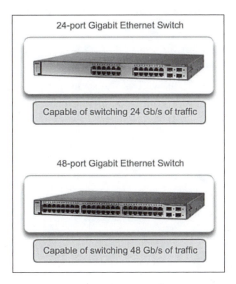

Figure 1-16   Forwarding Rate

Power over Ethernet (1.1.3.3)

Power over Ethernet (PoE) allows the switch to deliver power to a device over the existing Ethernet cabling. This feature can be used by IP phones and some wireless access points. The highlighted devices in Figure 1-17 have PoE ports.

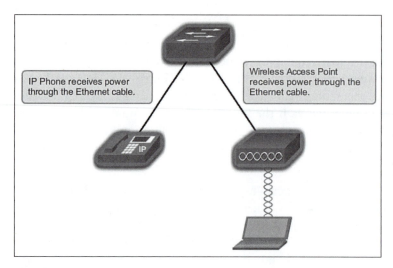

Figure 1-17 Power over Ethernet

PoE allows more flexibility when installing wireless access points and IP phones, allowing them to be installed anywhere that there is an Ethernet cable. A network administrator should ensure that the PoE features are required, because switches that support PoE are expensive.

The relatively new Cisco Catalyst 2960-C and 3560-C Series compact switches support PoE pass-through. PoE pass-through allows a network administrator to power PoE devices connected to the switch, as well as the switch itself, by drawing power from certain upstream switches. The highlighted switch in Figure 1-18 represents a Cisco Catalyst 2960-C.

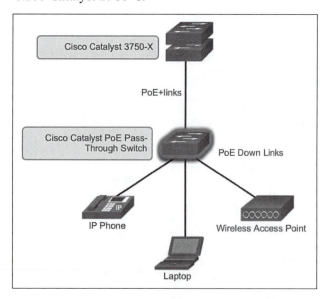

Figure 1-18 PoE Pass-Through

Cisco Catalyst Switch Breakdown (1.1.3.4)

While switches can be categorized in various ways, Cisco Catalyst switches are usually described in terms of the core-distribution-access hierarchy, as shown in Figure 1-19. The core and distribution layers often include the same types of switches, depending on the size of the network. Similarly, the distribution and access layers often include the same types of switches.

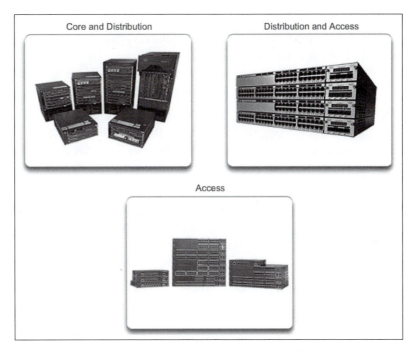

Figure 1-19   Switches in the Hierarchical Design Model

In general, the core and distribution layers incorporate four types of switches:

- **Cisco Catalyst 6500 Series Switches:** These switches scale to 4-terabit capacity with the Virtual Switching System, with up to 160 gigabits per slot; the switches are 100 Gigabit Ethernet ready, and support enhanced security, manageability, and wireless control.

- **Cisco Catalyst 4500E Series Switches:** These switches support modularity, offering 1.6-terabits-per-second capacity with the Virtual Switching System; these switches offer high availability bolstered by Control Plane Policing (CPP), and are ideal for collapsed distribution-access and small- to medium-distribution deployments.

- **Cisco Catalyst 4500-X Series Switches:** These switches are fixed aggregation switches for space-constrained environments, in a 1 RU form factor, and operate at 1.6-terabits-per-second capacity.

■ **Cisco Catalyst 3750-X Series Switches:** These switches are stackable fixed-configuration switches for smaller, restrictive deployments, with advanced Layer 3 and Layer 2 switching and security services, and support for Gigabit and 10 Gigabit Ethernet aggregation, including comprehensive support for Borderless Networks services.

The distribution and access layers typically incorporate the following types of switches:

■ **Cisco Catalyst 4500E Series Switches:** These switches come with high capacity (848 gigabits) and density (240 full Power Over Ethernet Plus ports), with 60 Watt Universal Power Over Ethernet to power a large range of devices, and high availability with Stateful Switchover (SSO).

■ **Cisco Catalyst 3750-X Series Switches:** These switches are stackable fixed-configuration switches, with StackWise Plus and StackPower for high availability and operational efficiency, service and network modules for service upgrades, and full Power Over Ethernet Plus and comprehensive Borderless Networks services.

■ **Cisco Catalyst 3560-X Series Switches:** These switches are fixed-configuration switches for campus and branch deployments, with high-availability and advanced security features, service and network modules for service upgrades, and full Power Over Ethernet Plus and comprehensive Borderless Networks services.

■ **Cisco Catalyst 3560 and 3560-C Series Compact Switches:** These are sleek, quiet switches that deliver comprehensive access services outside the wiring closet and support for Power Over Ethernet Plus, Cisco EnergyWise, and advanced QoS, as well as providing a unique PoE pass-through capability that eliminates the need for power outlets.

The access layer normally incorporates the following types of switches:

■ **Cisco Catalyst 2960 Series Switches:** These are stackable fixed-configuration Layer 2 switches that are a cost-effective solution for mid-sized organizations and branch offices, and provide full Power Over Ethernet Plus and baseline Borderless Networks services.

■ **Cisco Catalyst 2960 and 2960-C Series Compact Switches:** These are sleek, quiet switches that deliver baseline access services outside the wiring closet, with support for Power Over Ethernet Plus, Cisco EnergyWise, and advanced QoS, and provide unique PoE pass-through capability that eliminates the need for power outlets.

With such a wide selection of switches to choose from in the Catalyst product line, an organization can carefully determine the ideal combination to meet the needs of the employees and the customers.

Activity 1.1.3.5: Identify Switch Hardware

Go to the online course to perform this practice activity.

Lab 1.1.3.6: Selecting Switch Hardware

In this lab, you will complete the following objectives:

- Part 1: Explore Cisco Switch Products
- Part 2: Select an Access Layer Switch
- Part 3: Select a Distribution/Core Layer Switch

The Switched Environment (1.2)

In this section you learn about *frame forwarding* of LAN switches and the role of broadcast domains and collision domains in a switched environment.

Frame Forwarding (1.2.1)

Computer networking is enabled by switching. Often people make the mistake of thinking that switching is specific to LANs. In reality, switching is a generic concept that applies to any networking device with interfaces on it. Switching in a generic sense refers only to the use of some sort of table to instruct a networking device what port to use to send out a packet based on the port in which the packet entered, coupled with specific information embedded in the packet. It really is up to your imagination what a generic switch might use to switch packets; it comes down to the set of rules used to build the table.

Switching as a General Concept in Networking and Telecommunications (1.2.1.1)

The concept of switching and forwarding frames is universal in networking and telecommunications. Various types of switches are used in LANs, WANs, and the public switched telephone network (PSTN). The fundamental concept of switching refers to a device making a decision based on two criteria:

- *Ingress port*

- Some sort of address embedded in the frames or packets processed by the device

The decision on how a switch forwards traffic is made in relation to the flow of that traffic. The term *ingress* is used to describe where a frame enters the device on a port. The term *egress* is used to describe frames leaving the device from a particular port.

When a LAN switch makes a decision, it is based on the ingress port and the destination address of the message.

A LAN switch maintains a table that it uses to determine how to forward traffic through the switch. In Table 1-1, you see the information that a generic LAN switch might use to forward Ethernet frames.

Table 1-1   Generic LAN Switch

Port Table

Destination Address	Port
EE	1
AA	2
BA	3
EA	4
AC	5
AB	6

With Table 1-1, the following conclusions can be made:

- If a message enters port 1 and has a destination address of EA, the switch forwards the traffic out port 4.

- If a message enters port 5 and has a destination address of EE, the switch forwards the traffic out port 1.

- If a message enters port 3 and has a destination address of AB, the switch forwards the traffic out port 6.

The only intelligence of the LAN switch is its ability to use its table to forward traffic based on the ingress port and the destination address of a message. With a LAN switch, there is only one master switching table that describes a strict association between addresses and ports; therefore, a message with a given destination address always exits the same *egress port*, regardless of the ingress port it enters.

Cisco LAN switches forward Ethernet frames based on the destination MAC address of the frames.

Dynamically Populating a Switch MAC Address Table (1.2.1.2)

Switches use MAC addresses to direct network communications through the switch to the appropriate port toward the destination. A switch is made up of integrated circuits and the accompanying software that controls the data paths through the switch. For a switch to know which port to use to transmit a frame, it must first learn which devices exist on each port. As the switch learns the relationship of ports to devices, it builds a table called a MAC address or content addressable memory (CAM) table. CAM is a special type of memory used in high-speed searching applications.

LAN switches determine how to handle incoming data frames by maintaining the *MAC address table*. A switch builds its MAC address table by recording the MAC address of each device connected to each of its ports. The switch uses the information in the MAC address table to send frames destined for a specific device out the port that has been assigned to that device.

A switch populates the MAC address table based on source MAC addresses. When a switch receives an incoming frame with a destination MAC address that is not found in the MAC address table, the switch forwards the frame out of all ports (flooding) except for the ingress port of the frame. When the destination device responds, the switch adds the source MAC address of the frame and the port where the frame was received to the MAC address table. In networks with multiple interconnected switches, the MAC address table contains multiple MAC addresses for a single port connected to the other switches.

The following steps describe the process of building the MAC address table:

1. The switch receives a frame from PC 1 on Port 1 in Figure 1-20.

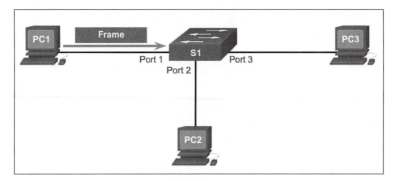

Figure 1-20   Receipt of a Frame

2. The switch examines the source MAC address and compares it to the MAC address table.

   ▪ If the address is not in the MAC address table, it associates the source MAC address of PC 1 with the ingress port (Port 1) in the MAC address table, as shown in Figure 1-21.

   ▪ If the MAC address table already has an entry for that source address, it resets the aging timer. An entry for a MAC address is typically kept for five minutes.

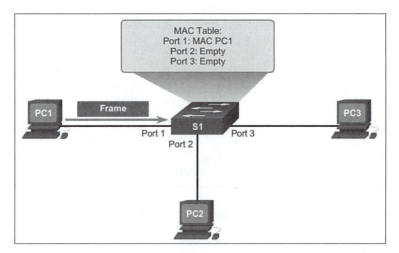

Figure 1-21   Parse Source MAC Address Against MAC Address Table

3. After the switch has recorded the source address information, the switch examines the destination MAC address.

   ▪ If the destination address is not in the MAC table or if it's a broadcast MAC address, as indicated by all Fs, the switch floods the frame to all ports except the ingress port, as shown in Figure 1-22.

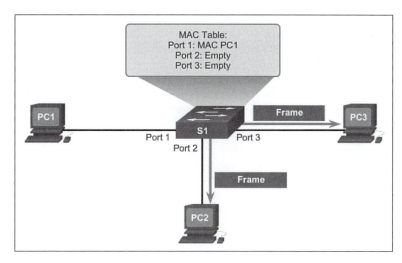

Figure 1-22   Switch Forwards Frame Out All Ports If Destination Is Not in MAC Address Table

4. The destination device (PC 3) replies to the frame with a unicast frame addressed to PC 1, as shown in Figure 1-23.

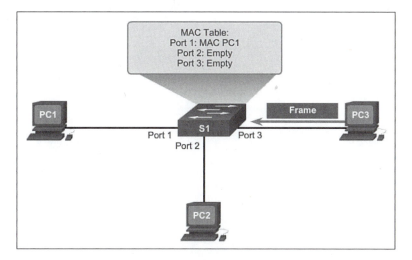

Figure 1-23   Frame Recipient Replies with Unicast Frame

5. The switch enters the source MAC address of PC 3 and the port number of the ingress port into the address table. The destination address of the frame and its associated egress port are found in the MAC address table, as shown in Figure 1-24.

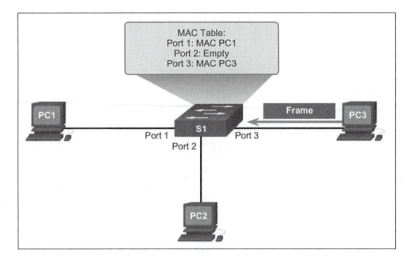

Figure 1-24   Switch Populates MAC Address Table with New Source MAC Address

6. The switch can now forward frames between these source and destination devices without flooding, because it has entries in the address table that identify the associated ports, as shown in Figure 1-25.

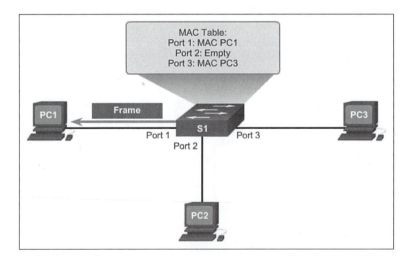

Figure 1-25   Switch Forwards Frame Out All Ports Associated with Original Sender

Switch Forwarding Methods (1.2.1.3)

As networks grew and enterprises began to experience slower network performance, Ethernet bridges (early versions of a switch) were added to networks to limit the size of the collision domains. In the 1990s, advancements in integrated circuit technologies allowed LAN switches to replace Ethernet bridges. These LAN switches were able to move the Layer 2 forwarding decisions from software to application-specific integrated circuits (ASIC). ASICs reduce the packet-handling time within the device and allow the device to handle an increased number of ports without degrading performance. This method of forwarding data frames at Layer 2 was referred to as *store-and-forward switching*. This term distinguished it from *cut-through switching*. These switching methods are explored in this section.

The store-and-forward method makes a forwarding decision on a frame after it has received the entire frame and checked the frame for errors using a mathematical error-checking mechanism known as a cyclic redundancy check (CRC). The CRC was invented by Wesley Peterson at IBM in 1961.

By contrast, the cut-through frame forwarding method begins the forwarding process after the destination MAC address of an incoming frame and the egress port have been determined.

Store-and-Forward Switching (1.2.1.4)

Store-and-forward switching has two primary characteristics that distinguish it from cut-through: error checking and automatic buffering.

Error Checking

A switch using store-and-forward switching performs an error check on an incoming frame. After receiving the entire frame on the ingress port, as shown in Figure 1-26, the switch compares the frame check sequence (FCS) value in the last field of the datagram against its own FCS calculations. The FCS is an error-checking process that helps to ensure that the frame is free of physical and data-link errors. If the frame is error-free, the switch forwards the frame. Otherwise, the frame is dropped.

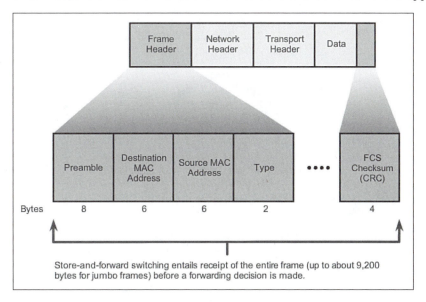

Figure 1-26 Store-and-Forward Switching

Automatic Buffering

The ingress port buffering process used by store-and-forward switches provides the flexibility to support any mix of Ethernet speeds. For example, handling an incoming frame traveling into a 100-Mb/s Ethernet port that must be sent out a 1-Gb/s interface would require using the store-and-forward method. With any mismatch in speeds between the ingress and egress ports, the switch stores the entire frame in a buffer, computes the FCS check, forwards it to the egress port buffer, and then sends it.

A store-and-forward switch drops frames that do not pass the FCS check and therefore does not forward invalid frames. By contrast, a cut-through switch can forward invalid frames because no FCS check is performed.

Cut-Through Switching (1.2.1.5)

An advantage to cut-through switching is the ability of the switch to start forwarding a frame earlier than store-and-forward switching. There are two primary characteristics of cut-through switching: rapid frame forwarding and fragment free.

Rapid Frame Forwarding

As indicated in Figure 1-27, a switch using the cut-through method can make a forwarding decision as soon as it has looked up the destination MAC address of the frame in its MAC address table. The switch does not have to wait for the rest of the frame to enter the ingress port before making its forwarding decision.

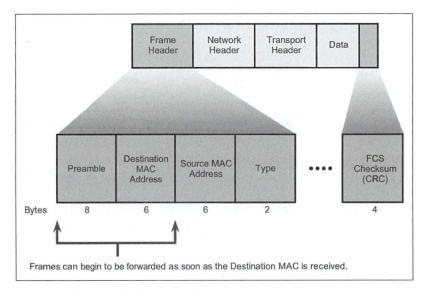

Figure 1-27   Cut-Through Switching

With today's MAC controllers and ASICs, a switch using the cut-through method can quickly decide whether it needs to examine a larger portion of a frame's headers for additional filtering purposes. For example, the switch can analyze past the first 14 bytes (the source MAC address, the destination MAC address, and the EtherType fields) and examine an additional 40 bytes to perform more sophisticated functions relative to IPv4 Layers 3 and 4.

The cut-through switching method does not drop most invalid frames. Frames with errors are forwarded to other segments of the network. If there is a high error rate (invalid frames) in the network, cut-through switching can have a negative impact on bandwidth, thus clogging bandwidth with damaged and invalid frames.

Fragment Free

Fragment free switching is a modified form of cut-through switching in which the switch waits for the collision window (64 bytes) to pass before forwarding the frame. This means that each frame will be checked into the data field to make sure that no fragmentation has occurred. Fragment free mode provides better error checking than cut-through, with practically no increase in latency.

The lower latency speed of cut-through switching makes it more appropriate for extremely demanding, high-performance computing (HPC) applications that require process-to-process latencies of 10 microseconds or less.

Interactive Graphic

Activity 1.2.1.6: Frame Forwarding Methods

Go to the online course to perform this practice activity.

Interactive Graphic

Activity 1.2.1.7: Switch It!

Go to the online course to perform this practice activity.

Switching Domains (1.2.2)

Access switches determine collision domains. Routers and multilayer switches determine broadcast domains. However, VLANs coincide with broadcast domains in a switched environment, so access switches also contribute to the determination of broadcast domains. In this topic, you will explore the relationship between collision domains and broadcast domains.

Collision Domains (1.2.2.1)

In hub-based Ethernet segments, network devices compete for the medium, because devices must take turns when transmitting. The network segments that share the same bandwidth between devices are known as *collision domains*, because when two or more devices within that segment try to communicate at the same time, collisions can occur.

It is possible, however, to use a switch device, operating at the OSI data link layer, to divide a network into segments and reduce the number of devices that compete for bandwidth. When a switch is used, each port represents a new segment. Each new segment is a new collision domain. More bandwidth is available to the devices on the segment, and collisions in one collision domain do not interfere with the other segments. This is also known as microsegmentation.

As shown in Figure 1-28, each switch port connects to a single PC or server, and each switch port represents a separate collision domain.

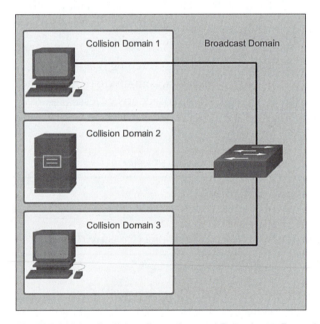

Figure 1-28   Collision Domains and Broadcast Domains

Broadcast Domains (1.2.2.2)

Although switches filter most frames based on MAC addresses, they do not filter broadcast frames. For other devices on the LAN to receive broadcast frames, switches must flood these frames out all ports except the one on which the broadcast was received. A collection of interconnected switches forms a single *broadcast domain*.

Only a network layer device, such as a router, can divide a Layer 2 broadcast domain. Routers are used to segment both collision and broadcast domains.

When a device sends a Layer 2 broadcast, the destination MAC address in the frame is set to all binary 1s. A frame with a destination MAC address of all binary 1s, or all Fs in hexadecimal, is received by all devices in the broadcast domain.

The Layer 2 broadcast domain is referred to as the MAC broadcast domain. The MAC broadcast domain consists of all devices on the LAN that receive broadcast frames from a host.

Video

Video 1.2.2.2: Broadcast Domains I

Go to the online course and view the first half of the animation.

When a switch receives a broadcast frame, it forwards the frame out each of its ports, except the ingress port where the broadcast frame was received. Each device connected to the switch receives a copy of the broadcast frame and processes it. Broadcasts are sometimes necessary for initially locating other devices and network services, but they also reduce network efficiency. Network bandwidth is used to propagate the broadcast traffic. Too many broadcasts and a heavy traffic load on a network can result in congestion: a slowdown in the network performance.

When two switches are connected together, the broadcast domain is increased.

Video

Video 1.2.2.2: Broadcast Domains II

Go to the online course and view the second half of the animation.

In this case, a broadcast frame is forwarded to all connected ports on switch S1. Switch S1 is connected to switch S2. The frame is then also propagated to all devices connected to switch S2.

Alleviating Network Congestion (1.2.2.3)

LAN switches have special characteristics that make them effective at alleviating network congestion. First, they allow the segmentation of a LAN into separate collision domains. Each port of the switch represents a separate collision domain and provides the full bandwidth to the device or devices that are connected to that port. Second, they provide full-duplex communication between devices. A full-duplex connection can carry transmitted and received signals at the same time. Full-duplex connections have dramatically increased LAN network performance and are required for 1-Gb/s Ethernet speeds and higher.

Switches interconnect LAN segments (collision domains), use a table of MAC addresses to determine the segment to which the frame is to be sent, and can lessen or eliminate collisions entirely. Following are some important characteristics of switches that contribute to alleviating network congestion:

- **High port density:** Switches have high port densities: 24- and 48-port switches are often just 1 rack unit (1.75 inches) in height and operate at speeds of 100 Mb/s, 1 Gb/s, and 10 Gb/s. Large enterprise switches can support many hundreds of ports.

- **Large frame buffers:** The ability to store more received frames before having to start dropping them is useful, particularly when there might be congested ports to servers or other parts of the network.

- **Port speed:** Depending on the cost of a switch, it might be possible to support a mixture of speeds. Ports of 100 Mb/s, and 1 or 10 Gb/s, are common (100 Gb/s is also possible).

- **Fast internal switching:** Having fast internal forwarding capabilities allows high performance. The method that is used can be a fast internal bus or shared memory, which affects the overall performance of the switch.

- **Low per-port cost:** Switches provide high port density at a lower cost. For this reason, LAN switches can accommodate network designs featuring fewer users per segment, therefore increasing the average available bandwidth per user.

Interactive Graphic

Activity 1.2.2.4: Circle the Domain

Go to the online course to perform this practice activity.

Summary (1.3)

Class Activity 1.3.1.1: It's Network Access Time

Use Packet Tracer for this activity. Internet connectivity is not required in this design. Work with a classmate to create two network designs to accommodate the following scenarios:

Scenario 1: Classroom Design (LAN)

- 15 student end devices represented by one or two PCs
- One instructor end device, preferably represented by a server
- Stream video presentations over a LAN connection

Scenario 2: Administrative Design (WAN)

- All requirements as listed in Scenario 1
- Access to and from a remote administrative server for video presentations and pushed updates for network application software

Both the LAN and WAN designs should fit on one Packet Tracer file screen. All intermediary devices should be labeled with the switch model (or name) and the router model (or name).

Save your work and be ready to justify your device decisions and layout to your instructor and the class.

Interactive Graphic

Activity 1.3.1.2: Basic Switch Configurations

Go to the online course to use the Syntax Checker to perform basic switch configurations.

Packet Tracer Activity 1.3.1.3: Skills Integration Challenge

As a recently hired LAN technician, your network manager has asked you to demonstrate your ability to configure a small LAN. Your tasks include configuring initial settings on two switches using the Cisco IOS and configuring IP address parameters on host devices to provide end-to-end connectivity. You are to use two switches and two hosts/PCs on a cabled and powered network.

We have seen that the trend in networks is toward convergence using a single set of wires and devices to handle voice, video, and data transmission. In addition, there has been a dramatic shift in the way businesses operate. No longer are employees constrained to physical offices or by geographic boundaries. Resources must now be seamlessly available anytime and anywhere. The Cisco Borderless Network architecture enables different elements, from access switches to wireless access points, to work together and allow users to access resources from any place at any time.

The traditional three-layer hierarchical design model divides the network into core, distribution, and access layers, and allows each portion of the network to be optimized for specific functionality. It provides modularity, resiliency, and flexibility, which provide a foundation that allows network designers to overlay security, mobility, and unified communication features. In some networks, having a separate core and distribution layer is not required. In these networks, the functionality of the core layer and the distribution layer is often collapsed together.

There are various types of switches used in business networks. It is important to deploy the appropriate types of switches based on network requirements. When selecting the type of switch, the network designer must choose between a fixed or modular configuration, and stackable or nonstackable. Another consideration is the thickness of the switch, which is expressed in number of rack units. A network administrator might choose to implement a multilayer switch. Multilayer switches are characterized by their ability to build a routing table, support a few routing protocols, and forward IP packets at a rate close to that of Layer 2 forwarding. Other switch features that should be considered include port density, forwarding rates, power capabilities (such as PoE), and scalability features.

Cisco LAN switches use ASICs to forward frames based on the destination MAC address. Before this can be accomplished, the switch must first use the source MAC address of incoming frames to build a MAC address table in content-addressable memory (CAM). If the destination MAC address is contained in this table, the frame is forwarded only to the specific destination port. In cases where the destination MAC address is not found in the MAC address table, the frames are flooded out all ports, except the one on which the frame was received.

Switches use either store-and-forward or cut-through switching. Store-and-forward reads the entire frame into a buffer and checks the CRC before forwarding the frame. Cut-through switching only reads the first portion of the frame and starts forwarding it as soon as the destination address is read. Although this is extremely fast, no error checking is done on the frame before forwarding.

Every port on a switch forms a separate collision domain, allowing extremely high-speed, full-duplex communication. Switch ports do not block broadcasts, and connecting switches together can extend the size of the broadcast domain, often resulting in degraded network performance.

Practice

The following activities provide practice with the topics introduced in this chapter. The Labs and Class Activities are available in the companion *Switched Networks Lab Manual* (ISBN 978-1-58713-372-5). The Packet Tracer Activities PKA files are found in the online course.

Class Activities

- Class Activity 1.0.1.2: Sent or Received Instructions
- Class Activity 1.3.1.1: It's Network Access Time

Labs

- Lab 1.1.3.6: Selecting Switch Hardware

Packet Tracer Activities

- Packet Tracer Activity 1.1.2.5: Comparing 2960 and 3560 Switches

Check Your Understanding Questions

Complete all the review questions listed here to test your understanding of the topics and concepts in this chapter. The appendix "Answers to 'Check Your Understanding' Questions" lists the answers.

1. What are the layers of the switch hierarchical design model? (Choose three.)

   A. Access

   B. Data link

   C. Core

   D. Network access

   E. Enterprise

   F. Distribution

2. Which of the following characteristics describe a converged network? (Choose two.)

    A. Support of voice and video, both using the same switch

    B. Separate wiring infrastructure for voice and video traffic

    C. Affordability for small and medium businesses

    D. Cheaper equipment cost

3. When an appropriate switch form factor for a network is being determined, what should be selected when fault tolerance and bandwidth availability are desired but the budget is limited?

    A. Stackable switch

    B. Nonstackable switch

    C. Fixed configuration switch

    D. Modular switch

4. Which cost-effective physical network topology design is recommended when building a three-tier campus network that connects three buildings?

    A. Bus

    B. Mesh

    C. Extended star

    D. Dual-ring

5. When the appropriate switch form factor for a network is being determined, what type of switch should be selected when future expansion is important and cost is not a limiting factor?

    A. Stackable switch

    B. 1-rack-unit switch

    C. Fixed configuration switch

    D. Modular switch

6. Fill in the blank. The technology that allows a switch to deliver power to a device like an IP phone or an access point through the data cable is known as

    _____.

7. Which of the following statements about Layer 2 Ethernet switches are true?
   (Choose two.)

   A. Layer 2 switches prevent broadcasts.

   B. Layer 2 switches have multiple collision domains.

   C. Layer 2 switches route traffic between different networks.

   D. Layer 2 switches decrease the number of broadcast domains.

   E. Layer 2 switches can send traffic based on the destination address.

8. A network administrator is researching enterprise-level switches to upgrade the
   network infrastructure. Which switching feature defines the overall amount of
   data that the switch can process each second?

   A. Forwarding rate

   B. Wire speed

   C. PoE

   D. Port density

9. Which option best describes a switching method?

   A. Cut-through: makes a forwarding decision after receiving the entire frame

   B. Store-and-forward: forwards the frame immediately after examining its desti-
      nation MAC address

   C. Cut-through: provides the flexibility to support any mix of Ethernet speeds

   D. Store-and-forward: ensures that the frame is free of physical and data-link
      errors

10. Which service is provided by an automated attendant feature on a converged
    network?

    A. Point-to-point video

    B. Call routing

    C. IT management interface

    D. Videoconferencing

11. A medium-sized company wants to add IP phones to its network. Should it con-
    sider buying a switch that supports PoE?

    A. Yes, because PoE increases port density.

    B. Yes, because PoE provides more flexibility in placing IP phones.

    C. No, because PoE has no effect on the use of VoIP devices on a network.

    D. Yes, because PoE adds Layer 3 functionality to a switch.

12. Which switching mode describes a switch that transfers a frame as soon as the destination MAC address is read?

A. Fragment free

B. Cut-through

C. Store-and-forward

D. Latency forwarding

CHAPTER 2

Basic Switching Concepts and Configuration

Objectives

Upon completion of this chapter, you will be able to answer the following questions:

- How do you configure the initial settings on a Cisco switch?

- How do you configure switch ports to meet network requirements?

- How do you configure the management VLAN switch virtual interface?

- How do you describe basic security attacks in a switched environment?

- How do you describe security best practices in a switched environment?

- How do you configure the port security feature to restrict network access?

Key Terms

This chapter uses the following key terms. You can find the definitions in the Glossary.

Introduction (2.0.1.1)

Switches are used to connect multiple devices together on the same network. In a properly designed network, LAN switches are responsible for directing and controlling the data flow at the access layer to networked resources.

Cisco switches are self-configuring, and no additional configurations are necessary for them to function out of the box. However, Cisco switches run Cisco IOS and can be manually configured to better meet the needs of the network. This includes adjusting port speed, bandwidth, and security requirements.

Additionally, Cisco switches can be managed both locally and remotely. To remotely manage a switch, it needs to have an IP address and default gateway configured. These are just two of the configurations discussed in this chapter.

Access layer switches operate at the access layer, where client network devices connect directly to the network and IT departments want uncomplicated network access for the users. It is one of the most vulnerable areas of the network because it is so exposed to the user. Switches need to be configured to be resilient to attacks of all types while they are protecting user data and allowing high-speed connections. *Port security* is one of the security features that Cisco-managed switches provide.

This chapter examines some of the basic switch configuration settings required to maintain a secure, available, switched LAN environment.

Class Activity 2.0.1.2: Stand by Me

When you arrived to class today, you were given a number by your instructor to use for this introductory class activity.

When class begins, your instructor will ask certain students with specific numbers to stand. Your job is to record the standing students' numbers for each scenario.

Scenario 1

Students with numbers starting with the number 5 should stand. Record the numbers of the standing students.

Scenario 2

Students with numbers ending in B should stand. Record the numbers of the standing students.

Scenario 3

The student with the number 505C should stand. Record the number of the standing student.

At the end of this activity, divide into small groups and record answers to the Reflection questions on the PDF for this activity.

Save your work and be prepared to share it with another student or the entire class.

Basic Switch Configuration (2.1)

Basic switch administration should be mastered by a switch administrator. This includes familiarity with the hardware as well as basic port configuration.

Configure a Switch with Initial Settings (2.1.1)

In this section, you learn the Cisco switch boot sequence, how to recover from a system crash, and how to configure the switch to support remote management.

Switch Boot Sequence (2.1.1.1)

After a Cisco switch is powered on, it goes through the following boot sequence:

1. The switch loads a power-on self-test (POST) program stored in ROM. POST checks the CPU subsystem. It tests the CPU, DRAM, and the portion of the flash device that makes up the flash file system.

2. The switch loads the boot loader software. The boot loader is a small program stored in ROM and is run immediately after the POST successfully completes.

3. The boot loader performs low-level CPU initialization. It initializes the CPU registers, which control where physical memory is mapped, the quantity of memory, and its speed.

4. The boot loader initializes the flash file system on the system board.

5. The boot loader locates and loads a default IOS operating system software image into memory and hands control of the switch over to the IOS.

The boot loader finds the Cisco IOS image and attempts to automatically boot by using information in the BOOT environment variable. If this variable is not set, the switch attempts to load and execute the first executable file it can by performing a recursive, depth-first search throughout the flash file system. In a depth-first search of the file system, the search begins at the first top-level directory. The search proceeds through the directory from the lowest level subdirectory, up the tree. If the search is unsuccessful, the next top-level directory is located and the bottom-up search pattern is repeated. On Catalyst 2960 Series switches, the image file is normally contained in a directory that has the same name as the image file (excluding the .bin file extension).

The IOS operating system then initializes the interfaces using the Cisco IOS commands found in the configuration file, startup-config, which is stored in NVRAM.

In Figure 2-1, the BOOT environment variable is set using the **boot system** global configuration mode command. Notice that the IOS is located in a distinct folder and the folder path is specified. Use the **show bootvar** command (**show boot** in older IOS versions) to see to what the current IOS boot file is set.

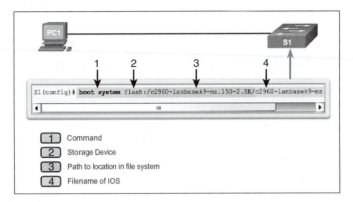

Figure 2-1   Configure BOOT Environment Variable

Recovering From a System Crash (2.1.1.2)

The boot loader provides access into the switch if the operating system cannot be used because of missing or damaged system files. The boot loader has a command line that provides access to the files stored in flash memory.

The boot loader can be accessed through a console connection following these steps:

Step 1.   Connect a PC by a console cable to the switch console port. Configure terminal emulation software to connect to the switch.

Step 2.   Unplug the switch power cord, because many Cisco switches do not have an on/off switch.

Step 3.   Reconnect the power cord to the switch and, within 15 seconds, press and hold down the **Mode** button while the System LED is still flashing green.

Step 4.   Continue pressing the **Mode** button until the System LED turns briefly amber and then solid green; then release the **Mode** button.

Step 5.   The boot loader **switch:** prompt appears in the terminal emulation software on the PC.

The **boot loader** command line supports commands to format the flash file system, reinstall the operating system software, and recover from a lost or forgotten password. For example, the **dir** command can be used to view a list of files within a specified directory, as shown in Figure 2-2.

```
Switch# dir flash:
Directory of flash:/

    2  -rwx    11607161   Mar 1 2013 03:10:47 +00:00  c2960-
lanbasek9-mz.150-2.SE.bin
    3  -rwx        1809   Mar 1 2013 00:02:48 +00:00  config.text
    5  -rwx        1919   Mar 1 2013 00:02:48 +00:00  private-
config.text
    6  -rwx       59416   Mar 1 2013 00:02:49 +00:00  multiple-fs

32514048 bytes total (20841472 bytes free)
Switch#
```

Figure 2-2   Directory Listing in Boot Loader

Note

In this example, the IOS is located in the root of the flash folder.

Switch LED Indicators (2.1.1.3)

Cisco Catalyst switches have several status LED indicator lights. You can use the switch LEDs to quickly monitor switch activity and its performance. Switches of different models and feature sets will have different LEDs, and their placement on the front panel of the switch can also vary.

Figure 2-3 shows the switch LEDs and the **Mode** button for a Cisco Catalyst 2960 switch. The **Mode** button is used to toggle through port status, port duplex, port speed, and PoE (if supported) status of the port LEDs. The following describes the purpose of the LED indicators and the meaning of their colors:

- **System LED:** Shows whether the system is receiving power and is functioning properly. If the LED is off, it means that the system is not powered on. If the LED is green, the system is operating normally. If the LED is amber, the system is receiving power but is not functioning properly.

- **Redundant Power System (RPS) LED:** Shows the RPS status. If the LED is off, the RPS is off or not properly connected. If the LED is green, the RPS is connected and ready to provide backup power. If the LED is blinking green, the RPS is connected but is unavailable because it is providing power to another device. If the LED is amber, the RPS is in standby mode or in a fault condition. If the LED is blinking amber, the internal power supply in the switch has failed, and the RPS is providing power.

- **Port Status LED:** Indicates that the port status mode is selected when the LED is green. This is the default mode. When selected, the port LEDs will display colors with different meanings. If the LED is off, there is no link, or the port was administratively shut down. If the LED is green, a link is present. If the LED is blinking green, there is activity and the port is sending or receiving data. If the LED is alternating green-amber, there is a link fault. If the LED is amber, the port is blocked to ensure that a loop does not exist in the forwarding domain and is not forwarding data (typically, ports will remain in this state for the first 30 seconds after being activated). If the LED is blinking amber, the port is blocked to prevent a possible loop in the forwarding domain.

■ **Port Duplex LED:** Indicates that the port duplex mode is selected when the LED is green. When selected, port LEDs that are off are in half-duplex mode. If the port LED is green, the port is in full-duplex mode.

■ **Port Speed LED:** Indicates that the port speed mode is selected. When selected, the port LEDs will display colors with different meanings. If the LED is off, the port is operating at 10 Mb/s. If the LED is green, the port is operating at 100 Mb/s. If the LED is blinking green, the port is operating at 1000 Mb/s.

■ **Power over Ethernet (PoE) Mode LED:** If PoE is supported, a PoE mode LED will be present. If the LED is off, it indicates that the PoE mode is not selected and that none of the ports have been denied power or placed in a fault condition. If the LED is blinking amber, the PoE mode is not selected but at least one of the ports has been denied power, or has a PoE fault. If the LED is green, it indicates that the PoE mode is selected and that the port LEDs will display colors with different meanings. If the port LED is off, the PoE is off. If the port LED is green, the PoE is on. If the port LED is alternating green-amber, PoE is denied because providing power to the powered device will exceed the switch power capacity. If the LED is blinking amber, PoE is off because of a fault. If the LED is amber, PoE for the port has been disabled.

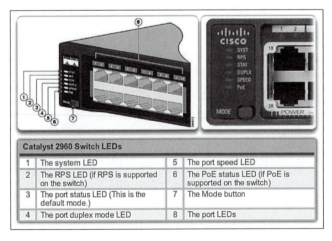

Catalyst 2960 Switch LEDs			
1	The system LED	5	The port speed LED
2	The RPS LED (if RPS is supported on the switch)	6	The PoE status LED (if PoE is supported on the switch)
3	The port status LED (This is the default mode.)	7	The Mode button
4	The port duplex mode LED	8	The port LEDs

Figure 2-3   Switch LEDs

Preparing for Basic Switch Management (2.1.1.4)

A console cable is used to connect a PC to the console port of a switch, as depicted in Figure 2-4. To remotely manage the switch, it must be initially configured through the console port.

To prepare a switch for remote management access, the switch must be configured with an IP address and a subnet mask. Keep in mind that to manage the switch from a remote network, the switch must be configured with a default gateway. This is very similar to configuring the IP address information on host devices. In Figure 2-4, the switch virtual interface (SVI) on S1 should be assigned an IP address. The SVI is a virtual interface, not a physical port on the switch.

SVI is a concept related to VLANs. VLANs are numbered logical groups to which physical ports can be assigned. Configurations and settings applied to a VLAN are also applied to all the ports assigned to that VLAN.

By default, the switch is configured to have the management of the switch controlled through VLAN 1. All ports are assigned to VLAN 1 by default. For security purposes, it is considered a best practice to use a VLAN other than VLAN 1 for the management VLAN.

Note that these IP settings are only for remote management access to the switch; the IP settings do not allow the switch to route Layer 3 packets.

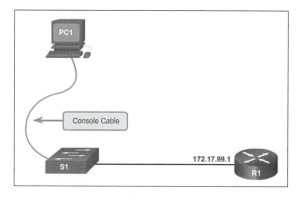

Figure 2-4   Preparing for Remote Management

Configuring Basic Switch Management Access with IPv4 (2.1.1.5)

To configure basic switch management access with IPv4, follow these steps:

Step 1.   Configure the management interface.

An IP address and subnet mask are configured on the management SVI of the switch from VLAN interface configuration mode. As shown in Table 2-1, the **interface vlan 99** command is used to enter interface configuration mode. The **ip address** command is used to configure the IP address. The **no shutdown** command enables the interface. In this example, VLAN 99 is configured with IP address 172.17.99.11.

Table 2-1   Cisco Switch Management Interface

Cisco Switch IOS Commands	
Enter global configuration mode.	S1# **configure terminal**
Enter interface configuration mode.	S1(config)# **interface vlan 99**
Configure the management interface IP address.	S1(config-if)# **ip address 172.17.99.11 255.255.255.0**
Enable the management interface.	S1(config-if)# **no shutdown**
Return to the privileged EXEC mode.	S1(config-if)# **end**
Save the running configuration file to the startup configuration file.	S1# **copy running-config startup-config**

The SVI for VLAN 99 will not appear as "up/up" until VLAN 99 is created and there is a device connected to a switch port associated with VLAN 99. To create a VLAN with the vlan_id of 99 and associate it to interface FastEthernet 0/1, use the following commands:

```
S1(config)# vlan 99
S1(config-vlan)# name Mgmt
S1(config)# interface f0/1
S1(config-if)# switchport access vlan 99
```

Step 2.   Configure the default gateway.

The switch should be configured with a default gateway if it will be managed remotely from networks not directly connected. The default gateway is the router the switch is connected to. The switch will forward its IP packets with destination IP addresses outside the local network to the default gateway. As shown in Table 2-2, R1 is the default gateway for S1. The interface on R1 connected to the switch has IP address 172.17.99.1. This address is the default gateway address for S1.

To configure the default gateway for the switch, use the **ip default-gateway** command, as shown in Figure 2-5. Enter the IP address of the default gateway. The default gateway is the IP address of the router interface to which the switch is connected. Use the **copy running-config startup-config** command to back up your configuration.

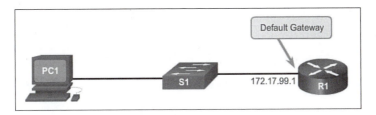

Figure 2-5   Default Gateway

Table 2-2   Configure Default Gateway for Switch

Cisco Switch IOS Commands	
Enter global configuration mode.	S1# **configure terminal**
Configure the default gateway for the switch.	S1(config)# **ip default-gateway 172.17.99.1**
Return to the privileged EXEC mode.	S1(config)# **end**
Save the running configuration file to the startup configuration file.	S1# **copy running-config startup-config**

Step 3.   Verify the configuration.

As shown in Figure 2-6, the **show ip interface brief** command is useful when determining the status of both physical and virtual interfaces. The output shown confirms that interface VLAN 99 has been configured with an IP address and subnet mask and that the interface status is "up."

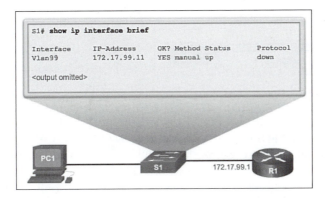

Figure 2-6   Verify Switch Management Interface Configuration

Lab 2.1.1.6: Configuring Basic Switch Settings

In this lab, you will complete the following objectives:

- Part 1: Cable the Network and Verify the Default Switch Configuration
- Part 2: Configure Basic Network Device Settings
- Part 3: Verify and Test Network Connectivity
- Part 4: Manage the MAC Address Table

Configure Switch Ports (2.1.2)

In general terms, switches are configured from the physical layer upward. The first set of tasks for switch configuration involves physical layer characteristics, such as duplex, speed, and pinouts.

Duplex Communication (2.1.2.1)

Figure 2-7 illustrates full-duplex and half-duplex communication.

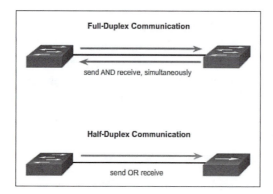

Figure 2-7   Duplex Communication

Full-duplex communication improves the performance of a switched LAN. Full-duplex communication increases effective bandwidth by allowing both ends of a connection to transmit and receive data simultaneously. This is also known as bidirectional. This method of optimizing network performance requires microsegmentation. A microsegmented LAN is created when a switch port has only one device connected and is operating at full-duplex. This results in a micro-size collision domain of a single device. However, because there is only one device connected, a microsegmented LAN is collision free.

Unlike full-duplex communication, half-duplex communication is unidirectional. Sending and receiving data do not occur at the same time. Half-duplex communication creates performance issues because data can flow in only one direction at a time, often resulting in collisions. Half-duplex connections are typically seen in older hardware, such as hubs. Full-duplex communication has replaced half-duplex in most hardware.

Most Ethernet and Fast Ethernet NICs sold today offer full-duplex capability. Gigabit Ethernet and 10-Gb NICs require full-duplex connections to operate. In full-duplex mode, the collision detection circuit on the NIC is disabled. Frames that are sent by the two connected devices cannot collide because the devices use two separate circuits in the network cable. Full-duplex connections require a switch that supports full-duplex configuration, or a direct connection using an Ethernet cable between two devices.

Configure Switch Ports at the Physical Layer (2.1.2.2)

Switch ports can be manually configured with specific duplex and speed settings. Use the **duplex** interface configuration mode command to manually specify the duplex mode for a switch port. Use the **speed** interface configuration mode command to manually specify the speed for a switch port. In Figure 2-8, ports F0/1 on switch S1 and S2 are manually configured with the **full** keyword for the **duplex** command, and the **100** keyword for the **speed** command.

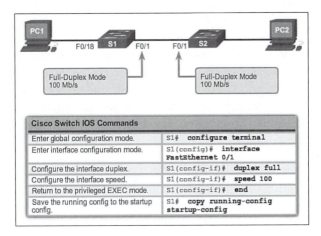

Figure 2-8   Configure Duplex and Speed

The default setting for both duplex and speed for switch ports on Cisco Catalyst 2960 and 3560 switches is auto. The 10/100/1000 ports operate in either half- or full-duplex mode when they are set to 10 or 100 Mb/s, but when they are set to 1000 Mb/s (1 Gb/s), they operate only in full-duplex mode. Autonegotiation is useful when the speed and duplex settings of the device connecting to the port are unknown or can change. When connecting to known devices, such as servers, dedicated workstations, or network devices, best practice is to manually set the speed and duplex settings.

When troubleshooting switch port issues, the duplex and speed settings should be checked.

Note

Mismatched settings for the duplex mode and speed of switch ports can cause connectivity issues. Autonegotiation failure creates mismatched settings.

All fiber-optic ports, such as 100BASE-FX ports, operate only at one preset speed and are always full-duplex.

Interactive Graphic

Activity 2.1.2.2: Configuring Duplex and Speed

Go to the online course to use the Syntax Checker in the second graphic to configure port F0/1 of switch S1.

Auto-MDIX (2.1.2.3)

Until recently, certain cable types (straight-through or crossover) were required when connecting devices. Switch-to-switch or switch-to-router connections required using different Ethernet cables. Using the automatic medium-dependent interface crossover (auto-MDIX) feature on an interface eliminates this problem. When auto-MDIX is enabled, the interface automatically detects the required cable connection type (straight-through or crossover) and configures the connection appropriately. When connecting to switches without the auto-MDIX feature, straight-through cables must be used to connect to devices such as servers, workstations, or routers, and crossover cables must be used to connect to other switches or repeaters.

With auto-MDIX enabled, either type of cable can be used to connect to other devices, and the interface automatically adjusts to communicate successfully. On newer Cisco routers and switches, the **mdix auto** interface configuration mode command enables the feature. When using auto-MDIX on an interface, the interface speed and duplex must be set to **auto** so that the feature operates correctly.

The commands to enable auto-MDIX are shown in Figure 2-9.

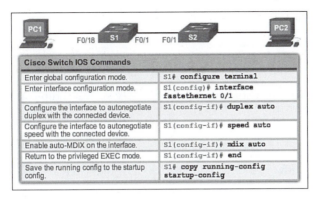

Figure 2-9   Configure Auto-MDIX

Note

The auto-MDIX feature is enabled by default on Catalyst 2960 and Catalyst 3560 switches, but it is not available on the older Catalyst 2950 and Catalyst 3550 switches.

To examine the auto-MDIX setting for a specific interface, use the **show controllers ethernet-controller** command with the **phy** keyword. To limit the output to lines referencing auto-MDIX, use the **include Auto-MDIX** filter. As shown in Figure 2-10, the output indicates On or Off for the feature.

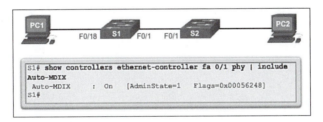

Figure 2-10   Verify Auto-MDIX

Activity 2.1.2.3: Enable Auto-MDIX

Go to the online course to use the Syntax Checker in the third graphic to configure port F0/1 on S2 for auto-MDIX.

Verifying Switch Port Configuration (2.1.2.4)

Table 2-3 describes some of the options for the **show** command that are helpful in verifying common configurable switch features.

Table 2-3   Common Verification Commands

Cisco Switch IOS Commands	
Display interface status configuration.	S1# **show interfaces** [*interface-id*]
Display current startup configuration.	S1# **show startup-config**
Display current operating configuration.	S1# **show running-config**
Display info about flash file system.	S1# **show flash**
Display system hardware and software status.	S1# **show version**
Display history of commands entered.	S1# **show history**
Display IP information about an interface.	S1# **show ip** [*interface-id*]
Display the MAC address table.	S1# **show mac address-table**

Figure 2-11 shows sample abbreviated output from the **show running-config** command. Use this command to verify that the switch has been correctly configured. As seen in the output for S1, some key information is shown:

- Fast Ethernet 0/18 interface is configured with the management VLAN 99.

- VLAN 99 is configured with an IP address of 172.17.99.11 255.255.255.0.

- Default gateway is set to 172.17.99.1.

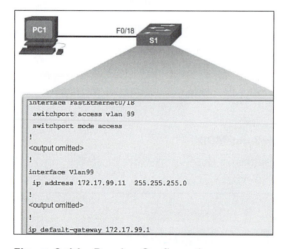

Figure 2-11   Running Configuration

The **show interfaces** command is another commonly used command that displays status and statistics information on the network interfaces of the switch. The **show interfaces** command is frequently used when configuring and monitoring network devices.

Figure 2-12 shows the output from the **show interfaces fastEthernet 0/18** command. The first line in the figure indicates that the FastEthernet 0/18 interface is up/up, meaning that it is operational. Farther down, the output shows that the duplex is full and the speed is 100 Mb/s.

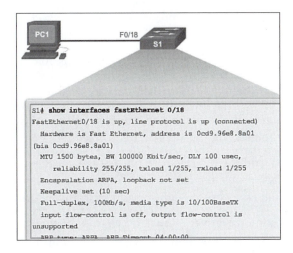

Figure 2-12   Interface Status

Network Access Layer Issues (2.1.2.5)

The output from the **show interfaces** command can be used to detect common media issues. One of the most important parts of this output is the display of the line and data-link protocol status. Example 2-1 indicates the summary line to check the status of an interface, and Table 2-4 describes the interface and line protocol status.

Example 2-1   Verify Interface Status

```
R1# show interfaces FastEthernet0/1
FastEthernet0/1 is up, line protocol is up
Hardware is Fast Ethernet, address is 0022.91c4.0e01 (bia 0022.91c4.0e01)
MTU 1500 bytes, BW 10000 Kbit, DLY 100 usec,
<output omitted>
```

Table 2-4   Verify Interface Status

Interface Status	Line Protocol Status	Link State
Up	Up	Operational
Down	Down	Interface Problem

The first parameter (FastEthernet0/1 is up) refers to the hardware layer and essentially reflects whether the interface is receiving the carrier detect signal from the other end. The second parameter (line protocol is up) refers to the data link layer and reflects whether the data link layer protocol keepalives are being received.

Based on the output of the **show interfaces** command, possible problems can be fixed as follows:

- If the interface is up and the line protocol is down, a problem exists. There could be an encapsulation type mismatch, the interface on the other end could be error-disabled, or there could be a hardware problem.

- If the line protocol and the interface are both down, a cable is not attached or some other interface problem exists. For example, in a back-to-back connection, the other end of the connection might be administratively down.

- If the interface is administratively down, it has been manually disabled (the **shutdown** command has been issued) in the active configuration.

Example 2-2 shows an example of the **show interfaces** command output. The example shows counters and statistics for the FastEthernet 0/1 interface.

Example 2-2   Verify Interface Counters

```
S1# show interfaces FastEthernet 0/1
FastEthernet0/1 is up, line protocol is up (connected)
Hardware is Fast Ethernet, address is 0021.d722.9f01 (bia 0021.d722.9f01)
MTU 1500 bytes, BW 100000 Kbit, DLY 100 usec,
<output omitted>
2295197 packets input, 305539992 bytes, 0 no buffer
Received 1925500 broadcasts (1903 multicasts)
0 runts, 0 giants, 0 throttles
3 input errors, 3 CRC, 0 frame, 0 overrun, 0 ignored
0 watchdog, 1903 multicast, 0 pause input
0 input packets with dribble condition detected
359464 packets output, 436549843 bytes, 0 underruns
8 output errors, 1790 collisions, 10 interface resets
0 babbles, 235 late collision, 0 deferred
<output omitted>
```

Some media errors are not severe enough to cause the circuit to fail, but do cause network performance issues. Table 2-5 explains some of these common errors, which can be detected by using the **show interfaces** command.

Table 2-5   Network Access Layer Issues

Error Type	Description
Input errors	Total number of errors. It includes runts, giants, no buffer, CRC, frame, overrun, and ignored counts.
Runts	Packets that are discarded because they are smaller than the minimum packet size for the medium. For example, any Ethernet packet that is less than 64 bytes is considered a runt.
Giants	Packets that are discarded because they exceed the maximum packet size for the medium. For example, any Ethernet packet that is greater than 1518 bytes is considered a giant.
CRC	CRC errors are generated when the calculated checksum is not the same as the checksum received.
Output errors	Sum of all errors that prevented the final transmission of datagrams out of the interface that is being examined.
Collisions	Number of messages retransmitted because of an Ethernet collision.
Late collisions	Jammed signal could not reach to ends.

"Input errors" is the sum of all errors in datagrams that were received on the interface being examined. This includes runts, giants, CRC, no buffer, frame, overrun, and ignored counts. The reported input errors from the **show interfaces** command include the following:

- **Runt frames:** Ethernet frames that are shorter than the 64-byte minimum allowed length are called runts. Malfunctioning NICs are the usual cause of excessive runt frames, but they can be caused by the same issues as excessive collisions.

- **Giants:** Ethernet frames that are longer than the maximum allowed length are called giants. Giants are caused by the same issues as those that cause runts.

- **CRC errors:** On Ethernet and serial interfaces, CRC errors usually indicate a media or cable error. Common causes include electrical interference, loose or damaged connections, or using the incorrect cabling type. If you see many CRC errors, there is too much noise on the link and you should inspect the cable for damage and length. You should also search for and eliminate noise sources, if possible.

"Output errors" is the sum of all errors that prevented the final transmission of datagrams out of the interface that is being examined. The reported output errors from the **show interfaces** command include the following:

- **Collisions:** Collisions in half-duplex operations are completely normal and you should not worry about them, as long as you are pleased with half-duplex operations. However, you should never see collisions in a properly designed and configured network that uses full-duplex communication. It is highly recommended that you use full-duplex unless you have older or legacy equipment that requires half-duplex.

- **Late collisions:** A late collision refers to a collision that occurs after 512 bits of the frame (the preamble) have been transmitted. Excessive cable lengths are the most common cause of late collisions. Another common cause is duplex misconfiguration. For example, you could have one end of a connection configured for full-duplex and the other for half-duplex. You would see late collisions on the interface that is configured for half-duplex. In that case, you must configure the same duplex setting on both ends. A properly designed and configured network should never have late collisions.

Troubleshooting Network Access Layer Issues (2.1.2.6)

Most issues that affect a switched network are encountered during the original implementation. Theoretically, after it is installed, a network continues to operate without problems. However, cabling gets damaged, configurations change, and new devices are connected to the switch that require switch configuration changes. Ongoing maintenance and troubleshooting of the network infrastructure are required.

To troubleshoot these issues when you have no connection or a bad connection between a switch and another device, follow this general process:

Use the **show interfaces** command to check the interface status.

If the interface is down:

- Check to make sure that the proper cables are being used. Additionally, check the cable and connectors for damage. If a bad or incorrect cable is suspected, replace the cable.

- If the interface is still down, the problem might be because of a mismatch in speed setting. The speed of an interface is typically autonegotiated; therefore, even if it is manually configured on one interface, the connecting interface should autonegotiate accordingly. If a speed mismatch does occur through misconfiguration or a hardware or software issue, that can result in the interface going down. Manually set the same speed on both connection ends if a problem is suspected.

If the interface is up, but issues with connectivity are still present:

- Using the **show interfaces** command, check for indications of excessive noise. Indications can include an increase in the counters for runts, giants, and CRC errors. If there is excessive noise, first find and remove the source of the noise, if possible. Also, verify that the cable does not exceed the maximum cable length and check the type of cable that is used. For copper cable, it is recommended that you use at least Category 5.

- If noise is not an issue, check for excessive collisions. If there are collisions or late collisions, verify the duplex settings on both ends of the connection. Much like the speed setting, the duplex setting is usually autonegotiated. If there does appear to be a duplex mismatch, manually set the duplex on both connection ends. It is recommended to use full-duplex if both sides support it.

Figure 2-13 summarizes switch media issues in a flowchart.

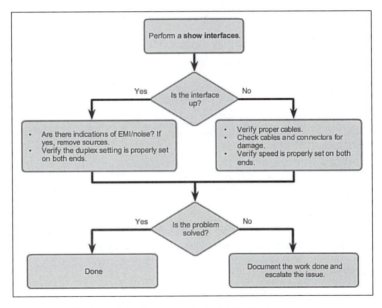

Figure 2-13   Troubleshooting Switch Media Issues

Switch Security: Management and Implementation (2.2)

Switch security is an integral part of network security. The features and technologies available on LAN switches have a wide variety of applications. Security is applied in a layered approach, and switches illustrate this with the configurable security options. In this section, the basic switch security features and technologies are introduced, including *Secure Shell (SSH)*, *DHCP snooping*, and port security.

Secure Remote Access (2.2.1)

Having in mind that network security is applied in layers, a primary consideration is that network administrators need to be able to configure network devices without worrying about hackers seeing what they are doing. In other words, network administrators need secure remote access. Secure Shell makes this possible.

SSH Operation (2.2.1.1)

Secure Shell (SSH) is a protocol that provides a secure (encrypted) management connection to a remote device. SSH should replace Telnet for management connections. Telnet is an older protocol that uses unsecure plaintext transmission of both the login authentication (username and password) and the data transmitted between the communicating devices. SSH provides security for remote connections by providing strong encryption when a device is authenticated (username and password) and also for the transmitted data between the communicating devices. SSH is assigned to TCP port 22. Telnet is assigned to TCP port 23.

In Figure 2-14, an attacker can monitor packets using Wireshark. A Telnet stream can be targeted to capture the username and password.

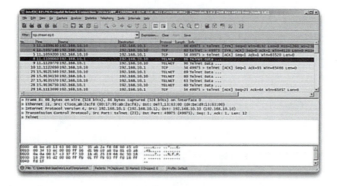

Figure 2-14 Wireshark Telnet Capture

In Figure 2-15, the attacker can capture the username and password of the administrator from the plaintext Telnet session.

Figure 2-16 shows the Wireshark view of an SSH session. The attacker can track the session using the IP address of the administrator device.

However, in Figure 2-17, the username and password are encrypted.

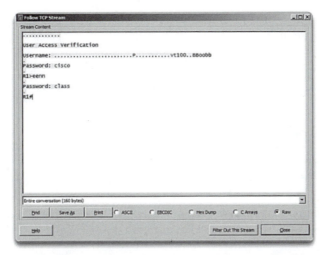

Figure 2-15 Plaintext Username and Password Captured

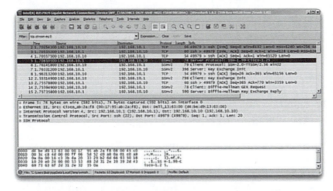

Figure 2-16 Wireshark SSH Capture

Figure 2-17 Username and Password Encrypted

To enable SSH on a Catalyst 2960 switch, the switch must be using a version of the IOS software including cryptographic (encrypted) features and capabilities. In Example 2-3, use the **show version** command on the switch to see which IOS the switch is currently running, and verify that the IOS filename includes the combination "k9", which indicates that it supports cryptographic (encrypted) features and capabilities.

Example 2-3 Cryptographic Image

```
S1# show version
Cisco IOS Software, C2960 Software (C2960-LANBASEK9-M), Version 15.0(2)SE, RELEASE
  SOFTWARE (fc1)
<output omitted>
```

Configuring SSH (2.2.1.2)

Before configuring SSH, be sure that the switch is minimally configured with a unique host name and the correct network connectivity settings.

Step 1.   Verify SSH support.

Use the **show ip ssh** command to verify that the switch supports SSH. If the switch is not running an IOS that supports cryptographic features, this command is unrecognized.

Step 2.   Configure the IP domain name.

Configure the IP domain name of the network using the **ip domain-name** *domain-name* global configuration mode command. In Figure 2-18, the *domain-name* value is **cisco.com**.

Step 3.   Generate RSA key pairs.

Generating an RSA key pair automatically enables SSH. Use the **crypto key generate rsa** global configuration mode command to enable the SSH server on the switch and generate an RSA key pair. When generating RSA keys, the administrator is prompted to enter a modulus length. Cisco recommends a minimum modulus size of 1024 bits (see the sample configuration in Figure 2-18). A longer modulus length is more secure, but it takes longer to generate and to use.

Note

To delete the RSA key pair, use the **crypto key zeroize rsa** global configuration mode command. After the RSA key pair is deleted, the SSH server is automatically disabled.

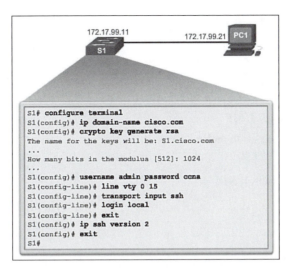

```
172.17.99.11          172.17.99.21  PC1
   S1
```

```
S1# configure terminal
S1(config)# ip domain-name cisco.com
S1(config)# crypto key generate rsa
The name for the keys will be: S1.cisco.com
...
How many bits in the modulus [512]: 1024
...
S1(config)# username admin password ccna
S1(config-line)# line vty 0 15
S1(config-line)# transport input ssh
S1(config-line)# login local
S1(config-line)# exit
S1(config)# ip ssh version 2
S1(config)# exit
S1#
```

Figure 2-18   Configure SSH for Remote Management

Step 4.   Configure user authentication.

The SSH server can authenticate users locally or using an authentication server. To use the local authentication method, create a username and password pair using the **username** *username* **password** *password* global configuration mode command. In the example, the user **admin** is assigned the password **ccna**.

Step 5.   Configure the vty lines.

Enable the SSH protocol on the vty lines using the **transport input ssh** line configuration mode command. The Catalyst 2960 has vty lines ranging from 0 to 15. This configuration prevents non-SSH (such as Telnet) connections and limits the switch to accept only SSH connections. Use the **line vty** global configuration mode command and then the **login local** line configuration mode command to require local authentication for SSH connections from the local username database.

Step 6.   Enable SSH version 2.

By default, SSH supports both versions 1 and 2. When supporting both versions, this is shown in the **show ip ssh** output as supporting version 1.99. Version 1 has known vulnerabilities. For this reason, it is recommended to enable only version 2. Enable SSH version using the **ip ssh version 2** global configuration command.

Interactive Graphic

Activity 2.2.1.2: Configure SSH

Go to the online course to use the Syntax Checker in the second graphic to configure SSH on S1.

Verifying SSH (2.2.1.3)

On a PC, an SSH client, such as PuTTY, is used to connect to an SSH server. For the examples in Figures 2-19, 2-20, and 2-21, the following have been configured:

- SSH enabled on switch S1

- Interface VLAN 99 (SVI) with IP address 172.17.99.11 on switch S1

- PC1 with IP address 172.17.99.21

In Figure 2-19, the PC initiates an SSH connection to the SVI VLAN IP address of S1.

Figure 2-19   Configure PuTTY SSH Client Connection Parameters

In Example 2-4 (and the related graphic in Figure 2-20), the user has been prompted for a username and password. Using the configuration from the previous example, the username **admin** and password **ccna** are entered. After entering the correct combination, the user is connected through SSH to the CLI on the Catalyst 2960 switch.

Figure 2-20   Remote Management SSH Connection

Example 2-4 PuTTY Window Text for Remote Management SSH Connection

```
Login as: admin
Using keyboard-interactive
authentication.
Password:

S1> enable
Password:
S1#
```

To display the version and configuration data for SSH on the device that you configured as an SSH server, use the **show ip ssh** command. In the example, SSH version 2 is enabled. To check the SSH connections to the device, use the **show ssh** command (see Figure 2-21).

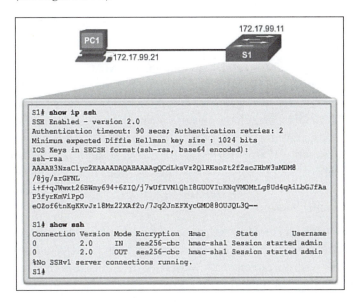

Figure 2-21 Verify SSH Status and Settings

Packet Tracer Activity 2.2.1.4: Configuring SSH

SSH should replace Telnet for management connections. Telnet uses insecure plaintext communications. SSH provides security for remote connections by providing strong encryption of all transmitted data between devices. In this activity, you will secure a remote switch with password encryption and SSH.

Security Concerns in LANs (2.2.2)

Modern networks are especially vulnerable to sophisticated attacks. It is more important than ever to be familiar with the common security attacks associated with the LAN environment. Fortunately, each type of attack has an effective means to mitigate the attack.

Common Security Attacks: MAC Address Flooding (2.2.2.1)

Basic switch security does not stop malicious attacks. Security is a layered process that is essentially never complete. The more aware the team of networking professionals within an organization is regarding security attacks and the dangers they pose, the better. Some types of security attacks are described here, but the details of how some of these attacks work are beyond the scope of this course. More detailed information is found in the CCNA WAN Technologies course and the CCNA Security course.

MAC Address Flooding

The MAC address table in a switch contains the MAC addresses associated with each physical port and the associated VLAN for each port. When a Layer 2 switch receives a frame, the switch looks in the MAC address table for the destination MAC address. All Catalyst switch models use a MAC address table for Layer 2 switching. As frames arrive on switch ports, the source MAC addresses are recorded in the MAC address table. If an entry exists for the MAC address, the switch forwards the frame to the correct port. If the MAC address does not exist in the MAC address table, the switch floods the frame out of every port on the switch, except the port where the frame was received.

The *MAC address flooding* behavior of a switch for unknown addresses can be used to attack a switch. This type of attack is called a MAC address table overflow attack. MAC address table overflow attacks are sometimes referred to as MAC flooding attacks and CAM table overflow attacks. The figures show how this type of attack works.

In Figure 2-22, host A sends traffic to host B. The switch receives the frames and looks up the destination MAC address in its MAC address table. If the switch cannot find the destination MAC in the MAC address table, the switch then copies the frame and floods (broadcasts) it out of every switch port, except the port where it was received.

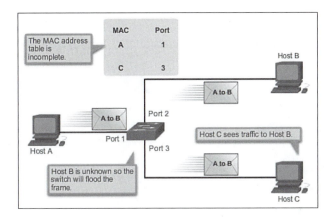

Figure 2-22 Switch Floods Frame for Unknown MAC Address

In Figure 2-23, host B receives the frame and sends a reply to host A. The switch then learns that the MAC address for host B is located on port 2 and records that information into the MAC address table.

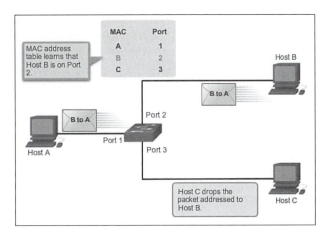

Figure 2-23 Switch Records MAC Address

Host C also receives the frame from host A to host B, but because the destination MAC address of that frame is host B, host C drops that frame.

As shown in Figure 2-24, any frame sent by host A (or any other host) to host B is forwarded to port 2 of the switch and not broadcast out every port.

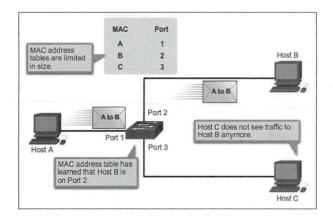

Figure 2-24 Switch Uses MAC Address Table to Forward Traffic

MAC address tables are limited in size. MAC flooding attacks make use of this limitation to overwhelm the switch with fake source MAC addresses until the switch MAC address table is full.

As shown in Figure 2-25, an attacker at host C can send frames with fake, randomly generated source and destination MAC addresses to the switch. The switch updates the MAC address table with the information in the fake frames. When the MAC address table is full of fake MAC addresses, the switch enters into what is known as fail-open mode. In this mode, the switch broadcasts all frames to all machines on the network. As a result, the attacker can see all the frames.

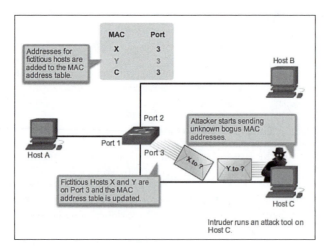

Figure 2-25 MAC Address Flooding Attack

Some network attack tools can generate up to 155,000 MAC entries on a switch per minute. Depending on the switch, the maximum MAC address table size varies.

As shown in Figure 2-26, as long as the MAC address table on the switch remains full, the switch broadcasts all received frames out of every port. In this example, frames sent from host A to host B are also broadcast out of port 3 on the switch and seen by the attacker at host C.

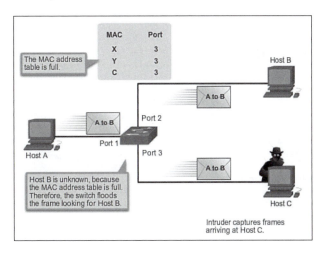

Figure 2-26   Switch Acts Like a Hub

One way to mitigate MAC address table overflow attacks is to configure port security.

Common Security Attacks: DHCP Spoofing (2.2.2.2)

Dynamic Host Control Protocol (DHCP) is the protocol that automatically assigns a host a valid IP address out of a DHCP pool. DHCP has been in use for nearly as long as TCP/IP has been the main protocol used within industry for allocating clients IP addresses. Two types of DHCP attacks can be performed against a switched network: *DHCP starvation attacks* and DHCP spoofing.

In DHCP starvation attacks, an attacker floods the DHCP server with DHCP requests to use up all the available IP addresses that the DHCP server can issue. After these IP addresses are issued, the server cannot issue any more addresses, and this situation produces a *denial of service (DoS)* attack as new clients cannot obtain network access. A DoS attack is any attack that is used to overload specific devices and network services with illegitimate traffic, thereby preventing legitimate traffic from reaching those resources.

In DHCP spoofing attacks, an attacker configures a fake DHCP server on the network to issue DHCP addresses to clients, as shown in Figure 2-27. The normal reason for this attack is to force the clients to use false Domain Name System (DNS) or Windows Internet Naming Service (WINS) servers and to make the clients use the attacker, or a machine under the control of the attacker, as their default gateway.

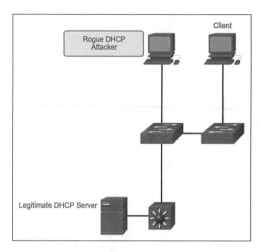

Figure 2-27   DHCP Spoofing

DHCP starvation is often used before a DHCP spoofing attack to deny service to the legitimate DHCP server, making it easier to introduce a fake DHCP server into the network.

To mitigate DHCP attacks, use the DHCP snooping and port security features on the Cisco Catalyst switches. These features are covered in a later topic.

Common Security Attacks: Leveraging CDP (2.2.2.3)

The *Cisco Discovery Protocol (CDP)* is a proprietary protocol that all Cisco devices can be configured to use. CDP discovers other Cisco devices that are directly connected, which allows the devices to autoconfigure their connection. In some cases, this simplifies configuration and connectivity.

By default, most Cisco routers and switches have CDP enabled on all ports. CDP information is sent in periodic, unencrypted broadcasts. This information is updated locally in the CDP database of each device. Because CDP is a Layer 2 protocol, CDP messages are not propagated by routers.

CDP contains information about the device, such as the IP address, IOS software version, platform, capabilities, and the native VLAN. This information can be used by an attacker to find ways to attack the network, typically in the form of a denial of service (DoS) attack.

Figure 2-28 is a portion of a Wireshark capture showing the contents of a CDP packet. The Cisco IOS Software version discovered through CDP, in particular, would allow the attacker to determine whether there were any security vulnerabilities specific to that particular version of IOS. Also, because CDP is not authenticated, an attacker could craft bogus CDP packets and send them to a directly connected Cisco device.

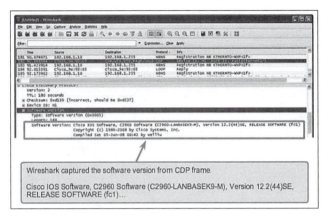

Wireshark captured the software version from CDP frame.

Cisco IOS Software, C2960 Software (C2960-LANBASEK9-M), Version 12.2(44)SE, RELEASE SOFTWARE (fc1)...

Figure 2-28   CDP Attack

It is recommended that you disable the use of CDP on devices or ports that do not need to use it by using the **no cdp run** global configuration mode command. CDP can be disabled on a per-port basis.

Telnet Attacks

The Telnet protocol is insecure and can be used by an attacker to gain remote access to a Cisco network device. There are tools available that allow an attacker to launch a brute force password-cracking attack against the vty lines on the switch.

Brute Force Password Attack

The first phase of a *brute force password attack* starts with the attacker using a list of common passwords and a program designed to try to establish a Telnet session using each word on the dictionary list. If the password is not discovered by the first phase, a second phase begins. In the second phase of a brute force attack, the attacker uses a program that creates sequential character combinations in an attempt to guess the password. Given enough time, a brute force password attack can crack almost all passwords used.

To mitigate against brute force password attacks, use strong passwords that are changed frequently. A strong password should have a mix of uppercase and lowercase letters and should include numerals and symbols (special characters). Access to the vty lines can also be limited using an access control list (ACL).

Telnet DoS Attack

Telnet can also be used to launch a DoS attack. In a Telnet DoS attack, the attacker exploits a flaw in the Telnet server software running on the switch that renders the Telnet service unavailable. This sort of attack prevents an administrator from remotely accessing switch management functions. This can be combined with other direct attacks on the network as part of a coordinated attempt to prevent the network administrator from accessing core devices during the breach.

Vulnerabilities in the Telnet service that permit DoS attacks to occur are usually addressed in security patches that are included in newer Cisco IOS revisions.

> **Note**
>
> It is a best practice to use SSH rather than Telnet for remote management connections.

Activity 2.2.2.4: Identify Common Security Attacks

Go to the online course to perform this practice activity.

Security Best Practices (2.2.3)

Network security *best practices* involve recommended procedures for network administrators to implement in their networks as common practice for ensuring a secure network. Of course, here the focus is on securing the LAN environment.

Best Practices (2.2.3.1)

Defending your network against attack requires vigilance and education. The following are best practices for securing a network:

- Develop a written security policy for the organization.

- Shut down unused services and ports.

- Use strong passwords and change them often.

- Control physical access to devices.

- Avoid using standard insecure HTTP websites, especially for login screens; instead use the more secure HTTPS.

- Perform backups and test the backed-up files on a regular basis.

- Educate employees about social engineering attacks, and develop policies to validate identities over the phone, through email, and in person.

- Encrypt and password-protect sensitive data.

- Implement security hardware and software, such as firewalls.

- Keep software up to date by installing security patches weekly or daily, if possible.

These methods, illustrated in Figure 2-29, are only a starting point for security management. Organizations must remain vigilant at all times to defend against continually evolving threats. Use network security tools to measure the vulnerability of the current network.

Figure 2-29 Security Best Practices

Network Security Tools and Testing (2.2.3.2)

Network security tools help a network administrator test a network for weaknesses. Some tools allow an administrator to assume the role of an attacker. Using one of these tools, an administrator can launch an attack against the network and audit the results to determine how to adjust security policies to mitigate those types of attacks. Security auditing and penetration testing are two basic functions that network security tools perform.

Network security testing techniques can be manually initiated by the administrator. Other tests are highly automated. Regardless of the type of testing, the staff that sets up and conducts the security testing should have extensive security and networking knowledge. This includes expertise in the following areas:

- Network security

- Firewalls

- Intrusion prevention systems

- Operating systems

- Programming

- Networking protocols (such as TCP/IP)

Network Security Audits (2.2.3.3)

Network security tools allow a network administrator to perform a security audit of a network. A *security audit* reveals the type of information an attacker can gather simply by monitoring network traffic.

For example, network security auditing tools allow an administrator to flood the MAC address table with fictitious MAC addresses. This is followed by an audit of the switch ports as the switch starts flooding traffic out of all ports. During the audit, the legitimate MAC address mappings are aged out and replaced with fictitious MAC address mappings. This determines which ports are compromised and not correctly configured to prevent this type of attack.

Timing is an important factor in performing the audit successfully. Different switches support varying numbers of MAC addresses in their MAC table. It can be difficult to determine the ideal number of spoofed MAC addresses to send to the switch. A network administrator also has to contend with the age-out period of the MAC address table. If the spoofed MAC addresses start to age out while performing a network audit, valid MAC addresses start to populate the MAC address table, limiting the data that can be monitored with a network auditing tool.

Network security tools can also be used for *penetration testing* against a network. Penetration testing is a simulated attack against the network to determine how vulnerable it would be in a real attack. This allows a network administrator to identify weaknesses within the configuration of networking devices and make changes to make the devices more resilient to attacks. There are numerous attacks that an administrator can perform, and most tool suites come with extensive documentation detailing the syntax needed to execute the desired attack.

Because penetration tests can have adverse effects on the network, they are carried out under very controlled conditions, following documented procedures detailed in a comprehensive network security policy. An off-line test bed network that mimics the actual production network is the ideal. The test bed network can be used by the networking staff to perform network penetration tests.

Switch Port Security (2.2.4)

A number of network attacks in the LAN environment can be mitigated with simple measures applied to switch ports on Cisco switches. DHCP snooping and Cisco port security help to mitigate MAC address flooding and DHCP attacks.

Secure Unused Ports (2.2.4.1)

A simple method that many administrators use to help secure the network from unauthorized access is to disable all unused ports on a switch. For example, if a

Catalyst 2960 switch has 24 ports and there are three Fast Ethernet connections in use, it is good practice to disable the 21 unused ports. Navigate to each unused port and issue the Cisco IOS **shutdown** command. If a port later needs to be reactivated, it can be enabled with the **no shutdown** command. Figure 2-30 shows partial output for this configuration.

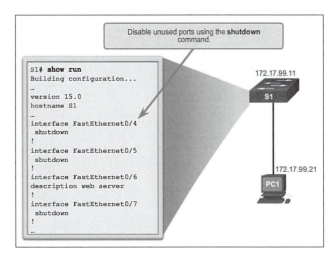

Figure 2-30   Disable Unused Ports

It is simple to make configuration changes to multiple ports on a switch. If a range of ports must be configured, use the **interface range** command:

```
Switch(config)# interface range type module/first-number – last-number
```

The process of enabling and disabling ports can be time-consuming, but it enhances security on the network and is well worth the effort.

DHCP Snooping (2.2.4.2)

DHCP snooping is a Cisco Catalyst feature that determines which switch ports can respond to DHCP requests. Ports are identified as trusted and untrusted. Trusted ports can source all DHCP messages, including DHCP offer and DHCP acknowledgment packets; untrusted ports can source requests only. Trusted ports host a DHCP server or can be an uplink toward the DHCP server. If a rogue device on an untrusted port attempts to send a DHCP offer packet into the network, the port is shut down. This feature can be coupled with DHCP options in which switch information, such as the port ID of the DHCP request, can be inserted into the DHCP request packet.

As shown in Figure 2-31, untrusted ports are those not explicitly configured as trusted. A DHCP binding table is built for untrusted ports. Each entry contains a client MAC address, IP address, lease time, binding type, VLAN number, and port ID recorded as clients make DHCP requests. The table is then used to filter subsequent

DHCP traffic. From a DHCP snooping perspective, untrusted access ports should not send any DHCP server messages.

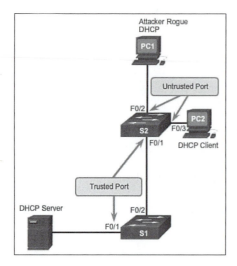

Figure 2-31   DHCP Snooping Operation

DHCP snooping allows the configuration of ports as trusted or untrusted. Trusted ports can send DHCP requests and acknowledgments. Untrusted ports can only forward DHCP requests. DHCP snooping enables the switch to build the DHCP binding table that binds a client MAC address, IP address, VLAN, and port ID.

The following configuration steps, illustrated in Figure 2-32, show how to implement DHCP snooping on a Catalyst 2960 switch:

Step 1.   Enable DHCP snooping using the **ip dhcp snooping** global configuration mode command.

Step 2.   Enable DHCP snooping for specific VLANs using the **ip dhcp snooping vlan** *number* command.

Step 3.   Define ports as trusted at the interface level by defining the trusted ports using the **ip dhcp snooping trust** command.

Step 4.   (Optional) Limit the rate at which an attacker can continually send bogus DHCP requests through untrusted ports to the DHCP server using the **ip dhcp snooping limit rate** *rate* command.

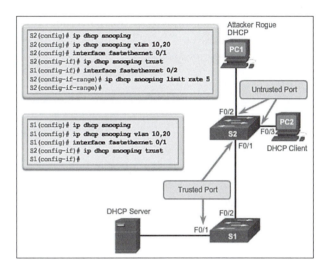

Figure 2-32   DHCP Snooping Configuration

Port Security: Operation (2.2.4.3)

All switch ports (interfaces) should be secured before the switch is deployed for production use. One way to secure ports is by implementing a feature called port security. Port security limits the number of valid MAC addresses allowed on a port. The MAC addresses of legitimate devices are allowed access, while other MAC addresses are denied.

Port security can be configured to allow one or more MAC addresses. If the number of MAC addresses allowed on the port is limited to one, only the device with that specific MAC address can successfully connect to the port.

If a port is configured as a secure port and the maximum number of MAC addresses is reached, any additional attempts to connect by unknown MAC addresses will generate a security violation.

Secure MAC Address Types

There are a number of ways to configure port security. The type of *secure MAC address* is based on the configuration and includes

- *Static secure MAC addresses*: MAC addresses that are manually configured on a port by using the **switchport port-security mac-address** *mac-address* interface configuration mode command. MAC addresses configured in this way are stored in the address table and are added to the running configuration on the switch.

- *Dynamic secure MAC addresses*: MAC addresses that are dynamically learned and stored only in the address table. MAC addresses configured in this way are removed when the switch restarts.

- *Sticky secure MAC addresses*: MAC addresses that can be dynamically learned or manually configured, and then stored in the address table and added to the running configuration.

Sticky Secure MAC Addresses

To configure an interface to convert dynamically learned MAC addresses to sticky secure MAC addresses and add them to the running configuration, you must enable sticky learning. Sticky learning is enabled on an interface by using the **switchport port-security mac-address sticky** interface configuration mode command.

When this command is entered, the switch converts all dynamically learned MAC addresses, including those that were dynamically learned before sticky learning was enabled, to sticky secure MAC addresses. All sticky secure MAC addresses are added to the address table and to the running configuration.

Sticky secure MAC addresses can also be manually defined. When sticky secure MAC addresses are configured by using the **switchport port-security mac-address sticky** *mac-address* interface configuration mode command, all specified addresses are added to the address table and the running configuration.

If the sticky secure MAC addresses are saved to the startup configuration file, when the switch restarts or the interface shuts down, the interface does not need to relearn the addresses. If the sticky secure addresses are not saved, they will be lost.

If sticky learning is disabled by using the **no switchport port-security mac-address sticky** interface configuration mode command, the sticky secure MAC addresses remain part of the address table as dynamic secure addresses, but are removed from the running configuration.

Note that port security features will not work until port security is enabled on the interface using the **switchport port-security** command.

Port Security: Violation Modes (2.2.4.4)

It is a security violation when either of these situations occurs:

- The maximum number of secure MAC addresses have been added to the address table for that interface, and a station whose MAC address is not in the address table attempts to access the interface.

- An address learned or configured on one secure interface is seen on another secure interface in the same VLAN.

An interface can be configured for one of three *violation modes*, specifying the action to be taken if a violation occurs:

- *Protect*: When the number of secure MAC addresses reaches the limit allowed on the port, packets with unknown source addresses are dropped until a sufficient number of secure MAC addresses are removed, or the number of maximum allowable addresses is increased. There is no notification that a security violation has occurred.

- *Restrict*: When the number of secure MAC addresses reaches the limit allowed on the port, packets with unknown source addresses are dropped until a sufficient number of secure MAC addresses are removed, or the number of maximum allowable addresses is increased. In this mode, there is a notification that a security violation has occurred.

- *Shutdown*: In this (default) violation mode, a port security violation causes the interface to immediately become error-disabled and turns off the port LED. It increments the violation counter. When a secure port is in the error-disabled state, it can be brought out of this state by entering the **shutdown** and **no shutdown** interface configuration mode commands.

Table 2-6 presents which kinds of data traffic are forwarded when one of the security violation modes is configured on a port.

Table 2-6   Port Security Violation Modes

Security Violation Modes

Violation Mode	Forwards Traffic	Sends Syslog Message	Increases Violation Counter	Shuts Down Port
Protect	No	No	No	No
Restrict	No	Yes	Yes	No
Shutdown	No	Yes	Yes	Yes

To change the violation mode on a switch port, use the **switchport port-security violation** {**protect** / **restrict** / **shutdown**} interface configuration mode command.

Port Security: Configuring (2.2.4.5)

Table 2-7 summarizes the default port security settings on a Cisco Catalyst switch.

Table 2-7 Port Security Defaults

Feature	Default Setting
Port security	Disabled on a port
Maximum number of secure MAC addresses	1
Restrict	Shutdown. The port shuts down when the maximum number of secure MAC addresses is exceeded.
Sticky address learning	Disabled

Figure 2-33 shows the Cisco IOS CLI commands needed to configure port security on the Fast Ethernet F0/18 port on the S1 switch. Notice that the example does not specify a violation mode. In this example, the violation mode is shutdown (the default mode).

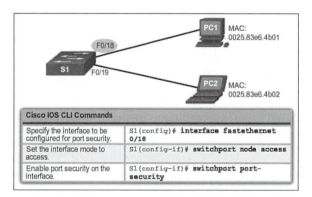

Figure 2-33 Configure Dynamic Port Security

Figure 2-34 shows how to enable sticky secure MAC addresses for port security on Fast Ethernet port 0/19 of switch S1. As stated earlier, the maximum number of secure MAC addresses can be manually configured. In this example, the Cisco IOS command syntax is used to set the maximum number of MAC addresses to 10 for port 0/19. The violation mode is set to shutdown, by default.

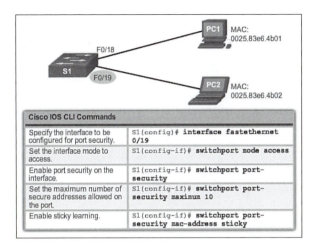

Figure 2-34   Configure Sticky Port Security

Port Security: Verifying (2.2.4.6)

After configuring port security on a switch, check each interface to verify that the port security is set correctly, and check to ensure that the static MAC addresses have been configured correctly.

Verify Port Security Settings

To display port security settings for the switch or for the specified interface, use the **show port-security** [**interface** *interface-id*] command. The output for the dynamic port security configuration is shown in Example 2-5. By default, there is one MAC address allowed on this port.

Example 2-5   Verify Dynamic MAC Addresses

```
S1# show port-security interface fastethernet 0/18
Port Security               : Enabled
Port Status               : Secure-up
Violation Mode          : Shutdown
Aging Time              : 0 mins
Aging Type              : Absolute
SecureStatic Address Aging       : Disabled
Maximum MAC Addresses            : 1
Total MAC Addresses          : 1
Configured MAC Addresses     : 0
Sticky MAC Addresses        : 0
Last Source Address:Vlan     : 0025.83e6.4b01:1
Security Violation Count     : 0
```

The output shown in Example 2-6 shows the values for the sticky port security settings. The maximum number of addresses is set to 10, as configured.

Example 2-6   Verify Sticky MAC Addresses

```
S1# show port-security interface fastethernet 0/19
Port Security               : Enabled
Port Status                 : Secure-up
Violation Mode            : Shutdown
Aging Time                : 0 mins
Aging Type                : Absolute
SecureStatic Address Aging     : Disabled
Maximum MAC Addresses          : 50
Total MAC Addresses        : 1
Configured MAC Addresses   : 0
Sticky MAC Addresses           : 1
Last Source Address:Vlan       : 0025.83e6.4b02:1
Security Violation Count   : 0
```

Note

The MAC address is identified as a sticky MAC address in Example 2-6.

Sticky MAC addresses are added to the MAC address table and to the running configuration. Port security with sticky MAC addresses retains dynamically learned MAC addresses during a link-down condition. If you enter the **copy running-config startup-config** command, port security with sticky MAC addresses saves dynamically learned MAC addresses in the startup config file and the port does not have to learn addresses from ingress traffic after bootup or a restart. As shown in Example 2-7, the sticky MAC for PC2 has been added to the running configuration for S1.

Example 2-7   Verify Sticky MAC Addresses in Running Configuration

```
S1# show run | begin FastEthernet 0/19
interface FastEthernet0/19
 switchport mode access
 switchport port-security maximum 50
 switchport port-security
 switchport port-security mac-address sticky
 switchport port-security mac-address sticky 0025.83e6.4b02
```

Verify Secure MAC Addresses

To display all secure MAC addresses configured on all switch interfaces, or on a specified interface with aging information for each, use the **show port-security address** command. As shown in Example 2-8, the secure MAC addresses are listed along with the types.

Example 2-8   Verify Secure MAC Addresses

```
S1# show port-security address
Secure Mac Address Table
-------------------------------------------------------------------

Vlan    Mac Address      Type             Ports    Remaining Age
                                                    (mins)

----    -----------      ----             -----    -------------
1       0025.83e6.4b01   SecureDynamic    Fa0/18   -
1       0025.83e6.4b02   SecureSticky     Fa0/19   -
-------------------------------------------------------------------
Total Addresses in System (excluding one mac per port) : 0
Max Addresses limit in System (excluding one mac per port
```

Ports in Error-Disabled State (2.2.4.7)

When a port is configured with port security, a violation can cause the port to become *error disabled*. When a port is error disabled, it is effectively shut down and no traffic is sent or received on that port. A series of port security–related messages display on the console, similar to those shown in Example 2-9.

Example 2-9   Port Security Violation Messages

```
Sep 20 06:44:54.966: %PM-4-ERR_DISABLE: psecure-violation error detected on Fa0/18,
  putting Fa0/18 in err-disable state
Sep 20 06:44:54.966: %PORT_SECURITY-2-PSECURE_VIOLATION: Security violation occurred,
  caused by MAC address 000c.292b.4c75 on port FastEthernet0/18.
Sep 20 06:44:55.973: %LINEPROTO-5-PPDOWN: Line protocol on Interface
FastEthernet0/18, changed state to down
Sep 20 06:44:56.971: %LINK-3-UPDOWN: Interface FastEthernet0/18, changed state to down
```

Note

The port protocol and link status is changed to down.

The port LED will change to orange. The **show interfaces** command identifies the port status as **err-disabled** (see Example 2-10). The output of the **show port-security interface** command now shows the port status as **secure-shutdown**. Because the port security violation mode is set to shutdown, the port with the security violation goes to the error-disabled state.

Example 2-10   Port Status

```
S1# show interface fa0/18 status
Port      Name   Status       Vlan  Duplex  Speed   Type
Fa0/18           err-disabled 1     auto    auto    10/100BaseTX
S1# show port-security interface fastethernet 0/18
Port Security                   : Enabled
Port Status                     : Secure-shutdown
Violation Mode          : Shutdown
Aging Time              : 0 mins
Aging Type              : Absolute
SecureStatic Address Aging      : Disabled
Maximum MAC Addresses           : 1
Total MAC Addresses       : 0
Configured MAC Addresses        : 0
Sticky MAC Addresses        : 0
Last Source Address:Vlan        : 000c.292b.4c75:1
Security Violation Count        : 1
```

The administrator should determine what caused the security violation before reenabling the port. If an unauthorized device is connected to a secure port, the port should not be reenabled until the security threat is eliminated. To reenable the port, use the **shutdown** interface configuration mode command (see Example 2-11). Then, use the **no shutdown** interface configuration command to make the port operational.

Example 2-11   Reenabling an Error-Disabled Port

```
S1(config)# interface FastEthernet 0/18
S1(config-if)# shutdown
Sep 20 06:57:28.532: %LINK-5-CHANGED: Interface FastEthernet0/18, changed state to
  administratively down
S1(config-if)# no shutdown
Sep 20 06:57:48.186: %LINK-3-UPDOWN: Interface FastEthernet0/18, changed state to up
Sep 20 06:57:49.193: %LINEPROTO-5-UPDOWN: Line protocol on Interface
FastEthernet0/18, changed state to up
```

Network Time Protocol (NTP) (2.2.4.8)

Having the correct time within networks is important. Correct time stamps are required to accurately track network events such as security violations. Additionally, clock synchronization is critical for the correct interpretation of events within syslog data files as well as for digital certificates.

Network Time Protocol (NTP) is a protocol that is used to synchronize the clocks of computer systems over packet-switched, variable-latency data networks. NTP allows network devices to synchronize their time settings with an NTP server. A group of NTP clients that obtain time and date information from a single source will have more consistent time settings.

A secure method of providing clocking for the network is for network administrators to implement their own private network master clocks, synchronized to UTC, using satellite or radio. However, if network administrators do not want to implement their own master clocks because of cost or other reasons, other clock sources are available on the Internet. NTP can get the correct time from an internal or external time source including the following:

- Local master clock
- Master clock on the Internet
- GPS or atomic clock

A network device can be configured as either an NTP server or an NTP client. To allow the software clock to be synchronized by an NTP time server, use the **ntp server** *ip-address* command in global configuration mode. A sample configuration is shown in Figure 2-35. Router R2 is configured as an NTP client, while Router R1 serves as an authoritative NTP server.

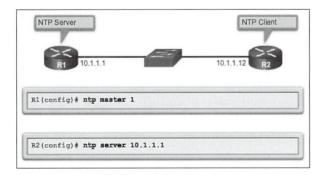

Figure 2-35   Port Status

To configure a device as having an NTP master clock to which peers can synchronize themselves, use the **ntp master** [*stratum*] command in global configuration mode. The stratum value is a number from 1 to 15 and indicates the NTP stratum number that the system will claim. If the system is configured as an NTP master and no stratum number is specified, it will default to stratum 8. If the NTP master cannot reach any clock with a lower stratum number, the system will claim to be synchronized at the configured stratum number, and other systems will be willing to synchronize to it using NTP.

To display the status of NTP associations, use the **show ntp associations** command in privileged EXEC mode. This command will indicate the IP address of any peer devices that are synchronized to this peer, statically configured peers, and stratum number. The **show ntp status** user EXEC command can be used to display such information as the NTP synchronization status, the peer that the device is synchronized to, and in which NTP strata the device is functioning. Example 2-12 displays the verification of NTP on Router R2.

Example 2-12   Configuring NTP

```
R2# show ntp associations


  address       ref clock     st    when    poll reach  delay  offset   disp
*~10.1.1.1      .LOCL.         1      13      64   377   1.472  6.071    3.629
 * sys.peer, # selected, + candidate, - outlyer, x falseticker, ~ configured


R2# show ntp status
Clock is synchronized, stratum 2, reference is 10.1.1.1
nominal freq is 119.2092 Hz, actual freq is 119.2092 Hz, precision is 2**17
reference time is D40ADC27.E644C776 (13:18:31.899 UTC Mon Sep 24 2012)
clock offset is 6.0716 msec, root delay is 1.47 msec
root dispersion is 15.41 msec, peer dispersion is 3.62 msec
loopfilter state is 'CTRL' (Normal Controlled Loop), drift is 0.000000091 s/s
system poll interval is 64, last update was 344 sec ago.***Insert Packet Tracer icon
  here.
```

Packet Tracer Activity 2.2.4.9: Configuring Switch Port Security

In this activity, you will configure and verify port security on a switch. Port security allows you to restrict a port's ingress traffic by limiting the MAC addresses that are allowed to send traffic into the port.

Packet Tracer Activity 2.2.4.10: Troubleshooting Switch Port Security

The employee who normally uses PC1 brought his laptop from home, disconnected PC1 and connected the laptop to the telecommunication outlet. After reminding him of the security policy that does not allow personal devices on the network, you now must reconnect PC1 and reenable the port.

Lab 2.2.4.11: Configuring Switch Security Features

In this lab, you will complete the following objectives:

- Part 1: Set Up the Topology and Initialize Devices
- Part 2: Configure Basic Device Settings and Verify Connectivity
- Part 3: Configure and Verify SSH Access on S1
- Part 4: Configure and Verify Security Features on S1

Summary (2.3)

Class Activity 2.3.1.1: Switch Trio

You are the network administrator for a small- to medium-sized business. Corporate headquarters for your business has mandated that security must be implemented on all switches in all offices. The memorandum delivered to you this morning states the following:

> "By Monday, April 18, 20xx, the first three ports of all configurable switches located in all offices must be secured with MAC addresses—one address will be reserved for the printer, one address will be reserved for the laptop in the office, and one address will be reserved for the office server.

> If a port's security is breached, we ask that you shut it down until the reason for the breach can be certified.

> Please implement this policy no later than the date stated in this memorandum. For questions, call 1.800.555.1212. Thank you. The Network Management Team."

Work with a partner in the class and create a Packet Tracer example to test this new security policy. After you have created your file, test it with at least one device to ensure that it is operational or validated.

Save your work and be prepared to share it with the entire class.

Packet Tracer Activity 2.3.1.2: Skills Integration Challenge

The network administrator asked you to configure a new switch. In this activity, you will use a list of requirements to configure the new switch with initial settings, SSH, and port security.

When a Cisco LAN switch is first powered on, it goes through the following boot sequence:

1. The switch loads a power-on self-test (POST) program stored in ROM. POST checks the CPU subsystem. It tests the CPU, DRAM, and the portion of the flash device that makes up the flash file system.

2. The switch loads the boot loader software. The boot loader is a small program stored in ROM and is run immediately after POST successfully completes.

3. The boot loader performs low-level CPU initialization. It initializes the CPU registers, which control where physical memory is mapped, the quantity of memory, and its speed.

4. The boot loader initializes the flash file system on the system board.

5. The boot loader locates and loads a default IOS operating system software image into memory and hands control of the switch over to the IOS.

The specific Cisco IOS file that is loaded is specified by the BOOT environmental variable. After the Cisco IOS is loaded, it uses the commands found in the startup config file to initialize and configure the interfaces. If the Cisco IOS files are missing or damaged, the boot loader program can be used to reload or recover from the problem.

The operational status of the switch is displayed by a series of LEDs on the front panel. These LEDs display such things as port status, duplex, and speed.

An IP address is configured on the SVI of the management VLAN to allow for remote configuration of the device. A default gateway belonging to the management VLAN must be configured on the switch using the **ip default-gateway** command. If the default gateway is not properly configured, remote management is not possible. It is recommended that Secure Shell (SSH) be used to provide a secure (encrypted) management connection to a remote device to prevent the sniffing of unencrypted usernames and passwords, which is possible when using protocols such as Telnet.

One of the advantages of a switch is that it allows full-duplex communication between devices, effectively doubling the communication rate. Although it is possible to specify the speed and duplex settings of a switch interface, it is recommended that the switch be allowed to set these parameters automatically to avoid errors.

Switch port security is a requirement to prevent such attacks as MAC address flooding and DHCP spoofing. Switch ports should be configured to allow only frames with specific source MAC addresses to enter. Frames from unknown source MAC addresses should be denied and cause the port to shut down to prevent further attacks.

Port security is only one defense against network compromise. There are ten best practices that represent the best insurance for a network:

- Develop a written security policy for the organization.

- Shut down unused services and ports.

- Use strong passwords and change them often.

- Control physical access to devices.

- Avoid using standard insecure HTTP websites, especially for login screens. Instead use the more secure HTTPS.

- Perform backups and test the backed-up files on a regular basis.

- Educate employees about social engineering attacks, and develop policies to validate identities over the phone, through email, and in person.

- Encrypt sensitive data and protect it with a strong password.

- Implement security hardware and software, such as firewalls.

- Keep IOS software up to date by installing security patches weekly or daily, if possible.

These methods are only a starting point for security management. Organizations must remain vigilant at all times to defend against continually evolving threats.

Practice

The following activities provide practice with the topics introduced in this chapter. The Labs and Class Activities are available in the companion *Switched Networks Lab Manual* (ISBN 978-1-58713-327-5). The Packet Tracer Activities PKA files are found in the online course.

Class Activities

- Class Activity 2.0.1.2: Stand by Me

- Class Activity 2.3.1.1: Switch Trio

Labs

- Lab 2.1.1.6: Configuring Basic Switch Settings

- Lab 2.2.4.11: Configuring Switch Security Features

Packet Tracer
Activity

Packet Tracer Activities

- Packet Tracer Activity 2.2.1.4: Configuring SSH

- Packet Tracer Activity 2.2.4.9: Configuring Switch Port Security

- Packet Tracer Activity 2.2.4.10: Troubleshooting Switch Port Security

- Packet Tracer Activity 2.3.1.2: Skills Integration Challenge

Check Your Understanding Questions

Complete all the review questions listed here to test your understanding of the topics and concepts in this chapter. The appendix "Answers to 'Check Your Understanding' Questions" lists the answers.

1. Which of the following options correctly associate the command with the paired behavior? (Choose three.)

   A. **switchport port-security violation protect:** Frames with unknown source addresses are dropped and a notification is sent.

   B. **switchport port-security violation restrict:** Frames with unknown source addresses are dropped and no notification is sent.

   C. **switchport port-security violation shutdown:** Frames with unknown source addresses result in the port becoming error-disabled and a notification is sent.

   D. **switchport port-security mac-address sticky:** Allows dynamically learned MAC addresses to be stored in the running configuration.

   E. **switchport port-security maximum:** Defines the number of MAC addresses associated with a port.

2. What advantage does SSH offer over Telnet when remotely connecting to a device?

   A. Encryption

   B. More connection lines

   C. Connection-oriented services

   D. Username and password authentication

3. Which option correctly associates the Layer 2 security attack with the description?

   A. MAC address flooding: broadcast requests for IP addresses with spoofed MAC addresses

   B. DHCP starvation: using Cisco-proprietary protocols to gain information about a switch

   C. CDP attack: the attacker fills the switch MAC address table with invalid MAC addresses

   D. Telnet attack: using brute force password attacks to gain access to a switch

4. The network administrator wants to configure an IP address on a Cisco switch. How does the network administrator assign the IP address?

    A. In privileged EXEC mode

    B. On the switch interface FastEthernet 0/0

    C. On the management VLAN virtual interface

    D. On the physical interface connected to the router or next-hop device

5. Why should a default gateway be assigned to a switch?

    A. So that there can be remote connectivity to the switch through such programs as Telnet and ping

    B. So that frames can be sent through the switch to the router

    C. So that frames generated from workstations and destined for remote networks can pass to a higher level

    D. So that other networks can be accessed from the command prompt of the switch

6. Which of the following tasks does autonegotiation in an Ethernet network accomplish? (Choose two.)

    A. Sets the link speed

    B. Sets the IP address

    C. Sets the link duplex mode

    D. Sets MAC address assignments on the switch port

    E. Sets the ring speed

7. The boot loader can be accessed through a console connection in a sequence of steps. Put the following steps in order.

    A. The boot loader **switch:** prompt appears in the terminal emulation software on the PC.

    B. Unplug the switch power cord.

    C. Connect a PC by console cable to the switch console port. Configure terminal emulation software to connect to the switch.

    D. Continue pressing the **Mode** button until the System LED turns briefly amber and then solid green; then release the **Mode** button.

    E. Reconnect the power cord to the switch and, within 15 seconds, press and hold down the **Mode** button while the System LED is still flashing green.

8. List three LED indicators on a Cisco Catalyst 2960 switch.

9. What are the default settings for duplex and speed on Cisco Catalyst 2960 and 3560 switches?

10. What feature on Cisco Catalyst 2960 enables switch ports to work with either crossover or straight-through cables?

11. A giant Ethernet frame is one that is greater than how many bytes?

12. An Ethernet frame that is smaller than 64 bytes is called a _____.

13. Assume that a Cisco Catalyst switch has an image that supports SSH. Assume that a host name and domain name are configured, that local authentication is properly configured, and that the vty lines support all protocols. Which command is required to have a functional SSH configuration?

    A. **ip ssh version 2** in global configuration mode

    B. **crypto key generate rsa** in global configuration mode

    C. **transport input ssh** in line VTY configuration mode

    D. **login local** in line vty configuration mode

    E. **ip domain-name** *<domain-name>* in global configuration mode

14. A network administrator has configured VLAN 99 as the management VLAN and has configured it with an IP address and subnet mask. The administrator issues the **show interface vlan 99** command and notices that the line protocol is down. Which action can change the state of the line protocol to up?

    A. Connect a host to an interface associated with VLAN 99.

    B. Configure a default gateway.

    C. Remove all access ports from VLAN 99.

    D. Configure a transport input method on the vty lines.

15. A network administrator plugs a PC into a switch port. The LED for that port changes to solid green. What statement best describes the current status of the port?

    A. There is a duplex mismatch error.

    B. There is a link fault error. This port is unable to forward frames.

    C. The port is operational and ready to transmit packets.

    D. This port has been disabled by management and is unable to forward frames.

    E. The flash memory is busy.

16. Describe a DHCP starvation attack.

17. List three best practices for securing a network. (Several answers are possible.)

18. What is an ideal environment to carry out penetration tests?

A. On the production network during nonpeak times

B. Under controlled conditions during business hours on the production network

C. On an off-line test bed network that mimics the actual production network

D. On a network environment simulated by software

19. What is the result of issuing the **no switchport port-security mac-address sticky** command on an interface with port security configured?

A. The sticky secure MAC addresses are removed from the address table and from the running configuration.

B. The sticky secure MAC addresses remain part of the address table but are removed from the running configuration.

C. The static secure MAC addresses are removed from the address table and from the running configuration.

D. The static secure MAC addresses remain part of the address table but are removed from the running configuration.

20. An attacker has bypassed physical security and was able to connect a laptop to an Ethernet interface on a switch. If all the switch ports are configured with port security and the violation mode is set to factory default, which action is taken against the attacker?

A. Packets with unknown source addresses are dropped, and there is no notification that a security violation has occurred.

B. Packets with unknown source addresses are dropped, and there is a notification that a security violation has occurred.

C. Packets with unknown source addresses are dropped, and the interface becomes error-disabled and turns off the port LED.

D. Packets with unknown source addresses are forwarded, and there is a notification to the syslog server.

CHAPTER 3

VLANs

Objectives

Upon completion of this chapter, you will be able to answer the following questions:

- How do you explain the purpose of VLANs in a switched network?

- How do you analyze the forwarding of frames by a switch based on VLAN configuration?

- How do you configure a switch port to be assigned to data and voice VLANs?

- How do you configure a trunk port on a LAN switch?

- How do you configure Dynamic Trunking Protocol (DTP)?

- How do you troubleshoot VLAN and trunk configurations in a switched network?

- How do you configure security features to mitigate attacks in a switched network?

- How do you explain security best practices for a switched network?

Key Terms

This chapter uses the following key terms. You can find the definitions in the Glossary.

Introduction (3.0.1.1)

Network performance is an important factor in the productivity of an organization. One of the technologies used to improve network performance is the separation of large broadcast domains into smaller ones. By design, routers will block broadcast traffic at an interface. However, routers normally have a limited number of LAN interfaces. A router's primary role is to move information between networks, not provide network access to end devices.

The role of providing access into a LAN is normally reserved for an access layer switch. A *virtual local-area network (VLAN)* can be created on a Layer 2 switch to reduce the size of broadcast domains, similar to a Layer 3 device. VLANs are commonly incorporated into network design, making it easier for a network to support the goals of an organization. While VLANs are primarily used within switched local-area networks, modern implementations of VLANs allow them to span MANs and WANs.

This chapter will cover how to configure, manage, and troubleshoot VLANs and *VLAN trunks*. It will also examine security considerations and strategies relating to VLANs and trunks, and best practices for VLAN design.

Class Activity 3.0.1.2: Vacation Station

You have purchased a three-floor vacation home at the beach for rental purposes. The floor plan is identical on each floor. Each floor offers one digital television for renters to use.

According to the local Internet service provider, only three stations can be offered within a television package. It is your job to decide which television packages you offer your guests.

- Divide the class into groups of three students per group.

- Choose three different stations to make one subscription package for each floor of your rental home.

- Complete the PDF for this activity.

- Share your completed group-reflection answers with the class.

VLAN Segmentation (3.1)

LAN switches and VLANs go hand in hand. When you look at the configuration of a router, you do not see references to VLANs; however, when you look at the configuration of a switch, you see frequent references to VLANs. Modern switches are structured around VLANs. VLANs are to switches as networks are to routers. Almost everything you do on a switch relates to VLANs. So, to a large extent, learning about switching is learning about VLANs. The day in the future when every port on every switch is on a separate Layer 3 network is the day that VLANs are no longer necessary—the need for VLANs is tied to the need to put multiple switch ports in one broadcast domain (in one VLAN).

Overview of VLANs (3.1.1)

This section provides a high-level introduction to VLANs, which sets the stage for the chapter.

VLAN Definitions (3.1.1.1)

Within a switched internetwork, VLANs provide segmentation and organizational flexibility. VLANs provide a way to group devices within a LAN. A group of devices within a VLAN communicate as if they were attached to the same wire. VLANs are based on logical connections, instead of physical connections.

VLANs allow an administrator to segment networks based on factors such as function, project team, or application, without regard for the physical location of the user or device, as seen in Figure 3-1. Devices within a VLAN act as if they are in their own independent network, even if they share a common infrastructure with other VLANs. Any switch port can belong to a VLAN, and unicast, broadcast, and multicast packets are forwarded and flooded only to end stations within the VLAN where the packets are sourced. Each VLAN is considered a separate logical network, and packets destined for stations that do not belong to the VLAN must be forwarded through a device that supports routing.

A VLAN creates a logical broadcast domain that can span multiple physical LAN segments. VLANs improve network performance by separating large broadcast domains into smaller ones. If a device in one VLAN sends a broadcast Ethernet frame, all devices in the VLAN receive the frame, but devices in other VLANs do not.

VLANs enable the implementation of access and security policies according to specific groupings of users. Each switch port can be assigned to only one VLAN (with the exception of a port connected to an IP phone or to another switch).

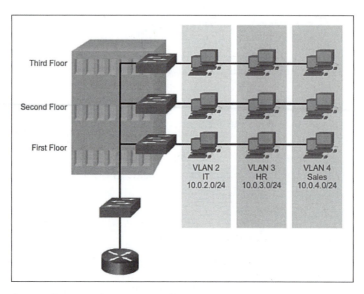

Figure 3-1   Defining VLAN Groups

Benefits of VLANs (3.1.1.2)

User productivity and network adaptability are important for business growth and success. VLANs make it easier to design a network to support the goals of an organization. The primary benefits of using VLANs are as follows:

- **Security:** Groups that have sensitive data are separated from the rest of the network, decreasing the chances of confidential information breaches. As shown in Figure 3-2, faculty computers are on VLAN 10 and completely separated from student and guest data traffic.

- **Cost reduction:** Cost savings result from reduced need for expensive network upgrades and more efficient use of existing bandwidth and uplinks.

- **Better performance:** Dividing flat Layer 2 networks into multiple logical workgroups (broadcast domains) reduces unnecessary traffic on the network and boosts performance.

- **Shrink broadcast domains:** Dividing a network into VLANs reduces the number of devices in the broadcast domain. As shown in Figure 3-2, there are six computers on this network but there are three broadcast domains: Faculty, Student, and Guest.

- **Improved IT staff efficiency:** VLANs make it easier to manage the network because users with similar network requirements share the same VLAN. When a new switch is provisioned, all the policies and procedures already configured for the particular VLAN are implemented when the ports are assigned. It is also easy for the IT staff to identify the function of a VLAN by giving it an appropriate name. In Figure 3-2, for easy identification, VLAN 10 has been named "Faculty," VLAN 20 is named "Student," and VLAN 30 "Guest."

- **Simpler project and application management:** VLANs aggregate users and network devices to support business or geographic requirements. Having separate functions makes managing a project or working with a specialized application easier; an example of such an application is an e-learning development platform for faculty.

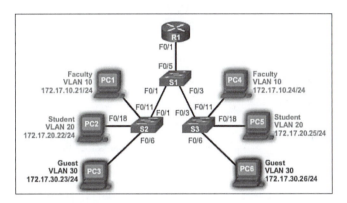

Figure 3-2   Benefits of VLANs

Each VLAN in a switched network corresponds to an IP network; therefore, VLAN design must take into consideration the implementation of a hierarchical network-addressing scheme. Hierarchical network addressing means that IP network numbers are applied to network segments or VLANs in an orderly fashion that takes the network as a whole into consideration. Blocks of contiguous network addresses are reserved for and configured on devices in a specific area of the network, as shown in Figure 3-2.

Types of VLANs (3.1.1.3)

There are a number of distinct types of VLANs used in modern networks. Some VLAN types are defined by traffic classes. Other types of VLANs are defined by the specific function that they serve.

Data VLAN

A *data VLAN* is a VLAN that is configured to carry user-generated traffic. A VLAN carrying voice or management traffic would not be a data VLAN. It is common practice to separate voice and management traffic from data traffic. A data VLAN is sometimes referred to as a *user VLAN*. Data VLANs are used to separate the network into groups of users or devices.

Default VLAN

All switch ports become a part of the default VLAN after the initial bootup of a switch loading the default configuration. Switch ports that participate in the *default VLAN* are part of the same broadcast domain. This allows any device connected to any switch port to communicate with other devices on other switch ports. The default VLAN for Cisco switches is VLAN 1. In Example 3-1, the **show vlan brief** command was issued on a switch running the default configuration. Notice that all ports are assigned to VLAN 1 by default.

VLAN 1 has all the features of any VLAN, except it cannot be renamed or deleted. By default, all Layer 2 control traffic is associated with VLAN 1.

Example 3-1   Default VLAN Configuration

```
Switch# show vlan brief

VLAN Name                             Status    Ports
---- -------------------------------- --------- -------------------------
1    default                          active    Fa0/1, Fa0/2, Fa0/3, Fa0/4
                                                Fa0/5, Fa0/6, Fa0/7, Fa0/8
                                                Fa0/9, Fa0/10, Fa0/11, Fa0/12
                                                Fa0/13, Fa0/14, Fa0/15, Fa0/16
                                                Fa0/17, Fa0/18, Fa0/19, Fa0/20
                                                Fa0/21, Fa0/22, Fa0/23, Fa0/24
                                                Gi0/1, Gi0/2
1002 fddi-default                     act/unsup
1003 token-ring-default               act/unsup
1004 fddinet-default                  act/unsup
1005 trnet-default                    act/unsup
```

Native VLAN

A *native VLAN* is assigned to an 802.1Q trunk port. Trunk ports are the links between switches that support the transmission of traffic associated with more than one VLAN. An 802.1Q trunk port supports traffic coming from many VLANs (tagged traffic), as well as traffic that does not come from a VLAN (untagged traffic). Tagged traffic refers to traffic that has a 4-byte tag inserted within the original Ethernet frame header, specifying the VLAN to which the frame belongs. The 802.1Q trunk port places untagged traffic on the native VLAN, which by default is VLAN 1.

Native VLANs are defined in the *IEEE 802.1Q* specification to maintain backward compatibility with untagged traffic common to legacy LAN scenarios. A native VLAN serves as a common identifier on opposite ends of a trunk link.

It is a best practice to configure the native VLAN as an unused VLAN, distinct from VLAN 1 and other VLANs. In fact, it is not unusual to dedicate a fixed VLAN to serve the role of the native VLAN for all trunk ports in the switched domain.

Management VLAN

A *management VLAN* is any VLAN configured to access the management capabilities of a switch. VLAN 1 is the management VLAN by default. To create the management VLAN, the switch virtual interface (SVI) of that VLAN is assigned an IP address and subnet mask, allowing the switch to be managed through HTTP, Telnet, SSH, or SNMP. Because the out-of-the-box configuration of a Cisco switch has VLAN 1 as the default VLAN, VLAN 1 would be a bad choice for the management VLAN.

In the past, the management VLAN for a 2960 switch was the only active SVI. On 15.x versions of the Cisco IOS for Catalyst 2960 Series switches, it is possible to have more than one active SVI. With Cisco IOS Release 15.x, the particular active SVI assigned for remote management must be documented. While theoretically a switch can have more than one management VLAN, having more than one increases exposure to network attacks.

In Example 3-1, all ports are currently assigned to the default VLAN 1. No native VLAN is explicitly assigned and no other VLANs are active; therefore the network is designed with the native VLAN the same as the management VLAN. This is considered a security risk.

Voice VLANs (3.1.1.4)

A separate VLAN is needed to support Voice over IP (VoIP). VoIP traffic requires

- Assured bandwidth to ensure voice quality
- Transmission priority over other types of network traffic
- Ability to be routed around congested areas on the network
- Delay of less than 150 ms across the network

To meet these requirements, the entire network has to be designed to support VoIP. The details of how to configure a network to support VoIP are beyond the scope of this course, but it is useful to summarize how a *voice VLAN* works between a switch, a Cisco IP Phone, and a computer.

In Figure 3-3, VLAN 150 is designed to carry voice traffic. The student computer PC5 is attached to the Cisco IP Phone, and the phone is attached to switch S3. PC5 is in VLAN 20, which is used for student data.

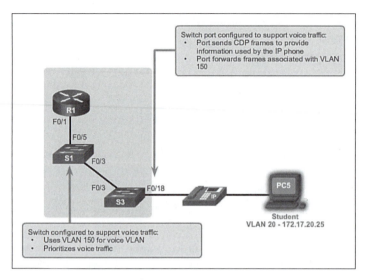

Figure 3-3 Voice VLAN

Packet Tracer Activity 3.1.1.5: Who Hears the Broadcast?

In this activity, a 24-port Catalyst 2960 switch is fully populated. All ports are in use. You will observe broadcast traffic in a VLAN implementation and answer some reflection questions.

VLANs in a Multiswitch Environment (3.1.2)

VLAN trunks are the connections in switched networks upon which all control traffic is transmitted and received. VLAN trunks carry data traffic for all VLANs in the switched network, unless restricted manually or with a pruning mechanism. Switches are interconnected with VLAN trunks. This section describes VLAN trunks.

VLAN Trunks (3.1.2.1)

A trunk is a point-to-point link between two network devices that carries more than one VLAN. A VLAN trunk extends VLANs across an entire network. Cisco supports IEEE 802.1Q for coordinating trunks on Fast Ethernet, Gigabit Ethernet, and 10-Gigabit Ethernet interfaces.

VLANs would not be very useful without VLAN trunks. VLAN trunks allow all VLAN traffic to propagate between switches so that devices that are in the same VLAN, but connected to different switches, can communicate without the intervention of a router.

A VLAN trunk does not belong to a specific VLAN; rather, it is a conduit for multiple VLANs between switches and routers. A trunk could also be used between a network device and server or other device that is equipped with an appropriate 802.1Q-capable NIC. By default, on a Cisco Catalyst switch, all VLANs are supported on a trunk port.

In Figure 3-4, the links between switches S1 and S2, and S1 and S3, are configured to transmit traffic coming from VLANs 10, 20, 30, and 99 across the network. This network could not function without VLAN trunks.

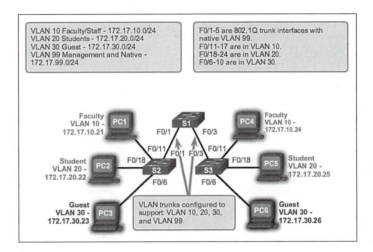

Figure 3-4   VLAN Trunks

Controlling Broadcast Domains with VLANs (3.1.2.2)

The behavior of broadcasts is affected by the presence of a switch. An ingress broadcast frame on a switch will only be forwarded out ports identified with the VLAN with which the frame is associated.

Network Without VLANs

In normal operation, when a switch receives a broadcast frame on one of its ports, it forwards the frame out all other ports except the port where the broadcast was received. In Figure 3-5, the entire network is configured in the same subnet (172.17.40.0/24) and no VLANs are configured. As a result, when the faculty computer (PC1) sends out a broadcast frame, switch S2 sends that broadcast frame out all of its ports. Eventually the entire network receives the broadcast because the network is one broadcast domain.

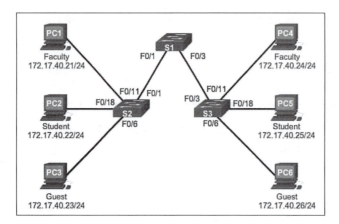

Figure 3-5   VLAN Trunks

Network with VLANs

As shown in Figure 3-6, the network has been segmented using two VLANs. Faculty devices are assigned to VLAN 10 and student devices are assigned to VLAN 20. When a broadcast frame is sent from the faculty computer, PC1, to switch S2, the switch forwards that broadcast frame only to those switch ports configured to support VLAN 10.

The ports that comprise the connection between switches S2 and S1 (ports F0/1), and between S1 and S3 (ports F0/3), are trunks and have been configured to support all the VLANs in the network. Port F0/18 is associated with VLAN 20, so S2 forwards the broadcast out port F0/1 but does not forward the broadcast out port F0/18, as shown in Figure 3-6.

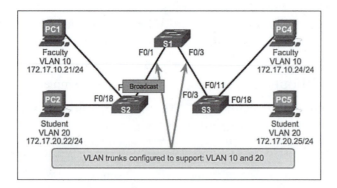

Figure 3-6   Broadcasts with VLAN Segmentation

When S1 receives the broadcast frame on port F0/1, S1 forwards that broadcast frame out of the only other port configured to support VLAN 10, which is port F0/3. When S3 receives the broadcast frame on port F0/3, it forwards the broadcast frame out of the only other port configured to support VLAN 10, which is port F0/11. The broadcast frame arrives at the only other computer in the network configured in VLAN 10, which is faculty computer PC4.

When VLANs are implemented on a switch, the transmission of unicast, multicast, and broadcast traffic from a host in a particular VLAN is restricted to the devices that are in that VLAN.

Tagging Ethernet Frames for VLAN Identification (3.1.2.3)

Catalyst 2960 Series switches are Layer 2 devices. They use the Ethernet frame header information to forward packets. They do not have routing tables. The standard Ethernet frame header does not contain information about the VLAN to which the frame belongs. Thus, when Ethernet frames are placed on a trunk, information about the VLANs to which they belong must be added. This process, called tagging, is accomplished by using the IEEE 802.1Q header, specified in the IEEE 802.1Q standard. The 802.1Q header includes a 4-byte tag inserted within the original Ethernet frame header, specifying the VLAN to which the frame belongs.

When the switch receives a frame on a port configured in access mode and assigned a VLAN, the switch inserts a VLAN tag in the frame header, recalculates the FCS, and sends the tagged frame out of a trunk port.

VLAN Tag Field Details

The VLAN tag field, shown in Figure 3-7, consists of a Type field, a Priority field, a Canonical Format Identifier field, and VLAN ID field:

- **Type:** A 2-byte value called the tag protocol ID (TPID) value. For Ethernet, it is set to hexadecimal 0x8100.

- **Priority:** A 3-bit value that supports level or service implementation.

- **Canonical Format Identifier (CFI):** A 1-bit identifier that enables Token Ring frames to be carried across Ethernet links.

- **VLAN ID (VID):** A 12-bit VLAN identification number that supports up to 4096 VLAN IDs.

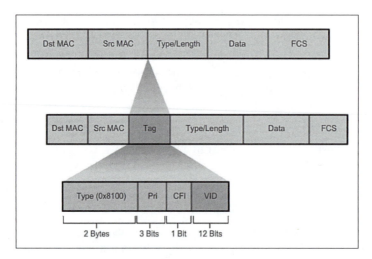

Figure 3-7   802.1Q VLAN Tag

After the switch inserts the Type and tag control information fields, it recalculates the FCS values and inserts the new FCS into the frame.

Native VLANs and 802.1Q Tagging (3.1.2.4)

The behavior of frames in the context of IEEE 802.1Q trunking is a vestige of the original standard, which was created when VLANs were still widely used. Essentially, the behavior is dictated by the assumption that a hub is connected between two switch ports that define a common VLAN trunk.

Tagged Frames on the Native VLAN

Some devices that support trunking add a VLAN tag to native VLAN traffic. Control traffic sent on the native VLAN should not be tagged. If an 802.1Q trunk port receives a tagged frame with the VLAN ID the same as the native VLAN, it drops the frame. Consequently, when configuring a switch port on a Cisco switch, configure devices so that they do not send tagged frames on the native VLAN. Devices from other vendors that support tagged frames on the native VLAN include IP phones, servers, routers, and non-Cisco switches.

Untagged Frames on the Native VLAN

When a Cisco switch trunk port receives untagged frames (which are unusual in a well-designed network), it forwards those frames to the native VLAN. If there are no devices associated with the native VLAN (which is not unusual) and there are no other trunk ports (which is not unusual), the frame is dropped. The default native

VLAN is VLAN 1. When configuring an 802.1Q trunk port, a default Port VLAN ID (PVID) is assigned the value of the native VLAN ID. All untagged traffic coming into or out of the 802.1Q port is forwarded based on the PVID value. For example, if VLAN 99 is configured as the native VLAN, the PVID is 99 and all untagged traffic is forwarded to VLAN 99. If the native VLAN has not been reconfigured, the PVID value is set to VLAN 1.

In Figure 3-8, PC1 is connected by a hub to an 802.1Q trunk link. PC1 sends untagged traffic, which the switches associate with the native VLAN configured on the trunk ports, and forwards accordingly. Tagged traffic on the trunk received by PC1 is dropped. This scenario reflects poor network design for several reasons: It uses a hub, it has a host connected to a trunk link, and it implies that the switches have access ports assigned to the native VLAN. But it illustrates the motivation for the IEEE 802.1Q specification for native VLANs as a means of handling legacy scenarios.

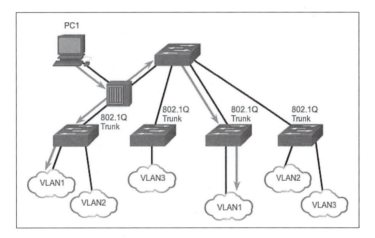

Figure 3-8   Native VLAN Forwarding Behavior

Voice VLAN Tagging (3.1.2.5)

Recall that to support VoIP, a separate voice VLAN is required.

An access port that is used to connect a Cisco IP Phone can be configured to use two separate VLANs: one VLAN for voice traffic and another VLAN for data traffic from a device attached to the phone. The link between the switch and the IP phone acts as a trunk to carry both voice VLAN traffic and data VLAN traffic.

The Cisco IP Phone contains an integrated three-port 10/100 switch. The ports provide dedicated connections to these devices:

- Port 1 connects to the switch or other VoIP device.

- Port 2 is an internal 10/100 interface that carries the IP phone traffic.

- Port 3 (access port) connects to a PC or other device.

On the switch, the access is configured to send Cisco Discovery Protocol (CDP) packets that instruct an attached IP phone to send voice traffic to the switch in one of three ways, depending on the type of traffic:

- In a voice VLAN tagged with a Layer 2 class of service (CoS) priority value

- In an access VLAN tagged with a Layer 2 CoS priority value

- In an access VLAN, untagged (no Layer 2 CoS priority value)

In Figure 3-9, the student computer PC5 is attached to a Cisco IP Phone, and the phone is attached to switch S3. VLAN 150 is designed to carry voice traffic, while PC5 is in VLAN 20, which is used for student data.

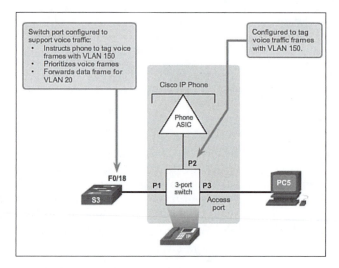

Figure 3-9   Voice VLAN Tagging

Sample Configuration

Example 3-2 shows sample output. A discussion of voice Cisco IOS commands is beyond the scope of this course, but the highlighted areas in the sample output show the F0/18 interface configured with a VLAN configured for data (VLAN 20) and a VLAN configured for voice (VLAN 150).

Example 3-2   Default VLAN Configuration

```
S1# show interfaces f0/18 switchport
Name: Fa0/18
Switchport: Enabled
Administrative Mode: dynamic auto
Operational Mode: down
Administrative Trunking Encapsulation: dot1q
Negotiation of Trunking: On
Access Mode VLAN: 20 (student)
Trunking Native Mode VLAN: 1 (default)
Administrative Native VLAN tagging: enabled
Voice VLAN: 150 (voice)
<output omitted>
```

Activity 3.1.2.6: VLAN Trunks in Action

Go to the online course to perform this practice activity.

Packet Tracer Activity 3.1.2.7: Investigating a VLAN Implementation

In this activity, you will observe how broadcast traffic is forwarded by the switches when VLANs are configured and when VLANs are not configured.

VLAN Implementations (3.2)

Network administrators who are responsible for portions of the switched network are familiar with the basic configuration tasks related to creating VLANs, configuring trunk links, associating voice and data VLANs with ports, and securing the VLAN implementation. This section describes the major tasks required to configure VLANs and trunks on switches in the network infrastructure.

VLAN Assignment (3.2.1)

The first step in configuring VLANs is to create the VLANs and to associate switch ports with VLANs.

VLAN Ranges on Catalyst Switches (3.2.1.1)

Different Cisco Catalyst switches support various numbers of VLANs. The number of supported VLANs is large enough to accommodate the needs of most organizations. For example, the Catalyst 2960 and 3560 Series switches support over 4000 VLANs. Normal-range VLANs on these switches are numbered 1 to 1005, and extended-range VLANs are numbered 1006 to 4094. Catalyst 2960 switches running Cisco IOS Release 15.x support extended-range VLANs.

Normal-Range VLANs

Normal range VLANs are usually the ones utilized in switched networks, because most networks do not need over 1000 VLANs!

- Used in small- and medium-sized business and enterprise networks.

- Identified by a VLAN ID between 1 and 1005.

- IDs 1002 through 1005 are reserved for Token Ring and FDDI VLANs.

- IDs 1 and 1002 to 1005 are automatically created and cannot be removed.

- Configurations are stored within a VLAN database file called vlan.dat. The vlan.dat file is located in the flash memory of the switch.

- The VLAN Trunking Protocol (VTP), which helps manage VLAN configurations between switches, can only learn and store normal-range VLANs.

Extended-Range VLANs

Extended range VLANs are primarily used in metropolitan service provider networks requiring over 1000 VLANs to support the various customers.

- Enable service providers to extend their infrastructure to a greater number of customers. Some global enterprises could be large enough to need extended-range VLAN IDs.

- Are identified by a VLAN ID between 1006 and 4094.

- Configurations are not written to the vlan.dat file.

- Support fewer VLAN features than normal-range VLANs.

- Are, by default, saved in the running configuration file.

- VTP does not learn extended-range VLANs.

Note

4096 is the upper bound for the number of VLANs available on Catalyst switches, because there are 12 bits in the VLAN ID field of the IEEE 802.1Q header.

Creating a VLAN (3.2.1.2)

When configuring normal-range VLANs, the configuration details are stored in flash memory on the switch in a file called vlan.dat. Flash memory is persistent and does not require the **copy running-config startup-config** command. However, because other details are often configured on a Cisco switch at the same time that VLANs are created, it is good practice to save running configuration changes to the startup configuration.

Table 3-1 displays the Cisco IOS command syntax used to add a VLAN to a switch and give it a name. Naming each VLAN is considered a best practice in switch configuration.

Table 3-1 Creating a VLAN

Cisco Switch IOS Commands	
Enter global configuration mode.	S1# **configure terminal**
Create a VLAN with a valid ID number.	S1(config)# **vlan vlan-id**
Specify a unique name to identify the VLAN.	S1(config-vlan)# **name vlan-name**
Return to privileged EXEC mode.	S1(config-vlan)# **end**

Figure 3-10 shows how the student VLAN (VLAN 20) is configured on switch S1. In the topology example, the student computer (PC2) has not been associated with a VLAN yet, but it does have an IP address of 172.17.20.22.

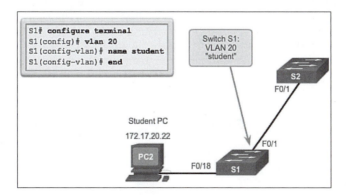

Figure 3-10 Sample VLAN Configuration

Interactive Graphic

Activity 3.2.1.2: Creating and Verifying VLANs

Go to the online course to use the Syntax Checker in the third graphic to create a VLAN and use the **show vlan brief** command to display the contents of the vlan.dat file.

In addition to entering a single VLAN ID, a series of VLAN IDs can be entered separated by commas, or a range of VLAN IDs separated by hyphens using the **vlan** *vlan-id* command. For example, use the following command to create VLANs 100, 102, 105, 106, and 107:

```
S1(config)# vlan 100,102,105-107
```

Assigning Ports to VLANs (3.2.1.3)

After creating a VLAN, the next step is to assign ports to the VLAN. An access port can belong to only one VLAN at a time. One exception to this rule is that of a port connected to an IP phone, in which case there are two VLANs associated with the port: one for voice and one for data.

Table 3-2 displays the syntax for defining a port to be an access port and assigning it to a VLAN. The **switchport mode access** command is optional but strongly recommended as a security best practice. With this command, the interface changes to permanent access mode.

Table 3-2   Assign Ports to VLANs

Cisco Switch IOS Commands	
Enter global configuration mode.	S1# **configure terminal**
Enter interface configuration mode.	S1(config)# **interface interface-id**
Set the port to access mode.	S1(config-if)# **switchport mode access**
Assign the port to a VLAN.	S1(config-if)# **switchport access vlan vlan-id**
Return to the privileged EXEC mode.	S1(config-if)# **end**

Note

Use the **interface range** command to simultaneously configure multiple interfaces.

In Figure 3-11, VLAN 20 is assigned to port F0/18 on switch S1; therefore, the student computer (PC2) is in VLAN 20. When VLAN 20 is configured on other switches, the network administrator knows to configure the other student computers to be in the same subnet as PC2 (172.17.20.0/24).

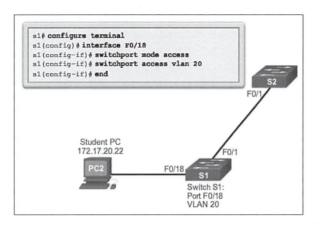

Figure 3-11   Sample Interface Configuration for VLANs

Activity 3.2.1.3: Assigning Ports to VLANs

Go to the online course to use the Syntax Checker in the third graphic to assign a VLAN and use the **show vlan brief** command to display the contents of the vlan.dat file.

The **switchport access vlan** command forces the creation of a VLAN if it does not already exist on the switch. For example, VLAN 30 is not present in the **show vlan brief** output of the switch. If the **switchport access vlan 30** command is entered on any interface with no previous configuration, the switch displays

```
% Access VLAN does not exist. Creating vlan 30
```

Changing VLAN Port Membership (3.2.1.4)

There are a number of ways to change VLAN port membership. Table 3-3 shows the syntax for changing a switch port to VLAN 1 membership with the **no switchport access vlan** interface configuration mode command.

Table 3-3   Removing a VLAN Assignment

Cisco Switch IOS Commands

Enter global configuration mode.	S1# **configure terminal**
Enter interface configuration mode.	S1(config)# **interface interface-id**
Remove the VLAN assignment from the port.	S1(config-if)# **no switchport access vlan**
Return to the privileged EXEC mode.	S1(config-if)# **end**

Interface F0/18 was previously assigned to VLAN 20. The **no switchport access vlan** command is entered for interface F0/18. Examine the output in the **show vlan brief** command, as shown in Example 3-3. The **show vlan brief** command displays the VLAN assignment and membership type for all switch ports. The **show vlan brief** command displays one line for each VLAN. The output for each VLAN includes the VLAN name, status, and switch ports.

Example 3-3   Sample VLAN Assignment Removal

```
S1(config)# interface f0/18
S1(config-if)# no switchport access vlan
S1(config-if)# do show vlan brief

VLAN Name                             Status    Ports
---- -------------------------------- --------- --------------------------
1    default                          active    Fa0/1, Fa0/2, Fa0/3, Fa0/4
                                                Fa0/5, Fa0/6, Fa0/7, Fa0/8
                                                Fa0/9, Fa0/10, Fa0/11, Fa0/12
                                                Fa0/13, Fa0/14, Fa0/15, Fa0/16
                                                Fa0/17, Fa0/18, Fa0/19, Fa0/20
                                                Fa0/21, Fa0/22, Fa0/23, Fa0/24
                                                Gi0/1, Gi0/2
20   student                          active
1002 fddi-default                     act/unsup
1003 token-ring-default               act/unsup
1004 fddinet-default                  act/unsup
1005 trnet-default                    act/unsup
```

VLAN 20 is still active, even though no ports are assigned to it. In Example 3-4, the **show interfaces f0/18 switchport** output verifies that the access VLAN for interface F0/18 has been reset to VLAN 1.

Example 3-4   Verification of VLAN Assignment Removal

```
S1# show interfaces f0/18 switchport
Name: Fa0/18
Switchport: Enabled
Administrative Mode: dynamic auto
Operational Mode: down
Administrative Trunking Encapsulation: dot1q
Negotiation of Trunking: On
Access Mode VLAN: 1 (default)
Trunking Native Mode VLAN: 1 (default)
<output omitted>
```

A port can easily have its VLAN membership changed. It is not necessary to first remove a port from a VLAN to change its VLAN membership. When an access port has its VLAN membership reassigned to another existing VLAN, the new VLAN membership simply replaces the previous VLAN membership. In Example 3-5, port F0/11 is assigned to VLAN 20.

Example 3-5   Changing VLAN Assignment

```
S1(config)# interface f0/11
S1(config-if)# switchport mode access
S1(config-if)# switchport access vlan 20
S1(config-if)# end
*Mar  31 09:33:26.058: %SYS-5-CONFIG_I: Configured from console by console
S1# show vlan brief

VLAN Name                             Status    Ports
---- -------------------------------- --------- -------------------------
1    default                          active    Fa0/1, Fa0/2, Fa0/3, Fa0/4
                                                Fa0/5, Fa0/6, Fa0/7, Fa0/8
                                                Fa0/9, Fa0/10, Fa0/12, Fa0/13
                                                Fa0/14, Fa0/15, Fa0/16, Fa0/17
                                                Fa0/18, Fa0/19, Fa0/20, Fa0/21
                                                Fa0/22, Fa0/23, Fa0/24, Gi0/1
                                                Gi0/2
20   student                          active    Fa0/11
1002 fddi-default                     act/unsup
1003 token-ring-default               act/unsup
1004 fddinet-default                  act/unsup
1005 trnet-default                    act/unsup
S1#
```

Interactive
Graphic

Activity 3.2.1.4: Creating and Verifying VLANs

Go to the online course to use the Syntax Checker in the fifth graphic to change
VLAN port membership.

Deleting VLANs (3.2.1.5)

In Example 3-6, the **no vlan** *vlan-id* global configuration mode command is used to
remove VLAN 20 from the switch. Switch S1 had a minimal configuration with all
ports in VLAN 1 and an unused VLAN 20 in the VLAN database. The **show vlan
brief** command verifies that VLAN 20 is no longer present in the vlan.dat file after
using the **no vlan 20** command.

Example 3-6   Deleting a VLAN

```
S1(config)# no vlan 20
S1(config)# end
S1#
*Mar  1 07:37:55.785: %SYS-5-CONFIG_I: Configured from console by console
S1# show vlan brief


VLAN Name                             Status    Ports
---- -------------------------------- --------- -------------------------------
1    default                          active    Fa0/1, Fa0/2, Fa0/3, Fa0/4
                                                Fa0/5, Fa0/6, Fa0/7, Fa0/8
                                                Fa0/9, Fa0/10, Fa0/12, Fa0/13
                                                Fa0/14, Fa0/15, Fa0/16, Fa0/17
                                                Fa0/18, Fa0/19, Fa0/20, Fa0/21
                                                Fa0/22, Fa0/23, Fa0/24, Gi0/1
                                                Gi0/2
1002 fddi-default                     act/unsup
1003 token-ring-default               act/unsup
1004 fddinet-default                  act/unsup
1005 trnet-default                    act/unsup
```

Caution

Before deleting a VLAN, be sure to first reassign all member ports to a different VLAN. Any
ports that are not moved to an active VLAN are unable to communicate with other hosts after
the VLAN is deleted and until they are assigned to an active VLAN.

Alternatively, the entire vlan.dat file can be deleted using the **delete flash:vlan.dat**
privileged EXEC mode command. The abbreviated command version (**delete vlan.
dat**) can be used if the vlan.dat file has not been moved from its default location.

After issuing this command and reloading the switch, the previously configured VLANs are no longer present. This effectively places the switch into its factory default condition concerning VLAN configurations.

> **Note**
>
> For a Catalyst switch, the **erase startup-config** command must accompany the **delete vlan.dat** command prior to reload to restore the switch to its factory default condition.

Verifying VLAN Information (3.2.1.6)

After a VLAN is configured, VLAN configurations can be validated using Cisco IOS **show** commands.

Table 3-4 displays the show vlan command options.

Table 3-4   show vlan Command

Cisco IOS CLI Command Syntax

show vlan [brief | id *vlan-id* **| name** *vlan-name* **| summary]**

Display one line for each VLAN with the VLAN name, status, and its ports.	**brief**
Display information about a single VLAN identified by VLAN ID number. For *vlan-id*, the range is 1 to 4094.	**id** *vlan-id*
Display information about a single VLAN identified by VLAN name. The VLAN name is an ASCII string from 1 to 32 characters.	**name** *vlan-name*
Display VLAN summary information.	**summary**

Table 3-5 displays the **show interfaces** command options.

Table 3-5   show interfaces Command

Cisco IOS CLI Command Syntax

show interfaces [*interface-id* **| vlan** *vlan-id***] | switchport**

Valid interfaces include physical ports (including type, module, and port number) and port channels. The port-channel range is 1 to 6.	*interface-id*
VLAN identification. The range is 1 to 4095.	**vlan** *vlan-id*
Display the administrative and operational status of a switching port, including port blocking and port protection settings.	**switchport**

In Example 3-7, the **show vlan name student** command produces output that is not easily interpreted. The preferable option is to use the **show vlan brief** command. The **show vlan summary** command displays the count of all configured VLANs. The output in Example 3-7 shows seven VLANs.

Example 3-7   Using the **show vlan** Command

```
S1# show vlan name student

VLAN Name                             Status    Ports
---- -------------------------------- --------- -------------------------
20   student                          active    Fa0/11
VLAN Type  SAID       MTU   Parent RingNo BridgeNo Stp  BrdgMode Trans1 Trans2
---- ----- ---------- ----- ------ ------ -------- ---- -------- ------ ------
20   enet  100020     1500  -      -      -        -    -        0      0


Remote SPAN VLAN
----------------
Disabled


Primary Secondary Type              Ports
------- --------- ----------------- -------------------------------------


S1# show vlan summary
Number of existing VLANs          : 7
 Number of existing VTP VLANs     : 7
 Number of existing extended VLANs : 0
```

The **show interfaces vlan** *vlan-id* command displays details that are beyond the scope of this course. The important information appears on the second line in Example 3-8, indicating that VLAN 20 is up.

Example 3-8   Using the **show interfaces vlan** Command

```
S1# show interfaces vlan 20
Vlan 20 is up, line protocol is down
  Hardware is EtherSVI, address is 0021.a1e0.78c1 (bia 0021.a1e0.78c1)
  MTU 1500 bytes, BW 1000000 Kbit, DLY 10 usec,
     reliability 255/255, txload 1/255, rxload 1/255
  Encapsulation ARPA, loopback not set
  Keepalive not supported
  ARP type: ARPA, ARP Timeout 04:00:00
  Last input never, output never, output hang never
  Last clearing of "show interface" counters never
  Input queue: 0/75/0/0 (size/max/drops/flushes); Total output drops: 0
```

```
    Queueing strategy: fifo
    Output queue: 0/40 (size/max)
    5 minute input rate 0 bits/sec, 0 packets/sec
    5 minute output rate 0 bits/sec, 0 packets/sec
       0 packets input, 0 bytes, 0 no buffer
       Received 0 broadcasts (0 IP multicasts)
       0 runts, 0 giants, 0 throttles
       0 input errors, 0 CRC, 0 frame, 0 overrun, 0 ignored
       0 packets output, 0 bytes, 0 underruns
       0 output errors, 0 interface resets
       0 output buffer failures, 0 output buffers swapped out
S1#
```

Activity 3.2.1.6: Using the show interfaces Command

Go to the online course to use the Syntax Checker in the fourth graphic to display the VLAN and switch port information, and verify VLAN assignments and mode.

Packet Tracer Activity 3.2.1.7: Configuring VLANs

VLANs are helpful in the administration of logical groups, allowing members of a group to be easily moved, changed, or added. This activity focuses on creating and naming VLANs, and assigning access ports to specific VLANs.

VLAN Trunks (3.2.2)

In this section, the elements of VLAN trunk configuration are explored. Remember that VLAN trunks carry all the control traffic between switches. VLAN trunks enable the communication between switches required for many of the technologies specific to the LAN switched environment.

Configuring IEEE 802.1Q Trunk Links (3.2.2.1)

A VLAN trunk is an OSI Layer 2 link between two switches that carries traffic for all VLANs (unless the allowed VLAN list is restricted manually or dynamically). To enable trunk links, configure the ports on either end of the physical link with parallel sets of commands.

To configure a switch port on one end of a trunk link, use the **switchport mode trunk** command. With this command, the interface changes to permanent trunking mode. The port enters into a *Dynamic Trunking Protocol (DTP)* negotiation to convert the link into a trunk link even if the interface connecting to it does not agree to the change. DTP is described in the next topic. In this course, the **switchport mode trunk** command is the only method implemented for trunk configuration.

The Cisco IOS command syntax to specify a native VLAN (other than VLAN 1) is shown in Table 3-6.

Table 3-6   802.1Q Trunk Configuration

Cisco Switch IOS Commands	
Enter global configuration mode.	S1# **configure terminal**
Enter interface configuration mode.	S1(config)# **interface** *interface-id*
Force the link to be a trunk link.	S1(config-if)# **switchport mode trunk**
Specify a native VLAN for 802.1Q trunks.	S1(config-if)# **switchport trunk native vlan** *vlan-id*
Specify the list of VLANs to be allowed on the trunk link.	S1(config-if)# **switchport trunk allowed vlan** *vlan-list*
Return to the privileged EXEC mode.	S1(config-if)# **end**

Use the Cisco IOS **switchport trunk allowed vlan** *vlan-list* command to specify the list of VLANs to be allowed on the trunk link.

In Figure 3-12, VLANs 10, 20, and 30 support the Faculty, Student, and Guest computers (PC1, PC2, and PC3). The native VLAN should also be changed from VLAN 1 and changed to another VLAN such as VLAN 99. By default, all VLANs are allowed across a trunk link. The **switchport trunk allowed vlan** command can be used to limit the allowed VLANs.

In Example 3-9, the F0/1 port on switch S1 is configured as a trunk port, assigns the native VLAN to VLAN 99, and specifies the trunk to only forward traffic for VLANs 10, 20, 30, and 99.

Example 3-9   Sample Trunk Configuration

```
S1(config)# interface FastEthernet0/1
S1(config-if)# switchport mode trunk
S1(config-if)# switchport trunk native vlan 99
S1(config-if)# switchport trunk allowed vlan 10,20,30
S1(config-if)# end
```

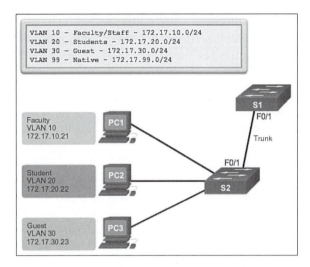

```
VLAN 10 - Faculty/Staff - 172.17.10.0/24
VLAN 20 - Students - 172.17.20.0/24
VLAN 30 - Guest - 172.17.30.0/24
VLAN 99 - Native - 172.17.99.0/24
```

Figure 3-12   Sample Interface Configuration for VLANs

Note

This configuration assumes the use of Cisco Catalyst 2960 switches, which automatically use 802.1Q encapsulation on trunk links. Other switches might require manual configuration of the encapsulation. Always configure both ends of a trunk link with the same native VLAN. If 802.1Q trunk configuration is not the same on both ends, Cisco IOS Software reports errors.

Resetting the Trunk to the Default State (3.2.2.2)

Table 3-7 shows the commands to remove the allowed VLANs and reset the native VLAN of the trunk. When reset to the default state, the trunk allows all VLANs and uses VLAN 1 as the native VLAN.

Table 3-7   Resetting Configured Values on Trunk Links

Cisco Switch IOS Commands	
Enter global configuration mode.	S1# **configure terminal**
Enter interface configuration mode.	S1(config)# **interface** *interface-id*
Force the link to be a trunk link.	S1(config-if)# **no switchport trunk allowed vlan**
Specify a native VLAN for 802.1Q trunks.	S1(config-if)# **no switchport trunk native vlan**
Return to the privileged EXEC mode.	S1(config-if)# **end**

Example 3-10 shows the commands used to reset all trunking characteristics of a trunking interface to the default settings. The **show interfaces f0/1 switchport** command reveals that the trunk has been reconfigured to a default state.

Example 3-10   Resetting Trunk Link

```
S1(config)# interface f0/1
S1(config-if)# no switchport trunk allowed vlan
S1(config-if)# no switchport trunk native vlan
S1(config-if)# end
S1# show interfaces f0/1 switchport
Name: Fa0/1
Switchport: Enabled
Administrative Mode: trunk
Operational Mode: trunk
Administrative Trunking Encapsulation: dot1q
Operational Trunking Encapsulation: dot1q
Negotiation of Trunking: On
Access Mode VLAN: 1 (default)
Trunking Native Mode VLAN: 1 (default)
Administrative Native VLAN tagging: enabled
<output omitted>
Administrative private-vlan trunk mappings: none
Operational private-vlan: none
Trunking VLANs Enabled: ALL
Pruning VLANs Enabled: 2-1001
<output omitted>
```

In Example 3-11, the sample output shows the commands used to remove the trunk feature from the F0/1 switch port on switch S1. The **show interfaces f0/1 switchport** command reveals that the F0/1 interface is now in static access mode.

Example 3-11   Return Port to Access Mode

```
S1(config)# interface f0/1
S1(config-if)# switchport mode access
S1(config-if)# end
S1# show interfaces f0/1 switchport
Name: Fa0/1
Switchport: Enabled
Administrative Mode: static access
Operational Mode: static access
Administrative Trunking Encapsulation: dot1q
Operational Trunking Encapsulation: native
Negotiation of Trunking: Off
```

```
Access Mode VLAN: 1 (default)
Trunking Native Mode VLAN: 1 (default)
Administrative Native VLAN tagging: enabled
<output omitted>
```

Verifying Trunk Configuration (3.2.2.3)

Example 3-12 displays the configuration of switch port F0/1 on switch S1. The configuration is verified with the **show interfaces** *interface-id* **switchport** command.

Example 3-12   Verifying Trunk Configuration

```
S1(config)# interface f0/1
S1(config-if)# switchport mode trunk
S1(config-if)# switchport trunk native vlan 99
S1(config-if)# end
S1# show interfaces f0/1 switchport
Name: Fa0/1
Switchport: Enabled
Administrative Mode: trunk
Operational Mode: trunk
Administrative Trunking Encapsulation: dot1q
Operational Trunking Encapsulation: dot1q
Negotiation of Trunking: On
Access Mode VLAN: 1 (default)
Trunking Native Mode VLAN: 99 (VLAN0099)
Administrative Native VLAN tagging: enabled
Voice VLAN: none
Administrative private-vlan host-association: none
Administrative private-vlan mapping: none
Administrative private-vlan trunk native VLAN: none
Administrative private-vlan trunk Native VLAN tagging: enabled
Administrative private-vlan trunk encapsulation: dot1q
Administrative private-vlan trunk normal VLANs: none
Administrative private-vlan trunk associations: none
Administrative private-vlan trunk mappings: none
Operational private-vlan: none
Trunking VLANs Enabled: ALL
Pruning VLANs Enabled: 2-1001
<output omitted>
```

The top highlighted area shows that port F0/1 has its administrative mode set to **trunk**. The port is in trunking mode. The next highlighted area verifies that the native VLAN is VLAN 99. Farther down in the output, the bottom highlighted area shows that all VLANs are enabled on the trunk.

Activity 3.2.2.3: Configuring and Verifying a VLAN Trunk

Go to the online course to use the Syntax Checker in the second graphic to configure a trunk supporting all VLANs on interface F0/1 with native VLAN 99. Verify the trunk configuration with the **show interfaces f0/1 switchport** command.

Packet Tracer
☐ Activity

Packet Tracer Activity 3.2.2.4: Configuring Trunks

Trunks are required to pass VLAN information between switches. A port on a switch is either an access port or a trunk port. Access ports carry traffic from a specific VLAN assigned to the port. A trunk port by default is a member of all VLANs; therefore, it carries traffic for all VLANs. This activity focuses on creating trunk ports and assigning them to a native VLAN other than the default.

Lab 3.2.2.5: Configuring VLANs and Trunking

In this lab, you will complete the following objectives:

- Part 1: Build the Network and Configure Basic Device Settings
- Part 2: Create VLANs and Assign Switch Ports
- Part 3: Maintain VLAN Port Assignments and the VLAN Database
- Part 4: Configure an 802.1Q Trunk Between the Switches
- Part 5: Delete the VLAN Database

Dynamic Trunking Protocol (3.2.3)

Networking technologies often involve both manual and automatic implementations. For example, routing, speed/duplex port configuration, and cable selection versus auto-MDIX illustrate this dichotomy of manual versus automatic. In LAN switching, Dynamic Trunking Protocol (DTP) is one of the first examples one encounters of manual versus automatic. With DTP, network administrators have the option to let neighboring switches autonegotiate trunk formation.

Introduction to DTP (3.2.3.1)

Ethernet trunk interfaces support different trunking modes. An interface can be set to trunking or nontrunking, or to negotiate trunking with the neighbor interface. Trunk negotiation is managed by the Dynamic Trunking Protocol (DTP), which operates on a point-to-point basis only between network devices.

DTP is a Cisco-proprietary protocol that is automatically enabled on Catalyst 2960 and Catalyst 3560 Series switches. Switches from other vendors do not support DTP. DTP manages trunk negotiation only if the port on the neighbor switch is configured in a trunk mode that supports DTP.

Caution

Some internetworking devices might forward DTP frames improperly, which can cause misconfigurations. To avoid this, turn off DTP on interfaces on a Cisco switch connected to devices that do not support DTP.

The default DTP configuration for Cisco Catalyst 2960 and 3560 switches is dynamic auto, as shown in Figure 3-13 on interface F0/3 of switches S1 and S3.

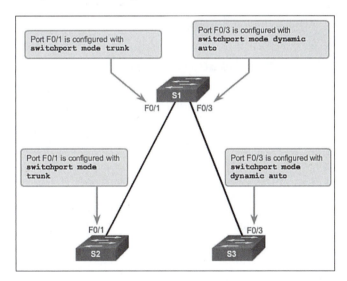

Figure 3-13   Initial DTP Configuration

To enable trunking from a Cisco switch to a device that does not support DTP, use the **switchport mode trunk** and **switchport nonegotiate** interface configuration mode commands. This causes the interface to become a trunk, but not generate DTP frames.

In Figure 3-14, the link between switches S1 and S2 becomes a trunk because the F0/1 ports on switches S1 and S2 are configured to ignore all DTP advertisements, and to come up in and stay in trunk port mode. The F0/3 ports on switches S1 and S3 are set to dynamic auto, so the negotiation results in the access mode state. This creates an inactive trunk link. When configuring a port to be in trunk mode, use the **switchport mode trunk** command. There is no ambiguity about which state the trunk is in; it is always on. With this configuration, it is easy to remember which state the trunk ports are in; if the port is supposed to be a trunk, the mode is set to trunk.

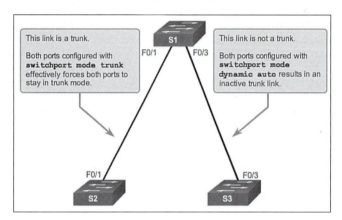

Figure 3-14   DTP Interaction Results

Negotiated Interface Modes (3.2.3.2)

Ethernet interfaces on Catalyst 2960 and Catalyst 3560 Series switches support different trunking modes with the help of DTP:

- **switchport mode access:** Puts the interface (access port) into permanent nontrunking mode and negotiates to convert the link into a nontrunk link. The interface becomes a nontrunk interface, regardless of whether the neighboring interface is a trunk interface.

- **switchport mode dynamic auto:** Makes the interface able to convert the link to a trunk link. The interface becomes a trunk interface if the neighboring interface is set to trunk or desirable mode. The default switch port mode for all Ethernet interfaces is **dynamic auto.**

- **switchport mode dynamic desirable:** Makes the interface actively attempt to convert the link to a trunk link. The interface becomes a trunk interface if the neighboring interface is set to trunk, desirable, or auto mode. This is the default switch port mode on older switches, such as the Catalyst 2950 and 3550 Series switches.

- **switchport mode trunk:** Puts the interface into permanent trunking mode and negotiates to convert the neighboring link into a trunk link. The interface becomes a trunk interface even if the neighboring interface is not a trunk interface.

- **switchport nonegotiate:** Prevents the interface from generating DTP frames. You can use this command only when the interface switch port mode is **access** or **trunk**. You must manually configure the neighboring interface as a trunk interface to establish a trunk link.

Table 3-8 illustrates the results of the DTP configuration options on opposite ends of a trunk link connected to Catalyst 2960 switch ports.

Table 3-8   DTP-Negotiated Interface Modes

	Dynamic Auto	**Dynamic Desirable**	**Trunk**	**Access**
Dynamic Auto	Access	Trunk	Trunk	Access
Dynamic Desirable	Trunk	Trunk	Trunk	Access
Trunk	Trunk	Trunk	Trunk	Limited Connectivity
Access	Access	Access	Limited Connectivity	Access

Configure trunk links statically whenever possible. The default DTP mode is dependent on the Cisco IOS Software version and on the platform. To determine the current DTP mode, issue the **show dtp interface** command, as shown in Example 3-13.

Example 3-13   Verifying DTP Mode

```
S1# show dtp interface f0/1
DTP information for FastEthernet0/1:
  TOS/TAS/TNS:                                  TRUNK/ON/TRUNK
  TOT/TAT/TNT:                                  802.1Q/802.1Q/802.1Q
  Neighbor address 1:                           0CD996D23F81
  Neighbor address 2:                           000000000000
  Hello timer expiration (sec/state):           12/RUNNING
  Access timer expiration (sec/state):          never/STOPPED
  Negotiation timer expiration (sec/state):     never/STOPPED
  Multidrop timer expiration (sec/state):       never/STOPPED
  FSM state:                                    S6:TRUNK
  # times multi & trunk                         0
  Enabled:                                      yes
  In STP:
<output omitted>
```

Interactive Graphic

Activity 3.2.3.2: Verifying DTP Mode

Go to the online course to use the Syntax Checker in the third graphic to determine the DTP mode on interface F0/1.

> **Note**
>
> A general best practice is to set the interface to **trunk** and **nonegotiate** when a trunk link is required. On links where trunking is not intended, DTP should be turned off.

Interactive Graphic

Activity 3.2.3.3: Predict DTP Behavior

Go to the online course to perform this practice activity.

Troubleshoot VLANs and Trunks (3.2.4)

A network administrator responsible for portions of the switched infrastructure is able to quickly diagnose and solve problems. Troubleshooting VLANs and VLAN trunks is standard practice in a switched environment.

IP Addressing Issues with VLAN (3.2.4.1)

Each VLAN must correspond to a unique IP subnet. If two devices in the same VLAN have different subnet addresses, they cannot communicate. This is a common problem, and it is easy to solve by identifying the incorrect configuration and changing the subnet address to the correct one.

In Figure 3-15, PC1 cannot connect to the Web/TFTP server shown.

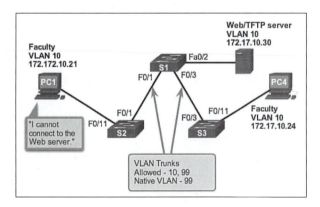

Figure 3-15   IP Issue Within VLAN

A check of the IP configuration settings of PC1 shown in Example 3-14 reveals the most common error in configuring VLANs: an incorrectly configured IP address. PC1 is configured with an IP address of 172.172.10.21, but it should have been configured with 172.17.10.21.

Example 3-14   Problem: Incorrect IP Address

```
PC1> ipconfig
   IPv4 Address. . . . . . . . . . . : 172.172.10.21
   Subnet Mask . . . . . . . . . . . : 255.255.0.0
   Default Gateway . . . . . . . . . : 0.0.0.0
```

The PC1 Fast Ethernet configuration dialog box shows the updated IP address of 172.17.10.21. In Figure 3-16, the output on the bottom reveals that PC1 has regained connectivity to the Web/TFTP server found at IP address 172.17.10.30.

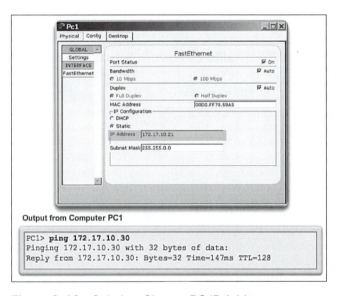

Figure 3-16   Solution: Change PC IP Address

Missing VLANs (3.2.4.2)

If there is still no connection between devices in a VLAN, but IP addressing issues have been ruled out, refer to the flowchart in Figure 3-17 to troubleshoot:

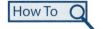

Step 1.   Use the **show vlan** command to check whether the port belongs to the expected VLAN. If the port is assigned to the wrong VLAN, use the **switchport access vlan** command to correct the VLAN membership. Use the **show mac address-table** command to check which addresses were learned on a particular port of the switch and to which VLAN that port is assigned.

Step 2.   If the VLAN to which the port is assigned is deleted, the port becomes inactive. Use the **show vlan** or **show interfaces switchport** command.

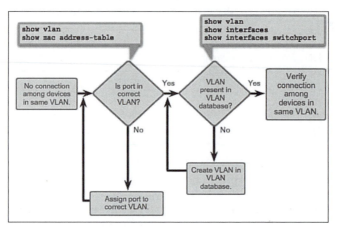

Figure 3-17   Missing VLAN

To display the MAC address table, use the **show macaddress-table** command. Example 3-15 shows MAC addresses that were learned on the F0/1 interface. It can be seen that MAC address 000c.296a.a21c was learned on interface F0/1 in VLAN 10. If this number is not the expected VLAN number, change the port VLAN membership using the **switchport access vlan** command.

Example 3-15   Missing VLAN

```
S1# show mac address-table interface FastEthernet 0/1
          Mac Address Table


Vlan    Mac Address       Type        Ports
----    -----------       --------    -----
  10    000c.296a.a21c    DYNAMIC     Fa0/1
  10    000f.34f9.9181    DYNAMIC     Fa0/1
Total Mac Addresses for this criterion: 2
S1# show interfaces FastEthernet 0/1 switchport
Name: Fa0/1
Switchport: Enabled
Administrative Mode: static access
Operational Mode: static access
Administrative Trunking Encapsulation: dot1q
Operational Trunking Encapsulation: native
Negotiation of Trunking: Off
Access Mode VLAN: 10 (Inactive)
Trunking Native Mode VLAN: 1 (default)
Administrative Native VLAN tagging: enabled
Voice VLAN: none
```

Each port in a switch belongs to a VLAN. If the VLAN to which the port belongs is deleted, the port becomes inactive. All ports belonging to the VLAN that was deleted are unable to communicate with the rest of the network. Use the **show interface f0/1 switchport** command to check whether the port is inactive. If the port is inactive, it is not functional until the missing VLAN is created using the **vlan** *vlan-id* command.

Introduction to Troubleshooting Trunks (3.2.4.3)

A common task of a network administrator is to troubleshoot trunk link formation or links incorrectly behaving as trunk links. Sometimes a switch port can behave like a trunk port even if it is not configured as a trunk port. For example, an access port might accept frames from VLANs different from the VLAN to which it is assigned. This is called VLAN leaking.

Figure 3-18 displays a flowchart of general trunk troubleshooting guidelines.

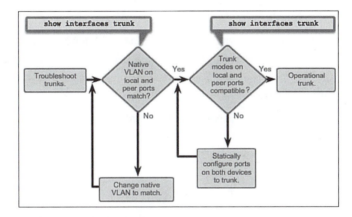

Figure 3-18   Troubleshooting Trunks

To troubleshoot issues when a trunk is not forming or when VLAN leaking is occurring, proceed as follows:

Step 1.   Use the **show interfaces trunk** command to check whether the local and peer native VLANs match. If the native VLAN does not match on both sides, VLAN leaking occurs.

Step 2.   Use the **show interfaces trunk** command to check whether a trunk has been established between switches. Statically configure trunk links whenever possible. Cisco Catalyst switch ports use DTP by default and attempt to negotiate a trunk link.

To display the status of the trunk and to display the native VLAN used on that trunk link, and to verify trunk establishment, use the **show interfaces trunk** command. Example 3-16 shows that the native VLAN on one side of the trunk link was changed to VLAN 2. If one end of the trunk is configured as native VLAN 99 and the other end is configured as native VLAN 2, a frame sent from VLAN 99 on one side is received on VLAN 2 on the other side. VLAN 99 leaks into the VLAN 2 segment.

Example 3-16   Troubleshooting Trunks

```
S1# show interfaces f0/1 trunk

Port        Mode            Encapsulation  Status      Native vlan
Fa0/1       auto            802.1q         trunking    2
<output omitted>
```

CDP displays a notification of a native VLAN mismatch on a trunk link with this message:

```
*Mar 1 06:45:26.232: %CDP-4-NATIVE_VLAN_MISMATCH: Native VLAN mismatch discovered on
FastEthernet0/1 (2), with S2 FastEthernet0/1 (99).
```

Connectivity issues occur in the network if a native VLAN mismatch exists. Data traffic for VLANs, other than the two native VLANs configured, successfully propagates across the trunk link, but data associated with either of the native VLANs does not successfully propagate across the trunk link.

As shown in Example 3-16, native VLAN mismatch issues do not keep the trunk from forming. To solve the native VLAN mismatch, configure the native VLAN to be the same VLAN on both sides of the link.

Common Problems with Trunks (3.2.4.4)

Trunking issues are usually associated with incorrect configurations. When configuring VLANs and trunks on a switched infrastructure, the following types of configuration errors are the most common:

- **Native VLAN mismatches:** Trunk ports are configured with different native VLANs. This configuration error generates console notifications, and causes control and management traffic to be misdirected. This poses a security risk. For example, one port might be configured with VLAN 99 and the other with VLAN 100.

- **Trunk mode mismatches:** One trunk port is configured in a mode that is not compatible for trunking on the corresponding peer port. This configuration error causes the trunk link to stop working. For example, both local and peer switch port modes might be configured as dynamic auto.

- **Allowed VLANs on trunks:** The list of allowed VLANs on a trunk has not been updated with the current VLAN trunking requirements. In this situation, unexpected traffic or no traffic is being sent over the trunk. For example, the list of allowed VLANs might not support current VLAN trunking requirements.

If an issue with a trunk is discovered and if the cause is unknown, start troubleshooting by examining the trunks for a native VLAN mismatch. If that is not the cause, check for trunk mode mismatches, and finally check for the allowed VLAN list on the trunk. The next several sections examine how to fix the common problems with trunks.

Trunk Mode Mismatches (3.2.4.5)

Trunk links are normally configured statically with the **switchport mode trunk** command. Cisco Catalyst switch trunk ports use DTP to negotiate the state of the link. When a port on a trunk link is configured with a trunk mode that is incompatible with the neighboring trunk port, a trunk link fails to form between the two switches.

In the scenario illustrated in Figure 3-19, PC4 cannot connect to the internal web server. The topology indicates a valid configuration. Why is there a problem?

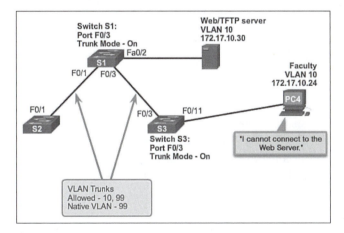

Figure 3-19 Scenario Topology

Check the status of the trunk ports on switch S1 using the **show interfaces trunk** command. The output shown in Example 3-17 reveals that interface Fa0/3 on switch S1 is not currently a trunk link. Examining the F0/3 interface reveals that the switch port is actually in dynamic auto mode. An examination of the trunks on switch S3 reveals that there are no active trunk ports. Further checking reveals that the Fa0/3 interface is also in dynamic auto mode. This explains why the trunk is down.

Example 3-17   Mismatched DTP Modes

```
S1# show interfaces trunk


Port          Mode                 Encapsulation  Status       Native vlan
Fa0/1         on                   802.1q         trunking     99


Port          Vlans allowed on trunk
Fa0/1         10,99


Port          Vlans allowed and active in management domain
Fa0/1         10,99


Port          Vlans in spanning tree forwarding state and not pruned
Fa0/1         10,99
S1# show interfaces f0/3 switchport
Name: Fa0/3
Switchport: Enabled
Administrative Mode: dynamic auto
<output omitted>
S3# show interfaces trunk
S3# show interfaces f0/3 switchport
Name: Fa0/3
Switchport: Enabled
Administrative Mode: dynamic auto
<output omitted>
```

To resolve the issue, reconfigure the trunk mode of the F0/3 ports on switches S1 and S3, as shown in Example 3-18. After the configuration change, the output of the **show interfaces** command indicates that the port on switch S1 is now in trunking mode. The output from PC4 indicates that it has regained connectivity to the Web/TFTP server found at IP address 172.17.10.30.

Example 3-18   Corrected Trunk Modes

```
S1(config)# interface f0/3
S1(config-if)# switchport mode trunk
S1(config-if)# end
S1# show interfaces f0/3 switchport
Name: Fa0/3
Switchport: Enabled
Administrative Mode: trunk
<output omitted>
S3(config)# interface f0/3
S3(config-if)# switchport mode trunk
```

```
S3(config-if)# end
S3# show interfaces f0/3 switchport
Name: Fa0/3
Switchport: Enabled
Administrative Mode: trunk
<output omitted>
S3# show interfaces trunk


Port            Mode                Encapsulation   Status       Native vlan
Fa0/3           on                  802.1q          trunking     99


Port            Vlans allowed on trunk
Fa0/3           10,99


Port            Vlans allowed and active in management domain
Fa0/3           10,99


Port            Vlans in spanning tree forwarding state and not pruned
Fa0/3           10,99
PC4> ping 172.17.10.30
Pinging 172.17.10.30 with 32 bytes of data:
Reply from 172.17.10.30: bytes=32 time=147ms TTL=128
<output omitted>
```

Incorrect VLAN List (3.2.4.6)

For traffic from a VLAN to be transmitted across a trunk, it must be allowed on the trunk. To do so, use the **switchport trunk allowed vlan** *vlan-id* command.

In Figure 3-20, VLAN 20 (Student) and PC5 have been added to the network. The documentation has been updated to show that the VLANs allowed on the trunk are 10, 20, and 99. In this scenario, PC5 cannot connect to the student email server.

Check the trunk ports on switch S1 using the **show interfaces trunk** command, as shown in Example 3-19. The command reveals that the interface F0/3 on switch S3 is correctly configured to allow VLANs 10, 20, and 99. An examination of the F0/3 interface on switch S1 reveals that interfaces F0/1 and F0/3 only allow VLANs 10 and 99. Someone updated the documentation but forgot to reconfigure the ports on the S1 switch.

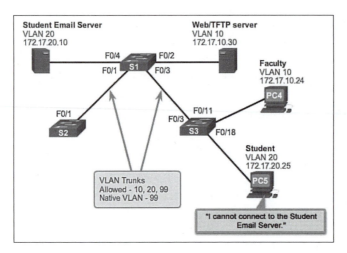

Figure 3-20   Scenario Topology

Example 3-19   Missing VLANs

```
S3# show interfaces trunk

Port        Mode            Encapsulation  Status       Native vlan
Fa0/3       on              802.1q         trunking     99


Port        Vlans allowed on trunk
Fa0/3       10,20,99


Port        Vlans allowed and active in management domain
Fa0/3       10,20,99


Port        Vlans in spanning tree forwarding state and not pruned
Fa0/3       10,20,99
S1# show interfaces trunk

Port        Mode            Encapsulation  Status       Native vlan
Fa0/1       on              802.1q         trunking     99
Fa0/3       on              802.1q         trunking     99


Port        Vlans allowed on trunk
Fa0/1       10,99
Fa0/3       10,99
<output omitted>
```

Reconfigure F0/1 and F0/3 on switch S1 using the **switchport trunk allowed vlan 10,20,99** command, as shown in Example 3-20. The output shows that VLANs 10, 20, and 99 are now added to the F0/1 and F0/3 ports on switch S1. The **show interfaces trunk** command is an excellent tool for revealing common trunking problems. PC5 has regained connectivity to the student email server found at IP address 172.17.20.10

Example 3-20 Corrected VLAN List

```
S1(config)# interface f0/1
S1(config-if)# switchport trunk allowed vlan 10,20,99
S1(config-if)# interface f0/3
S1(config-if)# switchport trunk allowed vlan 10,20,99
S1(config-if)# end
S1# show interfaces trunk


Port          Mode              Encapsulation  Status       Native vlan
Fa0/1         on                802.1q         trunking     99

Fa0/3         on                802.1q         trunking     99


Port          Vlans allowed on trunk
Fa0/1         10,20,99
Fa0/3         10,20,99
<output omitted>
PC5> ping 172.17.20.10
Pinging 172.17.10.30 with 32 bytes of data:
Reply from 172.17.10.30: bytes=32 time=147ms TTL=128
<output omitted>
```

Packet Tracer Activity 3.2.4.7: Troubleshooting a VLAN Implementation—Scenario 1

In this activity, you will troubleshoot connectivity problems between PCs on the same VLAN. The activity is complete when PCs on the same VLAN can ping each other. Any solution you implement must conform to the addressing table.

Packet Tracer Activity 3.2.4.8: Troubleshooting a VLAN Implementation—Scenario 2

In this activity, you will troubleshoot a misconfigured VLAN environment. The initial network has errors. Your objective is to locate and correct the errors in the configurations and establish end-to-end connectivity. Your final configuration should match the topology diagram and addressing table. The native VLAN for this topology is VLAN 56.

Lab 3.2.4.9: Troubleshooting VLAN Configurations

In this lab, you will complete the following objectives:

- Part 1: Build the Network and Configure Basic Device Settings
- Part 2: Troubleshoot VLAN 10
- Part 3: Troubleshoot VLAN 20

VLAN Security and Design (3.3)

The proliferation of network security certifications indicates that the importance of network security is growing. Every configuration, monitoring, maintenance, and troubleshooting procedure in a switched network must include an analysis of the security implications. VLANs and VLAN technologies play an integral role in the design and implementation of switched networks.

Attacks on VLANs (3.3.1)

A number of attacks are specific to the VLAN infrastructure. In this section, the various types of attacks involving VLANs are explored.

Switch Spoofing Attack (3.3.1.1)

There are a number of different types of VLAN attacks in modern switched networks. The VLAN architecture simplifies network maintenance and improves performance, but it also opens the door to abuse. It is important to understand the general methodology behind these attacks and the primary approaches to mitigate them.

VLAN hopping enables traffic from one VLAN to be seen by another VLAN. Switch spoofing is a type of VLAN hopping attack that works by taking advantage of an incorrectly configured trunk port. By default, trunk ports have access to all VLANs and pass traffic for multiple VLANs across the same physical link, generally between switches.

Figure 3-21 illustrates a *switch spoofing attack*.

In a basic switch spoofing attack, the attacker takes advantage of the fact that the default configuration of the switch port is dynamic auto. The network attacker configures a system to spoof itself as a switch. This spoofing requires that the network attacker be capable of emulating 802.1Q and DTP messages. By tricking a switch into thinking that another switch is attempting to form a trunk, an attacker can gain access to all the VLANs allowed on the trunk port.

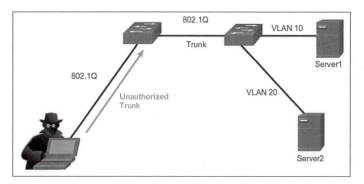

Figure 3-21   Switch Spoofing Attack

The best way to prevent a basic switch spoofing attack is to turn off trunking on all ports, except the ones that specifically require trunking. On the required trunking ports, disable DTP and manually enable trunking.

Double-Tagging Attack (3.3.1.2)

Another type of VLAN attack is a double-tagging (or double-encapsulated) VLAN hopping attack. This type of attack takes advantage of the way that hardware on most switches operates. Most switches perform only one level of 802.1Q deencapsulation, which allows an attacker to embed a hidden 802.1Q tag inside the frame. This tag allows the frame to be forwarded to a VLAN that the original 802.1Q tag did not specify. An important characteristic of the double-encapsulated VLAN hopping attack is that it works even if trunk ports are disabled, because a host typically sends a frame on a segment that is not a trunk link.

A *double-tagging attack*, illustrated in Figure 3-22, follows three steps:

1. The attacker sends a double-tagged 802.1Q frame to the switch. The outer header has the VLAN tag of the attacker, which is the same as the native VLAN of the trunk port. The assumption is that the switch processes the frame received from the attacker as if it were on a trunk port or a port with a voice VLAN (a switch should not receive a tagged Ethernet frame on an access port). For the purposes of this example, assume that the native VLAN is VLAN 10. The inner tag is the victim VLAN, in this case, VLAN 20.

2. The frame arrives on the switch, which looks at the first 4-byte 802.1Q tag. The switch sees that the frame is destined for VLAN 10, which is the native VLAN. The switch forwards the packet out on all VLAN 10 ports after stripping the VLAN 10 tag. On the trunk port, the VLAN 10 tag is stripped, and the packet is not retagged because it is part of the native VLAN. At this point, the VLAN 20 tag is still intact and has not been inspected by the first switch.

3. The second switch looks only at the inner 802.1Q tag that the attacker sent and sees that the frame is destined for VLAN 20, the target VLAN. The second switch sends the frame on to the victim port or floods it, depending on whether there is an existing MAC address table entry for the victim host.

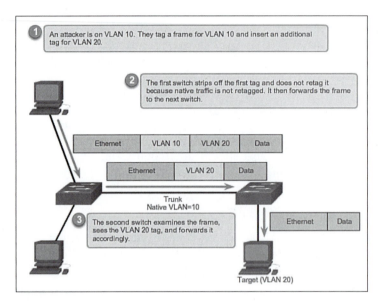

Figure 3-22   Double-Tagging Attack

This type of attack is unidirectional and works only when the attacker is connected to a port residing in the same VLAN as the native VLAN of the trunk port. Thwarting this type of attack is not as easy as stopping basic VLAN hopping attacks.

The best approach to mitigating double-tagging attacks is to ensure that the native VLAN of the trunk ports is different from the VLAN of any user ports. In fact, it is considered a security best practice to use a fixed VLAN that is distinct from all user VLANs in the switched network as the native VLAN for all 802.1Q trunks.

PVLAN Edge (3.3.1.3)

Some applications require that no traffic be forwarded at Layer 2 between ports on the same switch so that one neighbor does not see the traffic generated by another neighbor. In such an environment, the use of the *Private VLAN (PVLAN) Edge* feature, also known as *protected ports*, ensures that there is no exchange of unicast, broadcast, or multicast traffic between these ports on the switch, as shown in Figure 3-23.

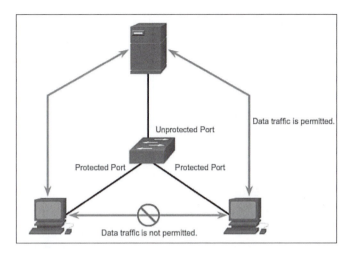

Figure 3-23 Private VLAN Edge

The PVLAN Edge feature has the following characteristics:

- A protected port does not forward any traffic (unicast, multicast, or broadcast) to any other port that is also a protected port, except for control traffic. Data traffic cannot be forwarded between protected ports at Layer 2.

- Forwarding behavior between a protected port and a nonprotected port proceeds as usual.

- Protected ports must be manually configured.

To configure the PVLAN Edge feature, enter the **switchport protected** command in interface configuration mode, as shown in Example 3-21. To disable protected port, use the **no switchport protected** interface configuration mode command. To verify the configuration of the PVLAN Edge feature, use the **show interfaces** *interface-id* **switchport** global configuration mode command.

Example 3-21 PVLAN Edge

```
S1(config)# interface g0/1
S1(config-if)# switchport protected
S1(config-if)# end
S1# show interfaces g0/1 switchport
Name: Gi0/1
Switchport: Enabled
Administrative Mode: dynamic auto
Operational Mode: down
Administrative Trunking Encapsulation: dot1q
Negotiation of Trunking: On
Access Mode VLAN: 1 (default)
```

```
Trunking Native Mode VLAN: 1 (default)
Administrative Native VLAN tagging: enabled
Voice VLAN: none
<output omitted>
Protected: true
Unknown unicast blocked: disabled
Unknown multicast blocked: disabled
Appliance trust: none
```

Activity 3.3.1.3: PVLAN Edge

Go to the online course to use the Syntax Checker in the third graphic to configure the PVLAN Edge feature on interface G0/1 and verify the configuration.

Activity 3.3.1.4: Identify the Type of VLAN Attacks

Go to the online course to perform this practice activity.

VLAN Best Practices (3.3.2)

VLAN best practices refer to those practices that any network administrator responsible for portions of a switched network should employ in his day-to-day work. These comprise standard operating procedures for switch practitioners.

VLAN Design Guidelines (3.3.2.1)

Cisco switches have a factory configuration in which default VLANs are preconfigured to support various media and protocol types. The default Ethernet VLAN is VLAN 1. It is a security best practice to configure all the ports on all switches to be associated with VLANs other than VLAN 1. This is usually done by configuring all unused ports to a *black hole VLAN* that is not used for anything on the network. All used ports are associated with VLANs distinct from VLAN 1 and distinct from the black hole VLAN. It is also a good practice to shut down unused switch ports to prevent unauthorized access.

A good security practice is to separate management and user data traffic. The management VLAN, which is VLAN 1 by default, should be changed to a separate, distinct VLAN. To communicate remotely with a Cisco switch for management purposes, the switch must have an IP address configured on the management VLAN. Users in other VLANs would not be able to establish remote access sessions to the switch unless they were routed into the management VLAN, providing an additional layer of security. Also, the switch should be configured to accept only encrypted SSH sessions for remote management.

All control traffic is sent on VLAN 1. Therefore, when the native VLAN is changed to something other than VLAN 1, all control traffic is tagged on IEEE 802.1Q VLAN trunks (tagged with VLAN ID 1). A recommended security practice is to change the native VLAN to a different VLAN than VLAN 1. The native VLAN should also be distinct from all user VLANs. Ensure that the native VLAN for an 802.1Q trunk is the same on both ends of the trunk link.

DTP offers four switch port modes: access, trunk, dynamic auto, and dynamic desirable. A general guideline is to disable autonegotiation. As a port security best practice, do not use the dynamic auto or dynamic desirable switch port modes.

Finally, voice traffic has stringent QoS requirements. If user PCs and IP phones are on the same VLAN, each tries to use the available bandwidth without considering the other device. To avoid this conflict, it is good practice to use separate VLANs for IP telephony and data traffic.

Lab 3.2.4.9: Troubleshooting VLAN Configurations

In this lab, you will complete the following objectives:

- Part 1: Build the Network and Configure Basic Device Settings
- Part 2: Implement VLAN Security on the Switches

Summary (3.4)

Class Activity 3.4.1.1: VLAN Plan

You are designing a VLAN switched network for your small- to medium-sized business.

Your business owns space on two floors of a high-rise building. The following elements need VLAN consideration and access for planning purposes:

- Management
- Finance
- Sales
- Human Resources
- Network administrator
- General visitors to your business location

You have two Cisco 3560-24PS switches.

Use a word processing software program to design your VLAN-switched network scheme.

Section 1 of your design should include the regular names of your departments, suggested VLAN names and numbers, and which switch ports would be assigned to each VLAN.

Section 2 of your design should list how security would be planned for this switched network.

When your VLAN plan is finished, complete the reflection questions from this activity's PDF.

Save your work. Be able to explain and discuss your VLAN design with another group or with the class.

Packet Tracer Activity 3.4.1.2: Skills Integration Challenge

In this activity, two switches are completely configured. On a third switch, you are responsible for assigning IP addressing to the SVI, configuring VLANs, assigning VLANs to interfaces, configuring trunking, and performing basic switch security.

This chapter introduced VLANs. VLANs are based on logical connections, instead of physical connections. VLANs are a mechanism to allow network administrators to create logical broadcast domains that can span across a single switch or multiple switches, regardless of physical proximity. This function is useful to reduce the size of broadcast domains or to allow groups of users to be logically grouped without the need to be physically located in the same place.

There are several types of VLANs:

- Default VLAN

- Management VLAN

- Native VLAN

- User/Data VLANs

- Black Hole VLAN

- Voice VLAN

On a Cisco switch, VLAN 1 is the default Ethernet VLAN, the default native VLAN, and the default management VLAN. Best practices suggest that the native and management VLANs be moved to another distinct VLAN and that unused switch ports be moved to a "black hole" VLAN for increased security.

The **switchport access vlan** command is used to create a VLAN on a switch. After creating a VLAN, the next step is to assign ports to the VLAN. The **show vlan brief** command displays the VLAN assignment and membership type for all switch ports. Each VLAN must correspond to a unique IP subnet.

Use the **show vlan** command to check whether the port belongs to the expected VLAN. If the port is assigned to the wrong VLAN, use the **switchport access vlan** command to correct the VLAN membership. Use the **show mac address-table** command to check which addresses were learned on a particular port of the switch and to which VLAN that port is assigned.

A port on a switch is either an access port or a trunk port. Access ports carry traffic from a specific VLAN assigned to the port. A trunk port by default is a member of all VLANs; therefore, it carries traffic for all VLANs.

VLAN trunks facilitate inter-switch communication by carrying traffic associated with multiple VLANs. IEEE 802.1Q frame tagging differentiates between Ethernet frames associated with distinct VLANs as they traverse common trunk links. To enable trunk links, use the **switchport mode trunk** command. Use the **show interfaces trunk** command to check whether a trunk has been established between switches.

Trunk negotiation is managed by the Dynamic Trunking Protocol (DTP), which operates on a point-to-point basis only, between network devices. DTP is a Cisco-proprietary protocol that is automatically enabled on Catalyst 2960 and Catalyst 3560 Series switches.

To place a switch into its factory default condition with one default VLAN, use the **delete flash:vlan.dat** and **erase startup-config** commands.

This chapter also examined the configuration, verification, and troubleshooting of VLANs and trunks using the Cisco IOS CLI and explored basic security and design considerations in the context of VLANs.

Practice

The following activities provide practice with the topics introduced in this chapter. The Labs and Class Activities are available in the companion *Switched Networks Lab Manual* (ISBN 978-1-58713-372-5). The Packet Tracer Activities PKA files are found in the online course.

Class Activities

- Class Activity 3.0.1.2: Vacation Station
- Class Activity 3.4.1.1: VLAN Plan

Labs

- Lab 3.2.2.5: Configuring VLANs and Trunking
- Lab 3.2.4.9: Troubleshooting VLAN Configurations

Packet Tracer
☐ **Activity**

Packet Tracer Activities

- Packet Tracer Activity 3.1.1.5: Who Hears the Broadcast?
- Packet Tracer Activity 3.1.2.7: Investigating a VLAN Implementation
- Packet Tracer Activity 3.2.1.7: Configuring VLANs
- Packet Tracer Activity 3.2.2.4: Configuring Trunks
- Packet Tracer Activity 3.2.4.7: Troubleshooting a VLAN Implementation—Scenario 1
- Packet Tracer Activity 3.2.4.8: Troubleshooting a VLAN Implementation—Scenario 2

Check Your Understanding Questions

Complete all the review questions listed here to test your understanding of the topics and concepts in this chapter. The appendix "Answers to 'Check Your Understanding' Questions" lists the answers.

1. For what reason would a network administrator use the **show interfaces trunk** command on a switch?

    A. To view the native VLAN

    B. To examine DTP negotiation as it occurs

    C. To verify port association with a particular VLAN

    D. To display an IP address for any existing VLAN

2. What is the purpose of the switch command **switchport access vlan 99**?

    A. To enable port security

    B. To make the port operational

    C. To assign the port to a particular VLAN

    D. To designate the VLAN that does not get tagged

    E. To assign the port to the default native VLAN (VLAN 99)

3. Which step should be performed first when deleting a VLAN that has member switch ports?

    A. Reload the switch.

    B. Implement the **delete vlan.dat** command.

    C. Reassign all VLAN member ports to a different VLAN.

    D. Back up the running config.

4. All access ports on a switch are configured with the administrative mode of dynamic auto. An attacker, connected to one of the ports, sends a malicious DTP frame. What is the intent of the attacker?

    A. VLAN hopping attack

    B. DHCP spoofing attack

    C. MAC flooding attack

    D. ARP poisoning attack

5. Which of the following statements accurately describe DTP? (Choose two.)

    A. DTP is a Cisco-proprietary protocol.

    B. DTP supports IEEE 802.1Q.

    C. Cisco switches require DTP to establish trunks.

    D. DTP must be enabled on only one side of the trunk link.

    E. Trunk ports that are configured for dynamic auto will request to enter the trunking state.

6. Match the action to the corresponding command.

    1. Assigns VLAN 10 for untagged traffic

    2. Activates the current interface as trunk

    3. Prohibits VLAN 10 on the trunk interface

    A. Switch(config-if)# **switchport trunk allowed vlan remove 10**

    B. Switch(config-if)# **switchport mode trunk**

    C. Switch(config-if)# **switchport trunk native vlan 10**

7. What is one way to prevent the VLAN hopping attack?

    A. Disable DTP negotiation on all ports.

    B. Change the native VLAN to an unused VLAN.

    C. Designate a different default VLAN.

    D. Remove all user VLANs from the trunk.

8. What security issue is of concern regarding the VLAN configuration of switches?

    A. All interfaces are in the same user VLAN.

    B. The management VLAN is using the same VLAN ID as a user VLAN is using.

    C. The "black hole" VLAN is not configured.

    D. The native VLAN has not been changed from the default setting.

9. In which location are the normal-range VLANs stored on a Cisco switch by default?

    A. Flash memory

    B. Startup config

    C. Running config

    D. RAM

10. Which of the following statements describe the benefits of VLANs? (Choose two.)

    A. VLANs improve network performance by regulating flow control and window size.

    B. VLANs enable switches to route packets to remote networks through VLAN ID filtering.

    C. VLANs reduce network cost by reducing the number of physical ports required on switches.

    D. VLANs improve network security by isolating users that have access to sensitive data and applications.

    E. VLANs divide a network into smaller logical networks, resulting in lower susceptibility to broadcast storms.

11. An administrator is investigating an inoperational trunk link between a Cisco switch and a switch from another vendor. After a few **show** commands, the administrator notices that the switches are not negotiating a trunk. What is a probable cause for this issue?

    A. Both switches are in trunk mode.

    B. Both switches are in nonegotiate mode.

    C. Switches from other vendors do not support DTP.

    D. DTP frames are flooding the entire network.

12. Which distinct type of VLAN is used by an administrator to access and configure a switch?

    A. Default VLAN

    B. Native VLAN

    C. Data VLAN

    D. Management VLAN

CHAPTER 4

LAN Redundancy

Objectives

Upon completion of this chapter, you will be able to answer the following questions:

- How do you describe the issues with implementing a redundant network?

- How do you describe IEEE 802.1D STP operation?

- How do you describe the different spanning tree varieties?

- How do you describe PVST+ operation in a switched LAN environment?

- How do you describe Rapid PVST+ operation in a switched LAN environment?

- How do you configure PVST+ in a switched LAN environment?

- How do you configure Rapid PVST+ in a switched LAN environment? 195

- How do you identify common STP configuration issues?

- How do you describe the purpose and operation of First Hop Redundancy Protocols?

- How do you describe the different varieties of First Hop Redundancy Protocols?

- Which Cisco IOS commands do you use to verify HSRP and GLBP implementations?

Key Terms

This chapter uses the following key terms. You can find the definitions in the Glossary.

Introduction (4.0.1.1)

Network redundancy is a key to maintaining network reliability. Multiple physical links between devices provide redundant paths. The network can then continue to operate when a single link or port has failed. Redundant links can also share the traffic load and increase capacity.

Multiple paths must be managed so that Layer 2 loops are not created, the best paths are chosen for use, and an alternate path is immediately available should a primary path fail. The Spanning Tree Protocols are used to manage Layer 2 redundancy.

Redundant devices, such as multilayer switches or routers, provide the capability for a client to use an alternate default gateway should the primary default gateway fail. A client can now have multiple paths to more than one possible default gateway. First Hop Redundancy Protocols are used to manage how a client is assigned a default gateway, and to be able to use an alternate default gateway should the primary default gateway fail.

This chapter focuses on the protocols used to manage these forms of redundancy. It also covers some of the potential redundancy problems and their symptoms.

Class Activity 4.0.1.2: Stormy Traffic

It is your first day on the job as a network administrator for a small- to medium-sized business. The previous network administrator left suddenly after a network upgrade took place for the business.

During the upgrade, a new switch was added. Because of the upgrade, many employees complain that they are having trouble accessing the Internet and servers on your network. In fact, most of them cannot access the network at all. Your corporate manager asks you to immediately research what could be causing these connectivity problems and delays.

So you take a look at the equipment operating on your network at your main distribution facility in the building. You notice that the network topology seems to be visually correct and that cables have been connected correctly, routers and switches are powered on and operational, and switches are connected together to provide backup or redundancy.

However, one thing you do notice is that all your switches' status lights are constantly blinking at a very fast pace to the point that they almost appear solid. You think you have found the problem with the connectivity issues that your employees are experiencing.

Use the Internet to research STP. As you research, take notes and describe:

- *Broadcast storm*
- Switching loops
- The purpose of STP
- Variations of STP

Complete the reflection questions that accompany the PDF file for this activity. Save your work and be prepared to share your answers with the class.

Spanning Tree Concepts (4.1)

Computer networking often involves the implementation of algorithms for the purpose of affecting a desired result. For example, each routing protocol is based on an algorithm. And algorithms such as Advanced Encryption Standard (AES) underlie wireless security. In this chapter, the Spanning Tree Protocol (STP) is explored; this protocol depends on the *spanning tree algorithm*.

STP Operation (4.1.2)

Spanning Tree Protocol is a term used to encompass not only the messages sent between switches, but also how switches use the information in the messages to make decisions and take actions to effect a desired result in the Layer 2 topology. In the realm of computer networking, when considering all the vendor implementations of STP and the behind-the-scenes operation, STP definitely comprises one of the most complex combinations of technologies, protocols, and algorithms.

Redundancy at OSI Layers 1 and 2 (4.1.1.1)

The three-tier hierarchical network design uses the core, distribution, and access layers with built-in redundancy to eliminate a single point of failure in the network. Multiple cabled paths between switches provide physical redundancy in a switched network. This improves the reliability and availability of the network. Having alternate physical paths for data to traverse the network makes it possible for users to access network resources, despite path disruption.

Here we illustrate how redundancy works in a network with three switches connected in a physical loop:

1. In Figure 4-1, PC1 is communicating with PC4 over a redundant network topology.

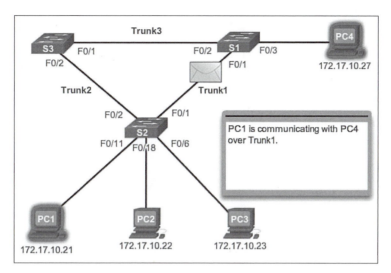

Figure 4-1   PC1 Communicating with PC4 over Trunk1

2. When the network link between S1 and S2 is disrupted, as shown in Figure 4-2, the path between PC1 and PC4 is automatically adjusted to compensate for the disruption.

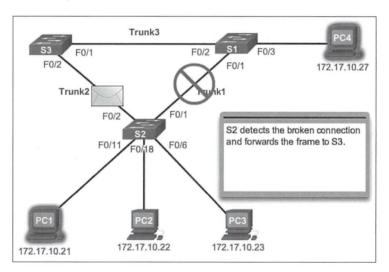

Figure 4-2   Trunk1 Is Broken Between S2 and S1

3. When the network connection between S1 and S2 is restored, the path is then readjusted to route traffic directly from S2 to S1 to get to PC4, as shown in Figure 4-1.

For many organizations, the availability of the network is essential to supporting business needs; therefore, the network infrastructure design is a critical business element. Path redundancy is a solution for providing the necessary availability of multiple network services by eliminating the possibility of a single point of failure.

> **Note**
>
> The OSI Layer 1 redundancy is illustrated using multiple links and devices, but more than just physical planning is required to complete the network setup. For the redundancy to work in a systematic way, the use of OSI Layer 2 protocols, such as STP, is also required.

Redundancy is an important part of hierarchical design for preventing disruption of network services to users. Redundant networks require adding physical paths, but logical redundancy must also be part of the design. However, redundant paths in a switched Ethernet network can cause both physical and logical Layer 2 loops.

Logical Layer 2 loops can occur because of the natural operation of switches; specifically, the learning and forwarding process. When multiple paths exist between two devices on a network, and there is no spanning tree implementation on the switches, a Layer 2 loop occurs. A Layer 2 loop can result in three primary issues:

- **MAC database instability:** Instability in the content of the MAC address table results from copies of the same frame being received on different ports of the switch. Data forwarding can be impaired when the switch consumes the resources that are coping with instability in the MAC address table.

- **Broadcast storms:** Without some loop-avoidance process, each switch flooding broadcasts endlessly. This situation is commonly called a broadcast storm.

- **Multiple frame transmission:** Multiple copies of unicast frames can be delivered to destination stations. Many protocols expect to receive only a single copy of each transmission. Multiple copies of the same frame can cause unrecoverable errors.

Issues with Layer 1 Redundancy: MAC Database Instability (4.1.1.2)

Ethernet frames do not have a time to live (TTL) attribute, like IP packets. As a result, if there is no mechanism enabled to block continued propagation of these frames on a switched network, they continue to propagate between switches endlessly, or until a link is disrupted and breaks the loop. This continued propagation between switches can result in MAC database instability. This can occur because of broadcast frames forwarding.

Broadcast frames are forwarded out all switch ports, except the original ingress port. This ensures that all devices in a broadcast domain are able to receive the frame. If there is more than one path for the frame to be forwarded out, an endless loop can result. When a loop occurs, it is possible for the MAC address table on a switch to constantly change with the updates from the broadcast frames, resulting in MAC database instability.

Here MAC database instability is illustrated:

1. PC1 sends out a broadcast frame to S2. S2 receives the broadcast frame on F0/11. When S2 receives the broadcast frame, it updates its MAC address table to record that PC1 is available on port F0/11, as shown in Figure 4-3.

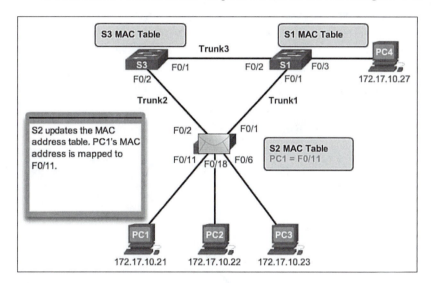

Figure 4-3 PC1 Sends Broadcast Frame

2. Because it is a broadcast frame, S2 forwards the frame out all ports, including Trunk1 and Trunk2, as shown in Figure 4-4. When the broadcast frame arrives at S3 and S1, they update their MAC address tables, as shown in Figure 4-5, to indicate that PC1 is available out port F0/1 on S1 and out port F0/2 on S3.

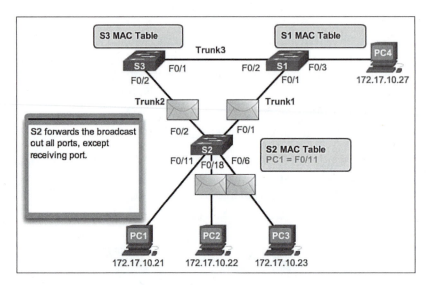

Figure 4-4   S2 Forwards Frame Copies Out All Noningress Ports

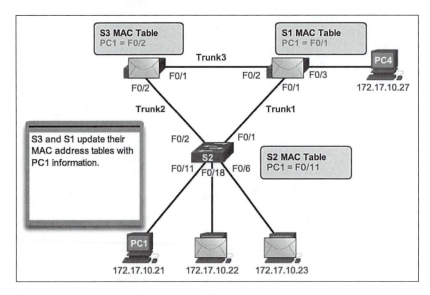

Figure 4-5   S1 and S3 Update MAC Address Tables

3. Because it is a broadcast frame, S3 and S1 forward the frame out all ports, except the ingress port, as shown in Figure 4-6. S3 sends the broadcast frame from PC1 to S1. S1 sends the broadcast frame from PC1 to S3. Each switch updates its MAC address table with the incorrect port for PC1, as shown in Figure 4-7.

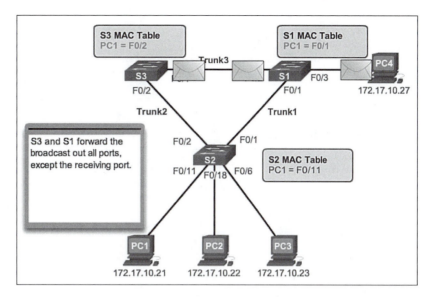

Figure 4-6   S1 and S3 Forward Frame Copies Out All Noningress Ports

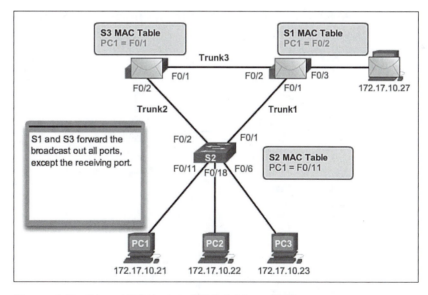

Figure 4-7   S1 and S3 Update MAC Address Tables

4. Each switch again forwards the broadcast frame out all its ports, except the ingress port, resulting in both switches forwarding the frame to S2, as shown in Figure 4-8.

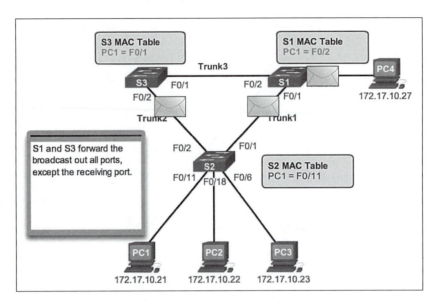

Figure 4-8 S1 and S3 Forward Frame Copies Out All Noningress Ports

5. When S2 receives the broadcast frames from S3 and S1, the MAC address table is updated again, this time with the last entry received from the other two switches. See Figure 4-9.

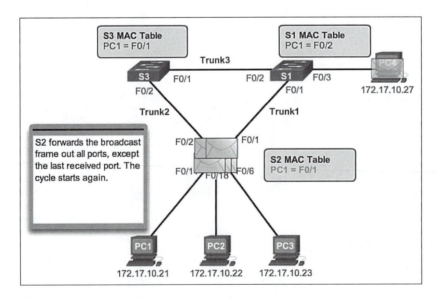

Figure 4-9 S2 Updates MAC Address Table

This process repeats until the loop is broken by physically disconnecting the connections causing the loop or powering down one of the switches in the loop. This creates a high CPU load on all switches caught in the loop. Because the same frames are constantly being forwarded back and forth between all switches in the loop, the CPU of the switch must process a lot of data. This slows performance on the switch when legitimate traffic arrives.

A host caught in a network loop is not accessible to other hosts on the network. Additionally, because of the constant changes in the MAC address table, the switch does not know out of which port to forward unicast frames. In the example illustrated in Figures 4-3 through 4-9, the switches will have the incorrect ports listed for PC1. Any unicast frame destined for PC1 loops around the network, just as the broadcast frames do. More and more frames looping around the network eventually create a broadcast storm.

Issues with Layer 1 Redundancy: Broadcast Storms (4.1.1.3)

A broadcast storm occurs when there are so many broadcast frames caught in a Layer 2 loop that all available bandwidth is consumed. Consequently, no bandwidth is available for legitimate traffic and the network becomes unavailable for data communication. This is an effective denial of service.

A broadcast storm is inevitable on a looped network. As more devices send broadcasts over the network, more traffic is caught within the loop, consuming resources. This eventually creates a broadcast storm that causes the network to fail.

There are other consequences of broadcast storms. Because broadcast traffic is forwarded out every port on a switch, all connected devices have to process all broadcast traffic that is being flooded endlessly around the looped network. This can cause the end device to malfunction because of the high processing requirements for sustaining such a high traffic load on the NIC.

When the network is fully saturated with Layer 2 broadcast traffic that is looping between the switches, new traffic is discarded by any switch in the topology because it is unable to process it.

Because devices connected to a network are regularly sending out broadcast frames, such as ARP requests, a broadcast storm can develop in seconds. As a result, when a loop is created, the switched network is quickly brought down.

Issues with Layer 1 Redundancy: Duplicate Unicast Frames (4.1.1.4)

Broadcast frames are not the only type of frames that are affected by loops. By exactly the same mechanism illustrated in Figures 4-3 through 4-9, unicast frames sent onto a looped network can result in duplicate frames arriving at the destination device.

Most upper-layer protocols are not designed to recognize, or cope with, duplicate transmissions. In general, protocols that make use of a sequence-numbering mechanism assume that the transmission has failed and that the sequence number has recycled for another communication session. Other protocols attempt to hand the duplicate transmission to the appropriate upper-layer protocol to be processed and possibly discarded.

Layer 2 LAN protocols, such as Ethernet, lack a mechanism to recognize and eliminate endlessly looping frames. Some Layer 3 protocols implement a TTL mechanism that limits the number of times a Layer 3 networking device can retransmit a packet. Lacking such a mechanism, Layer 2 devices continue to retransmit looping traffic indefinitely. A Layer 2 loop-avoidance mechanism, STP, was developed to address these problems.

To prevent these issues from occurring in a redundant network, some type of spanning tree must be enabled on the switches. Spanning tree is enabled by default on Cisco switches to prevent Layer 2 loops from occurring.

Packet Tracer
☐ Activity

Packet Tracer Activity 4.1.1.5: Examining a Redundant Design

In this activity, you will observe how STP operates by default and how it reacts when faults occur. Switches have been added to the network "out of the box." Cisco switches can be connected to a network without any additional action required by the network administrator. For the purpose of this activity, the bridge priority was modified.

STP Operation (4.1.2)

STP operation is based on the spanning tree algorithm. The better one understands the underlying algorithm used by STP, the easier it is to troubleshoot STP-related issues.

Spanning Tree Algorithm: Introduction (4.1.2.1)

Redundancy increases the availability of the network topology by protecting the network from a single point of failure, such as a failed network cable or switch. When physical redundancy is introduced into a design, loops and duplicate frames occur. Loops and duplicate frames have severe consequences for a switched network. STP was developed to address these issues.

STP ensures that there is only one logical path between all destinations on the network by intentionally blocking redundant paths that could cause a loop. A port is considered blocked when user data is prevented from entering or leaving that port. This does not include *bridge protocol data unit (BPDU)* frames that are used by

STP to prevent loops. Blocking the redundant paths is critical to preventing loops on the network. The physical paths still exist to provide redundancy, but these paths are disabled to prevent the loops from occurring. If the path is ever needed to compensate for a network cable or switch failure, STP recalculates the paths and unblocks the necessary ports to allow the redundant path to become active.

Normal STP operation is illustrated in this example, where all switches have STP enabled:

1. PC1 sends a broadcast out onto the network, as shown in Figure 4-10.

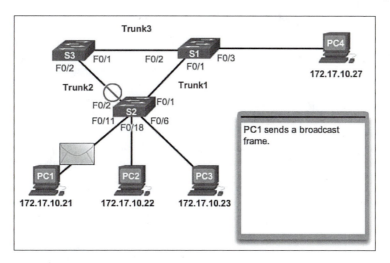

Figure 4-10   PC1 Sends Broadcast Frame with STP Enabled on All Switches

2. S2 is configured with STP and has set the port for Trunk2 to a blocking state. The blocking state prevents ports from being used to forward user data, thus preventing a loop from occurring. S2 forwards a broadcast frame out all switch ports, except the originating port from PC1 and the port for Trunk2.

3. S1 receives the broadcast frame and forwards it out all its switch ports, where it reaches PC4 and S3. S3 forwards the frame out the port for Trunk2 and S2 drops the frame. The Layer 2 loop is prevented.

In the next example, STP real-time redundancy is illustrated:

1. PC1 sends a broadcast out onto the network, as shown in Figure 4-10.

2. The broadcast is then forwarded around the network.

3. The trunk link between S2 and S1 fails, as pictured in Figure 4-11, resulting in the previous path being disrupted.

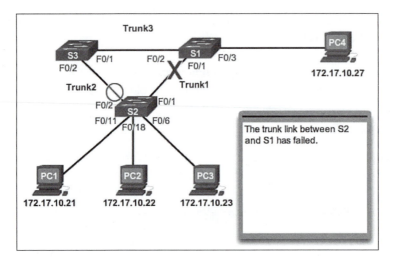

Figure 4-11   Trunk1 Fails

4. S2 unblocks the previously blocked port for Trunk2, as shown in Figure 4-12, and allows the broadcast traffic to traverse the alternate path around the network, permitting communication to continue. If this link comes back up, STP reconverges and the port on S2 is again blocked.

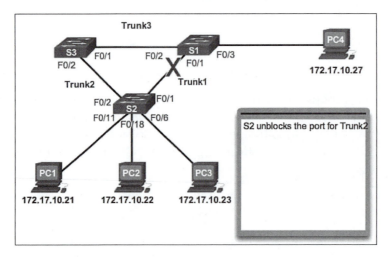

Figure 4-12   S2 Unblocks Port Previously Blocked by STP

STP prevents loops from occurring by configuring a loop-free path through the network using strategically placed "blocking-state" ports. The switches running STP are able to compensate for failures by dynamically unblocking the previously blocked ports and permitting traffic to traverse the alternate paths.

Up to now, we have used the term Spanning Tree Protocol and the acronym STP. The usage of the Spanning Tree Protocol term and the STP acronym can be misleading. Technically, these refer to the original 802.1D standard and its implementation. However, many professionals generically use these to refer to various implementations of spanning tree, such as *Rapid Spanning Tree Protocol (RSTP)* and *Multiple Spanning Tree Protocol (MSTP)*. In order to communicate spanning tree concepts correctly, it is important to refer to the particular implementation or standard in context. The latest IEEE documentation on spanning tree, IEEE-802-1D-2004, says "STP has now been superseded by the Rapid Spanning Tree Protocol (RSTP)." So one sees that the IEEE uses "STP" to refer to the original implementation of spanning tree and "RSTP" to describe the version of spanning tree specified in IEEE-802.1D-2004. In this curriculum, when the original Spanning Tree Protocol is the context of a discussion, the phrase "original 802.1D spanning tree" or simply "802.1D" is used to avoid confusion.

Note

STP is based on an algorithm invented by Radia Perlman while working for Digital Equipment Corporation, and published in the 1985 paper "An Algorithm for Distributed Computation of a Spanning Tree in an Extended LAN."

Spanning Tree Algorithm: Port Roles (4.1.2.2)

The spanning tree algorithm (STA) is used to determine which switch ports on a network must be put in the blocking state to prevent loops from occurring. The STA designates a single switch as the *root bridge* and uses it as the reference point for all path calculations. In Figure 4-13, the root bridge (switch S1) is chosen through an election process. All switches participating in spanning tree exchange BPDU frames to determine which switch has the lowest bridge ID (BID) on the network. The switch with the lowest BID automatically becomes the root bridge for the STA calculations.

Note

For simplicity, assume until otherwise indicated that all ports on all switches are assigned to VLAN 1. Each switch has a unique MAC address associated with VLAN 1.

A BPDU is a messaging frame exchanged by switches for STP. Each BPDU contains a BID that identifies the switch that sent the BPDU. The BID contains a priority value, the MAC address of the sending switch, and an optional extended system ID. The lowest BID value is determined by the combination of these three fields.

After the root bridge has been determined, the STA calculates the shortest path to it. Each switch uses the STA to determine which ports to block. While the STA determines the best paths to the root bridge for all switch ports in the broadcast domain, traffic is prevented from being forwarded through the network. The STA considers both path and *port costs* when determining which ports to block. The *path costs* are calculated using port cost values associated with port speeds for each switch port along a given path. The sum of the port cost values determines the overall path cost to the root bridge. If there is more than one path to choose from, STA chooses the path with the lowest path cost.

When the STA has determined which paths are most desirable relative to each switch, it assigns port roles to the participating switch ports. The *port roles* describe their relation in the network to the root bridge, shown in Figure 4-13, and whether they are allowed to forward traffic:

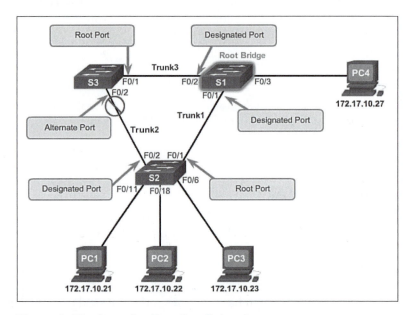

Figure 4-13   Spanning Tree Port Roles

- *Root ports*: Switch ports closest to the root bridge. In the figure, the root port on S2 is F0/1 configured for the trunk link between S2 and S1. The root port on S3 is F0/1, configured for the trunk link between S3 and S1. Root ports are selected on a per-switch basis.

- *Designated ports*: All nonroot ports that are still permitted to forward traffic on the network. In the figure, switch ports (F0/1 and F0/2) on S1 are designated ports. S2 also has its port F0/2 configured as a designated port. Designated ports are selected on a per-trunk basis. If one end of a trunk is a root port, the other end is a designated port. All ports on the root bridge are designated ports.

- *Alternate ports* and *backup ports*: Alternate ports and backup ports are configured to be in a blocking state to prevent loops. In the figure, the STA configured port F0/2 on S3 in the alternate role. Port F0/2 on S3 is in the blocking state. Alternate ports are selected only on trunk links where neither end is a root port. Notice in the figure that only one end of the trunk is blocked. This allows for faster transition to a forwarding state, when necessary. (Blocking ports only come into play when two ports on the same switch are connected to each other through a hub or single cable.)

- *Disabled ports*: A disabled port is a switch port that is shut down.

Spanning Tree Algorithm: Root Bridge (4.1.2.3)

As shown in Figure 4-14, every spanning tree instance (switched LAN or broadcast domain) has a switch designated as the root bridge. The root bridge serves as a reference point for all spanning tree calculations to determine which redundant paths to block.

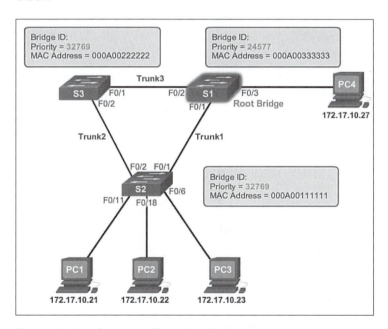

Figure 4-14 Spanning Tree Root Bridge

An election process determines which switch becomes the root bridge.

Figure 4-15 shows the BID fields. The BID is made up of a priority value, an extended system ID, and the MAC address of the switch.

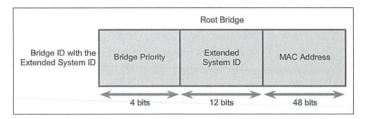

Figure 4-15   Bridge ID Fields

All switches in the broadcast domain participate in the election process. After a switch boots, it begins to send out BPDU frames every two seconds. These BPDUs contain the switch BID and the root ID.

As the switches forward their BPDU frames, adjacent switches in the broadcast domain read the root ID information from the BPDU frames. If the root ID from a BPDU received is lower than the root ID on the receiving switch, the receiving switch updates its root ID, identifying the adjacent switch as the root bridge. Actually, it might not be an adjacent switch, but could be any other switch in the broadcast domain. The switch then forwards new BPDU frames with the lower root ID to the other adjacent switches. Eventually, the switch with the lowest BID ends up being identified as the root bridge for the spanning tree instance.

There is a root bridge elected for each spanning tree instance. It is possible to have multiple distinct root bridges. If all ports on all switches are members of VLAN 1, there is only one spanning tree instance. The extended system ID plays a role in how spanning tree instances are determined.

Spanning Tree Algorithm: Path Cost (4.1.2.4)

When the root bridge has been elected for the spanning tree instance, the STA starts the process of determining the best paths to the root bridge from all destinations in the broadcast domain. The path information is determined by summing up the individual port costs along the path from the destination to the root bridge. Each "destination" is actually a switch port.

The default port costs are defined by the speed at which the port operates. As shown in Table 4-1, 10-Gb/s Ethernet ports have a port cost of 2, 1-Gb/s Ethernet ports have a port cost of 4, 100-Mb/s Fast Ethernet ports have a port cost of 19, and 10-Mb/s Ethernet ports have a port cost of 100.

Table 4-1 Port Costs

Link Speed	Cost (Revised IEEE Specification)	Cost (Previous IEEE Specification)
10 Gb/s	2	1
1 Gb/s	4	1
100 Mb/s	19	10
10 Mb/s	100	100

Note

As newer, faster Ethernet technologies enter the marketplace, the path cost values can change to accommodate the different speeds available. The nonlinear numbers in the table accommodate some improvements to the older Ethernet standard. The values have already been changed to accommodate the 10-Gb/s Ethernet standard. To illustrate the continued change associated with high-speed networking, Catalyst 4500 and 6500 switches support a longer path cost method. For example, 10 Gb/s has path cost 2000, 100 Gb/s has path cost 200, and 1 Tb/s has path cost 20.

Although switch ports have a default port cost associated with them, the port cost is configurable. The ability to configure individual port costs gives the administrator the flexibility to manually control the spanning tree paths to the root bridge.

To configure the port cost of an interface, enter the spanning-tree cost value command in interface configuration mode. The value can be between 1 and 200,000,000.

In the following code, switch port F0/1 has been configured with a port cost of 25 using the **spanning-tree cost 25** interface configuration mode command on the F0/1 interface.

```
S2(config)# interface f0/1
S2(config-router)# spanning-tree cost 25
```

To restore the port cost to the default value of 19, enter the **no spanning-tree cost** interface configuration mode command.

The path cost is equal to the sum of all the port costs along the path to the root bridge, as illustrated in Figure 4-16. Paths with the lowest cost become preferred, and all other redundant paths are blocked. In the example, the path cost from S2 to the root bridge S1 over path 1 is 19 (based on the IEEE-specified individual port cost), while the path cost over path 2 is 38. Because path 1 has a lower overall path cost to the root bridge, it is the preferred path. STP then configures the redundant path to be blocked, preventing a loop from occurring.

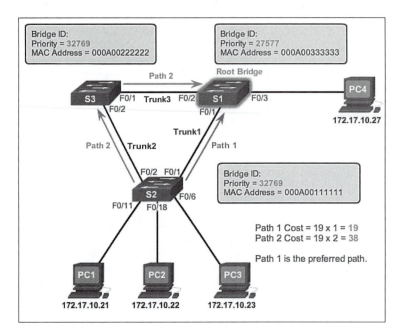

Figure 4-16   Path Cost Calculation

To verify the port and path cost to the root bridge, enter the **show spanning-tree** command, as shown in Example 4-1.

Example 4-1   Verifying Port and Path Cost

```
S2# show spanning-tree


VLAN0001
  Spanning tree enabled protocol ieee
  Root ID     Priority 27577
              Address       000A.0033.3333
              Cost          19
              Port          1
              Hello Time    2 sec  Max Age 20 sec  Forward Delay 15 sec

  Bridge ID   Priority    32769  (priority 32768 sys-id-ext 1)
              Address       000A.0011.1111
              Hello Time    2 sec  Max Age 20 sec  Forward Delay 15 sec
              Aging Time 300


Interface           Role Sts Cost       Prio.Nbr Type
----------------    ---- --- ---------  -------- --------------------------------
Fa0/1               Root FWD 19         128.1    Edge P2p
Fa0/2               Desg FWD 19         128.2    Edge P2p
```

The Cost field near the top of the output is the total path cost to the root bridge. This value changes depending on how many switch ports must be traversed to get to the root bridge. In the output, each interface is also identified with an individual port cost of 19.

802.1D BPDU Frame Format (4.1.2.5)

The spanning tree algorithm depends on the exchange of BPDUs to determine a root bridge. A BPDU frame contains 12 distinct fields that convey path and priority information used to determine the root bridge and paths to the root bridge.

Table 4-2 lists the BPDU fields:

- The first four fields identify the protocol, version, message type, and status flags.

- The next four fields are used to identify the root bridge and the cost of the path to the root bridge.

- The last four fields are all timer fields that determine how frequently BPDU messages are sent and how long the information received through the BPDU process (next topic) is retained.

Table 4-2 BPDU Fields

Field Number	Bytes	Field
1–4	2	Protocol ID
	1	Version
	1	Message Type
	1	Flags
5–8	8	Root ID
	4	Cost of path
	8	Bridge ID
	2	Port ID
9–12	2	Message age
	2	Max age
	2	Hello time
	2	Forward delay

The descriptions of the BPDU fields are

- **Protocol ID:** Type of protocol being used.

- **Version:** Version of STP.

- **Message Type:** Type of BPDU message (for example, configuration BPDU).

- **Flags:** Topology change (TC) bit, signaling a topology change in the event a path to the root bridge is disrupted; or topology change acknowledgment (TCA), acknowledging the receipt of a configuration message with the TC bit set.

- **Root ID:** Indicates the root bridge by listing its 2-byte priority followed by its 6-byte MAC address ID. When a switch first boots, the root ID is the same as the bridge ID; however, as the election process occurs, the lowest bridge ID replaces the local root ID to identify the root bridge switch.

- **Cost of path:** Cost of the path from the bridge sending the configuration message to the root bridge; the path cost field is updated by each switch along the path to the root bridge.

- **Bridge ID:** Priority and MAC address ID of the bridge sending the message. This label allows the root bridge to identify where the BPDU originated, as well as for identifying the multiple paths from the switch to the root bridge. When the root bridge receives more than one BPDU from a switch with different path costs, it knows that there are two distinct paths and uses the one path with the lower cost.

- **Port ID:** Port number from which the configuration message was sent; this field allows loops created by multiple attached bridges to be detected and corrected.

- **Message age:** Amount of time that has elapsed since the root sent the configuration message on which the current configuration message is based.

- **Max age:** Indicates when the current configuration message should be deleted. When the message age reaches the maximum age, the switch expires the current configuration and initiates a new election to determine a new root bridge, because it assumes that it has been disconnected from the root bridge. This is 20 seconds by default, but can be tuned to be between 6 and 40 seconds.

- **Hello time:** Time between root bridge configuration messages; the interval defines how long the root bridge waits between sending configuration message BPDUs. This is equal to 2 seconds by default, but can be tuned to be between 1 and 10 seconds.

- **Forward delay:** Length of time that bridges should wait before transitioning to a new state after a topology change. If a bridge transitions too soon, it is possible that not all network links will be ready to change their state and loops can result. This is by default equal to 15 seconds for each state, but can be tuned to be between 4 and 30 seconds.

Figure 4-17 shows a BPDU frame that was captured using Wireshark. In the example, the BPDU frame contains more fields than previously described. The BPDU message is encapsulated in an Ethernet frame when it is transmitted across the network. The 802.3 header indicates the source and destination addresses of the BPDU frame. This frame has a destination MAC address of 01:80:C2:00:00:00, which is a multicast address for the spanning tree group. When a frame is addressed with this MAC address, each switch that is configured for spanning tree accepts and reads the information from the frame; all other devices on the network disregard the frame.

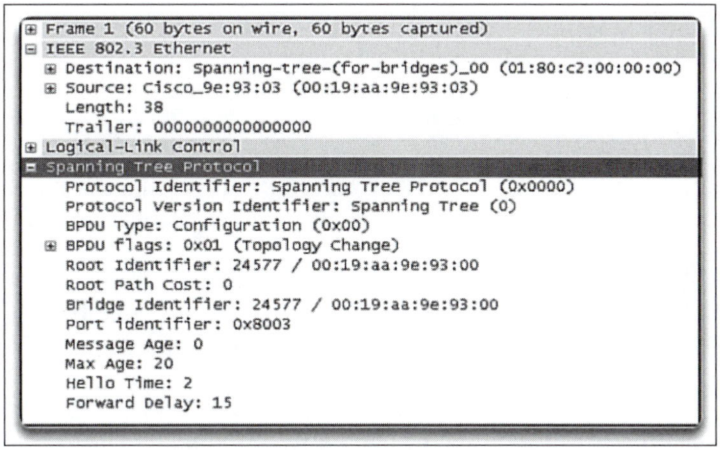

```
⊞ Frame 1 (60 bytes on wire, 60 bytes captured)
⊟ IEEE 802.3 Ethernet
  ⊞ Destination: Spanning-tree-(for-bridges)_00 (01:80:c2:00:00:00)
  ⊞ Source: Cisco_9e:93:03 (00:19:aa:9e:93:03)
    Length: 38
    Trailer: 0000000000000000
⊞ Logical-Link Control
⊟ Spanning Tree Protocol
    Protocol Identifier: Spanning Tree Protocol (0x0000)
    Protocol Version Identifier: Spanning Tree (0)
    BPDU Type: Configuration (0x00)
  ⊞ BPDU flags: 0x01 (Topology Change)
    Root Identifier: 24577 / 00:19:aa:9e:93:00
    Root Path Cost: 0
    Bridge Identifier: 24577 / 00:19:aa:9e:93:00
    Port Identifier: 0x8003
    Message Age: 0
    Max Age: 20
    Hello Time: 2
    Forward Delay: 15
```

Figure 4-17   BPDU Example

In the example, the root ID and the BID are the same in the captured BPDU frame. This indicates that the frame was captured from a root bridge. The timers are all set to the default values.

BPDU Propagation and Process (4.1.2.6)

Each switch in the broadcast domain initially assumes that it is the root bridge for a spanning tree instance, so the BPDU frames sent contain the BID of the local switch as the root ID. By default, BPDU frames are sent every two seconds after a switch is booted; that is, the default value of the Hello timer specified in the BPDU frame is two seconds. Each switch maintains local information about its own BID, the root ID, and the path cost to the root.

When adjacent switches receive a BPDU frame, they compare the root ID from the BPDU frame with the local root ID. If the root ID in the BPDU is lower than the local root ID, the switch updates the local root ID and the ID in its BPDU messages. These messages indicate the new root bridge on the network. The distance to the root bridge is also indicated by the path cost update. For example, if the BPDU was received on a Fast Ethernet switch port, the path cost would increment by 19. If the local root ID is lower than the root ID received in the BPDU frame, the BPDU frame is discarded.

After a root ID has been updated to identify a new root bridge, all subsequent BPDU frames sent from that switch contain the new root ID and updated path cost. That way, all other adjacent switches are able to see the lowest root ID identified at all times. As the BPDU frames pass between other adjacent switches, the path cost is continually updated to indicate the total path cost to the root bridge. Each switch in the spanning tree uses its path costs to identify the best possible path to the root bridge.

The following summarizes the BPDU process:

Note

Priority is the initial deciding factor when electing a root bridge. If the priorities of all the switches are the same, the device with the lowest MAC address becomes the root bridge.

1. Initially, each switch identifies itself as the root bridge. S2 forwards BPDU frames out all switch ports. The S2 BPDUs contain the bridge ID and the root ID of S2, indicating that it is the root bridge. See Figure 4-18.

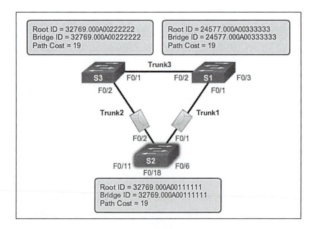

Figure 4-18 S2 Sends BPDUs on Trunk Links

2. When S3 receives a BPDU from switch S2, S3 compares its root ID with the BPDU frame it received. The priorities are equal, so the switch is forced to examine the MAC address portion to determine which MAC address has a lower value. Because S2 has a lower MAC address value, S3 updates its root ID with the S2 root ID. At that point, S3 considers S2 as the root bridge. See Figure 4-19.

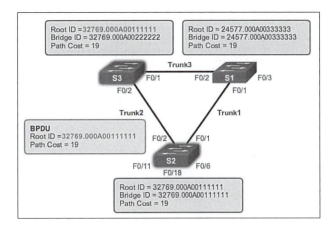

Figure 4-19 S3 Updates the Root Bridge ID

3. When S1 compares its root ID with the one in the received BPDU frame, it identifies its local root ID as the lower value and discards the BPDU from S2. S1 still considers itself the root bridge. See Figure 4-20.

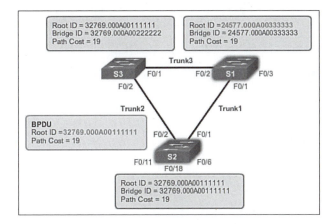

Figure 4-20 S1 Validates Its Role as Root Bridge

4. When S3 sends out its BPDU frames, the root ID contained in the BPDU frame is that of S2. See Figure 4-21.

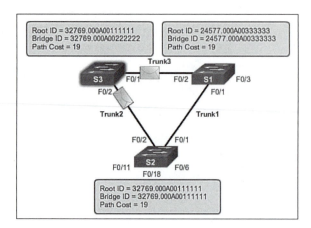

Figure 4-21   S3 Advertises That S2 Is the Root Bridge

5. When S2 receives the BPDU frame, it discards it after verifying that the root ID in the BPDU matched its local root ID. S2 does not update the path cost. See Figure 4-22.

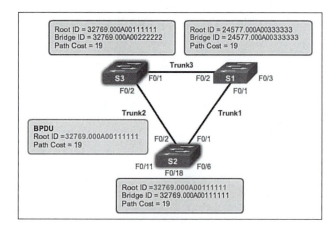

Figure 4-22   S2 Validates Its Role as the Root Bridge

6. Because S1 has a lower priority value in its root ID, it discards the BPDU frame received from S3. S1 does not update the path cost. See Figure 4-23.

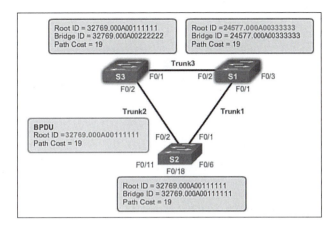

Figure 4-23   S1 Validates Its Role as the Root Bridge

7. S1 sends out its BPDU frames. The bridge ID and root ID of S1 indicate that it is the root bridge. See Figure 4-24.

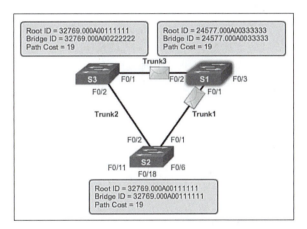

Figure 4-24   S1 Advertises Itself as Root Bridge

8. S3 identifies the root ID in the BPDU frame as having a lower value and, therefore, updates its root ID values to indicate that S1 is now the root bridge. S3 updates the path cost to 19 because the BPDU was received on a Fast Ethernet port. See Figure 4-25.

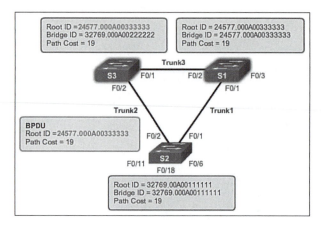

Figure 4-25 S3 Updates the Root Bridge ID

9. S2 identifies the root ID in the BPDU frame as having a lower value and, therefore, updates its root ID values to indicate that S1 is now the root bridge. S2 updates the path cost to 19 because the BPDU was received on a Fast Ethernet port. See Figure 4-26.

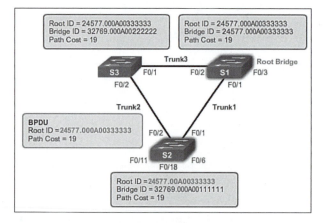

Figure 4-26 S2 Updates the Root Bridge ID

Extended System ID (4.1.2.7)

The bridge ID (BID) is used to determine the root bridge on a network. The BID field of a BPDU frame contains three separate fields:

- Bridge priority
- Extended system ID
- MAC address

Each field is used during the root bridge election.

Bridge Priority

The bridge priority is a customizable value that can be used to influence which switch becomes the root bridge. The switch with the lowest priority, which implies the lowest BID, becomes the root bridge because a lower priority value takes precedence. For example, to ensure that a specific switch is always the root bridge, set the priority to a lower value than the rest of the switches on the network. The default priority value for all Cisco switches is 32768. The range is 0 to 61440 in increments of 4096. Valid priority values are 0, 4096, 8192, 12288, 16384, 20480, 24576, 28672, 32768, 36864, 40960, 45056, 49152, 53248, 57344, and 61440. All other values are rejected. A bridge priority of 0 takes precedence over all other bridge priorities.

Extended System ID

Early implementations of IEEE 802.1D were designed for networks that did not use VLANs. There was a single common spanning tree across all switches. For this reason, in older Cisco switches, the extended system ID could be omitted in BPDU frames. As VLANs became common for network infrastructure segmentation, 802.1D was enhanced to include support for VLANs, requiring the VLAN ID to be included in the BPDU frame. VLAN information is included in the BPDU frame through the use of the extended system ID. All newer switches include the use of the extended system ID by default.

As shown in Figure 4-27, the bridge priority field is 2 bytes or 16 bits in length: 4 bits used for the bridge priority and 12 bits for the extended system ID, which identifies the VLAN participating in this particular STP process. Using these 12 bits for the extended system ID reduces the bridge priority to 4 bits. This process reserves the rightmost 12 bits for the VLAN ID and the far left 4 bits for the bridge priority. This explains why the bridge priority value can only be configured in multiples of 4096, or 2^{12}. If the far left bits are 0001, the bridge priority is 4096; if the far left bits are 1111, the bridge priority is 61440 (15 x 4096). The Catalyst 2960 and 3560 Series switches do not allow the configuration of a bridge priority of 65536 (16 x 4096) because they assume the use of a fifth bit that is unavailable because of the use of the extended system ID.

The extended system ID value is added to the bridge priority value in the BID to identify the priority and VLAN of the BPDU frame.

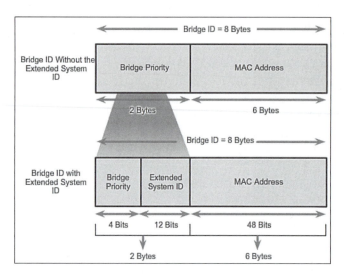

Figure 4-27   S2 Bridge ID Fields

When two switches are configured with the same priority and have the same extended system ID, the switch having the MAC address with the lowest hexadecimal value will have the lower BID. Initially, all switches are configured with the same default priority value. The MAC address is then the deciding factor on which switch is going to become the root bridge. To ensure that the root bridge decision best meets network requirements, it is recommended that the administrator configure the desired root bridge switch with a lower priority. This also ensures that the addition of new switches to the network does not trigger a new spanning tree election, which can disrupt network communication while a new root bridge is being selected.

In Figure 4-28, S1 has a lower priority than the other switches; therefore, it is preferred as the root bridge for that spanning tree instance.

When all switches are configured with the same priority, as is the case with all switches kept in the default configuration with a priority of 32768, the MAC address becomes the deciding factor for which switch becomes the root bridge, as shown in Figure 4-29.

Note

In the example, the priority of all the switches is 32769. The value is based on the 32768 default priority and the VLAN 1 assignment associated with each switch (32768+1).

The MAC address with the lowest hexadecimal value is considered to be the preferred root bridge. In the example, S2 has the lowest value for its MAC address and is, therefore, designated as the root bridge for that spanning tree instance.

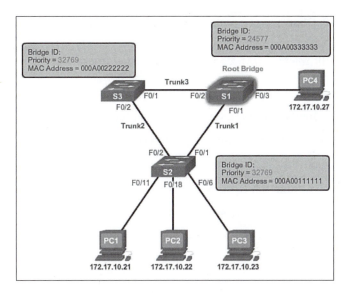

Figure 4-28   Root Bridge Decision Based on Bridge Priority

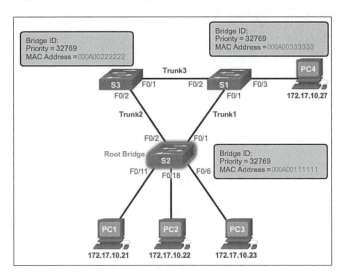

Figure 4-29   Root Bridge Decision Based on MAC Address

Activity 4.1.2.8: Identify 802.1D Port Roles

Go to the online course to perform this practice activity.

Video 4.1.2.9: Observing Spanning Tree Protocol Operation

Go to the online course and play the video to view STP characteristics, STP debugging, STP fault tolerance, and a broadcast storm without STP.

Lab 4.1.2.10: Building a Switched Network with Redundant Links

In this lab, you will complete the following objectives:

- Part 1: Build the Network and Configure Basic Device Settings
- Part 2: Determine the Root Bridge
- Part 3: Observe STP Port Selection Based on Port Cost
- Part 4: Observe STP Port Selection Based on Port Priority

Varieties of Spanning Tree Protocols (4.2)

A number of STP implementations have been deployed historically. Currently Cisco switches support three different STP modes. This section describes the various STP implementations.

Overview (4.2.1)

In this topic, the various STP options available on Cisco switches are introduced.

List of Spanning Tree Protocols (4.2.1.1)

Several varieties of spanning tree protocols have emerged since the original IEEE 802.1D. These varieties include

- **802.1D-1998:** This is the original IEEE 802.1D version that provides a loop-free topology in a network with redundant links. This specification assumes a Common Spanning Tree (CST), with one spanning tree instance for the entire bridged network, regardless of the number of VLANs.

- *PVST+ (Per-VLAN Spanning Tree+)*: This is a Cisco enhancement of the original 802.1D standard that provides a separate 802.1D spanning tree instance for each VLAN configured in the network. The separate instance supports *PortFast*, UplinkFast, BackboneFast, *BPDU guard*, BPDU filter, root guard, and loop guard.

- **802.1D-2004:** This is an updated version of the STP standard, incorporating *IEEE 802.1w*. IEEE 802.1D-2004 includes the RSTP specification.

- **Rapid Spanning Tree Protocol (RSTP) or IEEE 802.1w:** This is an evolution of STP that provides faster convergence than STP, adding new port roles and enhancing the BPDU exchange mechanism.

- *Rapid PVST+:* This is a Cisco enhancement of RSTP that uses PVST+. Rapid PVST+ provides a separate instance of 802.1w per VLAN. The separate instance supports PortFast, BPDU guard, BPDU filter, root guard, and loop guard.

- **Multiple Spanning Tree Protocol (MSTP):** This is an IEEE standard inspired by the earlier Cisco-proprietary *Multiple Instance STP (MISTP)* implementation. MSTP maps multiple VLANs into the same spanning tree instance. The Cisco implementation of MSTP is *Multiple Spanning Tree (MST)*, which provides up to 16 instances of RSTP and combines many VLANs with the same physical and logical topology into a common RSTP instance. Each instance supports PortFast, BPDU guard, BPDU filter, root guard, and loop guard.

A network professional, whose duties include switch administration, might be required to decide which type of spanning tree protocol to implement.

> **Note**
>
> The legacy Cisco-proprietary features UplinkFast and BackboneFast are not described in this course. These features are superseded by the implementation of Rapid PVST+, which incorporates these features as part of the implementation of the RSTP specification.

Characteristics of the Spanning Tree Protocols (4.2.1.2)

The following lists the characteristics of the various spanning tree protocols. The italicized words indicate whether the particular spanning tree protocol is a Cisco-proprietary or an IEEE standard implementation:

- **802.1D-1998:** Assumes one *IEEE 802.1D* spanning tree instance for the entire bridged network, regardless of the number of VLANs. Because there is only one instance, the CPU and memory requirements for this version are lower than for the other protocols. However, because there is only one instance, there is only one root bridge and one tree. Traffic for all VLANs flows over the same path, which can lead to suboptimal traffic flows. Because of the limitations of 802.1D, this version is slow to converge. This variety of spanning tree is often, unfortunately, referred to as "STP;" this is a source of confusion because STP is really a generic term encompassing the family of spanning tree protocols. To avoid confusion, one should be very specific about which standard or combination of standards is implemented in a given situation.

- **PVST+:** A *Cisco* enhancement of STP that provides a separate instance of the Cisco implementation of 802.1D for each VLAN that is configured in the network. The separate instance supports PortFast, UplinkFast, BackboneFast, BPDU guard, BPDU filter, root guard, and loop guard. Creating an instance for each VLAN increases the CPU and memory requirements, but allows for per-VLAN root bridges. This design allows the spanning tree to be optimized for the traffic of each VLAN. Convergence of this version is similar to the convergence of 802.1D. However, convergence is per-VLAN.

- **RSTP (or *IEEE 802.1w*):** An evolution of spanning tree that provides faster convergence than the original 802.1D implementation. This version addresses many convergence issues, but because it still provides a single instance of STP, it does not address the suboptimal traffic flow issues. To support that faster convergence, the CPU usage and memory requirements of this version are slightly higher than those of CST, but less than those of RSTP+.

- **Rapid PVST+:** A *Cisco* enhancement of RSTP that uses PVST+. It provides a separate instance of 802.1w per VLAN. The separate instance supports PortFast, BPDU guard, BPDU filter, root guard, and loop guard. This version addresses both the convergence issues and the suboptimal traffic flow issues. However, this version has the largest CPU and memory requirements.

- **MSTP:** The *IEEE 802.1s* standard, inspired by the earlier Cisco-proprietary MISTP implementation. To reduce the number of required STP instances, MSTP maps multiple VLANs that have the same traffic flow requirements into the same spanning tree instance.

- **MST:** The *Cisco* implementation of MSTP, which provides up to 16 instances of RSTP (802.1w) and combines many VLANs with the same physical and logical topology into a common RSTP instance. Each instance supports PortFast, BPDU guard, BPDU filter, root guard, and loop guard. The CPU and memory requirements of this version are less than those of Rapid PVST+, but more than those of RSTP.

Table 4-3 summarizes the various spanning tree protocol characteristics.

Table 4-3   Spanning Tree Protocol Characteristics

Protocol	Standard	Resources Needed	Convergence	Tree Calculation
"STP"	Protocol ID	Low	Slow	All VLANs
PVST+	Version	High	Slow	Per VLAN
RSTP	Message Type	Medium	Fast	All VLANs
Rapid PVST+	Flags	Very high	Fast	Per VLAN
MSTP	Root ID	Medium or high	Fast	Per Instance

The default spanning tree mode for Cisco Catalyst switches is PVST+, which is enabled on all ports. PVST+ has much slower convergence after a topology change than Rapid PVST+.

Note

It is important to distinguish between the legacy *IEEE 802.1D-1998* (and earlier) standard and the *IEEE 802.1D-2004* standard. IEEE 802.1D-2004 incorporates RSTP functionality, while IEEE 802.1D-1998 refers to the original implementation of the spanning tree algorithm. Newer Cisco switches running newer versions of the IOS, such as Catalyst 2960 switches with IOS Release 15.0, run PVST+ by default, but incorporate many of the specifications of IEEE 802.1D-2004 in this mode. To run rapid spanning tree on such a switch, it must be explicitly configured for rapid spanning tree mode. Also, one often hears the term *nondesignated port* used in the context of spanning tree operation. The term *nondesignated port* was never used in the IEEE documentation; IEEE has always used the term *alternate port* to indicate a port that is neither a root port nor a designated port.

Interactive Graphic

Activity 4.2.1.3: Identify Types of Spanning Tree Protocols

Go to the online course to perform this practice activity.

PVST+ (4.2.2)

This topic focuses on the Cisco-proprietary STP implementation, which is the default mode for Cisco switches. PVST+ implements one instance of the 802.1D-1998 standard on each VLAN. Keep in mind that RSTP is included in the 802.1D-2004 specification.

Overview of PVST+ (4.2.2.1)

The original IEEE 802.1D standard defines a Common Spanning Tree (CST) that assumes only one spanning tree instance for the entire switched network, regardless of the number of VLANs. A network running CST has these characteristics:

- No load sharing is possible. One uplink must block for all VLANs.

- The CPU is spared. Only one instance of spanning tree must be computed.

Cisco developed PVST+ so that a network can run an independent instance of the Cisco implementation of IEEE 802.1D for each VLAN in the network. With PVST+, it is possible for one trunk port on a switch to be blocking for a VLAN while not blocking for other VLANs. PVST+ can be used to implement Layer 2 load balancing. Because each VLAN runs a separate instance of STP, the switches in a PVST+ environment require greater CPU process and BPDU bandwidth consumption than a traditional CST implementation of STP.

In a PVST+ environment, spanning tree parameters can be tuned so that half of the VLANs forward on each uplink trunk. In Figure 4-30, port F0/3 on S2 is the forwarding port for VLAN 20, and F0/2 on S2 is the forwarding port for VLAN 10. This is accomplished by configuring one switch to be elected the root bridge for half of the VLANs in the network, and a second switch to be elected the root bridge for the other half of the VLANs. In the figure, S3 is the root bridge for VLAN 20, and S1 is the root bridge for VLAN 10. Multiple STP root bridges per VLAN increase redundancy in the network.

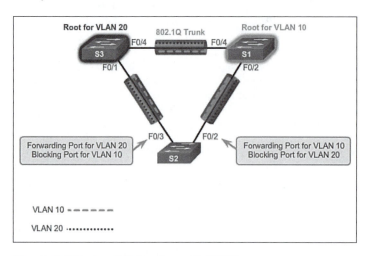

Figure 4-30   Load Balancing with PVST+

Networks running PVST+ have these characteristics:

- Optimum load balancing can result.

- One spanning tree instance for each VLAN maintained can mean a considerable waste of CPU cycles for all the switches in the network (in addition to the bandwidth that is used for each instance to send its own BPDU). This would only be problematic if a large number of VLANs are configured.

Port States and PVST+ Operation (4.2.2.2)

STP facilitates the logical loop-free path throughout the broadcast domain. The spanning tree is determined through the information learned by the exchange of the BPDU frames between the interconnected switches. To facilitate the learning of the logical spanning tree, each switch port transitions through five possible *port states* and three BPDU timers.

The spanning tree is determined immediately after a switch is finished booting up. If a switch port transitions directly from the blocking to the forwarding state without information about the full topology during the transition, the port can temporarily create a data loop. For this reason, STP introduces the five port states. Table 4-4 describes the following port states that ensure that no loops are created during the creation of the logical spanning tree:

- *Blocking*: The port is an alternate port and does not participate in frame forwarding. The port receives BPDU frames to determine the location and root ID of the root bridge switch and what port roles each switch port should assume in the final active STP topology.

- *Listening*: Listens for the path to the root. STP has determined that the port can participate in frame forwarding according to the BPDU frames that the switch has received thus far. At this point, the switch port not only receives BPDU frames, but it also transmits its own BPDU frames and informs adjacent switches that the switch port is preparing to participate in the active topology.

- *Learning*: Learns the MAC addresses. The port prepares to participate in frame forwarding and begins to populate the MAC address table.

- *Forwarding*: The port is considered part of the active topology. It forwards data frames and sends and receives BPDU frames.

- *Disabled*: The Layer 2 port does not participate in spanning tree and does not forward frames. The disabled state is set when the switch port is administratively disabled.

Table 4-4 summarizes the allowed operations associated with each port state.

Table 4-4 Spanning Tree Port States

Operation Allowed	Port State				
	Blocking	**Listening**	**Learning**	**Forwarding**	**Disabled**
Can receive and process BPDUs	Yes	Yes	Yes	Yes	No
Can forward data frames received on interface	No	No	No	Yes	No
Can forward data frames switched from another interface	No	No	No	Yes	No
Can learn MAC addresses	No	No	Yes	Yes	No

Note that the number of ports in each of the various states (blocking, listening, learning, or forwarding) can be displayed with the **show spanning-tree summary** command.

For each VLAN in a switched network, PVST+ performs four steps to provide a loop-free logical network topology:

1. **Elects one root bridge:** Only one switch can act as the root bridge (for a given VLAN). The root bridge is the switch with the lowest bridge ID. On the root bridge, all ports are designated ports (in particular, no root ports).

2. **Selects the root port on each nonroot bridge:** STP establishes one root port on each nonroot bridge. The root port is the lowest-cost path from the nonroot bridge to the root bridge, indicating the direction of the best path to the root bridge. Root ports are normally in the forwarding state.

3. **Selects the designated port on each segment:** On each link, STP establishes one designated port. The designated port is selected on the switch that has the lowest-cost path to the root bridge. Designated ports are normally in the forwarding state, forwarding traffic for the segment.

4. **The remaining ports in the switched network are alternate ports:** Alternate ports normally remain in the blocking state, to logically break the loop topology. When a port is in the blocking state, it does not forward traffic, but can still process received BPDU messages.

Extended System ID and PVST+ Operation (4.2.2.3)

In a PVST+ environment, the extended system ID, shown in Figure 4-31, ensures that each switch has a unique BID for each VLAN.

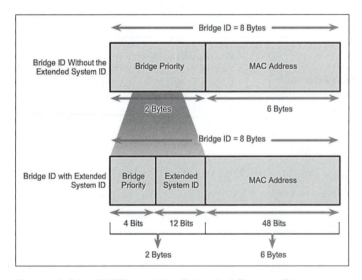

Figure 4-31   PVST+ and the Extended System ID

For example, the VLAN 2 default BID would be 32770 (priority 32768, plus the extended system ID of 2). If no priority has been configured, every switch has the same default priority and the election of the root for each VLAN is based on the MAC address. This method is a random means of selecting the root bridge.

There are situations where the administrator might want a specific switch to be selected as the root bridge. This can be for a variety of reasons, including that the switch is more centrally located within the LAN design, the switch has higher processing power, or the switch is simply easier to access and manage remotely. To manipulate the root bridge election, simply assign a lower priority to the switch that should be selected as the root bridge.

Interactive Graphic

Activity 4.2.2.4: Identifying PVST+ Operation

Go to the online course to perform this practice activity.

Rapid PVST+ (4.2.3)

Rapid PVST+ is the implementation of RSTP on Cisco switches. On Cisco switches, Rapid PVST+ implements a separate instance of RSTP for each VLAN. This section will detail the operation of Rapid PVST+.

Overview of Rapid PVST+ (4.2.3.1)

RSTP (IEEE 802.1w) is an evolution of the original 802.1D standard and is incorporated into the IEEE 802.1D-2004 standard. The 802.1w STP terminology remains primarily the same as the original IEEE 802.1D STP terminology. Most parameters have been left unchanged, so users familiar with STP can easily configure the new protocol. Rapid PVST+ is simply the Cisco implementation of RSTP on a per-VLAN basis. With Rapid PVST+, an independent instance of RSTP runs for each VLAN.

Figure 4-32 shows a network running RSTP. S1 is the root bridge with two designated ports in a forwarding state. RSTP supports a new port type: Port F0/3 on S2 is an alternate port in the *discarding* state (abbreviated DIS). Notice that there are no blocking ports. RSTP does not have a blocking port state. RSTP defines port states as discarding, learning, or forwarding.

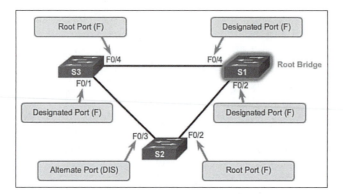

Figure 4-32   RSTP

RSTP speeds the recalculation of the spanning tree when the Layer 2 network topology changes. RSTP can achieve much faster convergence in a properly configured network, sometimes in as little as a few hundred milliseconds. RSTP redefines the type of ports and their state. If a port is configured to be an alternate port or a backup port, it can immediately change to forwarding state without waiting for the network to converge. The following briefly describes RSTP characteristics:

- RSTP is the preferred protocol for preventing Layer 2 loops in a switched network environment. Many of the differences were established by Cisco-proprietary enhancements to the original 802.1D. These enhancements, such as BPDUs carrying and sending information about port roles only to neighboring switches, require no additional configuration and generally perform better than the earlier Cisco-proprietary versions. They are now transparent and integrated in the protocol's operation.

- Cisco-proprietary enhancements to the original 802.1D, such as UplinkFast and BackboneFast, are not compatible with RSTP.

- RSTP (802.1w) supersedes the original 802.1D while retaining backward compatibility. Much of the original 802.1D terminology remains, and most parameters are unchanged. In addition, 802.1w is capable of reverting back to legacy 802.1D to interoperate with legacy switches on a per-port basis. For example, the RSTP spanning tree algorithm elects a root bridge in exactly the same way as the original 802.1D.

- RSTP keeps the same BPDU format as the original IEEE 802.1D, except that the version field is set to 2 to indicate RSTP, and the Flags field uses all 8 bits.

- RSTP is able to actively confirm that a port can safely transition to the forwarding state without having to rely on any timer configuration.

RSTP BPDU (4.2.3.2)

RSTP uses type 2, version 2 BPDUs. The original 802.1D STP uses type 0, version 0 BPDUs. However, a switch running RSTP can communicate directly with a switch running the original 802.1D STP. RSTP sends BPDUs and populates the flag byte in a slightly different manner than in the original 802.1D:

- Protocol information can be immediately aged on a port if Hello packets are not received for three consecutive Hello times, six seconds by default, or if the max age timer expires.

- Because BPDUs are used as a keepalive mechanism, three consecutively missed BPDUs indicate lost connectivity between a bridge and its neighboring root or designated bridge. The fast aging of the information allows failures to be detected quickly.

Note

Like STP, an RSTP switch sends a BPDU with its current information every Hello time period (two seconds, by default), even if the RSTP bridge does not receive any BPDUs from the root bridge.

As shown in Figure 4-33, RSTP uses the flag byte of version 2 BPDU:

- Bits 0 and 7 are used for topology change and acknowledgment as they are in the original 802.1D.

- Bits 1 and 6 are used for the Proposal Agreement process (used for rapid convergence).

- Bits from 2 to 5 encode the role and state of the port.

- Bits 4 and 5 are used to encode the port role using a 2-bit code.

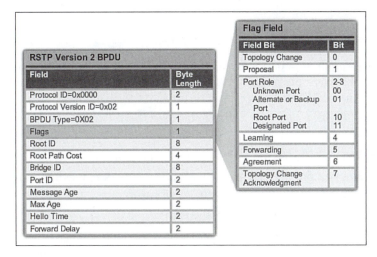

Figure 4-33   RSTP BPDU

Edge Ports (4.2.3.3)

An RSTP *edge port* is a switch port that is never intended to be connected to another switch device. It immediately transitions to the forwarding state when enabled.

The RSTP edge port concept corresponds to the PVST+ PortFast feature; an edge port is directly connected to an end station and assumes that no switch device is connected to it. RSTP edge ports should immediately transition to the forwarding state, thereby skipping the time-consuming original 802.1D listening and learning port states.

The Cisco RSTP implementation, Rapid PVST+, maintains the PortFast keyword, using the **spanning-tree portfast** command for edge port configuration. This makes the transition from the original 802.1D to RSTP seamless.

Figure 4-34 shows examples of ports that can be configured as edge ports.

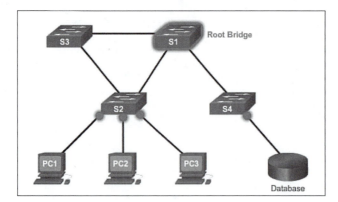

Figure 4-34 Edge Ports

Note

Configuring an edge port to be attached to another switch is not recommended. This can have negative implications for RSTP because a temporary loop can result, possibly delaying the convergence of RSTP.

Link Types (4.2.3.4)

The *link type* provides a categorization for each port participating in RSTP by using the duplex mode on the port. Depending on what is attached to each port, two different link types can be identified:

- *Point-to-Point link type*: A port operating in full-duplex mode typically connects a switch to a switch and is a candidate for rapid transition to forwarding state.

■ *Shared link type*: A port operating in half-duplex mode connects a switch to a hub that attaches multiple devices.

The link type can determine whether the port can immediately transition to the forwarding state, assuming that certain conditions are met. These conditions are different for edge ports and nonedge ports. Nonedge ports are categorized into two link types, point-to-point and shared. The link type is automatically determined, but can be overridden with an explicit port configuration using the **spanning-tree link-type parameter** command.

Edge port connections and point-to-point connections are candidates for rapid transition to the forwarding state. However, before the link-type parameter is considered, RSTP must determine the port role. Characteristics of port roles with regard to link types include the following:

■ Root ports do not use the link-type parameter. Root ports are able to make a rapid transition to the forwarding state as soon as the port is in sync.

■ Alternate and backup ports do not use the link-type parameter in most cases.

■ Designated ports make the most use of the link-type parameter. Rapid transition to the forwarding state for the designated port occurs only if the link-type parameter is set to point-to-point.

Interactive Graphic

Activity 4.2.3.5: Identify Port Roles in Rapid PVST+

Go to the online course to perform this practice activity.

Interactive Graphic

Activity 4.2.3.6: Compare PVST+ and Rapid PVST+

Go to the online course to perform this practice activity.

Spanning Tree Configuration (4.3)

This section describes how to configure PVST+ and Rapid PVST+.

PVST+ Configuration (4.3.1)

This topic describes how to configure PVST+.

Catalyst 2960 Default Configuration (4.3.1.1)

Table 4-5 shows the default spanning tree configuration for a Cisco Catalyst 2960 Series switch. Notice that the default spanning tree mode is PVST+.

Table 4-5   Default Switch Configuration

Feature	Default Setting
Enable state	Enabled on VLAN 1
Spanning-tree mode	PVST+ (Rapid PVST+ and MST are disabled.)
Switch priority	32768
Spanning-tree port priority (configurable on a per-interface basis)	128
Spanning-tree port cost (configurable on a per-port basis)	1000 Mb/s: 4 100 Mb/s: 19 10 Mb/s: 100
Spanning-tree VLAN port priority (configurable on a per-VLAN basis)	128
Spanning-tree VLAN port cost (configurable on a per-VLAN basis)	1000 Mb/s: 4 100 Mb/s: 19 10 Mb/s: 100
Spanning-tree timers	Hello time: 2 seconds Forward-delay time: 15 seconds Maximum-aging time: 20 seconds Transmit hold count: 6 BPDUs

Configuring and Verifying the Bridge ID (4.3.1.2)

When an administrator wants a specific switch to become a root bridge, the bridge priority value must be adjusted to ensure that it is lower than the bridge priority values of all the other switches on the network. There are two different methods to configure the bridge priority value on a Cisco Catalyst switch.

Method 1

To ensure that the switch has the lowest bridge priority value, use the **spanning-tree vlan vlan-id root primary** command in global configuration mode. The priority for the switch is set to the predefined value of 24,576 or to the highest multiple of 4096, less than the lowest bridge priority detected on the network.

If an alternate root bridge is desired, use the **spanning-tree vlan vlan-id root secondary** global configuration mode command. This command sets the priority for the switch to the predefined value of 28,672. This ensures that the alternate switch becomes the root bridge if the primary root bridge fails. This assumes that the rest of the switches in the network have the default 32,768 priority value defined.

In Figure 4-35, S1 has been assigned as the primary root bridge using the **spanning-tree vlan 1 root primary** command, and S2 has been configured as the secondary root bridge using the **spanning-tree vlan 1 root secondary** command.

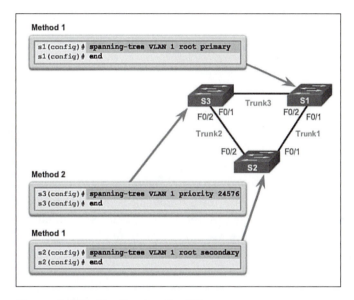

Figure 4-35   Configuring the BID

Method 2

Another method for configuring the bridge priority value is using the **spanning-tree vlan vlan-id priority value** global configuration mode command. This command gives more granular control over the bridge priority value. The priority value is configured in increments of 4096 between 0 and 61,440.

In Figure 4-35, S3 has been assigned a bridge priority value of 24,576 using the **spanning-tree vlan 1 priority 24576** command.

To verify the bridge priority of a switch, use the **show spanning-tree** command. In Example 4-2, the priority of S3 is seen to be 24,576. Also notice that the switch is designated as the root bridge for the spanning tree instance.

Example 4-2   Verify the BID

```
S3# show spanning-tree

VLAN0001
  Spanning tree enabled protocol ieee
  Root ID    Priority    24577
             Address     000A.0033.3333
             This bridge is the root
             Hello Time   2 sec  Max Age 20 sec  Forward Delay 15 sec

  Bridge ID  Priority    24577  (priority 24576 sys-id-ext 1)
             Address     000A.0033.3333
             Hello Time   2 sec  Max Age 20 sec  Forward Delay 15 sec
             Aging Time 300


Interface          Role Sts Cost      Prio.Nbr Type
---------------- ---- --- --------- -------- --------------------------------
Fa0/1              Desg FWD 4         128.1    P2p
Fa0/2              Desg FWD 4         128.2    P2p
```

Interactive Graphic

Activity 4.3.1.2: Configuring Duplex and Speed

Go to the online course to use the Syntax Checker in the third graphic to configure switches S1, S2, and S3. Using Method 2, configure S3 manually, setting the priority to 24,576 for VLAN 1. Using Method 1, configure S2 as the secondary root VLAN 1 and configure S1 as the primary root for VLAN 1. Verify the configuration with the **show spanning-tree** command on S1.

PortFast and BPDU Guard (4.3.1.3)

PortFast is a Cisco feature for PVST+ environments. When a switch port is configured with PortFast, that port transitions from the blocking to the forwarding state immediately, bypassing the usual 802.1D STP transition states (the listening and learning states). You can use PortFast on access ports to allow these devices to connect to the network immediately, rather than waiting for IEEE 802.1D STP to converge on each VLAN. Access ports are ports that are connected to a single workstation or to a server.

In a valid PortFast configuration, BPDUs should never be received, because that would indicate that another bridge or switch is connected to the port, potentially causing a spanning tree loop. Cisco switches support a feature called BPDU guard. When it is enabled, BPDU guard puts the port in an *error-disabled* state on receipt of a BPDU. This will effectively shut down the port. The BPDU guard feature provides a secure response to invalid configurations because you must manually put the interface back into service.

Cisco PortFast technology is useful for DHCP. Without PortFast, a PC can send a DHCP request before the port is in forwarding state, denying the host from getting a usable IP address and other information. Because PortFast immediately changes the state to forwarding, the PC always gets a usable IP address.

Note

Because the purpose of PortFast is to minimize the time that access ports must wait for spanning tree to converge, it should only be used on access ports, as indicated in Figure 4-36. If you enable PortFast on a port connecting to another switch, you risk creating a spanning tree loop.

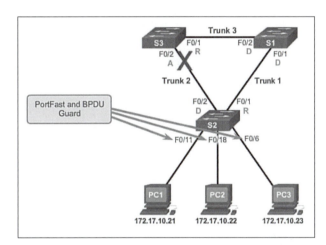

Figure 4-36 PortFast and BPDU Guard

To configure PortFast on a switch port, enter the **spanning-tree portfast** interface configuration mode command on each interface where PortFast is to be enabled, as shown in Example 4-3. The **spanning-tree portfast default** global configuration mode command enables PortFast on all nontrunking interfaces. Example 4-3 illustrates PortFast configuration.

Example 4-3 PortFast Configuration

```
S2(config)# interface fastEthernet 0/11
S2(config-if)# spanning-tree portfast
%Warning: portfast should only be enabled on ports connected to a single
 host. Connecting hubs, concentrators, switches, bridges, etc... to this
 interface  when portfast is enabled, can cause temporary bridging loops.
 Use with CAUTION

%Portfast has been configured on FastEthernet0/11 but will only
 have effect when the interface is in a non-trunking mode.
S2(config-if)#
```

To configure BPDU guard on a Layer 2 access port, use the **spanning-tree bpdu-guard enable** interface configuration mode command. The **spanning-tree portfast bpduguard default** global configuration command enables BPDU guard on all PortFast-enabled ports. BPDU guard configuration is illustrated here:

```
S2(config-if)# spanning-tree bpduguard enable
S2(config-if)#
```

To verify that PortFast and BPDU guard have been enabled for a switch port, use the **show running-config** command, as shown in Example 4-4.

Example 4-4 Verify BPDU Guard

```
S2# show running-config interface f0/11
Building configuration...

Current configuration : 90 bytes
!
interface FastEthernet0/11
 spanning-tree portfast
 spanning-tree bpduguard enable
end
S2#
```

PortFast and BPDU guard are disabled, by default, on all interfaces.

**Interactive
Graphic**

Activity 4.3.1.3: Verify PortFast and BPDU Guard Configuration

Go to the online course to use the Syntax Checker in the fourth graphic to configure and verify switches S1 and S2 with PortFast and BPDU guard.

PVST+ Load Balancing (4.3.1.4)

The topology in Figure 4-37 shows three switches with 802.1Q trunks connecting them. There are two VLANs, 10 and 20, that are being trunked across these links. The goal is to configure S3 as the root bridge for VLAN 20 and S1 as the root bridge for VLAN 10. Port F0/3 on S2 is the forwarding port for VLAN 20 and the blocking port for VLAN 10. Port F0/2 on S2 is the forwarding port for VLAN 10 and the blocking port for VLAN 20.

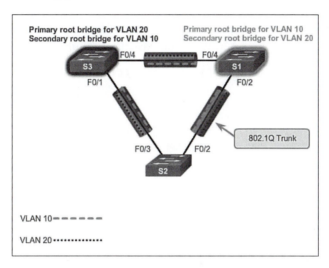

Figure 4-37   Configuring PVST+ Load Balancing

In addition to establishing a root bridge, it is also possible to establish a secondary root bridge. A secondary root bridge is a switch that can become the root bridge for a VLAN if the primary root bridge fails. Assuming that the other bridges in the VLAN retain their default STP priority, this switch becomes the root bridge if the primary root bridge fails.

The steps to configure PVST+ on this example topology are as follows:

Step 1.   Select the switches you want for the primary and secondary root bridges for each VLAN.

Step 2.   Configure the appropriate switch to be a primary bridge for the VLAN by using the **spanning-tree vlan number root primary** command.

Step 3.   Configure the appropriate switch to be a secondary bridge for the VLAN by using the **spanning-tree vlan number root secondary** command.

Another way to specify the root bridge is to set the spanning tree priority on each switch to the lowest value so that the switch is selected as the primary bridge for its associated VLAN.

In the following configurations, S3 is configured as the primary root bridge for VLAN 20 and the secondary root bridge for VLAN 10. S1 is configured as the primary root bridge for VLAN 10 and the secondary root bridge for VLAN 20. S2 retained its default STP priority.

```
S3(config)# spanning-tree vlan 20 root primary
S3(config)# spanning-tree vlan 10 root secondary
S1(config)# spanning-tree vlan 10 root primary
S1(config)# spanning-tree vlan 20 root secondary
```

This configuration enables *spanning tree load balancing*, with VLAN 10 traffic passing through S1 and VLAN 20 traffic passing through S3.

Another way to specify the root bridge is to set the spanning tree priority on each switch to the lowest value so that the switch is selected as the primary bridge for its associated VLAN, as shown here:

```
S3(config)# spanning-tree vlan 20 priority 4096
S1(config)# spanning-tree vlan 10 priority 4096
```

The switch priority can be set for any spanning tree instance. This setting affects the likelihood that a switch is selected as the root bridge. A lower value increases the probability that the switch is selected. The range is 0 to 61,440 in increments of 4096; all other values are rejected. For example, a valid priority value is 4096 x 2 = 8192.

The **show spanning-tree active** command displays spanning tree configuration details for the active interfaces only. The output shown in Example 4-5 is for S1 configured with PVST+. There are a number of Cisco IOS command parameters associated with the **show spanning-tree** command.

Example 4-5   Configure PVST+

```
S1# show spanning-tree active
<output omitted>
VLAN00010
  Spanning tree enabled protocol ieee
  Root ID    Priority    4106
             Address       0019.aa9e.b000
             This bridge is the root
             Hello Time   2 sec  Max Age 20 sec  Forward Delay 15 sec

  Bridge ID  Priority    4106   (priority 4096 sys-id-ext 10)
             Address       0019.aa9e.b000
             Hello Time   2 sec  Max Age 20 sec  Forward Delay 15 sec
             Aging Time 300
```

```
Interface        Role Sts Cost    Prio.Nbr Type
---------------- ---- --- -------- -------- --------------------------------
Fa0/2            Desg FWD 19       128.1    P2p
Fa0/4            Desg FWD 19       128.2    P2p
<output omitted>
S1#
```

In Example 4-6, the priority for VLAN 10 is 4096, the lowest of the three respective VLAN priorities.

Example 4-6   Verify PVST+

```
S1# show running-config
Building configuration...

Current configuration : 3377 bytes
!
version 12.2
<output omitted>
!
spanning-tree mode pvst
spanning-tree extend system-id
spanning-tree vlan 1 priority 24576
spanning-tree vlan 10 priority 4096
spanning-tree vlan 20 priority 28762
!
<output omitted>
```

Activity 4.3.1.4: Configure PVST+

Go to the online course to use the Syntax Checker in the sixth graphic to configure and verify spanning tree for S1 and S3.

Packet Tracer Activity 4.3.1.5: Configuring PVST+

In this activity, you will configure VLANs and trunks, and examine and configure the Spanning Tree Protocol primary and secondary root bridges. You will also optimize the switched topology using PVST+, PortFast, and BPDU guard.

Rapid PVST+ Configuration (4.3.2)

Rapid PVST+ configuration in large part parallels the configuration of PVST+.

Spanning Tree Mode (4.3.2.1)

Rapid PVST+ is the Cisco implementation of RSTP. It supports RSTP on a per-VLAN basis. The topology in Figure 4-38 has two VLANs: 10 and 20.

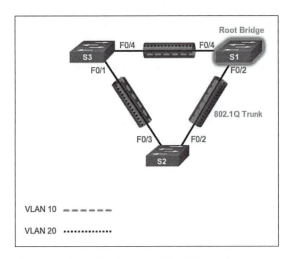

Figure 4-38   Configuring Rapid PVST+

Note
The default spanning tree configuration on a Catalyst 2960 Series switch is PVST+. A Catalyst 2960 switch supports PVST+, Rapid PVST+, and MST, but only one version can be active for all VLANs at any time.

Rapid PVST+ commands control the configuration of VLAN spanning tree instances. A spanning tree instance is created when an interface is assigned to a VLAN and is removed when the last interface is moved to another VLAN. As well, you can configure STP switch and port parameters before a spanning tree instance is created. These parameters are applied when a spanning tree instance is created.

Table 4-6 displays the Cisco IOS command syntax needed to configure Rapid PVST+ on a Cisco switch. The **spanning-tree mode rapid-pvst** global configuration mode command is the one required command for the Rapid PVST+ configuration. When specifying an interface to configure, valid interfaces include physical ports, VLANs, and port channels. The VLAN ID range is 1 to 4094 when the enhanced software image (EI) is installed and 1 to 1005 when the standard software image (SI) is installed. The port-channel range is 1 to 6.

Table 4-6   Cisco IOS Rapid PVST+ Commands

Cisco IOS Command Syntax	
Enter global configuration mode.	**configure terminal**
Configure Rapid PVST+ spanning-tree mode.	**spanning-tree mode rapid-pvst**
Enter interface configuration mode and specify an interface to configure. Valid interfaces include physical ports, VLANs, and port channels.	**interface** *interface-id*
Specify that the link type for this port is point-to-point.	**spanning-tree link-type point-to-point**
Return to privileged EXEC mode.	**end**
Clear all detected STPs and force the STP renegotiation with neighboring switches.	**clear spanning-tree detected-protocols**

Example 4-7 shows the Rapid PVST+ commands configured on S1.

Example 4-7   Configure Rapid PVST+

```
S1(config)# spanning-tree mode rapid-pvst
S1(config)# interface f0/2
S1(config-if)# spanning-tree link-type point-to-point
S1(config-if)# end
S1# clear spanning-tree detected-protocols
```

Example 4-8 shows the output of the **show spanning-tree vlan 10** command for VLAN 10 on switch S1. Notice that the BID priority is set to 4096. In the output, the statement "Spanning tree enabled protocol rstp" indicates that S1 is running Rapid PVST+. Because S1 is the root bridge for VLAN 10, all its interfaces are designated ports.

Example 4-8   Verify Rapid PVST+ Mode

```
S1# show spanning-tree vlan 10
VLAN00010
  Spanning tree enabled protocol rstp
  Root ID    Priority    4106
             Address     0019.aa9e.b000
             This bridge is the root
             Hello Time   2 sec  Max Age 20 sec  Forward Delay 15 sec

  Bridge ID  Priority    4106  (priority 4096 sys-id-ext 10)
             Address     0019.aa9e.b000
```

```
             Hello Time   2 sec  Max Age 20 sec  Forward Delay 15 sec
             Aging Time 300


Interface          Role Sts Cost      Prio.Nbr Type
---------------- ---- --- --------- -------- -------------------------------
Fa0/2                Desg LRN 19       128.1    P2p
Fa0/4                Desg LRN 19       128.2    P2p
<output omitted>
S1#
```

The **show running-config** command output is used to verify the Rapid PVST+ configuration on S1, as shown in Example 4-9.

Example 4-9   Verify Rapid PVST+

```
S1# show running-config
<output omitted>
!
spanning-tree mode rapid-pvst
spanning-tree extend system-id
spanning-tree vlan 1 priority 24576
spanning-tree vlan 10 priority 4096
spanning-tree vlan 20 priority 28762
!
<output omitted>
S1#
```

Note

Generally, it is unnecessary to configure the point-to-point *link-type* parameter for Rapid PVST+, because it is unusual to have a shared *link-type*. In most cases, the only difference between configuring PVST+ and Rapid PVST+ is the **spanning-tree mode rapid-pvst** command.

Packet Tracer Activity 4.3.2.2 Configuring Rapid PVST+

In this activity, you will configure VLANs and trunks, and examine and configure the primary and secondary root bridges. You will also optimize the spanning tree configuration by using Rapid PVST+, PortFast, and BPDU guard.

Lab 4.3.2.3: Configuring Rapid PVST+, PortFast, and BPDU Guard

In this lab, you will complete the following objectives:

- Part 1: Build the Network and Configure Basic Device Settings

- Part 2: Configure VLANs, Native VLANs, and Trunks

- Part 3: Configure the Root Bridge and Examine PVST+ Convergence

- Part 4: Configure Rapid PVST+, PortFast, and BPDU Guard, and Examine Convergence

STP Configuration Issues (4.3.3)

STP should be configured on Layer 2 switches to avoid broadcast storms associated with physical loops. Troubleshooting STP issues can be challenging. In this section, you learn some useful techniques.

Analyzing the STP Topology (4.3.3.1)

To analyze the STP topology, follow these steps, as shown in Figure 4-39:

Step 1. Discover the Layer 2 topology. Use network documentation if it exists or use the **show cdp neighbors** command to discover the Layer 2 topology.

Step 2. After discovering the Layer 2 topology, use STP knowledge to determine the expected Layer 2 path. It is necessary to know which switch is the root bridge.

Step 3. Use the **show spanning-tree vlan** *vlan-id* command to determine which switch is the root bridge.

Step 4. Use the **show spanning-tree vlan** *vlan-id* command on all switches to find out which ports are in the blocking or forwarding state and confirm your expected Layer 2 path.

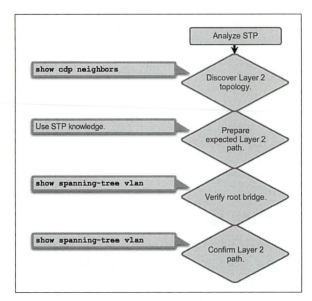

Figure 4-39   Analyzing the STP Topology

Expected Topology Versus Actual Topology (4.3.3.2)

In many networks, the optimal STP topology is determined as part of the network design and then implemented through manipulation of STP priority and cost values. Situations can occur where STP was not considered in the network design and implementation, or where it was considered or implemented before the network underwent significant growth and change. In such situations, it is important to know how to analyze the actual STP topology in the operational network.

A big part of troubleshooting consists of comparing the actual state of the network against the expected state of the network and spotting the differences to gather clues about the troubleshooting problem, as indicated in Figure 4-40. A network professional should be able to examine the switches and determine the actual topology, and be able to understand what the underling spanning tree topology should be.

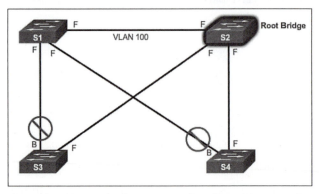

Figure 4-40   Verify That Actual Topology Matches Expected Topology

Overview of Spanning Tree Status (4.3.3.3)

Using the **show spanning-tree** command without specifying any additional options provides a quick overview of the status of STP for all VLANs that are defined on a switch. If interested only in a particular VLAN, limit the scope of this command by specifying that VLAN as an option.

Use the **show spanning-tree vlan** *vlan_id* command to get STP information for a particular VLAN. Use this command to get information about the role and status of each port on the switch. The example output in Figure 4-41 on switch S1 shows all three ports in the forwarding (FWD) state and the role of the three ports as either designated ports or root ports. Any ports being blocked display the output status as "BLK."

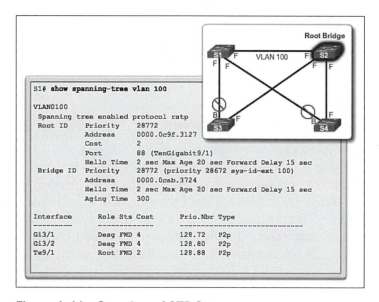

Figure 4-41   Overview of STP Status

The output also gives information about the BID of the local switch and the root ID, which is the BID of the root bridge.

Spanning Tree Failure Consequences (4.3.3.4)

With many protocols, a malfunction means that you lose the functionality that the protocol was providing. For example, if OSPF malfunctions on a router, connectivity to networks that are reachable through that router might be lost. This would generally not affect the rest of the OSPF network. If connectivity to the router is still available, it is possible to troubleshoot to diagnose and fix the problem.

With STP, there are two types of failure. The first is similar to the OSPF problem; STP might erroneously block ports that should have gone into the forwarding state.

Connectivity might be lost for traffic that would normally pass through this switch, but the rest of the network remains unaffected. The second type of failure is much more disruptive, as shown in Figure 4-42. It happens when STP erroneously moves one or more ports into the forwarding state.

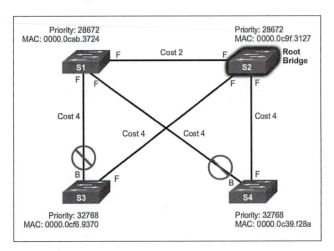

Figure 4-42   STP Failure Can Be Catastrophic

Remember that an Ethernet frame header does not include a TTL field, which means that any frame that enters a bridging loop continues to be forwarded by the switches indefinitely. The only exceptions are frames that have their destination address recorded in the MAC address table of the switches. These frames are simply forwarded to the port that is associated with the MAC address and do not enter a loop. However, any frame that is flooded by a switch enters the loop (see Figure 4-43). This can include broadcasts, multicasts, and unicasts with a globally unknown destination MAC address.

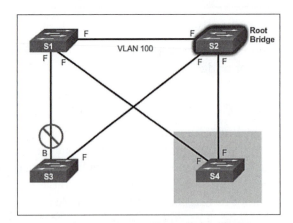

Figure 4-43   Erroneous Transition to Forwarding

What are the consequences and corresponding symptoms of STP failure (see Figure 4-44)?

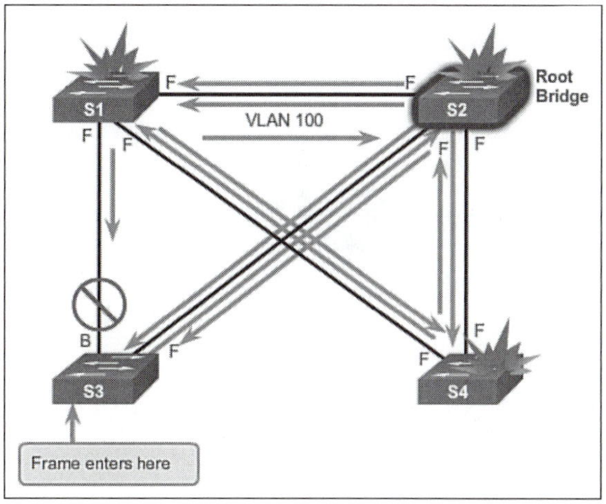

Figure 4-44   Consequences of STP Failure Are Severe

The load on all links in the switched LAN quickly starts increasing as more and more frames enter the loop. This problem is not limited to the links that form the loop, but also affects any other links in the switched domain because the frames are flooded on all links. When the spanning tree failure is limited to a single VLAN, only links in that VLAN are affected. Switches and trunks that do not carry that VLAN operate normally.

If the spanning tree failure has created a bridging loop, traffic increases exponentially. The switches will then flood the broadcasts out multiple ports. This creates copies of the frames every time the switches forward them.

When control plane traffic starts entering the loop (for example, OSPF Hellos or EIGRP Hellos), the devices that are running these protocols quickly start getting overloaded. Their CPUs approach 100 percent utilization while they are trying to process an ever-increasing load of control plane traffic. In many cases, the earliest indication of this broadcast storm in progress is that routers or Layer 3 switches are reporting control plane failures and that they are running at a high CPU load.

The switches experience frequent MAC address table changes. If a loop exists, a switch might see a frame with a certain source MAC address coming in on one port and then see another frame with the same source MAC address coming in on a different port a fraction of a second later. This will cause the switch to update the MAC address table twice for the same MAC address.

Because of the combination of very high load on all links and the switch CPUs running at maximum load, these devices typically become unreachable. This makes it very difficult to diagnose the problem while it is happening.

Repairing a Spanning Tree Problem (4.3.3.5)

One way to correct spanning tree failure is to manually remove redundant links in the switched network, either physically or through configuration, until all loops are eliminated from the topology, as shown in Figure 4-45. When the loops are broken, the traffic and CPU loads should quickly drop to normal levels, and connectivity to devices should be restored.

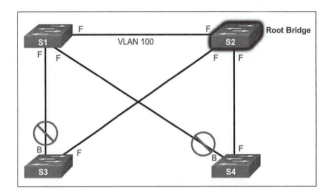

Figure 4-45   Repairing a Spanning Tree Problem

Although this intervention restores connectivity to the network, it is not the end of the troubleshooting process. All redundancy from the switched network has been removed, and now the redundant links must be restored.

If the underlying cause of the spanning tree failure has not been fixed, chances are that restoring the redundant links will trigger a new broadcast storm. Before restoring the redundant links, determine and correct the cause of the spanning tree failure. Carefully monitor the network to ensure that the problem is fixed.

Interactive Graphic

Activity 4.3.3.6: Troubleshoot STP Configuration Issues

Go to the online course to perform this practice activity.

First Hop Redundancy Protocols (4.4)

Just as Spanning Tree Protocols are used to support physical redundancy in a Layer 2 switched environment, and routers are used for Layer 3 redundancy in a routed network, *First Hop Redundancy Protocols (FHRP)* are used for redundancy at the portion of the network where access layer switches connect to routers or multilayer switches.

Concept of First Hop Redundancy Protocols (4.4.1)

In the history of networking, a number of solutions providing redundant default gateways for hosts and access layer switches have become available to network administrators. After the dust settled a bit, FHRPs have emerged as the preferred solution for this particular type of redundancy.

Default Gateway Limitations (4.4.1.1)

Spanning tree protocols enable physical redundancy in a Layer 2 switched network. However, a host at the access layer of a hierarchical network also benefits from alternate default gateways. If a router or router interface (that serves as a default gateway) fails, the hosts configured with that default gateway are isolated from outside networks. A mechanism is needed to provide alternate default gateways in switched networks where two or more routers are connected to the same VLANs.

> **Note**
>
> For the purposes of the discussion on router redundancy, there is no functional difference between a multilayer switch and a router at the distribution layer. In practice, it is common for a multilayer switch to act as the default gateway for each VLAN in a switched network. This discussion focuses on the functionality of *routing*, regardless of the physical device used.

In a switched network, each client receives only one default gateway. There is no way to configure a secondary gateway, even if a second path exists to carry packets off the local segment.

In Figure 4-46, R1 is responsible for routing packets from PC1. If R1 becomes unavailable, the routing protocols can dynamically converge. R2 now routes packets from outside networks that would have gone through R1. However, traffic from the inside network associated with R1, including traffic from workstations, servers, and printers configured with R1 as their default gateway, is still sent to R1 and dropped.

End devices are typically configured with a single IP address for a default gateway. This address does not change when the network topology changes. If that default gateway IP address cannot be reached, the local device is unable to send packets off the local network segment, effectively disconnecting it from the rest of the network. Even if a redundant router exists that could serve as a default gateway for that segment, there is no dynamic method by which these devices can determine the address of a new default gateway.

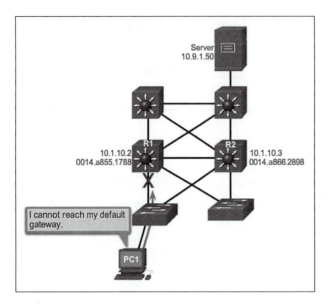

Figure 4-46   Default Gateway Limitations

Router Redundancy (4.4.1.2)

One way prevent a single point of failure at the default gateway is to implement a *virtual router*. To implement this type of router redundancy, multiple routers are configured to work together to present the illusion of a single router to the hosts on the LAN, as shown in Figure 4-47. By sharing an IP address and a MAC address, two or more routers can act as a single virtual router, as depicted in the figure.

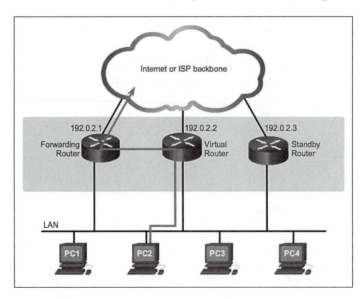

Figure 4-47   Router Redundancy

The IP address of the virtual router is configured as the default gateway for the workstations on a specific IP segment. When frames are sent from host devices to the default gateway, the hosts use ARP to resolve the MAC address that is associated with the IP address of the default gateway. The ARP resolution returns the MAC address of the virtual router. Frames that are sent to the MAC address of the virtual router can then be physically processed by the currently *active router* within the virtual router group. A protocol is used to identify two or more routers as the devices that are responsible for processing frames that are sent to the MAC or IP address of a single virtual router. Host devices send traffic to the address of the virtual router. The physical router that forwards this traffic is transparent to the host devices.

A redundancy protocol provides the mechanism for determining which router should take the active role in forwarding traffic. It also determines when the forwarding role must be taken over by a *standby router*. The transition from one forwarding router to another is transparent to the end devices.

The ability of a network to dynamically recover from the failure of a device acting as a default gateway is known as *first hop redundancy*.

Steps for Router Failover (4.4.1.3)

When the active router fails, the redundancy protocol transitions the standby router to the new active router role. These are the steps that take place when the active router fails, as shown in Figure 4-48:

1. The standby router stops seeing Hello messages from the forwarding router.

2. The standby router assumes the role of the forwarding router.

3. Because the new forwarding router assumes both the IP and MAC addresses of the virtual router, the host devices see no disruption in service.

Interactive Graphic

Activity 4.4.1.4: Identify FHRP Terminology

Go to the online course to perform this practice activity.

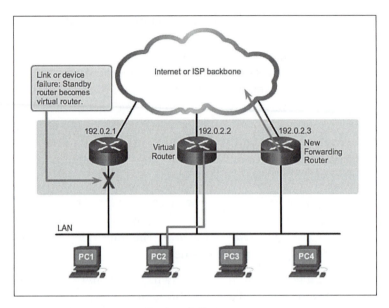

Figure 4-48   Steps for Router Failover

Varieties of First Hop Redundancy Protocols (4.4.2)

Just as there are a variety of Spanning Tree Protocols, there are a variety of First Hop Redundancy Protocols. The one to choose depends on the vendor equipment and the degree of redundancy required.

First Hop Redundancy Protocols (4.4.2.1)

The following list defines the options available for First Hop Redundancy Protocols:

- *Hot Standby Router Protocol (HSRP)*: A Cisco-proprietary FHRP designed to allow for transparent failover of a first-hop IPv4 device. HSRP provides high network availability by providing first-hop routing redundancy for IPv4 hosts on networks configured with an IPv4 default gateway address. HSRP is used in a group of routers for selecting an active device and a standby device. In a group of device interfaces, the active device is the device that is used for routing packets. The standby device is the device that takes over when the active device fails, or when preset conditions are met. The function of the HSRP standby router is to monitor the operational status of the HSRP group and to quickly assume packet-forwarding responsibility if the active router fails. The routers in an HSRP group share a *virtual IP address* and a *virtual MAC address*.

- *HSRP for IPv6*: This Cisco-proprietary FHRP provides the same functionality of HSRP, but in an IPv6 environment. An HSRP IPv6 group has a virtual MAC address derived from the HSRP group number and a virtual IPv6 link-local address derived from the HSRP virtual MAC address. Periodic router advertisements (RA) are sent for the HSRP virtual IPv6 link-local address when the HSRP group is active. When the group becomes inactive, these RAs stop after a final RA is sent.

- *Virtual Router Redundancy Protocol version 2 (VRRPv2)*: A nonproprietary election protocol that dynamically assigns responsibility for one or more virtual routers to the VRRP routers on an IPv4 LAN. This allows several routers on a multiaccess link to use the same virtual IPv4 address. A VRRP router is configured to run the VRRP protocol in conjunction with one or more other routers attached to a LAN. In a VRRP configuration, one router is elected as the virtual router master, with the other routers acting as backups, in case the virtual router master fails.

- **VRRPv3:** Provides the capability to support IPv4 and IPv6 addresses. VRRPv3 works in multivendor environments and is more scalable than VRRPv2.

- *Gateway Load Balancing Protocol (GLBP)*: A Cisco-proprietary FHRP that protects data traffic from a failed router or circuit, like HSRP and VRRP, while also allowing load balancing (also called load sharing) between a group of redundant routers.

- **GLBP for IPv6:** A Cisco-proprietary FHRP providing the same functionality of GLBP, but in an IPv6 environment. GLBP for IPv6 provides automatic router backup for IPv6 hosts configured with a single default gateway on a LAN. Multiple first-hop routers on the LAN combine to offer a single virtual first-hop IPv6 router while sharing the IPv6 packet-forwarding load.

- *ICMP Router Discovery Protocol (IRDP)*: Specified in RFC 1256, this is a legacy FHRP solution. IRDP allows IPv4 hosts to locate routers that provide IPv4 connectivity to other (nonlocal) IP networks.

Interactive Graphic

Activity 4.4.2.2: Identify the Type of FHRP

Go to the online course to perform this practice activity.

FHRP Verification (4.4.3)

In this section, the HSRP and GLBP verification commands are explored.

HSRP Verification (4.4.3.1)

An HSRP active router has the following characteristics:

- Responds to the default gateway's ARP requests with the virtual router's MAC.

- Assumes active forwarding of packets for the virtual router.

- Sends Hello messages.

- Knows the virtual router IP address.

An HSRP standby router has the following characteristics:

- Listens for periodic Hello messages.

- Assumes active forwarding of packets if it does not hear from the active router.

Use the **show standby** command to verify the HSRP state. The output shown in Example 4-10 indicates that the router is in the active state.

Example 4-10   Verify HSRP State

```
Router# show standby

Ethernet0/1 - Group 1
  State is Active
    2 state changes, last state change 00:30:59
  Virtual IP address is 10.1.0.20
    Secondary virtual IP address 10.1.0.21
  Active virtual MAC address is 0004.4d82.7981
    Local virtual MAC address is 0004.4d82.7981 (bia)
  Hello time 4 sec, hold time 12 sec
    Next hello sent in 1.412 secs
  Gratuitous ARP 14 sent, next in 7.412 secs
  Preemption enabled, min delay 50 sec, sync delay 40 sec
  Active router is local
  Standby router is 10.1.0.6, priority 75 (expires in 9.184 sec)
  Priority 95 (configured 120)
    Tracking 2 objects, 0 up
      Down Interface Ethernet0/2, pri 15
      Down Interface Ethernet0/3
  Group name is "HSRP1" (cfgd)
Follow by groups:
    Et1/0.3 Grp 2 Active 10.0.0.254 0000.0c07.ac02 refresh 30 secs (next 19.666)
    Et1/0.4 Grp 2 Active 10.0.0.254 0000.0c07.ac02 refresh 30 secs (next 19.491)
  Group name is "HSRP1", advertisement interval is 34 sec
```

GLBP Verification (4.4.3.2)

Although HSRP and VRRP provide gateway resiliency, for the standby members of the redundancy group, the upstream bandwidth is not used while the device is in standby mode.

Only the active router in HSRP and VRRP groups forwards traffic for the virtual MAC address. Resources that are associated with the standby router are not fully utilized. You can accomplish some load balancing with these protocols by creating multiple groups and assigning multiple default gateways, but this configuration creates an administrative burden.

GLBP is a Cisco-proprietary solution to allow automatic selection and simultaneous use of multiple available gateways in addition to automatic failover between those gateways. Multiple routers share the load of frames that, from a client perspective, are sent to a single default gateway address, as shown in Figure 4-49.

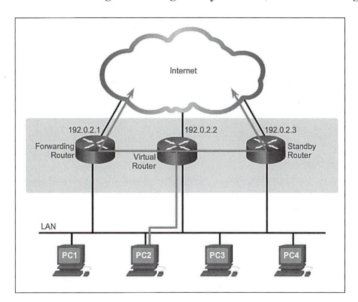

Figure 4-49   Gateway Load Balancing Protocol

With GLBP, you can fully utilize resources without the administrative burden of configuring multiple groups and managing multiple default gateway configurations. GLBP has the following characteristics:

- Allows full use of resources on all devices without the administrative burden of creating multiple groups.

- Provides a single virtual IP address and multiple virtual MAC addresses.

- Routes traffic to a single gateway distributed across routers.

- Provides automatic rerouting in the event of any failure.

Use the **show glbp** command to verify the GLBP status. The output shown in Example 4-11 shows that GLBP group 10 is in the active state with virtual IP address 10.21.8.10.

Example 4-11   Verify GLBP

```
Router# show glbp

FastEthernet0/0 - Group 10
  State is Active
    2 state changes, last state change 23:50:33
  Virtual IP address is 10.21.8.10
  Hello time 5 sec, hold time 18 sec
    Next hello sent in 4.300 secs
  Redirect time 1800 sec, forwarder time-out 28800 sec
  Authentication text "stringabc"
  Preemption enabled, min delay 60 sec
  Active is local
  Standby is unknown
  Priority 254 (configured)
  Weighting 105 (configured 110), thresholds: lower 95, upper 105
    Track object 2 state Down decrement 5
  Load balancing: host-dependent
  There is 1 forwarder (1 active)
  Forwarder 1
    State is Active
      1 state change, last state change 23:50:15
    MAC address is 0007.b400.0101 (default)
    Owner ID is 0005.0050.6c08
    Redirection enabled
    Preemption enabled, min delay 60 sec
    Active is local, weighting 105
<output omitted>
```

Interactive Graphic

Activity 4.4.3.3: HSRP and GLBP

Go to the online course to use the Syntax Checker to configure and verify HSRP and GLBP. Configuration of HSRP and GLBP are beyond the scope of this course. However, familiarity with the commands used to enable HSRP and GLBP aid in understanding the configuration output. For this reason, the Syntax Checker and subsequent lab are optional exercises.

Lab 4.4.3.4: Configuring HSRP and GLBP

In this lab, you will complete the following objectives:

- Part 1: Build the Network and Verify Connectivity
- Part 2: Configure First Hop Redundancy Using HSRP
- Part 3: Configure First Hop Redundancy Using GLBP

Summary (4.5)

Class Activity 4.5.1.1: Documentation Tree

The employees in your building are having difficulty accessing a web server on the network. You look for the network documentation that the previous network engineer used before he transitioned to a new job; however, you cannot find any network documentation.

Therefore, you decide to create your own network record-keeping system. You decide to start at the access layer of your network hierarchy. This is where redundant switches are located, as well as the company servers, printers, and local hosts.

You create a matrix to record your documentation and include access layer switches on the list. You also decide to document switch names, ports in use, cabling connections, root ports, designated ports, and alternate ports.

Problems that can result from a redundant Layer 2 network include broadcast storms, MAC database instability, and duplicate unicast frames. STP is a Layer 2 protocol that ensures that there is only one logical path between all destinations on the network by intentionally blocking redundant paths that could cause a loop.

STP sends BPDU frames for communication between switches. One switch is elected as the root bridge for each instance of spanning tree. An administrator can control this election by changing the bridge priority. Root bridges can be configured to enable spanning tree load balancing by VLAN or by a group of VLANs, depending on the spanning tree protocol used. STP then assigns a port role to each participating port using a path cost. The path cost is equal to the sum of all the port costs along the path to the root bridge. A port cost is automatically assigned to each port; however, it can also be manually configured. Paths with the lowest cost become preferred, and all other redundant paths are blocked.

PVST+ is the default configuration of IEEE 802.1D on Cisco switches. It runs one instance of STP for each VLAN. A newer, faster-converging spanning tree protocol, RSTP, can be implemented on Cisco switches on a per-VLAN basis in the form of Rapid PVST+. Multiple Spanning Tree (MST) is the Cisco implementation of Multiple Spanning Tree Protocol (MSTP), where one instance of spanning tree runs for a defined group of VLANs. Features, such as PortFast and BPDU guard, ensure that hosts in the switched environment are provided immediate access to the network without interfering with spanning tree operation.

First Hop Redundancy Protocols, such as HSRP, VRRP, and GLBP, provide alternate default gateways for hosts in the redundant router or multilayer switched environment. Multiple routers share a virtual IP address and MAC address that is used as the default gateway on a client. This ensures that hosts maintain connectivity in the event of the failure of one device serving as a default gateway for a VLAN or set of VLANs. When using HSRP or VRRP, one router is active or forwarding for a particular group while others are in standby mode. GLBP allows the simultaneous use of multiple gateways in addition to providing automatic failover.

Practice

The following activities provide practice with the topics introduced in this chapter. The Labs and Class Activities are available in the companion *Switched Networks Lab Manual* (ISBN 978-1-58713-372-5). The Packet Tracer Activities PKA files are found in the online course.

Class Activities

- Class Activity 4.0.1.2: Stormy Traffic
- Class Activity 4.5.1.1: Documentation Tree

Labs

- Lab 4.1.2.10: Building a Switched Network with Redundant Links
- Lab 4.3.2.3: Configuring Rapid PVST+, PortFast, and BPDU Guard
- Lab 4.4.3.4: Configuring HSRP and GLBP

Packet Tracer Activities

- Packet Tracer Activity 4.1.1.5: Examining a Redundant Design
- Packet Tracer Activity 4.3.1.5: Configuring PVST+
- Packet Tracer Activity 4.3.2.2 Configuring Rapid PVST+

Check Your Understanding Questions

Complete all the review questions listed here to test your understanding of the topics and concepts in this chapter. The appendix "Answers to 'Check Your Understanding' Questions" lists the answers.

1. During the implementation of Spanning Tree Protocol, all switches are rebooted by the network administrator. What is the first step of the spanning-tree election process?

   A. Each switch with a lower root ID than its neighbor will not send BPDUs.

   B. All the switches send out BPDUs advertising themselves as the root bridge.

   C. Each switch determines the best path to forward traffic.

   D. Each switch determines what port to block to prevent a loop from occurring.

2. Which of the following port states are used by Rapid PVST+? (Choose three.)

   A. Discarding

   B. Blocking

   C. Trunking

   D. Listening

   E. Learning

   F. Forwarding

3. After the election of the root bridge has been completed, how will switches find the best paths to the root bridge?

   A. Each switch will analyze the sum of the hops to reach the root and use the path with the fewest hops.

   B. Each switch will analyze the BID of all neighbors to reach the root and use the path through the lowest BID neighbors.

   C. Each switch will analyze the port states of all neighbors and use the designated ports to forward traffic to the root.

   D. Each switch will analyze the sum of all port costs to reach the root and use the path with the lowest cost.

4. What are expectations of configuring PortFast on a switch port? (Choose two.)

   A. The switch port immediately transitions from the listening to the forwarding state.

   B. The switch port immediately transitions from the blocking to the forwarding state.

   C. The switch port should never receive BPDUs from end stations that are connected to the port.

   D. The switch port immediately processes any BPDUs before transitioning to the forwarding state.

   E. The switch port sends DHCP requests before transitioning to the forwarding state.

5. An administrator is troubleshooting a switch and wants to verify whether it is a root bridge. What command can be used to do this?

   A. **show spanning-tree**

   B. **show running-config**

   C. **show startup-config**

   D. **show vlan**

6. When PVST is running over a switched network, which port state can participate in BPDU frame forwarding based on BPDUs received, but does not forward data frames?

   A. Blocking

   B. Listening

   C. Forwarding

   D. Disabled

7. Put in order the router failover stage steps that occur when an FHRP initiates a router failover process.

   A. The standby router stops seeing hello messages from the forwarding router.

   B. The standby router assumes the role of forwarding router.

   C. The new forwarding router assumes the IP and MAC addresses of the virtual router.

8. A network administrator is overseeing the implementation of First Hop Redundancy Protocols. Which of the following protocols will not be able to function with multivendor devices? (Choose two.)

   A. HSRP

   B. VRRP

   C. GLBP

   D. IRDP

9. Which of the following issues are the result of a broadcast storm? (Choose two.)

   A. During a broadcast storm, a switch will forward a received broadcast out every port on the switch.

   B. Because of high processing demands during a broadcast storm, communication can fail between end stations in the broadcast domain.

   C. In a network saturated with broadcast traffic, new traffic arriving at the switch will be forwarded into the broadcast domain, which further consumes available bandwidth.

   D. During a broadcast storm, constant changes to the MAC address table prevent a switch from accurately forwarding frames.

   E. During a broadcast storm, switches with high-speed interfaces will forward traffic in half-duplex mode to conserve available bandwidth.

10. What is the initial approach that should be used to troubleshoot a broadcast storm in a switched network?

    A. Replace all instances of STP with RSTP.

    B. Insert redundant links to replace the failed STP links.

    C. Replace the cables on failed STP links.

    D. Manually remove redundant links in the switched network.

11. What is an accurate description of redundancy?

    A. Configuring a router with a complete MAC address database to ensure that all frames can be forwarded to the correct destination

    B. Configuring a switch with proper security to ensure that all traffic forwarded through an interface is filtered.

    C. Designing a network to use multiple virtual devices to ensure that all traffic uses the best path through the internetwork

    D. Designing a network to use multiple paths between switches to ensure that there is no single point of failure

12. Fill in the blank.

    A. A Cisco enhancement of RSTP to provide a spanning-tree instance for each VLAN: *Rapide PVST+*

    B. The legacy standard for STP that runs all VLANs in a single spanning-tree instance: *STP*

    C. Allows multiple VLANs to run in a single spanning-tree instance: *MSTP*

13. When First Hop Redundancy Protocols are used, which of the following items will be shared by a set of routers that are presenting the illusion of being a single router? (Choose two.)

    A. Host name
    B. IP address
    C. BID
    D. Static route
    E. MAC address

Link Aggregation

Objectives

Upon completion of this chapter, you will be able to answer the following questions:

- How do you describe link aggregation?

- How do you describe EtherChannel technology?

- How do you configure link aggregation with EtherChannel?

- How do you troubleshoot link aggregation with EtherChannel?

Key Terms

This chapter uses the following key terms. You can find the definitions in the Glossary.

Introduction (5.0.1.1)

Link aggregation is the ability to create one logical link using multiple physical links between two devices. This allows load sharing among the physical links, rather than having STP block one or more of the links. EtherChannel is a form of link aggregation used in switched networks.

This chapter describes EtherChannel and the methods used to create an EtherChannel. An EtherChannel can be manually configured or can be negotiated by using the Cisco-proprietary protocol Port Aggregation Protocol (PAgP) or the IEEE 802.3ad–defined protocol Link Aggregation Control Protocol (LACP). The configuration, verification, and troubleshooting of EtherChannel are discussed.

Class Activity 5.0.1.2: Imagine This

It is the end of the work day. In your small- to medium-sized business, you are trying to explain to the network engineers about EtherChannel and how it looks when it is physically set up. The network engineers have difficulty envisioning how two switches could possibly be connected through several links that collectively act as one channel or connection. Your company is definitely considering implementing an EtherChannel network.

Therefore, you end the meeting with an assignment for the engineers. To prepare for the next day's meeting, they are to perform some research and bring to the meeting one graphic representation of an EtherChannel network connection. They are tasked with explaining how an EtherChannel network operates to the other engineers.

When researching EtherChannel, a good question to search for is "What does EtherChannel look like?" Prepare a few slides to demonstrate your research that will be presented to the network engineering group. These slides should provide a solid grasp of how EtherChannels are physically created within a network topology. Your goal is to ensure that everyone leaving the next meeting will have a good idea as to why he or she would consider moving to a network topology using EtherChannel as an option.

Link Aggregation Concepts (5.1)

In this section, you learn about the principle of link aggregation in a LAN switched environment. The concept of link aggregation is common throughout networking, with aggregation of serial links using PPP as well as the bundling of PSTN lines with trunks.

Link Aggregation (5.1.1)

In this topic, *link aggregation* is defined and the advantages of using link aggregation are explored. Although the term *EtherChannel* has roots in Cisco-proprietary technologies, the term has come to encompass both Cisco-proprietary and vendor-neutral implementations of link aggregation in a LAN switched environment incorporating Cisco switches.

Introduction to Link Aggregation (5.1.1.1)

In Figure 5-1, traffic coming from several links (usually 100 or 1000 Mb/s) aggregates on the access switch and must be sent to distribution switches. Because of the traffic aggregation, links with higher bandwidth must be available between the access and distribution switches.

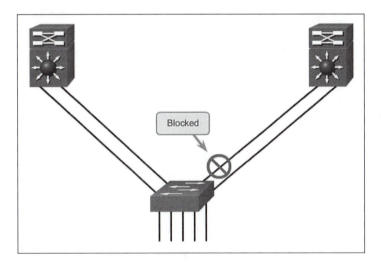

Figure 5-1   Redundant Links with STP

It might be possible to use faster links, such as 10 Gb/s, on the aggregated link between the access and distribution layer switches. However, adding faster links is expensive. Additionally, as the speed increases on the access links, even the fastest possible port on the aggregated link is no longer fast enough to aggregate the traffic coming from all access links.

It is also possible to multiply the number of physical links between the switches to increase the overall speed of switch-to-switch communication. However, by default, STP is enabled on switch devices. STP will block redundant links to prevent routing loops.

For these reasons, the best solution is to implement an EtherChannel configuration.

Advantages of EtherChannel (5.1.1.2)

EtherChannel technology was originally developed by Cisco as a LAN switch-to-switch technique of grouping several Fast Ethernet or Gigabit Ethernet ports into one logical channel. When an EtherChannel is configured, the resulting virtual interface is called a port channel. The physical interfaces are bundled together into a *port channel interface*. Network diagrams depict EtherChannel bundles, as shown in Figure 5-2.

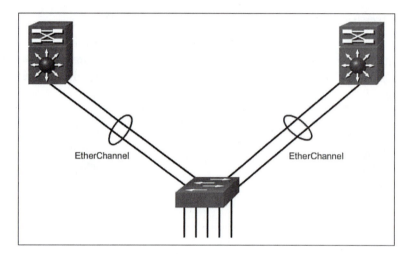

Figure 5-2   Depicting EtherChannel Bundles

EtherChannel technology has many advantages:

- Most configuration tasks can be done on the EtherChannel interface instead of on each individual port, ensuring configuration consistency throughout the links.

- EtherChannel relies on existing switch ports. There is no need to upgrade the link to a faster and more expensive connection to have more bandwidth.

- Load balancing takes place between links that are part of the same EtherChannel. Depending on the hardware platform, one or more load-balancing methods can be implemented. These methods include source MAC to destination MAC load balancing, or source IP to destination IP load balancing, across the physical links.

- EtherChannel creates an aggregation that is seen as one logical link. When several EtherChannel bundles exist between two switches, STP can block one of the bundles to prevent switching loops. When STP blocks one of the redundant links, it blocks the entire EtherChannel. This blocks all the ports belonging to that EtherChannel link. Where there is only one EtherChannel link, all physical links in the EtherChannel are active because STP sees only one (logical) link.

- EtherChannel provides redundancy because the overall link is seen as one logical connection. Additionally, the loss of one physical link within the channel does not create a change in the topology; therefore a spanning tree recalculation is not required. Assuming that at least one physical link is present, the EtherChannel remains functional, even if its overall throughput decreases because of a lost link within the EtherChannel.

EtherChannel Operation (5.1.2)

The two types of link aggregation in a switched environment are made possible with *Port Aggregation Protocol (PAgP)* and *Link Aggregation Control Protocol (LACP)*; PAgP is Cisco proprietary and LACP is vendor neutral. In this topic, you explore these two technologies.

Implementation Restrictions (5.1.2.1)

EtherChannel can be implemented by grouping multiple physical ports into one or more logical EtherChannel links.

> **Note**
>
> Interface types cannot be mixed. For example, Fast Ethernet and Gigabit Ethernet cannot be mixed within a single EtherChannel.

The EtherChannel provides full-duplex bandwidth up to 800 Mb/s (Fast EtherChannel) or 8 Gb/s (Gigabit EtherChannel) between one switch and another switch or host. Currently each EtherChannel can consist of up to eight compatibly configured Ethernet ports. The Cisco IOS switch can currently support six EtherChannels. However, as new IOSs are developed and platforms change, some cards and platforms might support increased numbers of ports within an EtherChannel link, as well as support an increased number of Gigabit EtherChannels. The concept is the same no matter the speeds or number of links that are involved. When configuring EtherChannel on switches, be aware of the hardware platform boundaries and specifications.

The original purpose of EtherChannel is to increase speed capability on aggregated links between switches. However, this concept was extended as EtherChannel technology became more popular, and now many servers also support link aggregation with EtherChannel. EtherChannel creates a one-to-one relationship; that is, one EtherChannel link connects only two devices. An EtherChannel link can be created between two switches or an EtherChannel link can be created between an EtherChannel-enabled server and a switch. However, traffic cannot be sent to two different switches through the same EtherChannel link.

The individual EtherChannel group member port configuration must be consistent on both devices. For example, for trunk ports, the allowed VLANs, native VLAN, and trunking mode have to match for an EtherChannel to form. If the physical ports of one side are configured as trunks, the physical ports of the other side must also be configured as trunks within the same native VLAN. Additionally, all ports in each EtherChannel link must be configured as Layer 2 ports.

Note

Layer 3 EtherChannels can be configured on Cisco Catalyst multilayer switches, such as the Catalyst 3560, but these are not explored in this course. A Layer 3 EtherChannel has a single IP address associated with the logical aggregation of switch ports in the EtherChannel.

Each EtherChannel has a logical port channel interface, as illustrated in Figure 5-3. A configuration applied to the port channel interface affects all physical interfaces that are assigned to that interface.

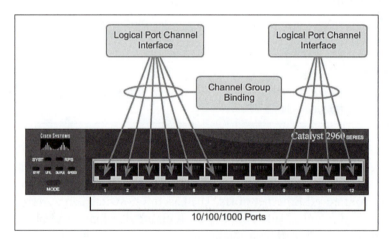

Figure 5-3   EtherChannel Implementation Restrictions

Port Aggregation Protocol (5.1.2.2)

EtherChannels can be formed through negotiation using one of two protocols, PAgP or LACP. These protocols allow ports with similar characteristics to form a channel through dynamic negotiation with adjoining switches.

Note

It is also possible to configure a static or unconditional EtherChannel without PAgP or LACP.

PAgP

PAgP is a Cisco-proprietary protocol that aids in the automatic creation of EtherChannel links. When an EtherChannel link is configured using PAgP, PAgP packets are sent between EtherChannel-capable ports to negotiate the forming of a channel. When PAgP identifies matched Ethernet links, it groups the links into an EtherChannel. The EtherChannel is then added to the spanning tree as a single port.

When enabled, PAgP also manages the EtherChannel. PAgP packets are sent every 30 seconds. PAgP checks for configuration consistency and manages link additions and failures between two switches. It ensures that when an EtherChannel is created, all ports have the same type of configuration.

Note

In EtherChannel, it is mandatory that all ports have the same speed, duplex setting, and VLAN information. Any port modification after the creation of the channel also changes all other channel ports.

PAgP helps create the EtherChannel link by detecting the configuration of each side and ensuring that links are compatible so that the EtherChannel link can be enabled when needed. Figure 5-4 indicates the success or failure of EtherChannel establishment based on the respective PAgP modes of the opposing interfaces.

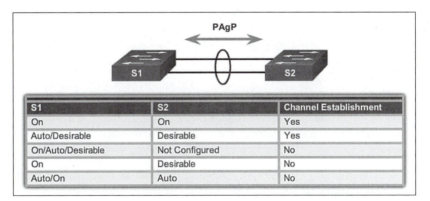

S1	S2	Channel Establishment
On	On	Yes
Auto/Desirable	Desirable	Yes
On/Auto/Desirable	Not Configured	No
On	Desirable	No
Auto/On	Auto	No

Figure 5-4   EtherChannel Establishment Based on PAgP Modes

The modes are described here:

- *On*: This mode forces the interface to channel without PAgP. Interfaces configured in the on mode do not exchange PAgP packets.

- **PAgP** *desirable*: This PAgP mode places an interface in an active negotiating state in which the interface initiates negotiations with other interfaces by sending PAgP packets.

- **PAgP** *auto*: This PAgP mode places an interface in a passive negotiating state in which the interface responds to the PAgP packets that it receives, but does not initiate PAgP negotiation.

The modes must be compatible on each side. If one side is configured to be in auto mode, it is placed in a passive state, waiting for the other side to initiate the EtherChannel negotiation. If the other side is also set to auto, the negotiation never starts and the EtherChannel does not form. If all modes are disabled by using the **no** command, or if no mode is configured, the EtherChannel is disabled.

The on mode manually places the interface in an EtherChannel, without any negotiation. It works only if the other side is also set to on. If the other side is set to negotiate parameters through PAgP, no EtherChannel forms, because the side that is set to on mode does not negotiate.

Link Aggregation Control Protocol (5.1.2.3)

LACP is part of an IEEE specification (802.3ad) that allows several physical ports to be bundled to form a single logical channel. LACP allows a switch to negotiate an automatic bundle by sending LACP packets to the peer. It performs a function similar to PAgP with Cisco EtherChannel. Because LACP is an IEEE standard, it can be used to facilitate EtherChannels in multivendor environments. On Cisco devices, both protocols are supported.

Note

LACP was originally defined as IEEE 802.3ad. However, LACP is now defined in the newer *IEEE 802.1AX-2008* standard for local- and metropolitan-area networks.

LACP provides the same negotiation benefits as PAgP. LACP helps create the EtherChannel link by detecting the configuration of each side and making sure that they are compatible so that the EtherChannel link can be enabled when needed. Figure 5-5 shows the modes for LACP. The figure indicates the success or failure of EtherChannel establishment based on the respective LACP modes of the opposing interfaces.

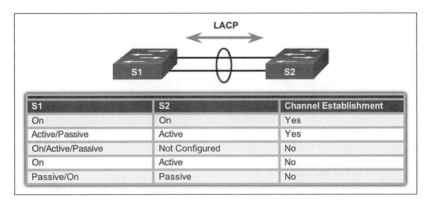

Figure 5-5 EtherChannel Establishment Based on LACP Modes

The modes are described here:

- *On*: This mode forces the interface to channel without LACP. Interfaces configured in the on mode do not exchange LACP packets.

- **LACP** *active*: This LACP mode places a port in an active negotiating state. In this state, the port initiates negotiations with other ports by sending LACP packets.

- **LACP** *passive*: This LACP mode places a port in a passive negotiating state. In this state, the port responds to the LACP packets that it receives, but does not initiate LACP packet negotiation.

Just as with PAgP, modes must be compatible on both sides for the EtherChannel link to form. The on mode is repeated, because it creates the EtherChannel configuration unconditionally, without PAgP or LACP dynamic negotiation.

<table>
<tr><td>Interactive
Graphic</td></tr>
</table>

Activity 5.1.2.4: Identify Terminology for PAgP and LACP Modes

Go to the online course to perform this practice activity.

Link Aggregation Configuration (5.2)

In this section you learn to configure, verify, and troubleshoot both PAgP-based and LACP-based EtherChannels.

Configuring EtherChannel (5.2.1)

This topic focuses on the configuration of PAgP-based and LACP-based EtherChannels.

Configuration Guidelines (5.2.1.1)

The following guidelines and restrictions are useful for configuring EtherChannel:

- **EtherChannel support:** All Ethernet interfaces on all modules must support EtherChannel with no requirement that interfaces be physically contiguous, or on the same module.

- **Speed and duplex:** Configure all interfaces in an EtherChannel to operate at the same speed and in the same duplex mode, as shown in Figure 5-6.

- **VLAN match:** All interfaces in the EtherChannel bundle must be assigned to the same VLAN, or be configured as a trunk, as shown in Figure 5-7.

- **Range of VLAN:** An EtherChannel supports the same allowed range of VLANs on all the interfaces in a trunking EtherChannel. If the allowed range of VLANs is not the same, the interfaces do not form an EtherChannel, even when set to auto or desirable mode.

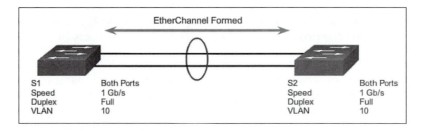

Figure 5-6   EtherChannel Establishment Succeeds

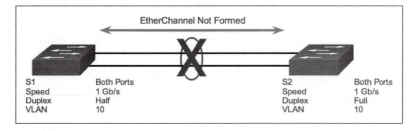

Figure 5-7   EtherChannel Establishment Fails

If these settings must be changed, configure them in port channel interface configuration mode. After the port channel interface is configured, any configuration that is applied to the port channel interface also affects individual interfaces. However, configurations that are applied to the individual interfaces do not affect the port channel interface. Therefore, making configuration changes to an interface that is part of an EtherChannel link can cause interface compatibility issues.

Configuring Interfaces (5.2.1.2)

The steps to configure EtherChannel with LACP are as follows:

Step 1. Specify the interfaces that comprise the EtherChannel group using the **interface range** *interface* global configuration mode command. The **range** keyword allows you to select several interfaces and configure them all together. A good practice is to start by shutting down those interfaces so that any incomplete configuration does not create activity on the link.

Step 2. Create the port channel interface with the **channel-group** *identifier* **mode active** command in interface range configuration mode. The identifier specifies a *channel group* number. The **mode active** keywords identify this as an LACP EtherChannel configuration.

Note

EtherChannel is disabled by default.

In Figure 5-8, EtherChannel is used to bundle FastEthernet0/1 and FastEthernet0/2 into interface port channel 1.

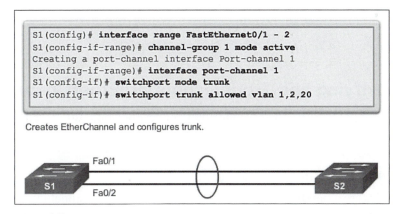

Figure 5-8   Configuring EtherChannel with LACP

To change Layer 2 settings on the port channel interface, enter port channel interface configuration mode using the **interface port-channel** command, followed by the interface identifier. In Figure 5-8, the EtherChannel is configured as a trunk interface with allowed VLANs specified, and interface port channel 1 is configured as a trunk with allowed VLANs 1, 2, and 20.

Activity 5.2.1.2: Configuring EtherChannel

Go to the online course to use the Syntax Checker in the second graphic to configure EtherChannel on switch S1.

Packet Tracer Activity 5.2.1.3: Configuring EtherChannel

Three switches have just been installed. There are redundant uplinks between the switches. Usually, only one of these links could be used; otherwise, a bridging loop might occur. However, using only one link utilizes only half of the available bandwidth. EtherChannel allows up to eight redundant links to be bundled together into one logical link. In this lab, you will configure Port Aggregation Protocol (PAgP), a Cisco EtherChannel protocol, and Link Aggregation Control Protocol (LACP), an IEEE 802.3ad open standard version of EtherChannel.

Lab 5.2.1.4: Configuring EtherChannel

In this lab, you will complete the following objectives:

- Part 1: Configure Basic Switch Settings
- Part 2: Configure PAgP
- Part 3: Configure LACP

Verifying and Troubleshooting EtherChannel (5.2.2)

This topic focuses on verifying and troubleshooting PAgP-based and LACP-based EtherChannels.

Verifying EtherChannel (5.2.2.1)

There are a number of commands to verify an EtherChannel configuration. First, the **show interface port-channel1** command displays the general status of the port channel interface. In Figure 5-9, the Port Channel 1 interface is up.

When several port channel interfaces are configured on the same device, use the **show etherchannel summary** command to simply display one line of information per port channel. In Example 5-1, the switch has one EtherChannel configured; group 1 uses LACP.

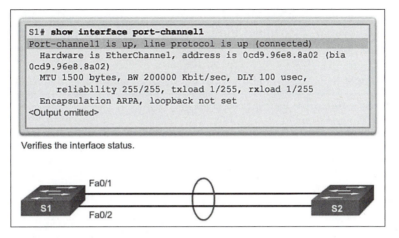

```
S1# show interface port-channel1
Port-channel1 is up, line protocol is up (connected)
  Hardware is EtherChannel, address is 0cd9.96e8.8a02 (bia
0cd9.96e8.8a02)
  MTU 1500 bytes, BW 200000 Kbit/sec, DLY 100 usec,
    reliability 255/255, txload 1/255, rxload 1/255
  Encapsulation ARPA, loopback not set
<Output omitted>
```

Verifies the interface status.

Figure 5-9   Verifying EtherChannel

Example 5-1   Verifying EtherChannel with a One-Line Summary per Channel Group

```
S1# show etherchannel summary
Flags:  D - down         P - bundled in port-channel
        I - stand-alone  s - suspended
        H - Hot-standby (LACP only)
        R - Layer3       S - Layer2
        U - in use       f - failed to allocate aggregator
        M - not in use, minimum links not met
        u - unsuitable for bundling
        w - waiting to be aggregated
        d - default port


Number of channel-groups in use: 1
Number of aggregators:           1


Group  Port-channel  Protocol     Ports
------+-------------+-----------+------------------------------------------
1      Po1(SU)        LACP        Fa0/1(P)    Fa0/2(P)
```

The interface bundle consists of the FastEthernet0/1 and FastEthernet0/2 interfaces. The group is a *Layer 2 EtherChannel* and it is in use, as indicated by the letters SU next to the port channel number.

Use the **show etherchannel port-channel** command to display information about a specific port channel interface, as shown in Example 5-2. In the example, the Port Channel 1 interface consists of two physical interfaces, FastEthernet0/1 and

FastEthernet0/2. It uses LACP in active mode. It is properly connected to another switch with a compatible configuration, which is why the port channel is said to be in use.

Example 5-2   Verifying EtherChannel by Displaying Port Channel Information

```
S1# show etherchannel port-channel
Channel-group listing:
----------------------
Group: 1
----------
Port-channels in the group:
--------------------------
Port-channel: Po1    (Primary Aggregator)
------------
Age of the Port-channel   = 0d:06h:23m:49s
Logical slot/port   = 2/1          Number of ports = 2
HotStandBy port = null
Port state          = Port-channel Ag-Inuse
Protocol            =   LACP
Port security       = Disabled
Ports in the Port-channel:
Index   Load   Port     EC state          No of bits
------+------+------+------------------+-----------
  0     55     Fa0/1    Active                4
  1     45     Fa0/2    Active                4
Time since last port bundled:      0d:05h:52m:59s      Fa0/2
Time since last port Un-bundled: 0d:05h:53m:05s      Fa0/2
```

On any physical interface member of an EtherChannel bundle, the **show interfaces etherchannel** command can provide information about the role of the interface in the EtherChannel, as shown in Example 5-3. The interface FastEthernet 0/1 is part of the EtherChannel bundle 1. The protocol for this EtherChannel is LACP.

Example 5-3   Verifying EtherChannel by Displaying the Role of a Particular Interface

```
S1# show interfaces f0/1 etherchannel
Port state     = Up Mstr Assoc In-Bndl
Channel group = 1              Mode = Active          Gcchange = -
Port-channel = Po1             GC  =   -              Pseudo port-channel = Po1
Port index    = 0              Load = 0x00            Protocol =   LACP
Flags: S - Device is sending Slow LACPDUs   F - Device is sending fast LACPDUs.
       A - Device is in active mode.        P - Device is in passive mode.
Local information:
                         LACP port    Admin    Oper    Port      Port
```

```
Port        Flags   State     Priority      Key       Key      Number      State
Fa0/1       SA      bndl      32768         0x1       0x1      0x102       0x3D
Partner's information:
                    LACP port                         Admin  Oper    Port    Port
Port        Flags   Priority  Dev ID           Age    key    Key     Number  State
Fa0/1       SA      32768     0cd9.96d2.4000   13s    0x0    0x1     0x102   0x3D
Age of the port in the current state: 0d:06h:06m:51s
```

Activity 5.2.2.1: Verifying EtherChannel

Go to the online course to use the Syntax Checker in the fifth graphic to verify EtherChannel on switch S1.

Troubleshooting EtherChannel (5.2.2.2)

All interfaces within an EtherChannel must have the same configuration of speed and duplex mode, native and allowed VLANs on trunks, and access VLAN on access ports:

- Assign all ports in the EtherChannel to the same VLAN, or configure them as trunks. Ports with different native VLANs cannot form an EtherChannel.

- When configuring an EtherChannel from trunk ports, verify that the trunking mode is the same on all the trunks. Inconsistent trunk modes on EtherChannel ports can cause EtherChannel not to function and ports to be shut down (errdisable state).

- An EtherChannel supports the same allowed range of VLANs on all the ports. If the allowed range of VLANs is not the same, the ports do not form an EtherChannel even when PAgP is set to the auto or desirable mode.

- The dynamic negotiation options for PAgP and LACP must be compatibly configured on both ends of the EtherChannel.

Note

It is easy to confuse PAgP or LACP with Dynamic Trunking Protocol (DTP), because they both are protocols used to automate behavior on trunk links. PAgP and LACP are used for link aggregation (EtherChannel). DTP is used for automating the creation of trunk links. When an EtherChannel trunk is configured, typically EtherChannel (PAgP or LACP) is configured first and then DTP.

In Figure 5-10, interfaces F0/1 and F0/2 on switches S1 and S2 are connected with an EtherChannel. The output indicates that the EtherChannel is down.

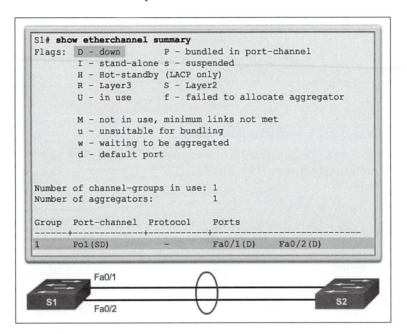

```
S1# show etherchannel summary
Flags:  D - down        P - bundled in port-channel
        I - stand-alone s - suspended
        H - Hot-standby (LACP only)
        R - Layer3       S - Layer2
        U - in use       f - failed to allocate aggregator

        M - not in use, minimum links not met
        u - unsuitable for bundling
        w - waiting to be aggregated
        d - default port


Number of channel-groups in use: 1
Number of aggregators:           1

Group  Port-channel  Protocol    Ports
------+-------------+-----------+-----------------------------
1      Po1(SD)           -        Fa0/1(D)    Fa0/2(D)
```

Fa0/1

S1

Fa0/2

S2

Figure 5-10   Troubleshooting EtherChannel

In Example 5-4, more detailed output indicates that there are incompatible PAgP modes configured on S1 and S2.

Example 5-4   Troubleshooting EtherChannel by Displaying Switch Configurations

```
S1# show run | begin interface Port-channel
interface Port-channel1
 switchport mode trunk
!
interface FastEthernet0/1
 switchport mode trunk
 channel-group 1 mode on
!
interface FastEthernet0/2
 switchport mode trunk
 channel-group 1 mode on
!
<output omitted>
S2# show run | begin interface Port-channel
interface Port-channel1
 switchport mode trunk
!
```

```
interface FastEthernet0/1
 switchport mode trunk
 channel-group 1 mode desirable
!
interface FastEthernet0/2
 switchport mode trunk
 channel-group 1 mode desirable
!
<output omitted>
```

In Example 5-5, the PAgP mode on the EtherChannel is changed to desirable and the EtherChannel becomes active.

Example 5-5   Changing the PAgP Mode to Resolve the EtherChannel Issue

```
S1(config)# no interface Port-channel 1
S1(config)# interface range f0/1 - 2
S1(config-if-range)# channel-group 1 mode desirable
Creating a port-channel interface Port-channel 1
S1(config-if-range)# no shutdown
S1(config-if-range)# interface Port-channel 1
S1(config-if)# switchport mode trunk
S1(config-if)# end
S1# show etherchannel summary
Flags:  D - down        P - bundled in port-channel
        I - stand-alone s - suspended
        H - Hot-standby (LACP only)
        R - Layer3       S - Layer2
        U - in use       f - failed to allocate aggregator
        M - not in use, minimum links not met
        u - unsuitable for bundling
        w - waiting to be aggregated
        d - default port
Number of channel-groups in use: 1
Number of aggregators:           1
Group  Port-channel  Protocol    Ports
------+-------------+-----------+-----------------------------------------------
1      Po1(SU)          PAgP     Fa0/1(P)    Fa0/2(P)
```

Note

EtherChannel and spanning tree must interoperate. For this reason, the order in which EtherChannel-related commands are entered is important, which is why (in Example 5-5) you see interface Port-Channel 1 removed and then re-added with the **channel-group** command, as opposed to directly changed. If one tries to change the configuration directly, spanning tree errors cause the associated ports to go into the blocking or errdisabled state.

Packet Tracer Activity 5.2.2.3: Troubleshooting EtherChannel

Four switches were recently configured by a junior technician. Users are complaining that the network is running slowly and would like you to investigate.

Lab 5.2.2.4: Troubleshooting EtherChannel

In this lab, you will complete the following objectives:

- Part 1: Build the Network and Load Device Configurations
- Part 2: Troubleshoot EtherChannel

Summary (5.3)

Class Activity 5.3.1.1: Linking Up

Many bottlenecks occur in your small- to medium-sized business network, even though you have configured VLANs, STP, and other network traffic options on the company's switches.

Instead of keeping the switches as they are currently configured, you would like to try EtherChannel as an option for at least part of the network to see whether it will decrease traffic congestion between your access and distribution layer switches.

Your company uses Catalyst 3560 switches at the distribution layer and Catalyst 2960 and 2950 switches at the access layer of the network. To verify whether these switches can perform EtherChannel, you visit the System Requirements to Implement EtherChannel on Catalyst Switches website. This site allows you to gather more information to determine whether EtherChannel is a good option for the equipment and network currently in place.

After researching the models, you decide to use a simulation software program to practice configuring EtherChannel before implementing it live on your network. As a part of this procedure, you ensure that the equipment simulated in Packet Tracer will support these practice configurations.

Packet Tracer Activity 5.3.1.2: Skills Integration Challenge

In this activity, two routers are configured to communicate with each other. You are responsible for configuring subinterfaces to communicate with the switches. You will configure VLANs, trunking, and EtherChannel with PVST. The Internet devices are all preconfigured.

EtherChannel aggregates multiple switched links together to load-balance over redundant paths between two devices. All ports in one EtherChannel must have the same speed, duplex setting, and VLAN information on all interfaces on the devices at both ends. Settings configured in the port channel interface configuration mode are also applied to the individual interfaces in that EtherChannel. Settings configured on individual interfaces are not applied to the EtherChannel or to the other interfaces in the EtherChannel.

PAgP is a Cisco-proprietary protocol that aids in the automatic creation of EtherChannel links. PAgP modes are on, PAgP desirable, and PAgP auto. LACP is part of an IEEE specification that also allows multiple physical ports to be bundled into one logical channel. The LACP modes are on, LACP active, and LACP passive. PAgP and LACP do not interoperate. The on mode is repeated in both PAgP and LACP because it creates an EtherChannel unconditionally, without the use of PAgP or LACP. The default for EtherChannel is that no mode is configured.

Practice

The following activities provide practice with the topics introduced in this chapter. The Labs and Class Activities are available in the companion *Switched Networks Lab Manual* (ISBN 978-1-58713-372-5). The Packet Tracer Activities PKA files are found in the online course.

Class Activities

- Class Activity 5.0.1.2: Imagine This
- Class Activity 5.3.1.1: Linking Up

Labs

- Lab 5.2.1.4: Configuring EtherChannel
- Lab 5.2.2.4: Troubleshooting EtherChannel

Packet Tracer
☐ Activity

Packet Tracer Activities

- Packet Tracer Activity 5.2.1.3: Configuring EtherChannel
- Packet Tracer Activity 5.2.2.3: Troubleshooting EtherChannel

Check Your Understanding Questions

Complete all the review questions listed here to test your understanding of the topics and concepts in this chapter. The appendix "Answers to 'Check Your Understanding' Questions" lists the answers.

1. What are advantages of using EtherChannel technology? (Choose three.)

    A. EtherChannel uses multiple logical links to provide redundancy.

    B. Configuration tasks can be done on the EtherChannel interface.

    C. There is no need to upgrade links to faster connections to increase bandwidth.

    D. Load balancing is not needed with EtherChannel.

    E. The Spanning Tree Protocol shuts down the unused interfaces in the bundle to avoid loops.

    F. A spanning tree recalculation is not required when a single link within the channel goes down.

2. See Figure 5-11. On the basis of the output that is shown, what can be determined about the EtherChannel bundle?

    A. The EtherChannel bundle is down.

    B. The EtherChannel bundle is operating at both Layer 2 and Layer 3.

    C. Two Gigabit Ethernet ports are used to form the EtherChannel.

    D. A Cisco-proprietary protocol was used to negotiate the EtherChannel link.

```
S_ATC_1.1# show etherchannel summary
Flags:  D - down         P - in port-channel
        I - stand-alone  s - suspended
        H - Hot-standby (LACP only)
        R - Layer3        S - Layer2
        U - in use        f - failed to allocate aggregator
        u - unsuitable for bundling
        w - waiting to be aggregated
        d - default port


Number of channel-groups in use: 1
Number of aggregators:           1

Group  Port-channel  Protocol    Ports
------+-------------+-----------+----------------------

1      Po1(SU)          PAgP     Fa0/1(P) Fa0/2(P)
```

Figure 5-11   EtherChannel Output

3. See Figure 5-12. An administrator wants to form an EtherChannel between the two switches by using the Port Aggregation Protocol. If switch S1 is configured to be in auto mode, which mode should be configured on S2 to form the EtherChannel?

   A. On

   B. Auto

   C. Desirable

   D. Off

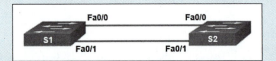

Figure 5-12   PAgP EtherChannel

4. Which of the following interface parameters must match for an EtherChannel to form? (Choose three.)

   A. Allowed VLANs

   B. EtherChannel mode

   C. Native VLAN

   D. PortFast mode

   E. Spanning tree state

   F. Trunking mode

5. What will happen if a network administrator puts a port that is part of an EtherChannel bundle into a different VLAN than the other ports in that bundle?

   A. The EtherChannel bundle will stay up only if PAgP is used.

   B. The EtherChannel bundle will stay up only if LACP is used.

   C. The EtherChannel bundle will stay up if either PAgP or LACP is used.

   D. The EtherChannel bundle will stay up if the ports were configured with no negotiation between the switches to form the EtherChannel.

   E. The EtherChannel will fail.

6. When a range of ports is being configured for EtherChannel, which mode will configure PAgP so that it initiates the EtherChannel negotiation?

   A. Active

   B. Auto

   C. Desirable

   D. Passive

7. See Figure 5-13. An administrator tried to implement an EtherChannel between two switches by grouping the six physical ports as shown. However, the administrator was not successful. What is the reason for that?

   A. An EtherChannel link can only be created between Layer 3 switches.

   B. An EtherChannel link can only be formed by grouping interfaces of the same type.

   C. An EtherChannel link can only be implemented on Gigabit Ethernet interfaces.

   D. An EtherChannel link can only be implemented on Fast Ethernet interfaces.

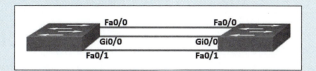

Figure 5-13   EtherChannel with Six Physical Ports

8. Which of the following protocols are used to implement EtherChannel? (Choose two.)

   A. Spanning Tree Protocol

   B. Rapid Spanning Tree Protocol

   C. Port Aggregation Protocol

   D. Link Aggregation Control Protocol

   E. Cisco Discovery Protocol

9. Fill in the blank. Which command displays only one line of information per port channel? _Show etherchannel summary_

10. Which statement is true about EtherChannel technology?

    A. Configuration tasks must be done on individual ports.

    B. EtherChannel relies on existing switch ports.

    C. Links must be upgraded to support EtherChannel.

    D. STP does not run on EtherChannel links.

CHAPTER 6

Inter-VLAN Routing

Objectives

Upon completion of this chapter, you will be able to answer the following questions:

- How do you describe the three primary options for enabling inter-VLAN routing?

- How do you configure legacy inter-VLAN routing?

- How do you configure router-on-a-stick inter-VLAN routing?

- How do you troubleshoot common inter-VLAN configuration issues?

- How do you troubleshoot common IP addressing issues in an inter-VLAN routed environment?

- How do you configure inter-VLAN routing using Layer 3 switching?

- How do you troubleshoot inter-VLAN routing in a Layer 3 switched environment?

Key Terms

This chapter uses the following key terms. You can find the definitions in the Glossary.

Introduction (6.0.1.1)

We have seen that using VLANs to segment a switched network provides improved performance, manageability, and security. Trunks are used to carry information for multiple VLANs between devices. However, because these VLANs segment the network, a Layer 3 process is required to allow traffic to move from one network segment to another.

Routing is the Layer 3 process of determining where to send data packets that are destined for addresses outside of the local network. The Layer 3 routing process can either be implemented using a router or a Layer 3 switch. These devices gather and maintain routing information to enable the transmission and receipt of data packets. The use of a Layer 3 device provides a method for controlling the flow of traffic between network segments, including network segments created by VLANs.

This chapter focuses on the methods used for the implementation of *inter-VLAN routing*. It includes configurations for both the use of a router and a Layer 3 switch. It also describes issues encountered when implementing inter-VLAN routing and standard troubleshooting techniques.

Class Activity 6.0.1.2: Switching to Local-Network Channels

You work for a small- to medium-size business. As the network administrator, you are responsible for ensuring that your network operates efficiently and securely.

Several years ago, you created VLANs on your only switch for two of your departments, Accounting and Sales. As the business has grown, it has become apparent that sometimes these two departments must share company files and network resources.

You discuss this scenario with network administrators in a few branches of your company. They tell you to consider using inter-VLAN routing.

Research the concept of inter-VLAN routing.

Design a simple presentation to show your manager how you would use inter-VLAN routing to allow the Accounting and Sales departments to remain separate, but share company files and network resources.

Inter-VLAN Routing Configuration (6.1)

This section focuses on the configuration of the first two of the three major methods of inter-VLAN routing: legacy, router-on-a-stick, and multilayer switching. First, the three methods of inter-VLAN routing are explained.

Inter-VLAN Routing Operation (6.1.1)

Inter-VLAN routing is one of those networking topics where understanding the underlying operation makes configuration of the participating devices quite intuitive.

What Is Inter-VLAN Routing? (6.1.1.1)

VLANs are used to segment switched networks. Layer 2 switches, such as the Catalyst 2960 Series, can be configured by a network professional with over 4000 VLANs. However, Layer 2 switches have very limited IPv4 and IPv6 functionality and cannot perform the routing function of routers. While Layer 2 switches are gaining more IP functionality, such as the ability to perform static routing, these switches do not support dynamic routing. With the large number of VLANs possible on these switches, static routing is insufficient.

A VLAN is a broadcast domain, so computers on separate VLANs are unable to communicate without the intervention of a routing device. Any device that supports Layer 3 routing, such as a router or a multilayer switch, can be used to perform the necessary routing functionality. Regardless of the device used, the process of forwarding network traffic from one VLAN to another VLAN using routing is known as inter-VLAN routing. Figure 6-1 illustrates router-based inter-VLAN routing as a process for forwarding network traffic from one VLAN to another VLAN using a router. Recall that a VLAN *is* a broadcast domain, so VLAN traffic stays within the VLAN without the intervention of a Layer 3 device.

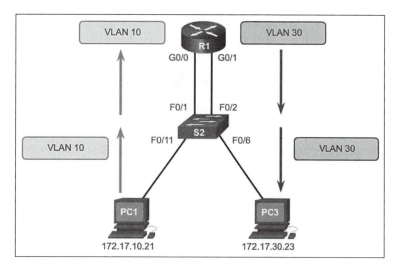

Figure 6-1   What Is Inter-VLAN Routing?

Legacy Inter-VLAN Routing (6.1.1.2)

Historically, the first solution for inter-VLAN routing relied on routers with multiple physical interfaces. Each interface had to be connected to a separate network and configured with a distinct subnet.

In this legacy approach, inter-VLAN routing is performed by connecting different physical router interfaces to different physical switch ports. The switch ports connected to the router are placed in access mode, and each physical interface is assigned to a different VLAN. Each router interface can then accept traffic from the VLAN associated with the switch interface that it is connected to, and traffic can be routed to the other VLANs connected to the other interfaces.

Figure 6-2 illustrates the topology for *legacy inter-VLAN routing*.

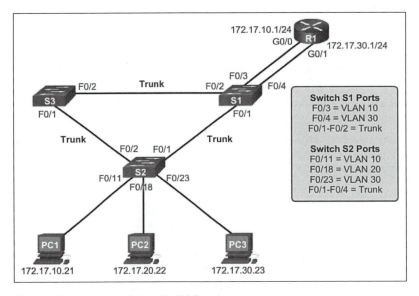

Figure 6-2   Legacy Inter-VLAN Routing

Video

Video 6.1.1.2: Legacy Inter-VLAN Routing

Go to the online course to view an animation of legacy inter-VLAN routing, with a router configured with two separate physical interfaces to interact with different VLANs and route between them.

Note

The legacy inter-VLAN method is not efficient and is generally no longer implemented in switched networks. It is shown in this course for explanation purposes only.

Router-on-a-Stick Inter-VLAN Routing (6.1.1.3)

While legacy inter-VLAN routing requires multiple physical interfaces on both the router and the switch, a more common, present-day implementation of inter-VLAN routing does not. Instead, some router software permits configuring a router interface as a trunk link, meaning that only one physical interface is required on the router and the switch to route packets between multiple VLANs.

Router-on-a-stick is a type of router configuration in which a single physical interface routes traffic between multiple VLANs on a network. As seen in Figure 6-3, the router is connected to switch S1 using a single, physical network connection (a trunk).

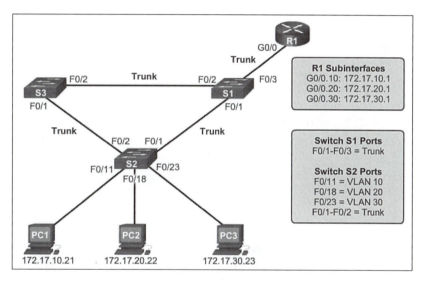

Figure 6-3   Router-on-a-Stick Inter-VLAN Routing

The router interface is configured to operate as a trunk link and is connected to a switch port that is configured in trunk mode. The router performs inter-VLAN routing by accepting VLAN-tagged traffic on the trunk interface coming from the adjacent switch, and then internally routing between the VLANs using subinterfaces. The router then forwards the routed traffic, VLAN-tagged for the destination VLAN, out the same physical interface as it used to receive the traffic.

Subinterfaces are software-based virtual interfaces, associated with a single physical interface. Subinterfaces are configured in software on a router, and each subinterface is independently configured with an IP address and VLAN assignment. Subinterfaces are configured for different subnets corresponding to their VLAN assignment to facilitate logical routing. After a routing decision is made based on the destination VLAN, the data frames are VLAN-tagged and sent back out the physical interface.

Video

Video 6.1.1.3: Router-on-a-Stick Inter-VLAN Routing

Go to the online course to view the animation of how router-on-a-stick performs its routing function.

Note

The router-on-a-stick method of inter-VLAN routing does not scale beyond 50 VLANs.

Multilayer Switch Inter-VLAN Routing (6.1.1.4)

The router-on-a-stick implementation of inter-VLAN routing requires only one physical interface on a router and one interface on a switch, simplifying the cabling of the router. However, in other implementations of inter-VLAN routing, a dedicated router is not required.

Multilayer switches can perform Layer 2 and Layer 3 functions, replacing the need for dedicated routers to perform basic routing on a network. Multilayer switches support dynamic routing and inter-VLAN routing, as illustrated in Figure 6-4.

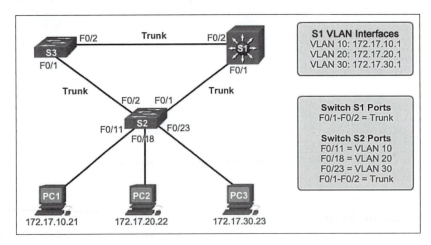

Figure 6-4   Switch-Based Inter-VLAN Routing

Video

Video 6.1.1.4: Switch-Based Inter-VLAN Routing

Go to the online course to view an animation of how a multilayer switch routes between VLANs.

To enable a multilayer switch to perform routing functions, the multilayer switch must have IP routing enabled.

Multilayer switching is more scalable than any other inter-VLAN routing implementation. This is because routers have a limited number of available ports to connect to networks. Additionally, for interfaces that are configured as a trunk line, limited amounts of traffic can be accommodated on that line at one time.

With a multilayer switch, traffic is routed internal to the switch device, which means that packets are not filtered down a single trunk line to obtain new VLAN-tagging information. A multilayer switch does not, however, completely replace the functionality of a router. Routers support a significant number of additional features, such as the ability to implement greater security controls. Rather, a multilayer switch can be thought of as a Layer 2 device that is upgraded to have some routing capabilities.

Note

In this course, configuring inter-VLAN routing on a switch is restricted to configuring static routes on a 2960 switch, which is the only routing functionality supported on the 2960 switches. The 2960 switch supports up to 16 static routes (including user-configured routes and the default route) and any directly connected routes and default routes for the management interface; the 2960 switch can have up to eight switch virtual interfaces (SVI) and an IP address can be assigned to each SVI. To enable the routing functionality on the 2960 switch, the **sdm prefer lanbase-routing** global configuration command must be entered and the switch must be reloaded. For a full-featured, relatively inexpensive multilayer switch, the Cisco Catalyst 3560 Series switches support the EIGRP, OSPF, and BGP routing protocols.

Interactive Graphic

Activity 6.1.1.5: Identify Types of Inter-VLAN Routing

Go to the online course to perform this practice activity.

Configure Legacy Inter-VLAN Routing (6.1.2)

In this topic, you learn how to configure inter-VLAN routing as it was done in the early 1990s before Ethernet interfaces on routers supported VLAN trunking. This information is more of historical interest than anything. The nice thing about legacy inter-VLAN routing configuration is that it reinforces the concept of routing between VLANs in a very physical way.

Configure Legacy Inter-VLAN Routing: Preparation (6.1.2.1)

Legacy inter-VLAN routing requires routers to have multiple physical interfaces, as depicted in Figure 6-5. The router accomplishes the routing by having each of its physical interfaces connected to a unique VLAN. Each interface is also configured with an IP address for the subnet associated with the particular VLAN to which it is connected. By configuring the IP addresses on the physical interfaces, network devices connected to each of the VLANs can communicate with the router using the physical interface connected to the same VLAN. In this configuration, network devices can use the router as a gateway to access the devices connected to the other VLANs.

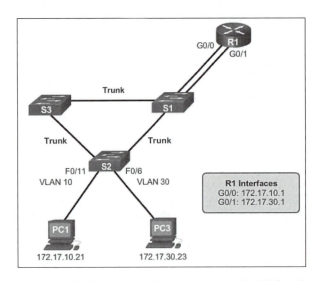

Figure 6-5   Router Interfaces and Inter-VLAN Routing

The routing process requires the source device to determine whether the destination device is local or remote to the local subnet. The source device accomplishes this by comparing the source and destination IP addresses against the subnet mask. When the destination IP address has been determined to be on a remote network, the source device must identify where it needs to forward the packet to reach the destination device. The source device examines the local routing table to determine where it needs to send the data. Devices use their default gateway as the Layer 2 destination for all traffic that must leave the local subnet. The default gateway is the route that the device uses when it has no other explicitly defined route to the destination network. The IP address of the router interface on the local subnet acts as the default gateway for the sending device.

When the source device has determined that the packet must travel through the local router interface on the connected VLAN, the source device sends out an ARP request to determine the MAC address of the local router interface. When the router sends its ARP reply back to the source device, the source device can use the MAC address to finish framing the packet before it sends it out on the network as unicast traffic.

Because the Ethernet frame has the destination MAC address of the router interface, the switch knows exactly which switch port to forward the unicast traffic out of to reach the router interface for that VLAN. When the frame arrives at the router, the router removes the source and destination MAC address information to examine the destination IP address of the packet. The router compares the destination address to entries in its routing table to determine where it needs to forward the data to reach its final destination. If the router determines that the destination network is a locally connected network, as is the case with inter-VLAN routing, the router sends an ARP request out the interface physically connected to the destination VLAN. The destination device responds to the router with its MAC address, which the router then uses to frame the packet. The router then sends the unicast traffic to the switch, which forwards it out the port where the destination device is connected.

Video

Video 6.1.2.1: Router Interfaces and Inter-VLAN Routing

Go to the online course to view an animation about how legacy inter-VLAN routing is accomplished.

Even though there are many steps in the process of inter-VLAN routing, when two devices on different VLANs communicate through a router, the entire process happens in a fraction of a second.

Configure Legacy Inter-VLAN Routing: Switch Configuration (6.1.2.2)

To configure legacy inter-VLAN routing, start by configuring the switch.

As shown in Figure 6-6, Router R1 is connected to switch ports F0/4 and F0/5.

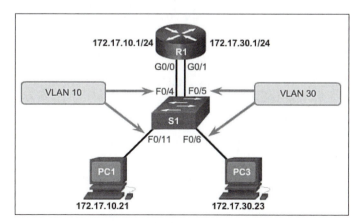

Figure 6-6   Configuring Legacy Inter-VLAN Routing

The command sequence for configuring switch S1 for legacy inter-VLAN routing is shown in Example 6-1. Ports F0/4 and F0/5 have been configured for VLANs 10 and 30, respectively.

Example 6-1   Legacy Inter-VLAN Routing Switch Configuration

```
S1(config)# vlan 10
S1(config-vlan)# vlan 30
S1(config-vlan)# interface f0/11
S1(config-if)# switchport access vlan 10
S1(config-if)# interface f0/4
S1(config-if)# switchport access vlan 10
S1(config-if)# interface f0/6
S1(config-if)# switchport access vlan 30
S1(config-if)# interface f0/5
S1(config-if)# switchport access vlan 30
S1(config-if)# end
```

Use the **vlan** *vlan-id* global configuration mode command to create VLANs. In Example 6-1, VLANs 10 and 30 were created on switch S1.

After the VLANs have been created, the switch ports are assigned to the appropriate VLANs. The **switchport access vlan** *vlan-id* command is executed from interface configuration mode on the switch for each interface to which the router connects.

In Example 6-1, interfaces F0/4 and F0/11 have been assigned to VLAN 10 using the **switchport access vlan 10** command. The same process is used to assign interface F0/5 and F0/6 on switch S1 to VLAN 30.

Configure Legacy Inter-VLAN Routing: Router Interface Configuration (6.1.2.3)

Next, the router can be configured to perform inter-VLAN routing.

Router interfaces are configured in a manner similar to configuring VLAN interfaces on switches. To configure a specific interface, change to interface configuration mode from global configuration mode.

As shown in Example 6-2, each interface of the router in Figure 6-6 is configured with an IP address using the **ip address** *ip-address subnet-mask* command in interface configuration mode. In Example 6-2, interface G0/0 is configured with IP address 172.17.10.1 and subnet mask 255.255.255.0 using the **ip address 172.17.10.1 255.255.255.0** command.

Example 6-2   Legacy Inter-VLAN Routing Router Configuration

```
R1(config)# interface g0/0
R1(config-if)# ip address 172.17.10.1 255.255.255.0
R1(config-if)# no shutdown
*Mar 20 01:42:12.951: %LINK-3-UPDOWN: Interface GigabitEthernet0/0, changed state to
  up
*Mar 20 01:42:13.951: %LINEPROTO-5-UPDOWN: Line protocol on Interface
  GigabitEthernet0/0, changed state to up
R1(config-if)# interface g0/1
R1(config-if)# ip address 172.17.30.1 255.255.255.0
R1(config-if)# no shutdown
*Mar 20 01:42:54.951: %LINK-3-UPDOWN: Interface GigabitEthernet0/1, changed state to
  up
*Mar 20 01:42:55.951: %LINEPROTO-5-UPDOWN: Line protocol on Interface
  GigabitEthernet0/1, changed state to up
```

Router interfaces are disabled by default and must be enabled using the **no shutdown** command before they are used. After the **no shutdown** interface configuration mode command has been issued, a notification displays, indicating that the interface state has changed to up. This indicates that the interface is now enabled.

The process is repeated for all router interfaces. Each router interface must be assigned to a unique subnet for routing to occur. In Example 6-2, the other router interface, G0/1, has been configured to use IP address 172.17.30.1, which is on a different subnet than interface G0/0.

After the IP addresses are assigned to the physical interfaces and the interfaces are enabled, the router is capable of performing inter-VLAN routing.

Examine the routing table using the **show ip route** command, as shown in Example 6-3.

Example 6-3   Verifying Legacy Inter-VLAN Routing on a Router

```
R1# show ip route
Codes: L - local, C - connected, S - static, R - RIP, M - mobile, B - BGP
       D - EIGRP, EX - EIGRP external, O - OSPF, IA - OSPF inter area
       N1 - OSPF NSSA external type 1, N2 - OSPF NSSA external type 2
       E1 - OSPF external type 1, E2 - OSPF external type 2
       i - IS-IS, su - IS-IS summary, L1 - IS-IS level-1, L2 - IS-IS level-2
       ia - IS-IS inter area, * - candidate default, U - per-user static route
       o - ODR, P - periodic downloaded static route, H - NHRP, l - LISP
       + - replicated route, % - next hop override
Gateway of last resort is not set

      172.17.0.0/16 is variably subnetted, 4 subnets, 2 masks
```

```
C        172.17.10.0/24 is directly connected, GigabitEthernet0/0
L        172.17.10.1/32 is directly connected, GigabitEthernet0/0
C        172.17.30.0/24 is directly connected, GigabitEthernet0/1
L        172.17.30.1/32 is directly connected, GigabitEthernet0/1
```

In Example 6-3, there are two routes visible in the routing table. One route is to the 172.17.10.0 subnet, which is attached to the local interface G0/0. The other route is to the 172.17.30.0 subnet, which is attached to the local interface G0/1. The router uses this routing table to determine where to send the traffic it receives. For example, if the router receives a packet on interface G0/0 destined for the 172.17.30.0 subnet, the router would identify that it should send the packet out interface G0/1 to reach hosts on the 172.17.30.0 subnet.

Notice the letter C to the left of each of the route entries for the VLANs. This letter indicates that the route is associated to a connected interface, which is also indicated in the route entry. Using the output in this example, if traffic was destined for the 172.17.30.0 subnet, the router would forward the traffic out interface G0/1.

Lab 6.1.2.4: Configuring Per-Physical-Interface Inter-VLAN Routing

In this lab, you will complete the following objectives:

- Part 1: Build the Network and Configure Basic Device Settings
- Part 2: Configure Switches with VLANs and Trunking
- Part 3: Verify Trunking, VLANs, Routing, and Connectivity

Configure Router-on-a-Stick Inter-VLAN Routing (6.1.3)

Before multilayer switch prices lowered enough that a small business could afford one, the most common form of inter-VLAN routing was provided by the "router-on-a-stick" method. This method of inter-VLAN routing served its purpose mostly during a short period of time, before the drop in multilayer switch prices and after the addition of router Ethernet interface support for VLAN trunking. Again, while it is not common anymore to use this method of inter-VLAN routing, this approach does effectively reinforce the concept of routing between VLANs, albeit in a manner not quite as physical as legacy inter-VLAN routing.

Configure Router-on-a-Stick: Preparation (6.1.3.1)

Legacy inter-VLAN routing using physical interfaces has a significant limitation. Routers have a limited number of physical interfaces to connect to different VLANs.

As the number of VLANs increases on a network, having one physical router interface per VLAN quickly exhausts the physical interface capacity of a router. An alternative in larger networks is to use VLAN trunking and *subinterfaces*. VLAN trunking allows a single physical router interface to route traffic for multiple VLANs. This technique is termed router-on-a-stick and uses virtual subinterfaces on the router to overcome the hardware limitations based on physical router interfaces.

Subinterfaces are software-based virtual interfaces that are assigned to physical interfaces. Each subinterface is configured independently with its own IP address and subnet mask. This allows a single physical interface to simultaneously be part of multiple logical networks.

When configuring inter-VLAN routing using the router-on-a-stick model, the physical interface of the router must be connected to a trunk link on the adjacent switch. On the router, subinterfaces are created for each unique VLAN on the network. Each subinterface is assigned an IP address specific to its subnet/VLAN and is also configured to tag frames for that VLAN. This way, the router can keep the traffic from each subinterface separated as it traverses the trunk link back to the switch.

Functionally, the router-on-a-stick model is the same as using the legacy inter-VLAN routing model, but instead of using the physical interfaces to perform the routing, subinterfaces of a single physical interface are used.

In Figure 6-7, PC1 wants to communicate with PC3. PC1 is on VLAN 10 and PC3 is on VLAN 30. For PC1 to communicate with PC3, PC1 must have its data routed through router R1 through subinterfaces.

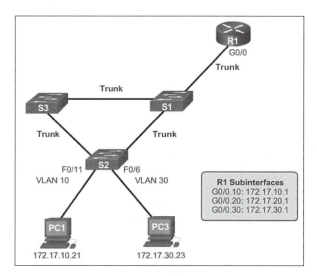

Figure 6-7 Router Subinterfaces and Inter-VLAN Routing

Video

Video 6.1.3.1: Router Subinterfaces and Inter-VLAN Routing

Go to the online course to view an animation about how subinterfaces are used to route between VLANs.

Using trunk links and subinterfaces decreases the number of router and switch ports used. Not only can this save money, but it can also reduce configuration complexity. Consequently, the router subinterface approach can scale to a much larger number of VLANs than a configuration with one physical interface per VLAN design.

Configure Router-on-a-Stick: Switch Configuration (6.1.3.2)

To enable inter-VLAN routing using router-on-a stick, start by enabling trunking on the switch port that is connected to the router.

In Figure 6-8, Router R1 is connected to switch S1 on trunk port F0/5. VLANs 10 and 30 are added to switch S1.

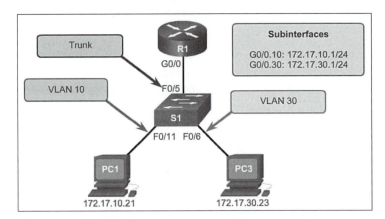

Figure 6-8 Configuring Router-on-a-Stick Inter-VLAN Routing

Because switch port F0/5 is configured as a trunk port, the port does not need to be assigned to any VLAN. To configure switch port F0/5 as a trunk port, execute the **switchport mode trunk** command in interface configuration mode for port F0/5.

> **Note**
>
> The router does not support the Dynamic Trunking Protocol (DTP), which is used by switches, so the following commands cannot be used: **switchport mode dynamic auto** or **switchport mode dynamic desirable**.

The router can now be configured to perform inter-VLAN routing.

Configure Router-on-a-Stick: Router Subinterface Configuration (6.1.3.3)

The configuration of the router is different when a router-on-a-stick configuration is used compared to legacy inter-VLAN routing. Figure 6-8 shows that multiple subinterfaces are configured.

Each subinterface is created using the **interface** *interface-id subinterface-id* global configuration mode command. The syntax for the subinterface is the physical interface, in this case **g0/0**, followed by a period and a subinterface number. The subinterface number is configurable, but it typically reflects the VLAN number. In Example 6-4, the subinterfaces use **10** and **30** as subinterface numbers to make it easier to remember the VLANs with which they are associated. Subinterface GigabitEthernet0/0.10 is created using the **interface g0/0.10** global configuration mode command.

Before assigning an IP address to a subinterface, the subinterface must be configured to operate on a specific VLAN using the **encapsulation dot1q** *vlan-id* command. In Example 6-4, subinterface G0/0.10 is assigned to VLAN 10.

Note

There is a **native** keyword option that can be appended to this command to set the IEEE 802.1Q native VLAN. In this example, the **native** keyword option was excluded to leave the native VLAN default to VLAN 1.

Next, assign the IP address for the subinterface using the **ip address** *ip-address subnet-mask* subinterface configuration mode command. In Example 6-4, subinterface G0/0.10 is assigned the IP address 172.17.10.1 using the **ip address 172.17.10.1 255.255.255.0** command.

This process is repeated for all router subinterfaces required to route between the VLANs configured on the network. Each router subinterface must be assigned an IP address on a unique subnet for routing to occur. For example, the other router subinterface, G0/0.30, is configured to use IP address 172.17.30.1, which is on a different subnet from subinterface G0/0.10.

After a physical interface is enabled, subinterfaces will automatically be enabled upon configuration. Subinterfaces do not need to be enabled with the **no shutdown** command at the subinterface configuration mode level of the Cisco IOS Software.

If the physical interface is disabled, all subinterfaces are disabled. In Example 6-4, the **no shutdown** command is entered in interface configuration mode for interface G0/0, which in turn enables all the configured subinterfaces.

Individual subinterfaces can be administratively shut down with the **shutdown** command. Also, individual subinterfaces can be enabled independently with the **no shutdown** command in subinterface configuration mode.

Example 6-4   Configuring Router-on-a-Stick Inter-VLAN Routing on a Router

```
R1(config)# interface g0/0.10
R1(config-subif)# encapsulation dot1q 10
R1(config-subif)# ip address 172.17.10.1 255.255.255.0
R1(config-subif)# interface g0/0.30
R1(config-subif)# encapsulation dot1q 30
R1(config-subif)# ip address 172.17.30.1 255.255.255.0
R1(config-subif)# interface g0/0
R1(config-if)# no shutdown
R1(config-if)# end
R1#
*Mar 20 06:32:03.777: %LINK-3-UPDOWN: Interface GigabitEthernet0/0, changed state to
  down
*Mar 20 06:32:04.217: %SYS-5-CONFIG_I: Configured from console by console
*Mar 20 06:32:06.929: %LINK-3-UPDOWN: Interface GigabitEthernet0/0, changed state to
  up
*Mar 20 06:32:07.929: %LINEPROTO-5-UPDOWN: Line protocol on Interface
  GigabitEthernet0/0, changed state to up
```

Configure Router-on-a-Stick: Verifying Subinterfaces (6.1.3.4)

By default, Cisco routers are configured to route traffic between local subinterfaces. As a result, routing does not specifically need to be enabled.

In Example 6-5, the **show vlans** command displays information about the Cisco IOS VLAN subinterfaces. The output shows the two VLAN subinterfaces, GigabitEthernet0/0.10 and GigabitEthernet0/0.30.

Example 6-5   Verifying Router-on-a-Stick Inter-VLAN Routing on a Switch

```
R1# show vlans
Virtual LAN ID:  1 (IEEE 802.1Q Encapsulation)
   vLAN Trunk Interface:   GigabitEthernet0/0
 This is configured as native Vlan for the following interface(s) :
GigabitEthernet0/0    Native-vlan Tx-type: Untagged
    Protocols Configured:   Address:          Received:        Transmitted:
        Other                                  0                1
    0 packets, 0 bytes input
    1 packets, 18 bytes output
```

```
Virtual LAN ID:  10 (IEEE 802.1Q Encapsulation)
   vLAN Trunk Interface:   GigabitEthernet0/0.10
   Protocols Configured:   Address:            Received:         Transmitted:
        IP                 172.17.10.1             0                   0
      Other                                        0                   1
   0 packets, 0 bytes input
   1 packets, 46 bytes output
Virtual LAN ID:  30 (IEEE 802.1Q Encapsulation)
   vLAN Trunk Interface:   GigabitEthernet0/0.30
   Protocols Configured:   Address:            Received:         Transmitted:
        IP                 172.17.30.1             0                   0
      Other                                        0                   1
   0 packets, 0 bytes input
   1 packets, 46 bytes output
```

Next, examine the routing table using the **show ip route** command, as shown in Example 6-6. In Example 6-6, the routes defined in the routing table indicate that they are associated with specific subinterfaces, rather than separate physical interfaces. There are two routes in the routing table. One route is to the 172.17.10.0 subnet, which is attached to the local subinterface G0/0.10. The other route is to the 172.17.30.0 subnet, which is attached to the local subinterface G0/0.30. The router uses this routing table to determine where to send the traffic it receives. For example, if the router received a packet on subinterface G0/0.10 destined for the 172.17.30.0 subnet, the router would identify that it should send the packet out subinterface G0/0.30 to reach hosts on the 172.17.30.0 subnet.

Example 6-6   Verifying Router-on-a-Stick Inter-VLAN Routing on a Router

```
R1# show ip route
Codes: L - local, C - connected, S - static, R - RIP, M - mobile, B - BGP
       D - EIGRP, EX - EIGRP external, O - OSPF, IA - OSPF inter area
       N1 - OSPF NSSA external type 1, N2 - OSPF NSSA external type 2
       E1 - OSPF external type 1, E2 - OSPF external type 2
       i - IS-IS, su - IS-IS summary, L1 - IS-IS level-1, L2 - IS-IS level-2
       ia - IS-IS inter area, * - candidate default, U - per-user static route
       o - ODR, P - periodic downloaded static route, H - NHRP, l - LISP
       + - replicated route, % - next hop override
Gateway of last resort is not set
     172.17.0.0/16 is variably subnetted, 4 subnets, 2 masks
C       172.17.10.0/24 is directly connected, GigabitEthernet0/0.10
L       172.17.10.1/32 is directly connected, GigabitEthernet0/0.10
C       172.17.30.0/24 is directly connected, GigabitEthernet0/0.30
L       172.17.30.1/32 is directly connected, GigabitEthernet0/0.30
```

Activity 6.1.3.4: Configuring Router-on-a-Stick Inter-VLAN Routing

Go to the online course to use the Syntax Checker in the third graphic to configure and verify router-on-a-stick on R1.

Configure Router-on-a-Stick: Verifying Routing (6.1.3.5)

After the router and switch have been configured to perform inter-VLAN routing, the next step is to verify host-to-host connectivity. Access to devices on remote VLANs can be tested using the **ping** command.

In Figure 6-8, a **ping** and a **tracert** are initiated from PC1 to the destination address of PC3. The outputs are shown in Example 6-7.

Example 6-7   Ping and Tracert on a PC

```
PC1> ping 172.17.30.23

Pinging 172.17.30.23 with 32 bytes of data:
Reply from 172.17.30.23: bytes=32 time=17ms TTL=127
Reply from 172.17.30.23: bytes=32 time=15ms TTL=127
Reply from 172.17.30.23: bytes=32 time=18ms TTL=127
Reply from 172.17.30.23: bytes=32 time=19ms TTL=127

Ping statistics for 172.17.30.23:
    Packets: Sent = 4, Received = 4, Lost = 0 (0% loss),
Approximate round trip times in milli-seconds:
    Minimum = 15ms, Maximum = 19ms, Average = 17ms

PC1> tracert
Tracing route to 172.17.30.23 over a maximum of 30 hops:
  1    9 ms     7 ms     9 ms      172.17.10.1
  2   16 ms    15 ms    16 ms      172.17.30.23
Trace complete.
```

Ping Test

The **ping** command sends an ICMP echo request to the destination address. When a host receives an ICMP echo request, it responds with an ICMP echo reply to confirm that it received the ICMP echo request. The **ping** command calculates the elapsed time using the difference between the time the echo request was sent and the time the echo reply was received. This elapsed time is used to determine the latency of the connection. Successfully receiving a reply confirms that there is a path between the sending device and the receiving device.

Tracert Test

Tracert is a useful utility for confirming the routed path taken between two devices. On UNIX systems, the utility is specified by **traceroute**. Tracert also uses ICMP to determine the path taken, but it uses ICMP echo requests with specific time-to-live values defined on the frame.

The time-to-live value determines exactly how many router hops away the ICMP echo is allowed to reach. The first ICMP echo request is sent with a time-to-live value set to expire at the first router on route to the destination device.

When the ICMP echo request times out on the first route, an ICMP message is sent back from the router to the originating device. The device records the response from the router and proceeds to send out another ICMP echo request, but this time with a greater time-to-live value. This allows the ICMP echo request to traverse the first router and reach the second device en route to the final destination. The process repeats recursively until finally the ICMP echo request is sent all the way to the final destination device. After the **tracert** utility finishes running, it displays a list of ingress router interfaces that the ICMP echo request reached on its way to the destination.

In Example 6-7, the **ping** utility was able to send an ICMP echo request to the IP address of PC3. Also, the **tracert** utility confirms that the path to PC3 is through the 172.17.10.1 subinterface IP address of Router R1.

Packet Tracer Activity 6.1.3.6: Configuring Router-on-a-Stick Inter-VLAN Routing

In this activity, you will check for connectivity prior to implementing inter-VLAN routing. You will then configure VLANs and inter-VLAN routing. Finally, you will enable trunking and verify connectivity between VLANs.

Lab 6.1.3.7: Configuring 802.1Q Trunk-Based Inter-VLAN Routing

In this lab, you will complete the following objectives:

- Part 1: Build the Network and Configure Basic Device Settings
- Part 2: Configure Switches with VLANs and Trunking
- Part 3: Configure Trunk-Based Inter-VLAN Routing

Troubleshoot Inter-VLAN Routing (6.2)

Troubleshooting legacy and router-on-a-stick inter-VLAN routing is a straightforward process.

Inter-VLAN Configuration Issues (6.2.1)

Primary inter-VLAN routing configuration issues include switch port and router interface issues.

Switch Port Issues (6.2.1.1)

There are several common switch misconfigurations that can arise when configuring routing between multiple VLANs.

When using the legacy routing model for inter-VLAN routing, ensure that the switch ports that connect to the router interfaces are configured with the correct VLANs. If a switch port is not configured for the correct VLAN, devices configured on that VLAN cannot connect to the router interface; therefore, those devices are unable to send data to the other VLANs.

As shown in Figure 6-9, PC1 and Router R1 interface G0/0 are configured to be on the same logical subnet, as indicated by their IP address assignment. However, the switch port F0/4 that connects to Router R1 interface G0/0 has not been configured and remains in the default VLAN. Because Router R1 is on a different VLAN than PC1, they are unable to communicate.

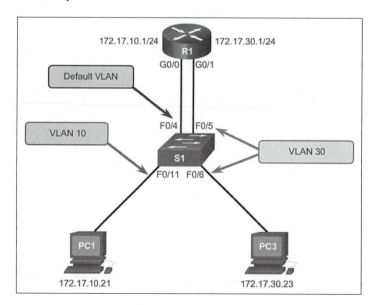

Figure 6-9   Switch Configuration Issues with Legacy Inter-VLAN Routing

To correct this problem, execute the **switchport access vlan 10** interface configuration mode command on switch port F0/4 on switch S1. When the switch port is configured for the correct VLAN, PC1 can communicate with Router R1 interface G0/0, which allows it to access the other VLANs connected to Router R1.

The Figure 6-10 topology shows the router-on-a-stick routing model. However, interface F0/5 on switch S1 is not configured as a trunk and is left in the default VLAN for the port. As a result, the router is unable to route between VLANs because each of its configured subinterfaces is unable to send or receive VLAN-tagged traffic.

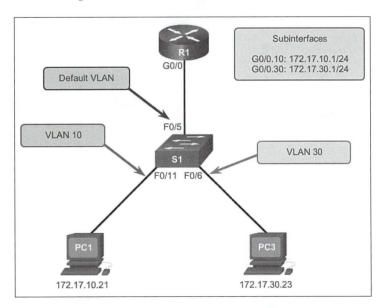

Figure 6-10   Switch Configuration Issues with Router-on-a-Stick Topology

To correct this problem, issue the **switchport mode trunk** interface configuration mode command on switch port F0/5 on S1. This converts the interface to a trunk port, allowing a trunk to be established between R1 and S1. When the trunk is successfully established, devices connected to each of the VLANs are able to communicate with the subinterface assigned to their VLAN, thus enabling inter-VLAN routing.

The Figure 6-11 topology shows that the trunk link between S1 and S2 is down. Because there is no redundant connection or path between the devices, all devices connected to S2 are unable to reach Router R1. As a result, all devices connected to S2 are unable to route to other VLANs through R1.

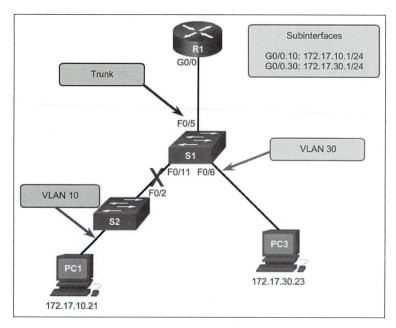

Figure 6-11 Redundancy Issues

To reduce the risk of a failed inter-switch link disrupting inter-VLAN routing, redundant links and alternate paths should be accounted for within the network design.

Verify Switch Configuration (6.2.1.2)

When a problem is suspected with a switch configuration, use the various verification commands to examine the configuration and identify the problem.

The screen output in Example 6-8 shows the results of the **show interfaces** *interface-id* **switchport** command. Assume that you have issued these commands because you suspect that VLAN 10 has not been assigned to port F0/4 on switch S1. The top highlighted area shows that port F0/4 on switch S1 is in access mode, but it does not show that it has been directly assigned to VLAN 10. The bottom highlighted area confirms that port F0/4 is still set to the default VLAN. The **show running-config** and the **show interfaces** *interface-id* **switchport** commands are useful for identifying VLAN assignment and port configuration issues.

Example 6-8 Verifying Switch Port Configuration

```
S1# show interfaces FastEthernet 0/4 switchport
Name: Fa0/4
Switchport: Enabled
Administrative Mode: static access
Operation Mode: up
Administrative Trunking Encapsulation: dot1q
```

```
Operational Trunking Encapsulation: native
Negotiation of Trunking: On
Access Mode VLAN: 1 (default)
Trunking Native Mode VLAN: 1 (default)
<output omitted>
```

Example 6-9 shows that after a device configuration has changed, communication between Router R1 and switch S1 has stopped. The link between the router and the switch is supposed to be a trunk link. The screen output shows the results of the **show interfaces** *interface-id* **switchport** and the **show running-config** commands. The top highlighted area confirms that port F0/4 on switch S1 is in access mode, not trunk mode. The bottom highlighted area also confirms that port F0/4 has been configured for access mode.

Example 6-9   Verifying Port Mode on a Switch

```
S1# show interfaces FastEthernet 0/4 switchport
Name: Fa0/4
Switchport: Enabled
Administrative Mode: static access
Operation Mode: down
Administrative Trunking Encapsulation: dot1q
Operational Trunking Encapsulation: native
<output omitted>
S1# show running-config
Building configuration...
<output omitted>
!
interface FastEthernet0/4
 switchport mode access
!
<output omitted>
```

Interface Issues (6.2.1.3)

When enabling inter-VLAN routing on a router, one of the most common configuration errors is to connect the physical router interface to the wrong switch port. This places the router interface in the incorrect VLAN and prevents it from reaching the other devices within the same subnet.

As shown in Figure 6-12, Router R1 interface G0/0 is connected to switch S1 port F0/9. Switch port F0/9 is configured for the default VLAN, not VLAN 10. This prevents PC1 from being able to communicate with the router interface. Therefore, it is unable to route to VLAN 30.

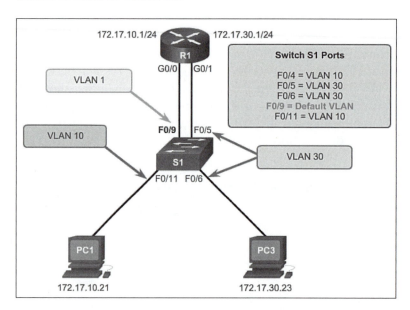

Figure 6-12   VLAN Issues

To correct this problem, physically connect the Router R1 interface G0/0 to switch S1 port F0/4. This puts the router interface in the correct VLAN and allows inter-VLAN routing. Alternately, change the VLAN assignment of switch port F0/9 to VLAN 10. This also allows PC1 to communicate with Router R1 interface G0/0.

Verify Router Configuration (6.2.1.4)

With router-on-a-stick configurations, a common problem is assigning the wrong VLAN ID to the subinterface.

As shown in Figure 6-13, Router R1 has been configured with the wrong VLAN on subinterface G0/0.10, preventing devices configured on VLAN 10 from communicating with subinterface G0/0.10. This subsequently prevents those devices from being able to send data to other VLANs on the network.

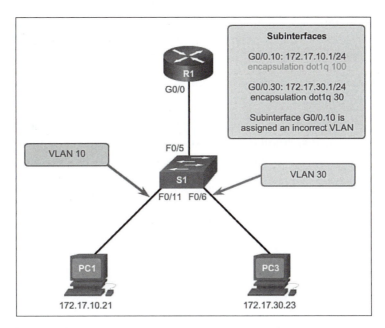

Figure 6-13 Router Subinterface Configuration Issues

Using the **show interfaces** and the **show running-config** commands can be useful in troubleshooting this type of issue, as shown in Example 6-10.

Example 6-10 Verifying Router Configuration

```
R1# show interfaces
<output omitted>
GigabitEthernet0/0.10 is up,line protocol is down (disabled)
 Encapsulation 802.1Q Virtual Lan,Vlan ID 100
 Last clearing of "show interfaces" counters never
<output omitted>
R1# show running-config
Building configuration...
Current configuration: 505 bytes
<output omitted>
!
interface GigabitEthernet0/0.10
 encapsulation dot1Q 100
 ip address 172.17.10.1 255.255.255.0
!
 interface GigabitEthernet0/0.30
<output omitted>
```

The **show interfaces** command produces a lot of output, making it sometimes difficult to see the problem, as shown in Example 6-10. However, the top highlighted section shows that the subinterface G0/0.10 on Router R1 uses VLAN 100.

The **show running-config** command confirms that subinterface G0/0.10 on Router R1 has been configured to allow access to VLAN 100 traffic and not VLAN 10.

To correct this problem, configure subinterface G0/0.10 to be on the correct VLAN using the **encapsulation dot1q 10** subinterface configuration mode command. When the subinterface has been assigned to the correct VLAN, it is accessible by devices on that VLAN and the router can perform inter-VLAN routing.

With proper verification, router configuration problems are quickly addressed, allowing inter-VLAN routing to function properly.

IP Addressing Issues (6.2.2)

As often as not, inter-VLAN routing configuration issues relate to IP addressing.

Errors with IP Addresses and Subnet Masks (6.2.2.1)

VLANs correspond to unique subnets on the network. For inter-VLAN routing to operate, a router must be connected to all VLANs, either by separate physical interfaces or by subinterfaces. Each interface, or subinterface, must be assigned an IP address that corresponds to the subnet to which it is connected. This permits devices on the VLAN to communicate with the router interface and enables the routing of traffic to other VLANs connected to the router.

The following are some common IP addressing errors:

- As shown in Figure 6-14, Router R1 has been configured with an incorrect IP address on interface G0/0. This prevents PC1 from being able to communicate with Router R1 on VLAN 10. To correct this problem, assign the correct IP address to Router R1 interface G0/0 using the **ip address 172.17.10.1 255.255.255.0** command. After the router interface has been assigned the correct IP address, PC1 can use the router interface as a default gateway for accessing other VLANs.

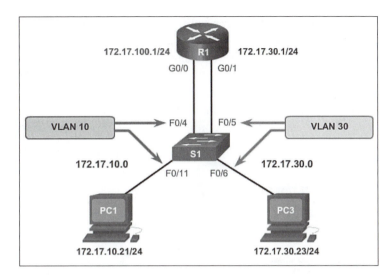

Figure 6-14 Incorrect IP Address on Router Interface

- In Figure 6-15, PC1 has been configured with an incorrect IP address for the subnet associated with VLAN 10. This prevents PC1 from being able to communicate with Router R1 on VLAN 10. To correct this problem, assign the correct IP address to PC1. Depending on the type of PC being used, the configuration details can be different.

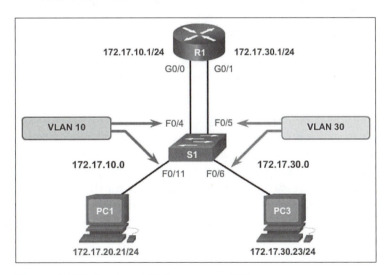

Figure 6-15 Incorrect IP Address on PC

■ In Figure 6-16, PC1 has been configured with the incorrect subnet mask. According to the subnet mask configured for PC1, PC1 is on the 172.17.0.0 network. The result is that PC1 calculates that PC3, with the IP address 172.17.30.23, is on the same subnet as PC1. PC1 does not forward traffic destined for PC3 to Router R1 interface G0/0; therefore, the traffic never reaches PC3. To correct this problem, change the subnet mask on PC1 to 255.255.255.0. Depending on the type of PC being used, the configuration details can be different.

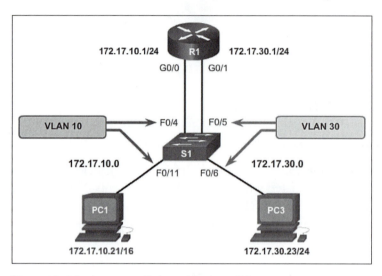

Figure 6-16   Incorrect Subnet Mask on PC

Verifying IP Address and Subnet Mask Configuration Issues (6.2.2.2)

Each interface, or subinterface, must be assigned an IP address corresponding to the subnet to which it is connected. A common error is to incorrectly configure an IP address for a subinterface. Example 6-11 displays the output of the **show running-config** command. The highlighted area shows that subinterface G0/0.10 on Router R1 has an IP address of 172.17.20.1. The VLAN for this subinterface should support VLAN 10 traffic. The IP address has been configured incorrectly. The **show ip interface** command is useful in this setting. The second highlight shows the incorrect IP address.

Example 6-11   Incorrect Router Subinterface IP Address

```
R1# show running-config
<output omitted>
!
interface GigabitEthernet0/0
 no ip address
 duplex auto
 speed auto
!
interface GigabitEthernet0/0.10
 encapsulation dot1Q 10
 ip address 172.17.20.1 255.255.255.0
!
interface GigabitEthernet0/0.30
<output omitted>
R1# show ip interface
<output omitted>
GigabitEthernet0/0.10 is up, line protocol is up
  Internet address is 172.17.20.1/24
   Broadcast address is 255.255.255.255
<output omitted>
```

Sometimes it is the end-user device, such as a personal computer, that is improperly configured. Figure 6-17 shows the displayed IP configuration for PC1. The IP address is 172.17.20.21, with a subnet mask of 255.255.255.0. But in this scenario, PC1 should be in VLAN 10, with an address of 172.17.10.21 and a subnet mask of 255.255.255.0.

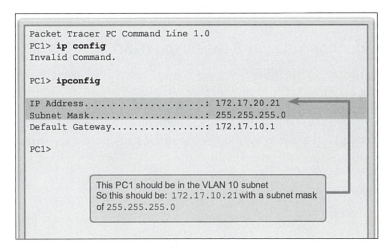

Figure 6-17   Incorrect IP Address on PC

Note

Although configuring subinterface IDs to match the VLAN number makes it easier to manage inter-VLAN configuration, it is not a requirement. When troubleshooting addressing issues, ensure that the subinterface is configured with the correct address for that VLAN.

Activity 6.2.2.3: Identify the Troubleshooting Command for an Inter-VLAN Routing Issue

Go to the online course to perform this practice activity.

Packet Tracer Activity 6.2.2.4: Troubleshooting Inter-VLAN Routing

In this activity, you will troubleshoot connectivity problems caused by improper configurations related to VLANs and inter-VLAN routing.

Layer 3 Switching (6.3)

By far the most common method for inter-VLAN routing is multilayer switching. In this section, you learn the basics of inter-VLAN routing with a multilayer switch.

Layer 3 Switching Operation and Configuration (6.3.1)

In this topic, you learn how inter-VLAN routing operates with multilayer switches. You also explore some basic configuration scenarios.

Introduction to Layer 3 Switching (6.3.1.1)

Router-on-a-stick is simple to implement because routers are usually available in every network. As shown in Figure 6-18, most enterprise networks use multilayer switches to achieve high-packet processing rates using hardware-based switching. Layer 3 switches usually have packet-switching throughputs in the millions of packets per second (pps), whereas traditional routers provide packet switching in the range of 100,000 pps to more than 1 million pps.

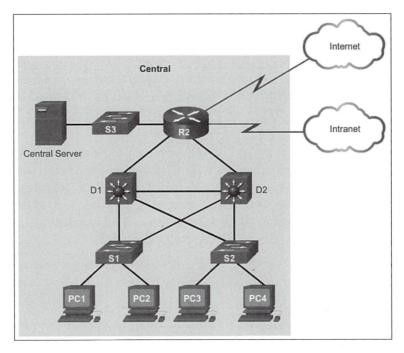

Figure 6-18 Multilayer Switches

All Catalyst multilayer switches support the following types of Layer 3 interfaces:

- *Routed port*: A pure Layer 3 interface similar to a physical interface on a Cisco IOS router.

- *Switch virtual interface (SVI)*: A virtual VLAN interface for inter-VLAN routing. In other words, SVIs are the virtual-routed VLAN interfaces.

High-performance switches, such as the Catalyst 6500 and Catalyst 4500, perform almost every function involving OSI Layer 3 and higher using hardware-based switching that is based on Cisco Express Forwarding.

All Layer 3 Cisco Catalyst switches support routing protocols, but several models of Catalyst switches require enhanced software for specific routing protocol features. Catalyst 2960 Series switches running IOS Release 12.2(55) or later support static routing.

Catalyst switches use different default settings for interfaces. All members of the Catalyst 3560 and 4500 families of switches use Layer 2 interfaces by default. Members of the Catalyst 6500 family of switches running Cisco IOS use Layer 3 interfaces by default. Default interface configurations do not appear in the running or startup configuration. Depending on which Catalyst family of switches is used, the **switchport** or **no switchport** interface configuration mode commands might be present in the running config or startup configuration files.

Inter-VLAN Routing with Switch Virtual Interfaces (6.3.1.2)

In the early days of switched networks, switching was fast (often at hardware speed, meaning that the speed was equivalent to the time it took to physically receive and forward frames onto other ports) and routing was slow (routing had to be processed in software). This prompted network designers to extend the switched portion of the network as much as possible. Access, distribution, and core layers were often configured to communicate at Layer 2. This topology created loop issues. To solve these issues, spanning-tree technologies were used to prevent loops while still enabling flexibility and redundancy in inter-switch connections.

However, as network technologies have evolved, routing has become faster and cheaper. Today, routing can be performed at wire speed. One consequence of this evolution is that routing can be transferred to the core and the distribution layers without impacting network performance.

Many users are in separate VLANs, and each VLAN is usually a separate subnet. Therefore, it is logical to configure the distribution switches as Layer 3 gateways for the users of each access switch VLAN. This implies that each distribution switch must have IP addresses matching each access switch VLAN.

As shown in Figure 6-19, Layer 3 (routed) ports are normally implemented between the distribution and the core layer. The network architecture depicted is not dependent on spanning tree because there are no physical loops in the Layer 2 portion of the topology.

An SVI is a virtual interface that is configured within a multilayer switch, as shown in Figure 6-20. An SVI can be created for any VLAN that exists on the switch. An SVI is considered to be virtual because there is no physical port dedicated to the interface. It can perform the same functions for the VLAN as a router interface would, and can be configured in much the same way as a router interface (that is, IP address, inbound/outbound ACLs, and so on). The SVI for the VLAN provides Layer 3 processing for packets to or from all switch ports associated with that VLAN.

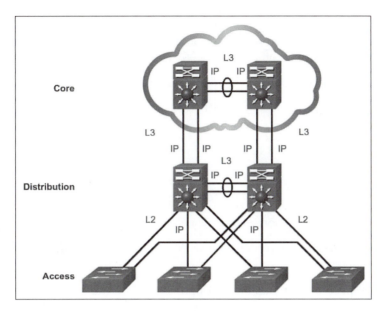

Figure 6-19   Switched Network Design

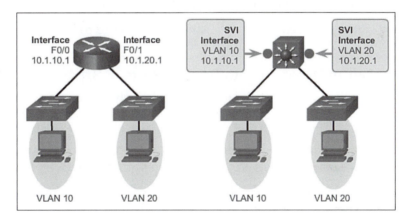

Figure 6-20   Switched Virtual Interface

By default, an SVI is created for the default VLAN (VLAN 10) to permit remote switch administration. Additional SVIs must be explicitly created. SVIs are created the first time the VLAN interface configuration mode is entered for a particular VLAN SVI, such as when the **interface vlan 10** command is entered. The VLAN number used corresponds to the VLAN tag associated with data frames on an 802.1Q encapsulated trunk or to the VLAN ID (VID) configured for an access port. When creating an SVI as a gateway for VLAN 10, name the SVI interface VLAN 10. Configure and assign an IP address to each VLAN SVI.

Whenever the SVI is created, ensure that particular VLAN is present in the VLAN database. In the figure, the switch should have VLAN 10 and VLAN 20 present in the VLAN database; otherwise, the SVI interface stays down.

The following are some of the reasons to configure SVI:

- To provide a gateway for a VLAN so that traffic can be routed into or out of that VLAN

- To provide Layer 3 IP connectivity to the switch

- To support routing protocol and bridging configurations

The following are some of the advantages of SVIs (the only disadvantage is that multilayer switches are more expensive):

- Much faster than router-on-a-stick, because everything is hardware switched and routed.

- No need for external links from the switch to the router for routing.

- Not limited to one link. Layer 2 EtherChannels can be used between the switches to get more bandwidth.

- Latency is much lower, because it does not need to leave the switch.

Inter-VLAN Routing with Routed Ports (6.3.1.4)

A routed port is a physical port that acts similarly to an interface on a router. Unlike an access port, a routed port is not associated with a particular VLAN. A routed port behaves like a regular router interface. Also, because Layer 2 functionality has been removed, Layer 2 protocols, such as STP, do not function on a routed interface. However, some protocols, such as LACP and EtherChannel, do function at Layer 3.

Unlike Cisco IOS routers, routed ports on a Cisco IOS switch do not support subinterfaces.

Routed ports are used for point-to-point links. Connecting WAN routers and connecting security devices are examples of the use of routed ports. In a switched network, routed ports are mostly configured between switches in the core and distribution layer. Figure 6-21 illustrates an example of routed ports in a campus switched network.

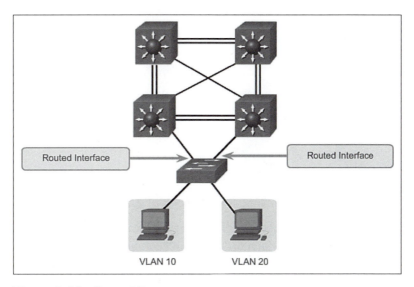

Figure 6-21   Routed Ports

To configure routed ports, use the **no switchport** interface configuration mode command on the appropriate ports. For example, the default configuration of the interfaces on Catalyst 3560 switches are Layer 2 interfaces, so they must be manually configured as routed ports. In addition, assign an IP address and other Layer 3 parameters as necessary. After assigning the IP address, verify that IP routing is globally enabled and that applicable routing protocols are configured.

Note

Routed ports are not supported on Catalyst 2960 Series switches.

Configuring Static Routes on a Catalyst 2960 Switch (6.3.1.5)

A Catalyst 2960 switch can function as a Layer 3 device because it supports routing between up to 8 VLANs and it supports up to 16 static routes.

The Cisco *Switch Database Manager (SDM)* provides multiple templates for the 2960 switch. The templates can be enabled to support specific roles depending on how the switch is used in the network. For example, the SDM *lanbase-routing template* can be enabled to allow the switch to route between VLANs and to support static routing. Figure 6-22 displays a topology where S1 and S2 are Catalyst 2960 switches.

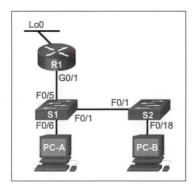

Figure 6-22 Catalyst 2960 Switches

In Example 6-12, the **show sdm prefer** command is entered on switch S1 and the *default template* is applied. The default template is the factory default setting for a Catalyst 2960 switch. The default template does not support static routing. If IPv6 addressing has been enabled, the template will be dual-ipv4-and-ipv6 by default.

Example 6-12 SDM Database Manager Template

```
S1# show sdm prefer
 The current template is "default" template.
 The selected template optimizes the resources in
 the switch to support this level of features for
 0 routed interfaces and 255 VLANs.
  number of unicast mac addresses:                 8K
  number of IPv4 IGMP groups:                      0.25K
  number of IPv4/MAC qos aces:                     0.125k
  number of IPv4/MAC security aces:                0.375k
```

The SDM template can be changed in global configuration mode with the **sdm prefer** command.

In Example 6-13, the *SDM template* options are displayed with the **sdm prefer ?** command. The SDM template is changed to lanbase-routing. The switch must be reloaded for the new template to take effect. Note the use of the **do** command to permit a command to be entered in a configuration mode distinct from the usual command configuration mode.

Example 6-13   SDM Template

```
S1# configure terminal
Enter configuration commands, one per line.  End with CNTL/Z.
S1(config)# sdm prefer ?
  default            Default bias
  dual-ipv4-and-ipv6  Support both IPv4 and IPv6
  lanbase-routing    Supports both IPv4 and IPv6 Static Routing
  qos                QoS bias
S1(config)# sdm prefer lanbase-routing
Changes to the running SDM preferences have been stored, but cannot take effect
until the next reload.
Use 'show sdm prefer' to see what SDM preference is currently active.
Switch(config)# do reload
System configuration has been modified. Save? [yes/no]: yes
Building configuration...
[OK]
Proceed with reload? [confirm]
*Mar 20 00:10:24.557: %SYS-5-RELOAD: Reload requested by console. Reload Reason:
  Reload command.
```

In Example 6-14, the lanbase-routing template is active on S1. With this template, static routing is supported for up to 16 static routes to remote networks, as indicated by the highlight.

Example 6-14   2960 Static Route Support

```
S1# show sdm prefer
 The current template is "lanbase-routing" template.
 The selected template optimizes the resources in
 the switch to support this level of features for
 0 routed interfaces and 255 VLANs.
  number of unicast mac addresses:                  4K
  number of IPv4 IGMP groups + multicast routes:    0.25K
  number of IPv4 unicast routes:                    0.75K
    number of directly-connected IPv4 hosts:        0.75K
    number of indirect IPv4 routes:                 16
  number of IPv6 multicast groups:                  0.375k
  number of directly-connected IPv6 addresses:      0.75K
    number of indirect IPv6 unicast routes:         16
  number of IPv4 policy based routing aces:         0
  number of IPv4/MAC qos aces:                      0.125k
  number of IPv4/MAC security aces:                 0.375k
  number of IPv6 policy based routing aces:         0
  number of IPv6 qos aces:                          0.375k
  number of IPv6 security aces:                     127
```

In Example 6-15, interface F0/6 on S1 is assigned to VLAN 2. The SVIs for VLANs 1 and 2 are also configured with IP addresses 192.168.1.1/24 and 192.168.2.1/24, respectively. IP routing is enabled with the **ip routing** global configuration mode command, and the routing table is displayed.

Example 6-15   Enabling IP Routing Functionality on a 2960 Switch

```
S1(config)# interface f0/6
S1(config-if)# switchport access vlan 2
S1(config-if)# interface vlan 1
S1(config-if)# ip address 192.168.1.1 255.255.255.0
S1(config-if)# interface vlan 2
S1(config-if)# ip address 192.168.2.1 255.255.255.0
S1(config-if)# no shutdown
Mar 20 01:00:25.021: %LINEPROTO-5-UPDOWN: Line protocol on Interface Vlan2, changed
  state to up
S1(config)# ip routing
S1(config)# do show ip route
Codes: L - local, C - connected, S - static, R - RIP, M - mobile, B - BGP
       D - EIGRP, EX - EIGRP external, O - OSPF, IA - OSPF inter area
       N1 - OSPF NSSA external type 1, N2 - OSPF NSSA external type 2
       E1 - OSPF external type 1, E2 - OSPF external type 2
       i - IS-IS, su - IS-IS summary, L1 - IS-IS level-1, L2 - IS-IS level-2
       ia - IS-IS inter area, * - candidate default, U - per-user static route
       o - ODR, P - periodic downloaded static route, H - NHRP, l - LISP
       + - replicated route, % - next hop override
Gateway of last resort is not set
      192.168.1.0/24 is variably subnetted, 2 subnets, 2 masks
C        192.168.1.0/24 is directly connected, Vlan1
L        192.168.1.1/32 is directly connected, Vlan1
      192.168.2.0/24 is variably subnetted, 2 subnets, 2 masks
C        192.168.2.0/24 is directly connected, Vlan2
L        192.168.2.1/32 is directly connected, Vlan2
```

Note

The **ip routing** command is automatically enabled on Cisco routers, but not on Catalyst 2960 switches with the lanbase-routing template. The corresponding command for IPv6, **ipv6 uni-cast-routing**, is disabled by default on Cisco routers and switches.

In Example 6-16, Router R1 has two IPv4 networks configured: Interface G0/1 has IP address 192.168.1.10/24, and loopback interface Lo0 has IP address 209.165.200.225/27. The **show ip route** command output is displayed.

Example 6-16 Router Participating in Routing with a Switch

```
R1# show ip route
Codes: L - local, C - connected, S - static, R - RIP, M - mobile, B - BGP
       D - EIGRP, EX - EIGRP external, O - OSPF, IA - OSPF inter area
       N1 - OSPF NSSA external type 1, N2 - OSPF NSSA external type 2
       E1 - OSPF external type 1, E2 - OSPF external type 2
       i - IS-IS, su - IS-IS summary, L1 - IS-IS level-1, L2 - IS-IS level-2
       ia - IS-IS inter area, * - candidate default, U - per-user static route
       o - ODR, P - periodic downloaded static route, H - NHRP, l - LISP
       + - replicated route, % - next hop override
Gateway of last resort is not set
      192.168.1.0/24 is variably subnetted, 2 subnets, 2 masks
C        192.168.1.0/24 is directly connected, GigabitEthernet0/1
L        192.168.1.10/32 is directly connected, GigabitEthernet0/1
      209.165.200.0/24 is variably subnetted, 2 subnets, 2 masks
C        209.165.200.224/27 is directly connected, Loopback0
L        209.165.200.225/32 is directly connected, Loopback0
```

A default route is configured on S1 in Example 6-17, and the **show ip route** command output is displayed.

Example 6-17 Configuring a Static Route on a 2960

```
S1(config)# ip route 0.0.0.0 0.0.0.0 192.168.1.10
S1(config)# do show ip route
Codes: L - local, C - connected, S - static, R - RIP, M - mobile, B - BGP
       D - EIGRP, EX - EIGRP external, O - OSPF, IA - OSPF inter area
       N1 - OSPF NSSA external type 1, N2 - OSPF NSSA external type 2
       E1 - OSPF external type 1, E2 - OSPF external type 2
       i - IS-IS, su - IS-IS summary, L1 - IS-IS level-1, L2 - IS-IS level-2
       ia - IS-IS inter area, * - candidate default, U - per-user static route
       o - ODR, P - periodic downloaded static route, H - NHRP, l - LISP
       + - replicated route, % - next hop override
Gateway of last resort is 192.168.1.10 to network 0.0.0.0
S*    0.0.0.0/0 [1/0] via 192.168.1.10
      192.168.1.0/24 is variably subnetted, 2 subnets, 2 masks
C        192.168.1.0/24 is directly connected, Vlan1
L        192.168.1.1/32 is directly connected, Vlan1
      192.168.2.0/24 is variably subnetted, 2 subnets, 2 masks
C        192.168.2.0/24 is directly connected, Vlan2
L        192.168.2.1/32 is directly connected, Vlan2
```

A static route to the remote network 192.168.2.0/24 (VLAN 2) is configured on R1 in Example 6-18, and the **show ip route** command output is displayed.

Example 6-18   Final Routing Table on Router

```
R1(config)# ip route 192.168.2.0 255.255.255.0 g0/1
R1(config)# do show ip route
Codes: L - local, C - connected, S - static, R - RIP, M - mobile, B - BGP
       D - EIGRP, EX - EIGRP external, O - OSPF, IA - OSPF inter area
       N1 - OSPF NSSA external type 1, N2 - OSPF NSSA external type 2
       E1 - OSPF external type 1, E2 - OSPF external type 2
       i - IS-IS, su - IS-IS summary, L1 - IS-IS level-1, L2 - IS-IS level-2
       ia - IS-IS inter area, * - candidate default, U - per-user static route
       o - ODR, P - periodic downloaded static route, H - NHRP, l - LISP
       + - replicated route, % - next hop override
Gateway of last resort is not set
       192.168.1.0/24 is variably subnetted, 2 subnets, 2 masks
C         192.168.1.0/24 is directly connected, GigabitEthernet0/1
L         192.168.1.10/32 is directly connected, GigabitEthernet0/1
S      192.168.2.0/24 is directly connected, GigabitEthernet0/1
       209.165.200.0/24 is variably subnetted, 2 subnets, 2 masks
C         209.165.200.224/27 is directly connected, Loopback0
L         209.165.200.225/32 is directly connected, Loopback0
```

In Figure 6-22, PC-A is configured with IP address 192.168.2.2/24 in VLAN 2 and PC-B is configured with IP address 192.168.1.2/24 in VLAN 1. PC-B is now able to ping both PC-A and the loopback interface on R1, as shown in Example 6-19.

Example 6-19   Host Connectivity

```
Microsoft Windows [version 6.1.7601 ]
Copyright <c> 2009 Microsoft corporation. All rights reserved.
C:\Users\NetAcad> ping 192.168.2.2
Pinging 192.168.2.2 with 32 bytes of data :
Reply from 192.168.2.2: bytes=32 times=2ms TTL=127
Reply from 192.168.2.2: bytes=32 times<1ms TTL=127
Reply from 192.168.2.2: bytes=32 times<1ms TTL=127
Reply from 192.168.2.2: bytes=32 times<1ms TTL=127
Ping statistics for 192.168.2.2:
    Packets: Sent = 4, Received = 4, Lost = 0 <0% loss>,
Approximate round trip times in milli-seconds:
    Minimum = 0ms, Maximum = 2ms, Average = 0ms


C:\Users\NetAcad> ping 209.165.200.225
Pinging 209.165.200.225 with 32 bytes of data :
```

```
Reply from 209.165.200.225: bytes=32 times<1ms TTL=255
Reply from 209.165.200.225: bytes=32 times=1ms TTL=255
Reply from 209.165.200.225: bytes=32 times<1ms TTL=255
Reply from 209.165.200.225: bytes=32 times<1ms TTL=255
Ping statistics for 209.165.200.225:
    Packets: Sent = 4, Received = 4, Lost = 0 <0% loss>,
Approximate round trip times in milli-seconds:
    Minimum = 0ms, Maximum = 1ms, Average = 0ms
C:\Users\NetAcad>
```

Interactive Graphic

Activity 6.3.1.5: Static Routing on a 2960

Go to the online course to use the Syntax Checker in the ninth graphic to configure static routing on S1.

Troubleshoot Layer 3 Switching (6.3.2)

Troubleshooting Layer 3 switching is analogous to troubleshooting legacy and router-on-a-stick inter-VLAN routing. The difference is that the interfaces are SVIs on a switch rather than physical interfaces or Ethernet subinterfaces on a router.

Layer 3 Switch Configuration Issues (6.3.2.1)

The issues common to legacy inter-VLAN routing and router-on-a-stick inter-VLAN routing are also manifested in the context of Layer 3 switching. To troubleshoot Layer 3 switching issues, the following items should be checked for accuracy:

- **VLANs:** VLANs must be defined across all the switches. VLANs must be enabled on the trunk ports. Ports must be in the right VLANs.

- **SVIs:** SVIs must have the correct IP address or subnet mask. SVIs must be up. SVIs must match with the VLAN number.

- **Routing:** Routing must be enabled. Each interface or network should be added to the routing protocol.

- **Hosts:** Hosts must have the correct IP address or subnet mask. Hosts must have a default gateway associated with an SVI or routed port.

To troubleshoot the Layer 3 switching problems, be familiar with the implementation and design layout of the topology, such as the one shown in Figure 6-23.

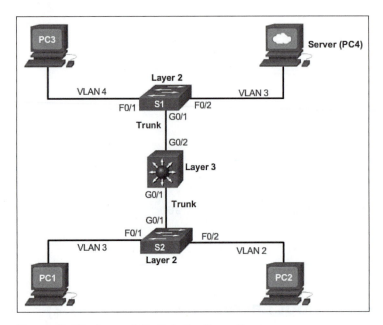

Figure 6-23   Layer 3 Switch Configuration Issues

Example: Troubleshooting Layer 3 Switching (6.3.2.2)

Company XYZ is adding a new floor, floor 5, to the network, as illustrated in Figure 6-24. Based on this, the current requirements are to make sure that the users on floor 5 can communicate with users on other floors. Currently, users on floor 5 cannot communicate with users on other floors. The following is an implementation plan to install a new VLAN for users on floor 5 and to ensure that the VLAN is routing to other VLANs.

There are four steps to implementing a new VLAN:

Step 1.   Create a new VLAN 500 on the fifth-floor switch and on the distribution switches. Name this VLAN.

Step 2.   Identify the ports needed for the users and switches. Set the **switchport access vlan** command to **500** and ensure that the trunk between the distribution switches is properly configured and that VLAN 500 is allowed on the trunk.

Step 3.   Create an SVI interface on the distribution switches and ensure that IP addresses are assigned.

Step 4.   Verify connectivity.

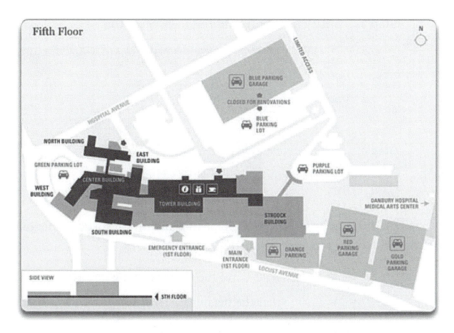

Figure 6-24   Layer 3 Switch Implementation and Troubleshooting Plan

The troubleshooting plan checks for the following:

Step 1.   Verify that all VLANs have been created:

- Was the VLAN created on all the switches?

- Verify with the **show vlan** command.

Step 2.   Ensure that ports are in the right VLAN and trunking is working as expected:

- Did all access ports have the **switchport access VLAN 500** command added?

- Were there any other ports that should have been added? If so, make those changes.

- Were these ports previously used? If so, ensure that there are no extra commands enabled on these ports that can cause conflicts. If not, is the port enabled?

- Are any user ports set to trunks? If so, issue the **switchport mode access** command.

- Are the trunk ports set to trunk mode?

- Is manual pruning of VLANs configured? If so, ensure that the trunks necessary to carry VLAN 500 traffic have the VLAN in the allowed statements.

Step 3.   Verify SVI configurations (if necessary):

- Is the SVI already created with the correct IP address and subnet mask?

- Is it enabled?

- Is routing enabled?

- Is this SVI added in the routing protocol?

Step 4.   Verify connectivity:

- Are all the links between switches in trunk mode?

- Is VLAN 500 allowed on all trunks?

- Is spanning tree blocking any of the participating links?

- Are the ports enabled?

- Do the hosts have the right default gateways assigned?

- Ensure that the default route or some routing protocol is enabled if necessary.

Activity 6.3.2.3: Troubleshoot Layer 3 Switching Issues

Go to the online course to perform this practice activity.

Lab 6.3.2.4: Configuring Per-Physical-Interface Inter-VLAN Routing

In this lab, you will complete the following objectives:

- Part 1: Build the Network and Load Device Configurations

- Part 2: Troubleshoot the Inter-VLAN Routing Configuration

- Part 3: Verify VLAN Configuration, Port Assignment, and Trunking

- Part 4: Test Layer 3 Connectivity

Summary (6.4)

Class Activity 6.4.1.1: The Inside Track

Your company has just purchased a three-level building. You are the network administrator and must design the company inter-VLAN routing network scheme to serve a few employees on each floor.

Floor 1 is occupied by the HR Department, Floor 2 is occupied by the IT Department, and Floor 3 is occupied by the Sales Department. All departments must be able to communicate with each other, but at the same time have their own separate working networks.

You brought three Cisco 2960 switches and a Cisco 1941 series router from the old office location to serve network connectivity in the new building. New equipment is non-negotiable.

Refer to the PDF for this activity for further instructions.

Packet Tracer Activity 6.4.1.2: Skills Integration Challenge

In this activity, you will demonstrate and reinforce your ability to implement inter-VLAN routing, including configuring IP addresses, VLANs, trunking, and subinterfaces.

Inter-VLAN routing is the process of routing traffic between different VLANs, using either a dedicated router or a multilayer switch. Inter-VLAN routing facilitates communication between devices isolated by VLAN boundaries.

Legacy inter-VLAN routing depended on a physical router port being available for each configured VLAN. This has been replaced by the router-on-a-stick topology that relies on an external router with subinterfaces trunked to a Layer 2 switch. With the router-on-a-stick option, appropriate IP addressing and VLAN information must be configured on each logical subinterface and a trunk encapsulation must be configured to match that of the trunking interface of the switch.

Another option is the multilayer inter-VLAN option using Layer 3 switching. Layer 3 switching involves SVIs and routed ports. Layer 3 switching is normally configured at the distribution and core layers of the hierarchical design model. Layer 3 switching with SVIs is a form of inter-VLAN routing. A routed port is a physical port that acts similarly to an interface on a router. Unlike an access port, a routed port is not associated with a particular VLAN.

Catalyst 2960 switches can be used in multilayer inter-VLAN routing. These switches support static routing, but dynamic routing protocols are not supported. SDM templates are required for enabling IP routing on 2960 switches.

Troubleshooting inter-VLAN routing with a router or a Layer 3 switch is similar. Common errors involve VLAN, trunk, Layer 3 interface, and IP address configurations.

Practice

The following activities provide practice with the topics introduced in this chapter. The Labs and Class Activities are available in the companion *Switched Networks Lab Manual* (ISBN 978-1-58713-327-5). The Packet Tracer Activities PKA files are found in the online course.

Class Activities

- Class Activity 6.0.1.2: Switching to Local-Network Channels
- Class Activity 6.4.1.1: The Inside Track

Labs

- Lab 6.1.2.4: Configuring Per-Physical-Interface Inter-VLAN Routing
- Lab 6.1.3.7: Configuring 802.1Q Trunk-Based Inter-VLAN Routing
- Lab 6.3.2.4: Troubleshooting Inter-VLAN Routing

Packet Tracer Activities

- Packet Tracer Activity 6.1.3.6: Configuring Router-on-a-Stick Inter-VLAN Routing
- Packet Tracer Activity 6.2.2.4: Troubleshooting Inter-VLAN Routing

Check Your Understanding Questions

Complete all the review questions listed here to test your understanding of the topics and concepts in this chapter. The appendix "Answers to 'Check Your Understanding' Questions" lists the answers.

1. Which scalable method must be implemented to provide inter-VLAN routing on a switched network with more than 1000 VLANs?

   A. Configuring static routes on a Layer 2 switch device

   B. Routing traffic internally to a Layer 3 switch device

   C. Connecting each physical router interface to a different physical switch port, with each switch port assigned to a different VLAN

   D. Connecting a router interface to a switch port that is configured in trunk mode to route packets between VLANs, with each VLAN assigned to a router subinterface

2. Fill in the blank. Do not use abbreviated commands. The _____ parameter can be added to the **show interfaces** *interface-id* command to display the administrative and operational switch interface mode.

3. See Example 6-20. A network administrator has configured router CiscoVille with these commands to provide inter-VLAN routing. What type of port will be required on a switch that is connected to interface g0/0 on router CiscoVille to allow inter-VLAN routing?

Example 6-20 Router-on-a-Stick

```
R1(config)# interface g0/0.10
R1(config-subif)# encapsulation dot1q 10
R1(config-subif)# ip address 192.168.10.254 255.255.255.0
R1(config-subif)# interface g0/0.20
R1(config-subif)# encapsulation dot1q 20
R1(config-subif)# ip address 192.168.20.254 255.255.255.0
R1(config-subif)# interface g0/0
R1(config-if)# no shutdown
```

   A. Routed port

   B. Access port

   C. Trunk port

   D. SVI

4. See Figure 6-25. An administrator is troubleshooting a router-on-a-stick network that should have the following requirements:

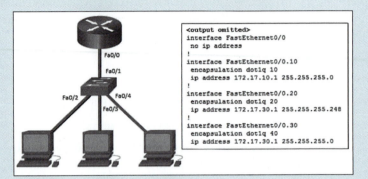

```
<output omitted>
interface FastEthernet0/0
 no ip address
!
interface FastEthernet0/0.10
 encapsulation dot1q 10
 ip address 172.17.10.1 255.255.255.0
!
interface FastEthernet0/0.20
 encapsulation dot1q 20
 ip address 172.17.30.1 255.255.255.248
!
interface FastEthernet0/0.30
 encapsulation dot1q 40
 ip address 172.17.30.1 255.255.255.0
```

Figure 6-25 Router-on-a-Stick

VLAN ID	Network	Subnet Mask	Subinterface	Default Gateway
10	172.17.10.0	255.255.255.0	F0/0.10	172.17.10.1
20	172.17.20.0	255.255.255.0	F0/0.20	172.17.20.1
30	172.17.30.0	255.255.255.0	F0/0.30	172.17.30.1

Which of the following errors can be identified from the **show running-config** command output from the router? (Choose two.)

A. There is no IP address that is configured for the router physical interface.

B. The VLAN ID for VLAN 30 is improperly configured.

C. A command to configure the router physical interface as a trunk is missing.

D. The IP address and subnet mask are improperly configured for VLAN 20.

E. The **no shutdown** command was not issued on subinterfaces.

5. See Figure 6-26. Which implementation of inter-VLAN routing does this topology use?

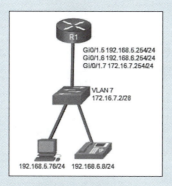

Figure 6-26   Inter-VLAN Routing

    A. Interdomain

    B. Router-on-a-stick

    C. Multiple physical interfaces

    D. Routing through a multilayer switch

6. See Figure 6-27. Inter-VLAN communication between VLAN 10, VLAN 20, and VLAN 30 is not successful. What is the problem?

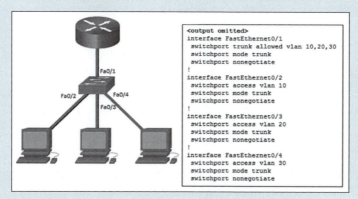

Figure 6-27   Multiple Physical Interfaces on a Router

    A. The access interfaces do not have IP addresses, and each should be configured with an IP address.

    B. The FastEthernet0/2, FastEthernet0/3, and FastEthernet0/4 interfaces are configured as trunk.

    C. The switch interface FastEthernet0/1 is configured to not negotiate and should be configured to negotiate.

    D. The switch interfaces FastEthernet0/2, FastEthernet0/3, and FastEthernet0/4 are configured to not negotiate and should be configured to negotiate.

7. See Figure 6-28. Fill in the blank. Use dot notation. PC0 has been assigned the last valid host address in the subnet. The IPv4 address for PC0 will be

_____.

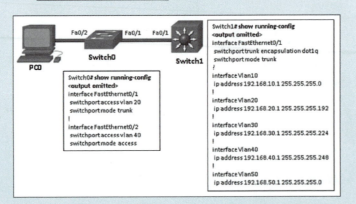

Figure 6-28   IP Addressing

8. See Example 6-21. What is the cause of the error that is displayed in the configuration of inter-VLAN routing on router CiscoVille?

Example 6-21   Error with Router-on-a-Stick

```
R1(config)# interface g0/0.10
R1(config-subif)# encapsulation dot1q 10
R1(config-subif)# ip address 192.168.10.254 255.255.255.0
R1(config-subif)# interface g0/0.20
R1(config-subif)# ip address 192.168.20.254 255.255.255.0
%Configuring IP routing on a LAN subinterface is only allowed if that subinterface is
    already configured as part of an IEEE 802.10, IEEE 802.1Q, or ISL vLAN.
```

A. The g0/0 interface does not support inter-VLAN routing.

B. The **no shutdown** command has not been configured.

C. The IP address on CiscoVille is incorrect.

D. The **encapsulation dot1Q 20** command has not been configured.

9. A PC is to access a web server on another network. Which inter-VLAN method will provide the highest bandwidth at Layer 3 and also provide a default gateway for the PC?

A. Router-on-a-stick

B. Multilayer switch with routing enabled

C. Trunked interface between the router and the switch

D. Multiple physical interfaces on the router, all connected to a Layer 2 switch

10. What is the meaning of the number 10 in the **encapsulation dot1Q 10 native** router subinterface command?

A. The interface number

B. The subinterface number

C. The subnet number

D. The VLAN ID

11. Which option should be used after the **sdm prefer** configuration command to enable static routing on Cisco Catalyst 2960 switches?

A. Switch(config)# **sdm prefer qos**

B. Switch(config)# **sdm prefer default**

C. Switch(config)# **sdm prefer lanbase-routing**

D. Switch(config)# **sdm prefer dual-ipv4-and-ipv6**

12. A network administrator enters the following command sequence on a Cisco 3560 switch. What is the purpose of these commands?

```
Switch(config)# interface gigabitethernet 0/1
Switch(config-if)# no switchport
```

A. To shut down the g0/1 port

B. To make the g0/1 port a routed port

C. To enable the g0/1 port as a switch virtual interface

D. To enable the g0/1 port as a bridge virtual interface

Objectives

Upon completion of this chapter, you will be able to answer the following questions:

- How do you describe the operation of DHCPv4 in a small- to medium-sized business network?

- How do you configure a router as a DHCPv4 server?

- How do you configure a router as a DHCPv4 client?

- How do you troubleshoot a DHCP configuration for IPv4 in a switched network?

- How do you explain the operation of DHCPv6?

- How do you configure stateless DHCPv6 for a small- to medium-sized business?

- How do you configure stateful DHCPv6 for a small- to medium-sized business?

- How do you troubleshoot a DHCP configuration for IPv6 in a switched network?

Key Terms

This chapter uses the following key terms. You can find the definitions in the Glossary.

Introduction (7.0.1.1)

Every device that connects to a network needs a unique IP address. Network administrators assign static IP addresses to routers, servers, printers, and other network devices whose locations (physical and logical) are not likely to change. These are usually devices that provide services to users and devices on the network; therefore, the addresses assigned to them should remain constant. Additionally, static addresses enable administrators to manage these devices remotely. It is easier for network administrators to access a device when they can easily determine its IP address.

However, computers and users in an organization often change locations, physically and logically. It can be difficult and time consuming for administrators to assign new IP addresses every time an employee moves. Additionally, for mobile employees working from remote locations, manually setting the correct network parameters can be challenging. Even for desktop clients, the manual assignment of IP addresses and other addressing information presents an administrative burden, especially as the network grows.

Introducing a *Dynamic Host Configuration Protocol (DHCP)* server to the local network simplifies IP address assignment to both desktop and mobile devices. Using a centralized *DHCP server* enables organizations to administer all dynamic IP address assignments from a single server. This practice makes IP address management more effective and ensures consistency across the organization, including branch offices.

DHCP is available for both IPv4 (*DHCPv4*) and for IPv6 (*DHCPv6*). This chapter explores the functionality, configuration, and troubleshooting of both DHCPv4 and DHCPv6.

Class Activity 7.0.1.2: Own or Lease?

This chapter presents the concept of using the DHCP process in a small- to medium-sized business network. This modeling activity describes how very basic wireless integrated services router (ISR) devices work using the DHCP process.

Visit http://ui.linksys.com/WRT54GL/4.30.0/Setup.htm, which is a web-based simulator that helps you learn to configure DHCP using a Linksys wireless 54GL router. To the right of the simulator (in the blue description column), there are two **More** hyperlinks that you can follow to read information about configuring DHCP settings on this particular ISR simulator.

Practice configuring the ISR's

- Host name

- Local IP address with subnet mask

- DHCP (enable and disable)

- Starting IP address

- Maximum number of users to receive an IP DHCP address

- Lease time

- Time zone (use yours or a favorite as an alternative)

When you have completed configuring the settings as listed for this assignment, take a screen shot of your settings by pressing the **PrtScrn** key. Copy and place your screen shot into a word processing document. Save it and be prepared to discuss your configuration choices with the class.

Dynamic Host Configuration Protocol v4 (7.1)

DHCPv4 is widely deployed across the world in organizations that are still using IPv4. It is a very reliable technology that saves untold hours of reconfiguration on end devices, especially given the proliferation of smart phones, tablets, and wireless LANs.

DHCPv4 Operation (7.1.1)

Relative to most networking protocols, the operation of DHCP is simple. Because of its simplicity, it is not difficult to get a DHCPv4 solution up and running within an organization.

Introducing DHCPv4 (7.1.1.1)

DHCPv4 assigns IPv4 addresses and other network configuration information dynamically. Because desktop clients typically make up the bulk of network nodes, DHCPv4 is an extremely useful and timesaving tool for network administrators.

A dedicated DHCPv4 server, as shown in Figure 7-1, is scalable and relatively easy to manage. However, in a small branch or SOHO location, a Cisco router can be configured to provide DHCPv4 services without the need for a dedicated server. A Cisco IOS feature set (called Easy IP) offers an optional, full-featured DHCPv4 server.

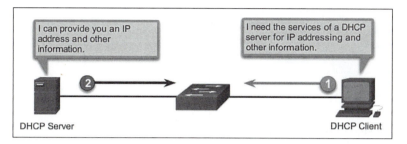

Figure 7-1 Dynamic Host Configuration Protocol

DHCPv4 includes three different address allocation mechanisms to provide flexibility when assigning IP addresses:

- *Manual Allocation*: The administrator assigns a preallocated IPv4 address to the client, and DHCPv4 communicates only the IPv4 address to the device.

- *Automatic Allocation*: DHCPv4 automatically assigns a static IPv4 address permanently to a device, selecting it from a pool of available addresses: the *DHCP pool*. There is no lease, and the address is permanently assigned to the device.

- *Dynamic Allocation*: DHCPv4 dynamically assigns, or leases, an IPv4 address from a pool of addresses for a limited period of time chosen by the server, or until the client no longer needs the address.

Dynamic allocation is the most commonly used DHCPv4 mechanism and is the focus of this section. When using dynamic allocation, clients lease the information from the server for an administratively defined period, as shown in Figure 7-1. Administrators configure DHCPv4 servers to set the leases to time out at different intervals. The lease is typically anywhere from 24 hours to a week or more. When the lease expires, the client must ask for another address, although the client is typically reassigned the same address.

DHCPv4 Operation (7.1.1.2)

As shown in Figure 7-2, DHCPv4 works in a client/server mode. When a client communicates with a DHCPv4 server, the server assigns or leases an IPv4 address to that client. The client connects to the network with that leased IP address until the lease expires. The client must contact the DHCP server periodically to extend the lease. This lease mechanism ensures that clients that move or power off do not keep addresses that they no longer need. When a lease expires, the DHCP server returns the address to the pool where it can be reallocated as necessary.

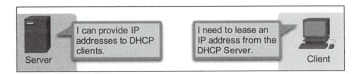

Figure 7-2 DHCPv4 Operation

Lease Origination

When the client boots (or otherwise wants to join a network), it begins a four-step process to obtain a *DHCP lease*. As shown in Figure 7-3, a client starts the process with a broadcast DHCPDISCOVER message with its own MAC address to discover available DHCPv4 servers.

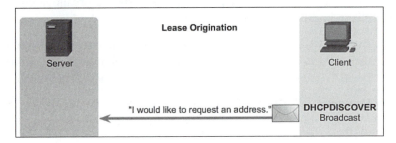

Figure 7-3 DHCPDISCOVER

DHCP Discover (DHCPDISCOVER)

The *DHCPDISCOVER* message finds DHCPv4 servers on the network. Because the client has no valid IPv4 information at bootup, it uses Layer 2 and Layer 3 broadcast addresses to communicate with the server.

DHCP Offer (DHCPOFFER)

When the DHCPv4 server receives a DHCPDISCOVER message, it reserves an available IPv4 address to lease to the client. The server also creates an ARP entry consisting of the MAC address of the requesting client and the leased IPv4 address of the client. As shown in Figure 7-4, the DHCPv4 server sends the *binding* DHCPOFFER message to the requesting client. The *DHCPOFFER* message is sent as a unicast, using the Layer 2 MAC address of the server as the source address and the Layer 2 MAC address of the client as the destination.

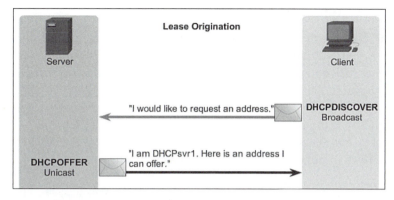

Figure 7-4   DHCPOFFER

DHCP Request (DHCPREQUEST)

When the client receives the DHCPOFFER from the server, it sends back a
DHCPREQUEST message, as shown in Figure 7-5. This message is used for
both *lease origination* and *lease renewal*. When used for lease origination, the
DHCPREQUEST serves as a binding acceptance notice to the selected server for the
parameters it has offered and an implicit decline to any other servers that might have
provided the client a binding offer.

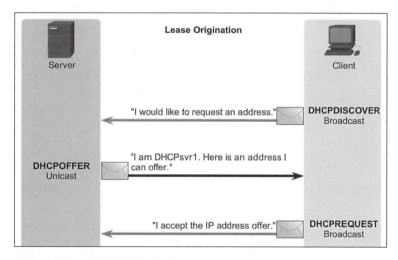

Figure 7-5   DHCPREQUEST

Many enterprise networks use multiple DHCPv4 servers. The DHCPREQUEST message is sent in the form of a broadcast to inform this DHCPv4 server and any other
DHCPv4 servers about the accepted offer.

DHCP Acknowledgment (DHCPACK)

On receiving the DHCPREQUEST message, the server verifies the lease information with an ICMP ping to that address to ensure that it is not being used already, creates a new ARP entry for the client lease, and replies with a unicast *DHCPACK* message, as shown in Figure 7-6. The DHCPACK message is a duplicate of the DHCPOFFER, except for a change in the message type field. When the client receives the DHCPACK message, it logs the configuration information and performs an ARP lookup for the assigned address. If there is no reply to the ARP, the client knows that the IPv4 address is valid and starts using it as its own.

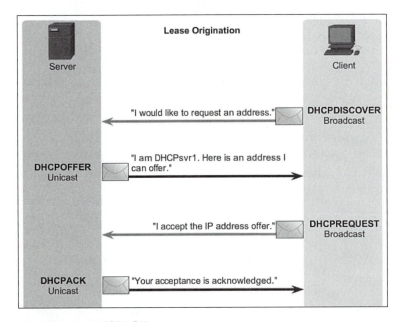

Figure 7-6   DHCPACK

Lease Renewal

Lease renewal involves a DHCP request and a DHCP acknowledgment.

DHCP Request (DHCPREQUEST)

As shown in Figure 7-7, when the lease has expired, the client sends a DHCPREQUEST message directly to the DHCPv4 server that originally offered the IPv4 address. If a DHCPACK is not received within a specified amount of time, the client broadcasts another DHCPREQUEST so that one of the other DHCPv4 servers can extend the lease.

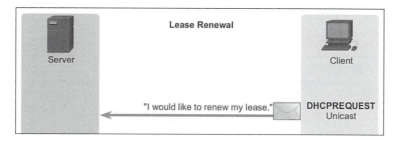

Figure 7-7   DHCPREQUEST for Lease Renewal

DHCP Acknowledgment (DHCPACK)

On receiving the DHCPREQUEST message, the server verifies the lease information by returning a DHCPACK, as shown in Figure 7-8.

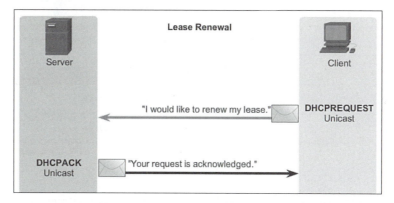

Figure 7-8   DHCPACK for Lease Renewal

DHCPv4 Message Format (7.1.1.3)

The DHCPv4 message format is used for all DHCPv4 transactions. DHCPv4 messages are encapsulated within the UDP transport protocol. DHCPv4 messages sent from the client use UDP source port 68 and destination port 67. DHCPv4 messages sent from the server to the client use UDP source port 67 and destination port 68.

Table 7-1 shows the format of a DHCPv4 message.

Table 7-1 DHCPv4 Message Format

8	16	24	32
OP Code (1)	Hardware Type (1)	Hardware Address Length (1)	Hops (1)
Transaction Identifier			
Seconds – 2 bytes		Flags – 2 bytes	
Client IP Address (CIADDR) – 4 bytes			
Your IP Address (YIADDR) – 4 bytes			
Server IP Address (SIADDR) – 4 bytes			
Gateway IP Address (GIADDR) – 4 bytes			
Client Hardware Address (CHADDR) – 16 bytes			
Server Name (SNAME) – 64 bytes			
Boot Filename – 128 bytes			
DHCP Options - variable			

The fields are as follows:

- **Operation (OP) Code:** Specifies the general type of message. A value of 1 indicates a request message; a value of 2 is a reply message.

- **Hardware Type:** Identifies the type of hardware used in the network. For example, 1 is Ethernet, 15 is Frame Relay, and 20 is a serial line. These are the same codes used in ARP messages.

- **Hardware Address Length:** Specifies the length of the address.

- **Hops:** Controls the forwarding of messages. Set to 0 by a client before transmitting a request.

- **Transaction Identifier:** Used by the client to match the request with replies received from DHCPv4 servers.

- **Seconds:** Identifies the number of seconds elapsed since a client began attempting to acquire or renew a lease. Used by DHCPv4 servers to prioritize replies when multiple client requests are outstanding.

- **Flags:** Used by a client that does not know its IPv4 address when it sends a request. Only one of the 16 bits is used, which is the broadcast flag. A value of 1 in this field tells the DHCPv4 server or relay agent receiving the request that the reply should be sent as a broadcast.

- **Client IP Address:** Used by a client during lease renewal when the address of the client is valid and usable, not during the process of acquiring an address. The client puts its own IPv4 address in this field if and only if it has a valid IPv4 address while in the bound state; otherwise, it sets the field to 0.

- **Your IP Address:** Used by the server to assign an IPv4 address to the client.

- **Server IP Address:** Used by the server to identify the address of the server that the client should use for the next step in the bootstrap process, which might or might not be the server sending this reply. The sending server always includes its own IPv4 address in a special field called the Server Identifier DHCPv4 option.

- **Gateway IP Address:** Routes DHCPv4 messages when DHCPv4 relay agents are involved. The gateway address facilitates communications of DHCPv4 requests and replies between the client and a server that are on different subnets or networks.

- **Client Hardware Address:** Specifies the physical layer of the client.

- **Server Name:** Used by the server sending a DHCPOFFER or DHCPACK message. The server can optionally put its name in this field. This can be a simple text nickname or a DNS domain name, such as dhcpserver.netacad.net.

- **Boot Filename:** Optionally used by a client to request a particular type of boot file in a DHCPDISCOVER message. Used by a server in a DHCPOFFER to fully specify a boot file directory and file name.

- **DHCP Options:** Holds DHCP options, including several parameters required for basic DHCP operation. This field is variable in length. Both client and server can use this field.

DHCPv4 Discover and Offer Messages (7.1.1.4)

If a client is configured to receive its IPv4 settings dynamically and wants to join the network, it requests addressing values from the DHCPv4 server. The client transmits a DHCPDISCOVER message on its local network when it boots or senses an active network connection. Because the client has no way of knowing the subnet to which it belongs, the DHCPDISCOVER message is an IPv4 broadcast (destination IPv4 address of 255.255.255.255). The client does not have a configured IPv4 address yet, so the source IPv4 address of 0.0.0.0 is used.

As shown in Figure 7-9, the client IPv4 address (*CIADDR*), default gateway address (*GIADDR*), and subnet mask are all marked to indicate that the address 0.0.0.0 is used. The DHCP server is on the same segment and will receive the broadcast. The server notes that the GIADDR field is blank and infers that the client is on the same segment; the server also notes the hardware address of the client that sourced the broadcast message.

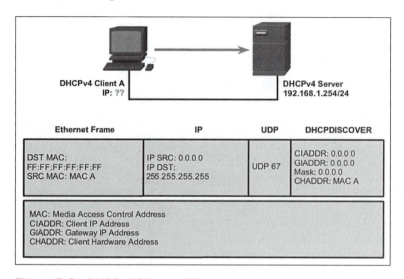

Figure 7-9   DHCPv4 Discover Message

Note

Unknown information is sent as 0.0.0.0.

When the DHCPv4 server receives the DHCPDISCOVER message, it responds with a DHCPOFFER message. This message contains initial configuration information for the client, including the IPv4 address that the server offers, the subnet mask, the lease duration, and the IPv4 address of the DHCPv4 server making the offer.

The DHCPOFFER message can be configured to include other information, such as the lease renewal time and DNS address.

As shown in Figure 7-10, the DHCP server responds to the DHCPDISCOVER message by assigning values to the CIADDR and subnet mask, as well as other global parameters. The frame is constructed using the client hardware address (*CHADDR*) and sent to the requesting client.

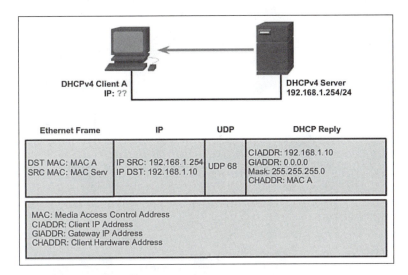

Figure 7-10 DHCPv4 Offer Message

The client and server send acknowledgment messages, and the process is complete.

Activity 7.1.1.5: Identify the Steps in DHCPv4 Operation

Go to the online course to perform this practice activity.

Configuring a Basic DHCPv4 Server (7.1.2)

Fortunately, Cisco routers can be configured as DHCP servers. This is useful in small networks, where a dedicated DHCP server is not needed.

Configuring a Basic DHCPv4 Server (7.1.2.1)

A Cisco router running Cisco IOS Software can be configured to act as a DHCPv4 server. The Cisco IOS DHCPv4 server assigns and manages IPv4 addresses from specified address pools within the router to DHCPv4 clients. The topology shown in Figure 7-11 is used to illustrate this functionality.

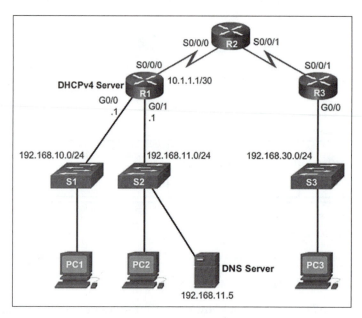

Figure 7-11   Router R1 as a DHCPv4 Server

To configure a DHCPv4 server with Cisco IOS, follow these steps:

Step 1.   Exclude IPv4 addresses.

Step 2.   Configure a DHCPv4 pool.

Step 3.   Configure specific tasks.

Step 1. Exclude IPv4 Addresses

The router functioning as the DHCPv4 server assigns all IPv4 addresses in a DHCPv4 address pool unless configured to exclude specific addresses. Typically, some IPv4 addresses in a pool are assigned to network devices that require static address assignments. Therefore, these IPv4 addresses should not be assigned to other devices. To exclude specific addresses, use the **ip dhcp excluded-address** *low-address* [*high-address*] command, as shown in Example 7-1. A single address or a range of addresses can be excluded by specifying the low address and high address of the range. Excluded addresses should include the addresses assigned to routers, servers, printers, and other devices that have been manually configured.

Example 7-1   Excluding IPv4 Addresses

```
R1(config)# ip dhcp excluded-address 192.168.10.1 192.168.10.9
R1(config)# ip dhcp excluded-address 192.168.10.254
```

Step 2. Configure a DHCPv4 Pool

Configuring a DHCPv4 server involves defining a pool of addresses to assign. As shown in Example 7-2, the **ip dhcp pool** *pool-name* command creates a pool with the specified name and puts the router in DHCPv4 configuration mode, which is identified by the prompt Router(dhcp-config)#.

Example 7-2   Configuring a DHCPv4 Pool

```
R1(config)# ip dhcp pool LAN-POOL-1
R1(dhcp-config)#
```

Step 3. Configure Specific Tasks

Table 7-2 lists the tasks to complete the DHCPv4 pool configuration. Some of these are optional, while others must be configured. The address pool and default gateway router must be configured. Use the **network** statement to define the range of available addresses. Use the **default-router** command to define the default gateway router. Typically, the gateway is the LAN interface of the router closest to the client devices. One gateway is required, but you can list up to eight addresses if there are multiple gateways. Other DHCPv4 pool commands are optional. For example, the IPv4 address of the DNS server that is available to a DHCPv4 client is configured using the **dns-server** command. The **domain-name** *domain* command is used to define the domain name. The duration of the DHCPv4 lease can be changed using the **lease** command. The default lease value is one day. The **netbios-name-server** command is used to define the NetBIOS WINS server.

Table 7-2   Configuring Specific DHCP Tasks

Task	Command
Define the address pool (required)	**network** *network-number [mask	/prefix-length]*
Define the default router or gateway (required)	**default-router** *address [address2...address8]*
Define a DNS server (optional)	**dns-server address** *[address2...address8]*
Define the domain name (optional)	**domain-name** *domain*
Define the duration of the DHCP lease (optional)	**lease** *{days [hours] [minutes]	infinite}*
Define the NetBIOS WINS server (optional)	**netbios-name-server** *address [address2...address8]*

DHCPv4 Example

A sample configuration with basic DHCPv4 parameters configured on Router R1, a DHCPv4 server for the 192.168.10.0/24 LAN, is shown in Example 7-3 using the example topology from Figure 7-11.

Example 7-3   DHCPv4 Example

```
R1(config)# ip dhcp excluded-address 192.168.10.1 192.168.10.9
R1(config)# ip dhcp excluded-address 192.168.10.254
R1(config)# ip dhcp pool LAN-POOL-1
R1(dhcp-config)# network 192.168.10.0 255.255.255.0
R1(dhcp-config)# default-router 192.168.10.1
R1(dhcp-config)# dns-server 192.168.11.5
R1(dhcp-config)# ip domain-name example.com
R1(dhcp-config)# end
R1#
```

Disabling DHCPv4

The DHCPv4 service is enabled, by default, on versions of Cisco IOS Software that support it. To disable the service, use the **no service dhcp** global configuration mode command. Use the **service dhcp** global configuration mode command to reenable the DHCPv4 server process. Enabling the service has no effect if the parameters are not configured.

Activity 7.1.2.1: Configuring a DHCPv4 Server

Go to the online course to use the Syntax Checker in the sixth graphic to configure similar DHCPv4 parameters on R1 for the 192.168.11.0/24 LAN.

Verifying DHCPv4 (7.1.2.2)

The topology shown in Figure 7-11 is used in the output for this continued example DHCPv4 implementation. R1 has been configured to provide DHCPv4 services. PC1 has not been powered up and, therefore, does not have an IP address.

As shown in Example 7-4, the **show running-config | section dhcp** command output displays the DHCPv4 commands configured on R1. The **| section** parameter displays only the commands associated with DHCPv4 configuration.

Example 7-4 Verifying DHCPv4 by Inspecting the Running Config File

```
R1# show running-config | section dhcp
ip dhcp excluded-address 192.168.10.1 192.168.10.9
ip dhcp excluded-address 192.168.10.254
ip dhcp excluded-address 192.168.11.1 192.168.11.9
ip dhcp excluded-address 192.168.11.254
ip dhcp pool LAN-POOL-1
 network 192.168.10.0 255.255.255.0
 default-router 192.168.10.1
 dns-server 192.168.11.5
 domain-name example.com
ip dhcp pool LAN-POOL-2
 network 192.168.11.0 255.255.255.0
 default-router 192.168.11.1
 dns-server 192.168.11.5
 domain-name example.com
R1#
```

As shown in Example 7-5, the operation of DHCPv4 can be verified using the **show ip dhcp binding** command. This command displays a list of all IPv4 address–to–MAC address bindings that have been provided by the DHCPv4 service. The second command in Example 7-5, **show ip dhcp server statistics**, is used to verify that messages are being received or sent by the router. This command displays count information regarding the number of DHCPv4 messages that have been sent and received.

Example 7-5 Before DHCPv4 with **show ip dhcp** Commands

```
R1# show ip dhcp binding
Bindings from all pools not associated with VRF:
IP address          Client-ID/              Lease expiration        Type
                    Hardware address/
                    User name
R1# show ip dhcp server statistics
Memory usage        23543
Address pools       1
Database agents     0
Automatic bindings  0
Manual bindings     0
Expired bindings    0
Malformed messages  0
Secure arp entries  0


Message             Received
BOOTREQUEST         0
```

```
DHCPDISCOVER          0
DHCPREQUEST           0
DHCPDECLINE           0
DHCPRELEASE           0
DHCPINFORM            0


Message             Sent
BOOTREPLY             0
DHCPOFFER             0
DHCPACK               0
DHCPNAK               0
R1#
```

As seen in the output for these commands, currently there are no bindings and the statistics indicate no messages sent or received. At this point, no devices have requested DHCPv4 services from Router R1.

In Example 7-6, the commands are issued after PC1 and PC2 have been powered on and have completed the booting process.

Example 7-6 After DHCPv4 with **show ip dhcp** Commands

```
R1# show ip dhcp binding
Bindings from all pools not associated with VRF:
IP address      Client-ID/        Lease expiration        Type
                Hardware address/
                User name
192.168.10.10   0100.e018.5bdd.35    May 28 2013 01:06 PM Automatic
192.168.11.10   0100.b0d0.d817.e6    May 28 2013 01:10 PM Automatic
R1# show ip dhcp server statistics
Memory usage        25307
Address pools       2
Database agents     0
Automatic bindings  2
Manual bindings     0
Expired bindings    0
Malformed messages  0
Secure arp entries  0


Message             Received
BOOTREQUEST           0
DHCPDISCOVER          8
DHCPREQUEST           3
DHCPDECLINE           0
```

```
DHCPRELEASE          0
DHCPINFORM           0


Message              Sent
BOOTREPLY            0
DHCPOFFER            3
DHCPACK              3
DHCPNAK              0
R1#
```

Notice that the binding information now displays that the IPv4 addresses of 192.168.10.10 and 192.168.11.10 have been bound to MAC addresses. The statistics are also displaying DHCPDISCOVER, DHCPREQUEST, DHCPOFFER, and DHCPACK activity.

As shown in Example 7-7, the **ipconfig /all** command, when issued on PC1, displays the TCP/IP parameters. Because PC1 was connected to the network segment 192.168.10.0/24, it automatically received a DNS suffix, IPv4 address, subnet mask, default gateway, and DNS server address from that pool. No router interface configuration is required. If a PC is connected to a network segment that has a DHCPv4 pool available, the PC can obtain an IPv4 address from the appropriate pool automatically.

Example 7-7   Verifying the DHCPv4 Client

```
C:\Documents and Settings\Administrator> ipconfig /all


Windows IP Configuration


Ethernet Adapter Local Area Connection

   Connection-specific DNS Suffix.: example.com
   Description ...................: SiS 900 PCI Fast Ethernet Adapter
   Physical Address...............: 00-E0-18-5B-DD-35
   Dhcp Enabled ..................: Yes
   Autoconfiguration Enabled......: Yes
   IP Address ....................: 192.168.10.10
   Subnet Mask....................: 255.255.255.0
   Default Gateway................: 192.168.10.1
   DHCP Server ...................: 192.168.10.1
   Lease Obtained.................: Monday,May 27,2013 1:06:22PM
   Lease Expires .................: Tuesday,May 28,2013 1:06:22PM
   DNS Servers   . . . . . . . . .: 192.168.11.5
```

DHCPv4 Relay (7.1.2.3)

In a complex hierarchical network, enterprise servers are usually located in a server farm. These servers can provide DHCP, DNS, TFTP, and FTP services for the network. Network clients are not typically on the same subnet as those servers. To locate the servers and receive services, clients often use broadcast messages.

In Figure 7-12, PC1 is attempting to acquire an IPv4 address from a DHCP server using a broadcast message. In this scenario, Router R1 is not configured as a DHCPv4 server and does not forward the broadcast. Because the DHCPv4 server is located on a different network, PC1 cannot receive an IP address using DHCP.

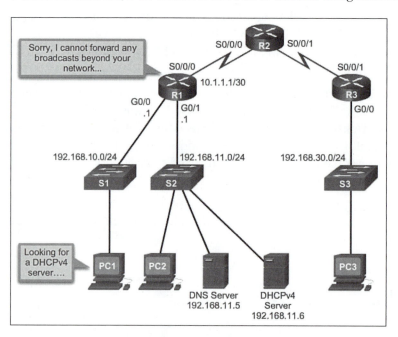

Figure 7-12 DHCP Relay Needed

In Example 7-8, PC1 is attempting to renew its IPv4 address. To do so, the **ipconfig / release** command is issued. Notice that the IPv4 address is released and the address is shown to be 0.0.0.0. Next, the **ipconfig /renew** command is issued. This command causes PC1 to broadcast a DHCPDISCOVER message. The output shows that PC1 is unable to locate the DHCPv4 server. Because routers do not forward broadcasts, the request is not successful.

Example 7-8   No IPv4 Address

```
C:\Documents and Settings\Administrator> ipconfig /release


Windows IP Configuration


Ethernet adapter Local Area Connection:
  Connection-specific DNS Suffix.:
  IP Address ....................: 0.0.0.0
  Subnet Mask...................: 0.0.0.0
  Default Gateway...............:


C:\Documents and Settings\Administrator> ipconfig /renew


Windows IP Configuration
An error occurred while renewing interface Local Area Connection:
unable to contact our DHCP server. Request has timed out.
```

As a solution to this problem, an administrator can add DHCPv4 servers on all the
subnets. However, running these services on several computers creates additional cost
and administrative overhead.

A better solution is to configure a Cisco IOS helper address. This solution enables
a router to forward DHCPv4 broadcasts to the DHCPv4 server. When a router for-
wards address assignment/parameter requests, it is acting as a *DHCP relay agent*.
In the example topology, PC1 would broadcast a request to locate a DHCPv4 server.
If R1 was configured as a DHCPv4 relay agent, it would forward the request to the
DHCPv4 server located on subnet 192.168.11.0.

As shown in Example 7-9, the interface on R1 receiving the broadcast is configured
with the **ip helper-address** interface configuration mode command. The address of
the DHCPv4 server is configured as the only parameter.

Example 7-9   DHCPv4 Relay Commands

```
R1(config)# interface g0/0
R1(config-if)# ip helper-address 192.168.11.6
R1(config-if)# end
R1# show ip interface g0/0
GigabitEthernet0/0 is up, line protocol is up
  Internet address is 192.168.10.1/24
  Broadcast address is 255.255.255.255
  Address determined by setup command
  MTU is 1500 bytes
  Helper address is 192.168.11.6
<output omitted>
```

When R1 has been configured as a DHCPv4 relay agent, it accepts broadcast requests for the DHCPv4 service and then forwards those requests as a unicast to the IPv4 address 192.168.11.6. The **show ip interface** command is used to verify the configuration.

As shown in Example 7-10, PC1 is now able to acquire an IPv4 address from the DHCPv4 server.

Example 7-10   Renew IPv4 Address

```
C:\Documents and Settings\Administrator> ipconfig /release


Windows IP Configuration


Ethernet adapter Local Area Connection:
  Connection-specific DNS Suffix.:
  IP Address ....................: 0.0.0.0
  Subnet Mask....................: 0.0.0.0
  Default Gateway................:

C:\Documents and Settings\Administrator> ipconfig /renew


Windows IP Configuration


Ethernet adapter Local Area Connection:
  Connection-specific DNS Suffix.:
  IP Address ....................: 192.168.10.11
  Subnet Mask....................: 255.255.255.0
  Default Gateway................: 192.168.10.1
```

DHCPv4 is not the only service that the router can be configured to relay. By default, the **ip helper-address** command forwards the following eight UDP services:

- Port 37: Time
- Port 49: TACACS
- Port 53: DNS
- Port 67: DHCP/BOOTP client
- Port 68: DHCP/BOOTP server
- Port 69: TFTP
- Port 137: NetBIOS name service
- Port 138: NetBIOS datagram service

Interactive Graphic

Activity 7.1.2.3: Configuring DHCPv4 Relay

Go to the online course to use the Syntax Checker in the fifth graphic to configure the DHCPv4 relay commands on the correct router so that PC3 can receive IPv4 addressing information from the DHCPv4 server. Refer back to Figure 7-11 to view the network topology.

Lab 7.1.2.4: Configuring Basic DHCPv4 on a Router

In this lab, you will complete the following objectives:

- Part 1: Build the Network and Configure Basic Device Settings
- Part 2: Configure a DHCPv4 Server and a DHCP Relay Agent

Lab 7.1.2.5: Configuring Basic DHCPv4 on a Switch

In this lab, you will complete the following objectives:

- Part 1: Build the Network and Configure Basic Device Settings
- Part 2: Change the SDM Preference
- Part 3: Configure DHCPv4
- Part 4: Configure DHCP for Multiple VLANs
- Part 5: Enable IP Routing

Configure DHCPv4 Client (7.1.3)

For the same reasons that one configures an end device as a *DHCP client*, it is often useful to configure a router as a DHCP client.

Configuring a Router as DHCPv4 Client (7.1.3.1)

Sometimes, Cisco routers in *small office/home office (SOHO)* and branch sites have to be configured as DHCPv4 clients in a similar manner to client computers. The method used depends on the ISP. However, in its simplest configuration, the Ethernet interface is used to connect to a cable or DSL modem. To configure an Ethernet interface as a DHCP client, use the **ip address dhcp** interface configuration mode command.

In Example 7-11, assume that an ISP has been configured to provide select customers with IP addresses from the 209.165.201.0/27 network range. After the G0/1 interface is configured with the **ip address dhcp** command, the **show ip interface g0/1** command confirms that the interface is up and that the address was allocated by a DHCPv4 server.

Example 7-11   DHCPv4 Relay Commands

```
SOHO(config)# interface g0/1
SOHO(config-if)# ip address dhcp
SOHO(config-if)# no shutdown
SOHO(config-if)#
*Jan 31 17:31:11.507: %DHCP-6-ADDRESS_ASSIGN: Interface GigabitEthernet0/1 assigned
  DHCP address 209.165.201.12, mask 255.255.255.224, hostname SOHO
SOHO(config-if)# end
SOHO# show ip interface g0/1
GigabitEthernet0/1 is up, line protocol is up
  Internet address is 209.165.201.12/27
  Broadcast address is 255.255.255.255
  Address determined by DHCP <output omitted>
```

Activity 7.1.3.1: Configuring a Router as a DHCP Client

Interactive
Graphic

Go to the online course to use the Syntax Checker in the second graphic to configure the interface that is connected to the ISP to acquire an address from the DHCP server.

Configuring a SOHO Router as a DHCPv4 Client (7.1.3.2)

Typically, small broadband routers for home use, such as Linksys routers, can be configured to connect to an ISP using a DSL or cable modem. In most cases, SOHO routers are set to acquire an IPv4 address automatically from the ISP.

For example, Figure 7-13 shows the default WAN setup page for a Linksys EA6500 router. Notice that the Internet connection type is set to Automatic Configuration - DHCP. This means that when the router is connected to a cable modem, for example, it is a DHCPv4 client and requests an IPv4 address from the ISP.

Note

The MAC Address Clone feature uses a specified address as the source MAC address on the ISP-facing interface of the router. Many ISPs assign IPv4 addresses based on the MAC address of the device during the initial installation. When a different device, such as a SOHO router, is connected to the ISP, the ISP might require that the MAC address of the original device be configured on the WAN interface.

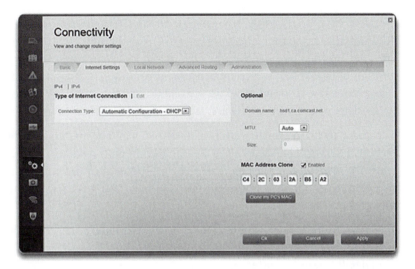

Figure 7-13 SOHO Router GUI

Packet Tracer
☐ **Activity**

Packet Tracer Activity 7.1.3.3: Configuring DHCPv4 Using Cisco IOS

A dedicated DHCP server is scalable and relatively easy to manage, but it can be costly to have one at every location in a network. However, a Cisco router can be configured to provide DHCP services without the need for a dedicated server. Cisco routers use the Cisco IOS feature set, Easy IP, as an optional, full-featured DHCP server. Easy IP leases configurations for 24 hours by default. As the network technician for your company, you are tasked with configuring a Cisco router as a DHCP server to provide dynamic allocation of addresses to clients on the network. You are also required to configure the edge router as a DHCP client so that it receives an IP address from the ISP network.

Troubleshoot DHCPv4 (7.1.4)

Troubleshooting DHCPv4 involves IP address conflicts, physical connectivity of devices, testing with static IP addresses, verifying switch port configuration, and testing DHCPv4 on a common subnet or VLAN. Also, troubleshooting DHCPv4 entails the use of the appropriate **show** and **debug** commands.

Troubleshooting Tasks (7.1.4.1)

DHCPv4 problems can arise for a multitude of reasons, such as software defects in operating systems, NIC drivers, or DHCP relay agents, but the most common are configuration issues. Because of the number of potentially problematic areas, a systematic approach to troubleshooting is required.

Troubleshooting Task 1: Resolve IPv4 Address Conflicts

An IPv4 address lease can expire on a client still connected to a network. If the client does not renew the lease, the DHCPv4 server can reassign that IPv4 address to another client. When the client reboots, it requests an IPv4 address. If the DHCPv4 server does not respond quickly, the client uses the last IPv4 address. The situation then arises where two clients are using the same IPv4 address, creating a conflict.

The **show ip dhcp conflict** command displays all address conflicts recorded by the DHCPv4 server. The server uses the **ping** command to detect clients. The client uses Address Resolution Protocol (ARP) to detect conflicts. If an address conflict is detected, the address is removed from the pool and not assigned until an administrator resolves the conflict.

The following output displays IP addresses that have conflicts with the DHCP server. It shows the detection method and detection time for conflicting IP addresses that the DHCP server has offered.

```
R1# show ip dhcp conflict
IP address Detection Method Detection time
192.168.10.32 Ping Feb 16 2013 12:28 PM
192.168.10.64 Gratuitous ARP Feb 23 2013 08:12 AM
```

Troubleshooting Task 2: Verify Physical Connectivity

First, use the **show interfaces** *interface-id* command to confirm that the router interface acting as the default gateway for the client is operational. If the state of the interface is anything other than up, the port does not pass traffic, including DHCP client requests.

Troubleshooting Task 3: Test Connectivity Using a Static IP Address

When troubleshooting any DHCPv4 issue, verify network connectivity by configuring static IPv4 address information on a client workstation. If the workstation is unable to reach network resources with a statically configured IPv4 address, the root cause of the problem is not DHCPv4. At this point, network connectivity troubleshooting is required.

Troubleshooting Task 4: Verify Switch Port Configuration

If the DHCPv4 client is unable to obtain an IPv4 address from the DHCPv4 server on startup, attempt to obtain an IPv4 address from the DHCPv4 server by manually forcing the client to send a DHCPv4 request.

Note

If there is a switch between the client and the DHCPv4 server, and the client is unable to obtain the DHCP configuration, switch port configuration issues might be the cause. These causes can include issues from trunking and channeling, STP, and RSTP. PortFast configuration and edge port configurations resolve the most common DHCPv4 client issues that occur with an initial installation of a Cisco switch.

Troubleshooting Task 5: Test DHCPv4 Operation on the Same Subnet or VLAN

It is important to distinguish whether DHCPv4 is functioning correctly when the client is on the same subnet or VLAN as the DHCPv4 server. If DHCPv4 is working correctly when the client is on the same subnet or VLAN, the problem might be the DHCP relay agent. If the problem persists, even with testing DHCPv4 on the same subnet or VLAN as the DHCPv4 server, the problem might actually be with the DHCPv4 server.

Verify Router DHCPv4 Configuration (7.1.4.2)

When the DHCPv4 server is located on a separate LAN from the client, the router interface facing the client must be configured to relay DHCPv4 requests by configuring the IPv4 helper address. If the IPv4 helper address is not configured properly, client DHCPv4 requests are not forwarded to the DHCPv4 server.

Follow these steps to verify the router configuration:

Step 1. Verify that the **ip helper-address** command is configured on the correct interface. It must be present on the inbound interface of the LAN containing the DHCPv4 client workstations and must be directed to the correct DHCPv4 server. In Example 7-12, the output of the **show running-config** command verifies that the DHCPv4 relay IPv4 address is referencing the DHCPv4 server address at 192.168.11.6. The **show ip interface** command can also be used to verify the DHCPv4 relay on an interface.

Example 7-12   Verifying DHCPv4 Relay and DHCPv4 Services

```
R1# show running-config | section interface GigabitEthernet0/0
interface GigabitEthernet0/0
 ip address 192.168.10.1 255.255.255.0
 ip helper-address 192.168.11.6
 duplex auto
 speed auto
R1# show running-config | include no service dhcp
R1#
```

Step 2. Verify that the global configuration command **no service dhcp** has not been configured. This command disables all DHCP server and relay functionality on the router. The **service dhcp** command does not appear in the running config because it is the default configuration. In Example 7-12, the **show running-config | include no service dhcp** command verifies that the DHCPv4 service is enabled because there is no match for the **show running-config | include no service dhcp** command. If the service had been disabled, the **no service dhcp** command would be displayed in the output.

Debugging DHCPv4 (7.1.4.3)

On routers configured as DHCPv4 servers, the DHCPv4 process fails if the router is not receiving requests from the client. As a troubleshooting task, verify that the router is receiving the DHCPv4 request from the client. This troubleshooting step involves configuring an ACL for debugging output.

Example 7-13 shows an extended ACL permitting only packets with UDP destination ports of 67 or 68. These are the typical ports used by DHCPv4 clients and servers when sending DHCPv4 messages. The extended ACL is used with the **debug ip packet** command to display only DHCPv4 messages.

Example 7-13 Verifying DHCPv4 using Router **debug** Commands

```
R1(config)# access-list 100 permit udp any any eq 67
R1(config)# access-list 100 permit udp any any eq 68
R1(config)# end
R1# debug ip packet 100
IP packet debugging is on for access list 100
*IP: s=0.0.0.0 (GigabitEthernet0/1), d=255.255.255.255, len 333, rcvd 2
*IP: s=0.0.0.0 (GigabitEthernet0/1), d=255.255.255.255, len 333, stop process pak for
  forus packet
*IP: s=192.168.11.1 (local), d=255.255.255.255 (GigabitEthernet0/1), len 328, sending
  broad/multicast
<output omitted>
R1# debug ip dhcp server events
DHCPD: returned 192.168.10.11 to address pool LAN-POOL-1
DHCPD: assigned IP address 192.168.10.12 to client 0100.0103.85e9.87.
DHCPD: checking for expired leases.
DHCPD: the lease for address 192.168.10.10 has expired.
DHCPD: returned 192.168.10.10 to address pool LAN-POOL-1
```

The output in the example shows that the router is receiving DHCP requests from the client. The source IP address is 0.0.0.0 because the client does not yet have an IP address. The destination is 255.255.255.255 because the DHCP discovery message from the client is sent as a broadcast. This output only shows a summary of the packet and not the DHCPv4 message itself. Nevertheless, the router did receive a broadcast packet with the source and destination IP and UDP ports that are correct for DHCPv4. The complete debug output shows all the packets in the DHCPv4 communications between the DHCPv4 server and client.

Another useful command for troubleshooting DHCPv4 operation is the **debug ip dhcp server events** command. This command reports server events, like address assignments and database updates. It is also used for decoding DHCPv4 receptions and transmissions.

Lab 7.1.4.4: Troubleshooting DHCPv4

In this lab, you will complete the following objectives:

- Part 1: Build the Network and Configure Basic Device Settings
- Part 2: Troubleshoot DHCPv4 Issues

Dynamic Host Configuration Protocol for IPv6 (DHCPv6) (7.2)

DHCPv6 is a bit more complex than DHCPv4. There are more options with IPv6 for addressing hosts, as you learn in this section.

SLAAC and DHCPv6 (7.2.1)

Stateless Address Autoconfiguration is a new option not available with IPv4. On the other hand, DHCPv6 is similar in that a DHCP server is involved. Interestingly, the degree to which the DHCP server is involved with DHCPv6 is configurable.

Stateless Address Autoconfiguration (SLAAC) (7.2.1.1)

Similar to IPv4, IPv6 global unicast addresses can be configured manually or dynamically. However, there are two methods in which IPv6 global unicast addresses can be assigned dynamically:

- *Stateless Address Autoconfiguration (SLAAC)*, as shown in Figure 7-14
- Dynamic Host Configuration Protocol for IPv6 (*Stateful DHCPv6*)

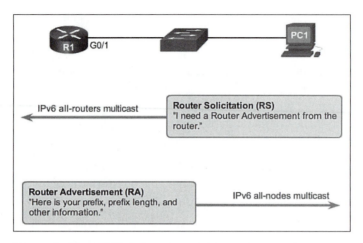

Figure 7-14 ICMPv6 Stateless Address Autoconfiguration

Introducing SLAAC

SLAAC is a method in which a device can obtain an IPv6 global unicast address without the services of a DHCPv6 server. At the core of SLAAC is *Internet Control Message Protocol version 6 (ICMPv6)*. ICMPv6 is similar to ICMPv4 but includes additional functionality and is a much more robust protocol. SLAAC uses ICMPv6 Router Solicitation and Router Advertisement messages to provide addressing and other configuration information that would normally be provided by a DHCP server:

- *Router Solicitation (RS)* **message:** When a client is configured to obtain its addressing information automatically using SLAAC, the client sends an RS message to the router. The RS message is sent to the IPv6 all-routers multicast address FF02::2.

- *Router Advertisement (RA)* **message:** RA messages are sent by routers to provide addressing information to clients configured to obtain their IPv6 addresses automatically. The RA message includes the prefix and prefix length of the local segment. A client uses this information to create its own IPv6 global unicast address. A router sends an RA message periodically, or in response to an RS message. By default, Cisco routers send RA messages every 200 seconds. RA messages are always sent to the IPv6 all-nodes multicast address FF02::1.

As the name indicates, SLAAC is stateless. A stateless service means that no server maintains network address information. Unlike DHCP, there is no SLAAC server that knows which IPv6 addresses are being used and which ones are available.

SLAAC Operation (7.2.1.2)

A router must be enabled as an IPv6 router before it can send RA messages. To enable IPv6 routing, a router is configured with the following command:

```
Router(config)# ipv6 unicast-routing
```

1. In the example topology shown in Figure 7-15, PC1 is configured to obtain IPv6 address information automatically. Since booting, PC1 has not received an RA message, so it sends an RS message to the all-routers multicast address to inform the local IPv6 router that it needs an RA.

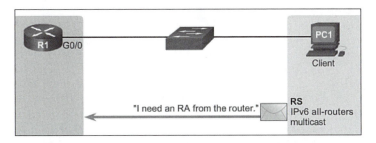

Figure 7-15   Client Sends Router Solicitation Message

2. As shown in Figure 7-16, R1 receives the RS message and responds with an RA message. Included in the RA message are the prefix and prefix length of the network. The RA message is sent to the IPv6 all-nodes multicast address FF02::1, with the link-local address of the router as the IPv6 source address.

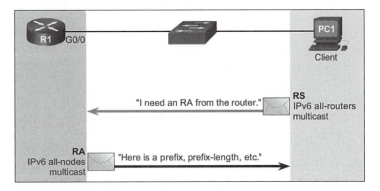

Figure 7-16   Router Sends Router Advertisement Message

3. PC1 receives the RA message containing the prefix and prefix length for the local network. PC1 will use this information to create its own IPv6 global unicast address. PC1 now has a 64-bit network prefix, but needs a 64-bit *Interface ID (IID)* to create a global unicast address.

There are two ways PC1 can create its own unique IID:

- **EUI-64:** Using the EUI-64 process, PC1 will create an IID using its 48-bit MAC address.

- **Randomly generated:** The 64-bit IID can be a random number generated by the client operating system.

As shown in Figure 7-17, PC1 can create a 128-bit IPv6 global unicast address by combining the 64-bit prefix with the 64-bit IID. PC1 will use the link-local address of the router as its IPv6 default gateway address.

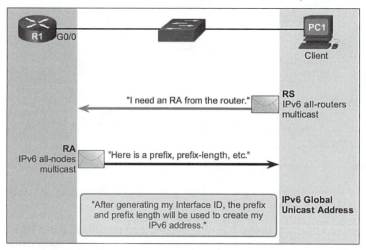

Figure 7-17   Client Creates Global Unicast Address

4. Because SLAAC is a stateless process, before PC1 can use this newly created IPv6 address, it must verify that it is unique. As shown in Figure 7-18, PC1 sends an ICMPv6 Neighbor Solicitation message with its own address as the target IPv6 address. If no other devices respond with a Neighbor Advertisement message, the address is unique and can be used by PC1. If a Neighbor Advertisement is received by PC1, the address is not unique and the operating system has to determine a new Interface ID to use.

This process is part of *ICMPv6 Neighbor Discovery* and is known as *Duplicate Address Detection (DAD)*.

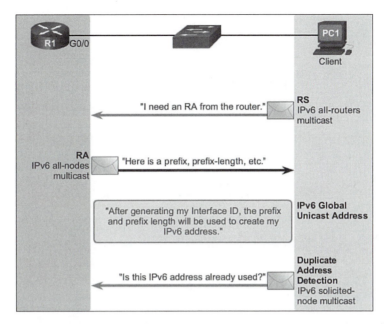

Figure 7-18   Client Performs Duplicate Address Detection

SLAAC and DHCPv6 (7.2.1.3)

The decision of whether a client is configured to obtain its IPv6 address information automatically using SLAAC, DHCPv6, or a combination of both depends on the settings within the RA message.

The two flags are the Managed Address Configuration flag (*M flag*) and the Other Configuration flag (*O flag*).

Using different combinations of the M and O flags, RA messages have one of three addressing options for the IPv6 device, as shown in Figure 7-19:

- SLAAC (Router Advertisement only)
- Stateless DHCPv6 (Router Advertisement and DHCPv6)
- Stateful DHCPv6 (DHCPv6 only)

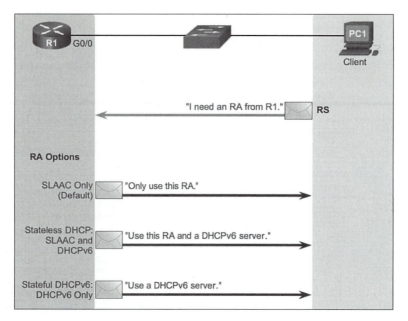

Figure 7-19   SLAAC and DHCPv6

Regardless of the option used, it is recommended by RFC 4861 that all IPv6 devices perform Duplicate Address Detection (DAD) on any unicast address, including addresses configured using SLAAC or DHCPv6.

Note

Although the RA message specifies the process the client should use in obtaining an IPv6 address dynamically, the client operating system can choose to ignore the RA message and use the services of a DHCPv6 server exclusively.

SLAAC Option (7.2.1.4)

The first option, SLAAC (Router Advertisements only), is the default option on Cisco routers. Both the M flag and the O flag are set to 0 in the RA, as shown in Figure 7-20.

This option instructs the client to use the information in the RA message exclusively. This includes prefix, prefix length, DNS server, MTU, and default gateway information. There is no further information available from a DHCPv6 server. The IPv6 global unicast address is created by combining the prefix from the RA and an Interface ID using either EUI-64 or a randomly generated value.

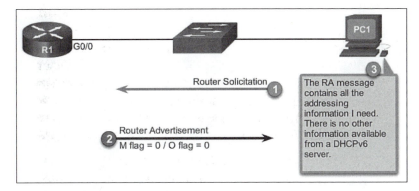

Figure 7-20   SLAAC Option

RA messages are configured on an individual interface of a router. To reenable an interface for SLAAC that might have been set to another option, the M and O flags need to be reset to their initial values of 0. This is done using the following interface configuration mode commands:

```
Router(config-if)# no ipv6 nd managed-config-flag
Router(config-if)# no ipv6 nd other-config-flag
```

Stateless DHCPv6 Option (7.2.1.5)

Although DHCPv6 is similar to DHCPv4 in what it provides, the two protocols are independent of each other. DHCPv6 is defined in RFC 3315. There has been a lot of work done on this specification over the years as indicated by the fact that the DHCPv6 RFC has the highest revision number of any Internet draft.

The second option, *stateless DHCPv6* (Router Advertisement and DHCPv6), informs the client to use the information in the RA message for addressing, but additional configuration parameters are available from a DHCPv6 server.

Using the prefix and prefix length in the RA message, along with EUI-64 or a randomly generated IID, the client creates its IPv6 global unicast address.

The client will then communicate with a stateless DHCPv6 server to obtain additional information not provided in the RA message. This can be a list of DNS server IPv6 addresses, for example. This process is known as stateless DHCPv6 because the server is not maintaining any client state information (that is, a list of available and allocated IPv6 addresses). The stateless DHCPv6 server is only providing configuration parameters for clients, not IPv6 addresses.

For stateless DHCPv6, the O flag is set to 1 and the M flag is left at the default setting of 0, as shown in Figure 7-21. The O flag value of 1 is used to inform the client that additional configuration information is available from a stateless DHCPv6 server.

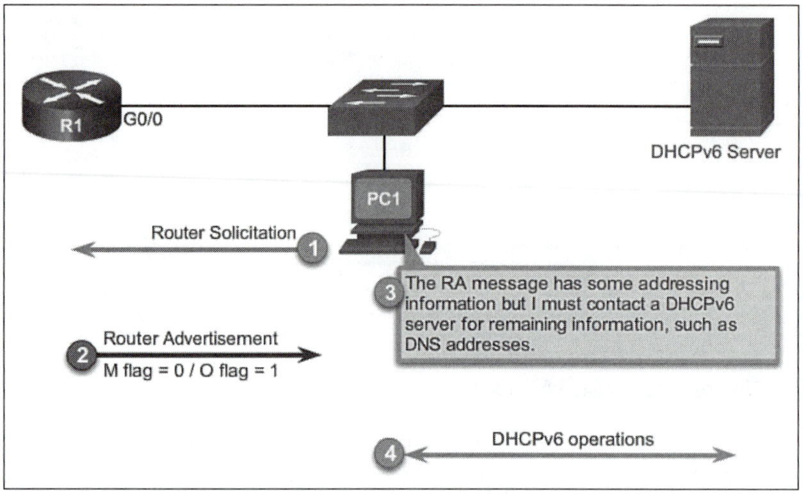

Figure 7-21   Stateless DHCPv6 Option

To modify the RA message sent on the interface of a router to indicate stateless DHCPv6, use the following command:

```
Router(config-if)# ipv6 nd other-config-flag
```

Stateful DHCPv6 Option (7.2.1.6)

The third option, Stateful DHCPv6 (DHCPv6 only) is the most similar to DHCPv4. In this case, the RA message informs the client not to use the information in the RA message. All addressing information and configuration information must be obtained from a stateful DHCPv6 server. This is known as stateful DHCPv6 because the DHCPv6 server maintains IPv6 state information. This is similar to a DHCPv4 server allocating addresses for IPv4.

The M flag indicates whether or not to use stateful DHCPv6. The O flag is not involved, as shown in Figure 7-22.

The following command is used to change the M flag from 0 to 1 to signify stateful DHCPv6:

```
Router(config-if)# ipv6 nd managed-config-flag
```

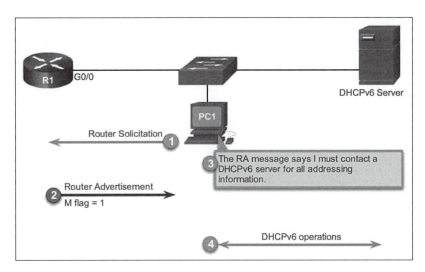

Figure 7-22   Stateful DHCPv6 Option

DHCPv6 Operations (7.2.1.7)

As shown in Figure 7-23, stateless or stateful DHCPv6, or both, begin with an ICMPv6 RA message from the router. The RA message might have been a periodic message or solicited by the device using an RS message.

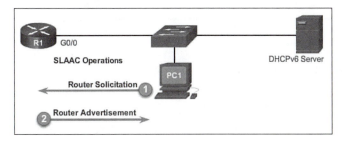

Figure 7-23   DHCPv6 Operations

If stateless or stateful DHCPv6 is indicated in the RA message, the device begins DHCPv6 client/server communications.

DHCPv6 Communications

When stateless DHCPv6 or stateful DHCPv6 is indicated by the RA, DHCPv6 operation is invoked. DHCPv6 messages are sent over UDP. DHCPv6 messages from the server to the client use UDP destination port 546. The client sends DHCPv6 messages to the server using UDP destination port 547.

The client, now a DHCPv6 client, needs to locate a DHCPv6 server. In Figure 7-24, the client sends a *DHCPv6 SOLICIT* message to the reserved IPv6 multicast all-DHCPv6-servers address FF02::1:2. This multicast address has link-local scope, which means that routers do not forward the messages to other networks.

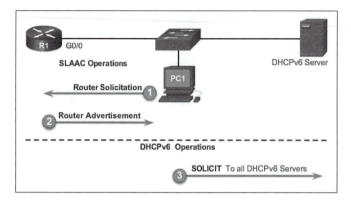

Figure 7-24   DHCPv6 SOLICIT Message

One or more DHCPv6 servers respond with a *DHCPv6 ADVERTISE* message, as shown in Figure 7-25. The ADVERTISE message informs the DHCPv6 client that the server is available for DHCPv6 service.

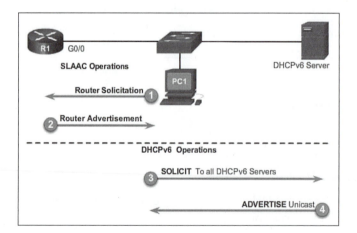

Figure 7-25   DHCPv6 ADVERTISE Message

In Figure 7-26, the client responds with a *DHCPv6 REQUEST* or INFORMATION-REQUEST message to the server, depending on whether it is using stateful or stateless DHCPv6:

- **Stateless DHCPv6 client:** The client sends a *DHCPv6 INFORMATION-REQUEST* message to the DHCPv6 server requesting only configuration parameters, such as a DNS server address. The client generated its own IPv6 address using the prefix from the RA message and a self-generated Interface ID.

■ **Stateful DHCPv6 client:** The client sends a DHCPv6 REQUEST message to the server to obtain an IPv6 address and all other configuration parameters from the server.

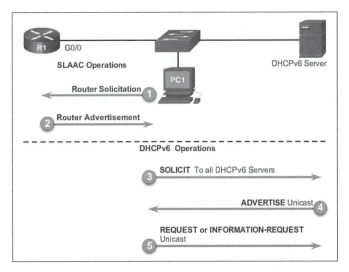

Figure 7-26   DHCPv6 REQUEST or INFORMATION-REQUEST Message

The server sends a *DHCPv6 REPLY* to the client containing the information requested in the REQUEST or INFORMATION-REQUEST message, as shown in Figure 7-27.

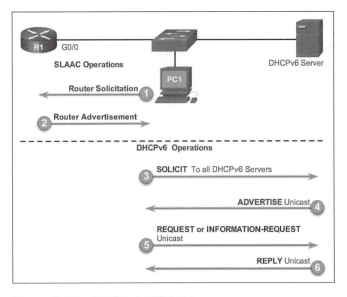

Figure 7-27   DHCPv6 REPLY Message

Interactive Graphic

Activity 7.2.1.8: Identify the Steps in DHCPv6 Operation

Go to the online course to perform this practice activity.

Stateless DHCPv6 (7.2.2)

The first of two DHCPv6 options is the stateless DHCPv6 option.

Configuring a Router as a Stateless DHCPv6 Server (7.2.2.1)

To configure a DHCPv6 server with Cisco IOS, follow these steps:

How To

Step 1.   Enable IPv6 routing.

Step 2.   Configure a DHCPv6 pool.

Step 3.   Configure pool parameters.

Step 4.   Configure the DHCPv6 interface.

Step 1. Enable IPv6 Routing

The **ipv6 unicast-routing** command is required to enable IPv6 routing:

```
R1(config)# ipv6 unicast-routing
```

This command is not necessary for the router to be a stateless DHCPv6 server, but is required for sending ICMPv6 RA messages.

Step 2. Configure a DHCPv6 Pool

The **ipv6 dhcp pool** *pool-name* command creates a pool and enters the router in DHCPv6 configuration mode, which is identified by the Router(config-dhcpv6)# prompt:

```
R1(config)# ipv6 dhcp pool pool-name
R1(config-dhcpv6)#
```

Step 3. Configure Pool Parameters

During the SLAAC process, the client received the information it needed to create an IPv6 global unicast address. The client also received the default gateway information using the source IPv6 address from the RA message, which is the link-local address of the router. However, the stateless DHCPv6 server can be configured to provide other information that might not have been included in the RA message, such as DNS server address and the domain name:

```
R1(config-dhcpv6)# dns-server dns-server-address
R1(config-dhcpv6)# domain-name domain-name
```

Step 4. Configure the DHCPv6 Interface

The **ipv6 dhcp server** *pool-name* interface configuration mode command binds the DHCPv6 pool to the interface. The router responds to stateless DHCPv6 requests on this interface with the information contained in the pool. The O flag needs to be changed from 0 to 1 using the **ipv6 nd other-config-flag** interface command:

```
R1(config)# interface type number
R1(config-if)# ipv6 dhcp server pool-name
R1(config-if)# ipv6 nd other-config-flag
```

RA messages sent on this interface indicate that additional information is available from a stateless DHCPv6 server.

DHCPv6 Stateless Server Example

Example 7-14 shows a sample stateless DHCPv6 server configuration for Router R1, pictured in Figure 7-28. R1 is configured as a stateless DHCPv6 server. Notice that Router R3 is shown as a DHCPv6 client. R3 is configured as a client to help verify the stateless DHCPv6 operations.

Figure 7-28   Configuring Router R1 as a Stateless DHCPv6 Server

Example 7-14   Stateless DHCPv6 Server Configuration

```
R1(config)# ipv6 unicast-routing
R1(config)# ipv6 dhcp pool IPV6-STATELESS
R1(config-dhcpv6)# dns-server 2001:db8:cafe:aaaa::5
R1(config-dhcpv6)# domain-name example.com
R1(config-dhcpv6)# exit
R1(config)# interface g0/1
R1(config-if)# ipv6 address 2001:db8:cafe:1::1/64
R1(config-if)# ipv6 dhcp server IPV6-STATELESS
R1(config-if)# ipv6 nd other-config-flag
```

Configuring a Router as a Stateless DHCPv6 Client (7.2.2.2)

In Example 7-15, Router R3, pictured in Figure 7-28, is configured as a stateless DHCPv6 client. This is not a typical scenario and is used for demonstration purposes only. Typically, a stateless DHCPv6 client is a device, such as a computer, tablet, mobile device, or webcam.

Example 7-15   Stateless DHCPv6 Client Configuration

```
R3(config)# interface g0/1
R1(config-if)# ipv6 enable
R1(config-if)# ipv6 address autoconfig
```

The client router needs an IPv6 link-local address on the interface to send and receive IPv6 messages, such as RS messages and DHCPv6 messages. The link-local address of a router is created automatically when IPv6 is enabled on the interface. This can happen when a global unicast address is configured on the interface or by using the **ipv6 enable** command. After the router receives a link-local address, it can send RS messages and participate in DHCPv6.

In this example, the **ipv6 enable** command is used because the router does not yet have a global unicast address.

The **ipv6 address autoconfig** command enables automatic configuration of IPv6 addressing using SLAAC. An RA message is then used to inform the client router to use stateless DHCPv6.

Verifying Stateless DHCPv6 (7.2.2.3)

The stateless DHCPv6 server and the stateless DHCPv6 client configurations can be verified with select **show** and **debug** commands.

Verifying the Stateless DHCPv6 Server

In Example 7-16, referencing Figure 7-28, the **show ipv6 dhcp pool** command verifies the name of the DHCPv6 pool and its parameters. The number of active clients is 0, because there is no state being maintained by the server.

Example 7-16   Verifying Stateless DHCPv6 Server Configuration

```
R1# show ipv6 dhcp pool
DHCPv6 pool: IPV6-STATELESS
  DNS server: 2001:DB8:CAFE:AAAA::5
  Domain name: example.com
  Active clients: 0
```

The **show running-config** command can also be used to verify all the commands that were previously configured.

Verifying the Stateless DHCPv6 Client

In Example 7-17, referencing Figure 7-28, Router R3 is used as a stateless DHCPv6 client. The output from the **show ipv6 interface** command shows that the router has "Stateless address autoconfig enabled" and has an IPv6 global unicast address. The IPv6 global unicast address was created using SLAAC, which includes the prefix contained in the RA message. The interface ID was generated using EUI-64. DHCPv6 was not used to assign the IPv6 address.

Example 7-17   Verifying Stateless DHCPv6 Client Configuration with **show ipv6 interface**

```
R3# show ipv6 interface g0/1
GigabitEthernet0/1 is up, line protocol is up
  IPv6 is enabled, link-local address is FE80::32F7:DFF:FE25:2DE1
  No Virtual link-local address(es):
  Stateless address autoconfig enabled
  Global unicast address(es):
    2001:DB8:CAFE:1:32F7:DFF:FE25:2DE1, subnet is 2001:DB8:CAFE:1::/64 [EUI/CAL/PRE]
      valid lifetime 2591935 preferred lifetime 604735
  Joined group address(es):
    FF02::1
    FF02::1:FF25:2DE1
  MTU is 1500 bytes
  ICMP error messages limited to one every 100 milliseconds
  ICMP redirects are enabled
  ICMP unreachables are sent
  ND DAD is enabled, number of DAD attempts: 1
  ND reachable time is 30000 milliseconds (using 30000)
  ND NS retransmit interval is 1000 milliseconds
  Default router is FE80::D68C:B5FF:FECE:A0C1 on GigabitEthernet0/1
```

The default router information is also from the RA message. This was the source IPv6 address of the packet that contained the RA message and the link-local address of the router.

The output from the **debug ipv6 dhcp detail** command in Example 7-18 shows the DHCPv6 messages exchanged between the client and the server. In this example, the command has been entered on the client. The INFORMATION-REQUEST message is shown because it is sent from a stateless DHCPv6 client. Notice that the client,

Router R3, is sending the DHCPv6 messages from its link-local address to the All_DHCPv6_Relay_Agents_and_Servers address FF02::1:2.

Example 7-18   Verifying Stateless DHCPv6 Client Configuration with **debug ipv6 dhcp detail**

```
R3# debug ipv6 dhcp detail
   IPv6 DHCP debugging is on (detailed)
R3#
*Feb  3 02:39:10.454: IPv6 DHCP: Sending INFORMATION-REQUEST to FF02::1:2 on
  GigabitEthernet0/1
*Feb  3 02:39:10.454: IPv6 DHCP: detailed packet contents
*Feb  3 02:39:10.454:   src FE80::32F7:DFF:FE25:2DE1
*Feb  3 02:39:10.454:   dst FF02::1:2 (GigabitEthernet0/1)
*Feb  3 02:39:10.454:   type INFORMATION-REQUEST(11), xid 12541745
<Some output omitted for brevity>
*Feb  3 02:39:10.454: IPv6 DHCP: Adding server FE80::D68C:B5FF:FECE:A0C1
*Feb  3 02:39:10.454: IPv6 DHCP: Processing options
*Feb  3 02:39:10.454: IPv6 DHCP: Configuring DNS server 2001:DB8:CAFE:AAAA::5
*Feb  3 02:39:10.454: IPv6 DHCP: Configuring domain name example.com
*Feb  3 02:39:10.454: IPv6 DHCP: DHCPv6 changes state from INFORMATION-REQUEST to IDLE
  (REPLY_RECEIVED) on GigabitEthernet0/1
```

The debug output displays all the DHCPv6 messages sent between the client and the server, including the DNS server and domain name options that were configured on the server.

Interactive Graphic

Activity 7.2.2.3: Configuring and Verifying Stateless DHCPv6

Go to the online course to use the Syntax Checker in the fourth graphic to configure and verify stateless DHCPv6 on the router.

Stateful DHCPv6 Server (7.2.3)

The second of two DHCPv6 options is the stateful DHCPv6 option.

Configuring a Router as a Stateful DHCPv6 Server (7.2.3.1)

Configuring a stateful DHCPv6 server is similar to configuring a stateless server. The most significant difference is that a stateful server also includes IPv6 addressing information similar to a DHCPv4 server.

To configure a DHCPv6 server with Cisco IOS, follow these steps:

Step 1.   Enable IPv6 routing.

Step 2.   Configure a DHCPv6 pool.

Step 3.   Configure pool parameters.

Step 4.   Configure the DHCPv6 interface.

Step 1. Enable IPv6 Routing

As with stateless DHCPv6, the **ipv6 unicast-routing** command is required to enable IPv6 routing. This command is not necessary for the router to be a stateful DHCPv6 server, but is required for sending ICMPv6 RA messages.

Step 2. Configure a DHCPv6 Pool

As with stateless DHCPv6, the **ipv6 dhcp pool** *pool-name* command creates a pool and enters the router in DHCPv6 configuration mode, which is identified by the Router(config-dhcpv6)# prompt.

Step 3. Configure Pool Parameters

With stateful DHCPv6, all addressing and other configuration parameters must be assigned by the DHCPv6 server. Example 7-19 illustrates configuration commands for the DHCPv6 pool parameters. The **address** *prefix/length* command is used to indicate the pool of addresses to be allocated by the server. The **lifetime** option indicates the valid and preferred lease times in seconds. As with stateless DHCPv6, the client uses the source IPv6 address from the packet that contained the RA message.

Example 7-19   Configure DHCPv6 Pool Parameters

```
Router(config-dhcpv6)# address prefix/length [lifetime valid-lifetime preferred-
  lifetime | infinite]
Router(config-dhcpv6)# dns-server dns-server-address
Router(config-dhcpv6)# domain-name domain-name
```

Other information provided by the stateful DHCPv6 server typically includes the DNS server address and the domain name.

Step 4. Configure the DHCPv6 Interface

Example 7-20 illustrates interface configuration commands for the DHCPv6. The **ipv6 dhcp server** *pool-name* interface command binds the DHCPv6 pool to the interface. The router responds to stateless DHCPv6 requests on this interface with the information contained in the pool. The M flag needs to be changed from 0 to 1 using the interface command **ipv6 nd managed-config-flag**. This informs the device not to use SLAAC but to obtain IPv6 addressing and all configuration parameters from a stateful DHCPv6 server.

Example 7-20   Configure DHCPv6 Interface

```
Router(config)# interface type number
Router(config-if)# ipv6 dhcp server pool-name
Router(config-if)# ipv6 nd managed-config-flag
```

DHCPv6 Stateful Server Example

Example 7-21 shows a sample stateful DHCPv6 server configuration for Router R1, pictured in Figure 7-29. Notice that a default gateway is not specified because the router will automatically send its own link-local address as the default gateway. Router R3 is configured as a client to help verify the stateful DHCPv6 operations.

Figure 7-29   Configuring Router R1 as a Stateful DHCPv6 Server

Example 7-21   Stateful DHCPv6 Server Configuration

```
R1(config)# ipv6 unicast-routing
R1(config)# ipv6 dhcp pool IPV6-STATEFUL
R1(config-dhcpv6)# address prefix 2001:DB8:CAFE:1::/64 lifetime infinite
R1(config-dhcpv6)# dns-server 2001:db8:cafe:aaaa::5
R1(config-dhcpv6)# domain-name example.com
R1(config-dhcpv6)# exit
R1(config)# interface g0/1
R1(config-if)# ipv6 address 2001:db8:cafe:1::1/64
R1(config-if)# ipv6 dhcp server IPV6-STATEFUL
R1(config-if)# ipv6 nd managed-config-flag
```

Configuring a Router as a Stateful DHCPv6 Client (7.2.3.2)

In Example 7-22, referencing Figure 7-29, the **ipv6 enable** interface configuration mode command is used to allow the router to receive a link-local address to send RS messages and participate in DHCPv6.

Example 7-22 Stateful DHCPv6 Client Configuration

```
R3(config)# interface g0/1
R3(config-if)# ipv6 enable
R3(config-if)# ipv6 address dhcp
```

The **ipv6 address dhcp** interface configuration mode command enables the router to behave as a DHCPv6 client on this interface.

Verifying Stateful DHCPv6 (7.2.3.3)

The stateful DHCPv6 server and the stateful DHCPv6 client configurations can be verified with select **show** commands.

Verifying the Stateful DHCPv6 Server

In Example 7-23, referencing Figure 7-29, the **show ipv6 dhcp pool** command verifies the name of the DHCPv6 pool and its parameters. The number of active clients is 1, which reflects client R3 receiving its IPv6 global unicast address from this server.

Example 7-23 Verifying Stateful DHCPv6 Client Configuration with **show ipv6 dhcp pool**

```
R1# show ipv6 dhcp pool
DHCPv6 pool: IPV6-STATEFUL
  Address allocation prefix: 2001:DB8:CAFE:1::/64 valid 4294967295 preferred
  4294967295 (1 in use, 0 conflicts)
  DNS server: 2001:DB8:CAFE:AAAA::5
  Domain name: example.com
  Active clients: 1
```

The **show ipv6 dhcp binding** command, as shown in Example 7-24, displays the automatic binding between the link-local address of the client and the address assigned by the server. FE80::32F7:DFF:FE25:2DE1 is the link-local address of the client. In this example, this is the G0/1 interface of R3. This address is bound to the IPv6 global unicast address, 2001:DB8:CAFE:1:5844:47B2:2603:C171, which was assigned by R1, the DHCPv6 server. This information is maintained by a stateful DHCPv6 server and not by a stateless DHCPv6 server.

Example 7-24   Verifying Stateful DHCPv6 Client Configuration with **show ipv6 dhcp binding**

```
R1# show ipv6 dhcp binding
Client: FE80::32F7:DFF:FE25:2DE1
  DUID: 0003000130F70D252DE0
  Username : unassigned
  IA NA: IA ID 0x00040001, T1 43200, T2 69120
    Address: 2001:DB8:CAFE:1:5844:47B2:2603:C171
            preferred lifetime INFINITY, valid lifetime INFINITY,
```

Verifying the Stateful DHCPv6 Client

The output from the **show ipv6 interface** command shown in Example 7-25 verifies the IPv6 global unicast address on DHCPv6 client R3 that was assigned by the DHCPv6 server. The default router information is not from the DHCPv6 server, but was determined by using the source IPv6 address from the RA message. Although the client does not use the information contained in the RA message, it is able to use the source IPv6 address for its default gateway information.

Example 7-25   Verifying Stateful DHCPv6 Client Configuration with **show ipv6 interface**

```
R3# show ipv6 interface g0/1
GigabitEthernet0/1 is up, line protocol is up
  IPv6 is enabled, link-local address is FE80::32F7:DFF:FE25:2DE1
  No Virtual link-local address(es):
  Global unicast address(es):
    2001:DB8:CAFE:1:5844:47B2:2603:C171, subnet is 2001:DB8:CAFE:1:5844:47B2:2603
:C171/128
  Joined group address(es):
    FF02::1
    FF02::1:FF03:C171
    FF02::1:FF25:2DE1
  MTU is 1500 bytes
  ICMP error messages limited to one every 100 milliseconds
  ICMP redirects are enabled
  ICMP unreachables are sent
  ND DAD is enabled, number of DAD attempts: 1
  ND reachable time is 30000 milliseconds (using 30000)
  ND NS retransmit interval is 1000 milliseconds
  Default router is FE80::D68C:B5FF:FECE:A0C1 on GigabitEthernet0/1
```

Activity 7.2.3.3: Configuring and Verifying Stateful DHCPv6

Go to the online course to use the Syntax Checker in the fourth graphic to configure
and verify stateful DHCPv6.

Configuring a Router as a DHCPv6 Relay Agent (7.2.3.4)

If the DHCPv6 server is located on a different network than the client, the IPv6 router can be configured as a DHCPv6 relay agent. The configuration of a DHCPv6 relay
agent is similar to the configuration of an IPv4 router as a DHCPv4 relay.

Note

Although the configuration of a DHCPv6 relay agent is similar to DHCPv4, IPv6 router or
relay agents forward DHCPv6 messages slightly differently than DHCPv4 relays. The messages and the process are beyond the scope of this curriculum.

Figure 7-30 shows an example topology where a DHCPv6 server is located
on the 2001:DB8:CAFE:1::/64 network. The network administrator wants to
use this DHCPv6 server as a central, stateful DHCPv6 server to allocate IPv6
addresses to all clients. Therefore, clients on other networks, such as PC1 on the
2001:DB8:CAFE:A::/64 network, must communicate with the DHCPv6 server.

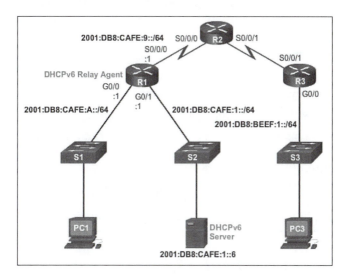

Figure 7-30   DHCPv6 Relay Agent

DHCPv6 messages from clients are sent to the IPv6 multicast address FF02::1:2
All_DHCPv6_Relay_Agents_and_Servers address. This address has link-local scope,
which means that routers do not forward these messages. The router must be configured as a DHCPv6 relay agent to enable the DHCPv6 client and server to communicate.

Configuring the DHCPv6 Relay Agent

As shown in Example 7-26, a DHCPv6 relay agent is configured using the **ipv6 dhcp relay destination** command. This command is configured on the interface facing the DHCPv6 client using the address of the DHCPv6 server as the destination.

Example 7-26   DHCPv6 Relay Agent Commands

```
R1(config)# interface g0/0
R1(config-if)# ipv6 dhcp relay destination 2001:db8:cafe:1::6
R1(config-if)# end
R1# show ipv6 dhcp interface g0/0
GigabitEthernet0/0 is in relay mode
  Relay destinations:
    2001:DB8:CAFE:1::6
```

The **show ipv6 dhcp interface** command verifies that the G0/0 interface is in relay mode with 2001:DB8:CAFE:1::6 configured as the DHCPv6 server.

Interactive Graphic

Activity 7.2.3.4: Configuring a DHCPv6 Relay Agent

Go to the online course to use the Syntax Checker in the third graphic to configure the DHCPv6 relay commands on the correct router so that PC3 can receive IPv6 addressing information from the DHCPv6 server. Refer to Figure 7-30 to view the network topology.

Lab 7.2.3.5: Configuring Stateless and Stateful DHCPv6

In this lab, you will complete the following objectives:

- Part 1: Build the Network and Configure Basic Device Settings
- Part 2: Configure the Network for SLAAC
- Part 3: Configure the Network for Stateless DHCPv6
- Part 4: Configure the Network for Stateful DHCPv6

Troubleshoot DHCPv6 (7.2.4)

Troubleshooting DHCPv6 involves IP address conflicts, address allocation methods, testing with static IP addresses, verifying switch port configuration, and testing DHCPv6 on a common subnet or VLAN. Also, troubleshooting DHCPv6 entails the use of the appropriate **show** and **debug** commands.

Troubleshooting Tasks (7.2.4.1)

Troubleshooting DHCPv6 is similar to troubleshooting DHCPv4.

Troubleshooting Task 1: Resolve Conflicts

An IPv6 address lease can expire on a client that still needs to connect to the network. The **show ipv6 dhcp conflict** command displays any address conflicts logged by the stateful DHCPv6 server. If an IPv6 address conflict is detected, the client typically removes the address and generates a new address using either SLAAC or stateful DHCPv6.

Troubleshooting Task 2: Verify Allocation Method

The **show ipv6 interface** *interface* command can be used to verify the method of address allocation prescribed in the RA message as indicated by the settings of the M and O flags. This information is displayed in the last lines of the output. If a client is not receiving its IPv6 address information from a stateful DHCPv6 server, it could be due to incorrect M and O flags in the RA message.

Troubleshooting Task 3: Test with a Static IPv6 Address

When troubleshooting any DHCP issue, whether it is DHCPv4 or DHCPv6, network connectivity can be verified by configuring a static IP address on a client workstation. In the case of IPv6, if the workstation is unable to reach network resources with a statically configured IPv6 address, the root cause of the problem is not SLAAC or DHCPv6. At this point, network connectivity troubleshooting is required.

Troubleshooting Task 4: Verify Switch Port Configuration

If the DHCPv6 client is unable to obtain information from a DHCPv6 server, verify that the switch port is enabled and is operating correctly.

> **Note**
>
> If there is a switch between the client and the DHCPv6 server, and the client is unable to obtain the DHCP configuration, switch port configuration issues might be the cause. These causes can include issues from trunking and channeling, STP, and RSTP. PortFast and edge port configurations resolve the most common DHCPv6 client issues that occur with an initial installation of a Cisco switch.

Troubleshooting Task 5: Test DHCPv6 Operation on the Same Subnet or VLAN

If the stateless or stateful DHCPv6 server is functioning correctly, but is on a different IPv6 network or VLAN than the client, the problem might be with the DHCPv6 relay agent. The client-facing interface on the router must be configured with the **ipv6 dhcp relay destination** command.

Verify Router DHCPv6 Configuration (7.2.4.2)

The router configurations for stateless and stateful DHCPv6 services have many similarities but also include significant differences.

Stateful DHCPv6

Example 7-27 shows the configuration commands for stateful DHCPv6 services.

Example 7-27   Stateful DHCPv6 Services

```
R1(config)# ipv6 unicast-routing
R1(config)# ipv6 dhcp pool IPV6-STATEFUL
R1(config-dhcpv6)# address prefix 2001:DB8:CAFE:1::/64 lifetime infinite
R1(config-dhcpv6)# dns-server 2001:db8:cafe:aaaa::5
R1(config-dhcpv6)# domain-name example.com
R1(config-dhcpv6)# exit
R1(config)# interface g0/1
R1(config-if)# ipv6 address 2001:db8:cafe:1::1/64
R1(config-if)# ipv6 dhcp server IPV6-STATEFUL
R1(config-if)# ipv6 nd managed-config-flag
```

A router configured for stateful DHCPv6 services has the **address prefix** command to provide addressing information.

For stateful DHCPv6 services, the **ipv6 nd managed-config-flag** interface configuration mode command is used. In this instance, the client ignores the addressing information in the RA message and communicates with a DHCPv6 server for both addressing and other information.

Stateless DHCPv6

Example 7-28 shows the configuration commands for stateless DHCPv6 services.

Example 7-28   Stateless DHCPv6 Services

```
R1(config)# ipv6 unicast-routing
R1(config)# ipv6 dhcp pool IPV6-STATELESS
R1(config-dhcpv6)# dns-server 2001:db8:cafe:aaaa::5
R1(config-dhcpv6)# domain-name example.com
R1(config-dhcpv6)# exit
R1(config)# interface g0/1
R1(config-if)# ipv6 address 2001:db8:cafe:1::1/64
R1(config-if)# ipv6 dhcp server IPV6-STATELESS
R1(config-if)# ipv6 nd other-config-flag
```

For stateless DHCPv6 services, the **ipv6 nd other-config-flag** interface configuration mode command is used. This informs the device to use SLAAC for addressing information and a stateless DHCPv6 server for other configuration parameters.

The **show ipv6 interface** command can be used to view the current configuration for the allocation method. Example 7-29 illustrates how to view the allocation method in each of the cases: SLAAC, stateless DHCPv6, and stateful DHCPv6, respectively.

Example 7-29   Viewing Allocation Method

```
R1# show ipv6 interface g0/1
GigabitEthernet0/1 is up, line protocol is up
  IPv6 is enabled, link-local address is FE80::D68C:B5FF:FECE:A0C1
<output omitted>
  Hosts use stateless autoconfig for addresses.
R1# show ipv6 interface g0/1
GigabitEthernet0/1 is up, line protocol is up
  IPv6 is enabled, link-local address is FE80::D68C:B5FF:FECE:A0C1
<output omitted>
  Hosts use DHCP to obtain other configuration.
R1# show ipv6 interface g0/1
GigabitEthernet0/1 is up, line protocol is up
  IPv6 is enabled, link-local address is FE80::D68C:B5FF:FECE:A0C1
<output omitted>
  Hosts use DHCP to obtain routable addresses.
```

Debugging DHCPv6 (7.2.4.3)

When the router is configured as a stateless or stateful DHCPv6 server, the **debug ipv6 dhcp detail** command is useful to verify the receipt and transmission of DHCPv6 messages. As shown in Example 7-30, a stateful DHCPv6 router has received a SOLICIT message from a client. The router is using the addressing information in its IPV6-STATEFUL pool for binding information.

Example 7-30   Debugging DHCPv6

```
R1# debug ipv6 dhcp detail
   IPv6 DHCP debugging is on (detailed)
R1#
*Feb  3 21:27:41.123: IPv6 DHCP: Received SOLICIT from FE80::32F7:DFF:FE25:2DE1 on
  GigabitEthernet0/1
*Feb  3 21:27:41.123: IPv6 DHCP: detailed packet contents
*Feb  3 21:27:41.123:   src FE80::32F7:DFF:FE25:2DE1 (GigabitEthernet0/1)
*Feb  3 21:27:41.127:   dst FF02::1:2
*Feb  3 21:27:41.127:   type SOLICIT(1), xid 13190645
*Feb  3 21:27:41.127:   option ELAPSED-TIME(8), len 2
*Feb  3 21:27:41.127:     elapsed-time 0
*Feb  3 21:27:41.127:   option CLIENTID(1), len 10
*Feb  3 21:27:41.127:     000
*Feb  3 21:27:41.127: IPv6 DHCP: Using interface pool IPV6-STATEFUL
*Feb  3 21:27:41.127: IPv6 DHCP: Creating binding for FE80::32F7:DFF:FE25:2DE1 in pool
  IPV6-STATEFUL
<output omitted>
```

Lab 7.2.4.4: Troubleshooting DHCPv6

In this lab, you will complete the following objectives:

- Part 1: Build the Network and Configure Basic Device Settings
- Part 2: Troubleshoot IPv6 Connectivity
- Part 3: Troubleshoot Stateless DHCPv6

Summary (7.3)

 Class Activity 7.3.1.1: IoE and DHCP

This chapter presents the concept of using the DHCP process in a small- to medium-sized business network; however, DHCP also has other uses!

With the advent of the Internet of Everything (IoE), any device in your home that is capable of wired or wireless connectivity to a network will be able to be accessed from just about anywhere.

Using Packet Tracer for this modeling activity, perform the following tasks:

- Configure a Cisco 1941 router (or DHCP-server-capable ISR device) for IPv4 or IPv6 DHCP addressing.

- Think of five devices in your home that you would like to receive IP addresses from the router's DHCP service. Set the end devices to claim DHCP addresses from the DHCP server.

- Show the output validating that each end device secures an IP address from the server. Save your output information through a screen capture program or press the **PrtScrn** key.

- Present your findings to a fellow classmate or to the class.

 Packet Tracer Activity 7.3.1.2: Skills Integration Challenge

In this culminating activity, you will configure VLANs, trunks, Easy IP DHCP, and DHCP relay agents and configure a router as a DHCP client.

All nodes on a network require a unique IP address to communicate with other devices. The static assignment of IP addressing information on a large network results in an administrative burden that can be eliminated by using DHCPv4 or DHCPv6 to dynamically assign IPv4 and IPv6 addressing information respectively.

DHCPv4 includes three different address allocation mechanisms to provide flexibility when assigning IP addresses:

- **Manual Allocation:** The administrator assigns a preallocated IPv4 address to the client, and DHCPv4 communicates only the IPv4 address to the device.

- **Automatic Allocation:** DHCPv4 automatically assigns a static IPv4 address permanently to a device, selecting it from a pool of available addresses. There is no lease, and the address is permanently assigned to the device.

■ **Dynamic Allocation:** DHCPv4 dynamically assigns, or leases, an IPv4 address from a pool of addresses for a limited period of time as configured on the server, or until the client no longer needs the address.

Dynamic allocation is the most commonly used DHCPv4 mechanism and involves the exchange of several different packets between the DHCPv4 server and the DHCPv4 client, resulting in the lease of valid addressing information for a predefined period of time.

Messages originating from the client (DHCPDISCOVER, DHCPREQUEST) are broadcast to allow all DHCPv4 servers on the network to hear the client request for, and receipt of, addressing information. Messages originating from the DHCPv4 server (DHCPOFFER, DHCPACK) are sent as unicasts directly to the client requesting the information.

There are two methods available for the dynamic configuration of IPv6 global unicast addresses.

■ Stateless Address Autoconfiguration (SLAAC)

■ Dynamic Host Configuration Protocol for IPv6 (Stateful DHCPv6)

With stateless autoconfiguration, the client uses information provided by the IPv6 RA message to automatically select and configure a unique IPv6 address. The stateless DHCPv6 option informs the client to use the information in the RA message for addressing, but additional configuration parameters are available from a DHCPv6 server.

Stateful DHCPv6 is similar to DHCPv4. In this case, the RA message informs the client not to use the information in the RA message. All addressing information and configuration information is obtained from a stateful DHCPv6 server. The DHCPv6 server maintains IPv6 state information similar to a DHCPv4 server allocating addresses for IPv4.

If the DHCP server is located on a different network segment than the DHCP client, it is necessary to configure a relay agent. The relay agent forwards specific broadcast messages originating from a LAN segment to a specified server located on a different LAN segment (in this case, a DHCP broadcast message would be forwarded to a DHCP server).

Troubleshooting issues with DHCPv4 and DHCPv6 involves the same tasks:

■ Resolve address conflicts

■ Verify physical connectivity

- Test connectivity using a static IP address
- Verify switch port configuration
- Test operation on the same subnet or VLAN

Practice

The following activities provide practice with the topics introduced in this chapter. The Labs and Class Activities are available in the companion *Switched Networks Lab Manual* (ISBN 978-1-58713-327-5). The Packet Tracer Activities PKA files are found in the online course.

Class Activities

- Class Activity 7.0.1.2: Own or Lease?
- Class Activity 7.3.1.1: IoE and DHCP

Labs

- Lab 7.1.2.4: Configuring Basic DHCPv4 on a Router
- Lab 7.1.2.5: Configuring Basic DHCPv4 on a Switch
- Lab 7.1.4.4: Troubleshooting DHCPv4
- Lab 7.2.3.5: Configuring Stateless and Stateful DHCPv6
- Lab 7.2.4.4: Troubleshooting DHCPv6

Packet Tracer
☐ **Activity**

Packet Tracer Activities

- Packet Tracer Activity 7.1.3.3: Configuring DHCPv4 Using Cisco IOS

Check Your Understanding Questions

Complete all the review questions listed here to test your understanding of the topics and concepts in this chapter. The appendix "Answers to 'Check Your Understanding' Questions" lists the answers.

1. What is the most likely scenario in which the WAN interface of a router would be configured as a DHCP client to be assigned a dynamic IP address from an ISP?

   A. There is a web server for public access on the LAN that is attached to the router.

   B. The router is also the gateway for a LAN.

   C. It is a SOHO or home broadband router.

   D. The router is configured as a DHCP server.

2. List the four DHCP message types for the DHCPv4 process in order.

3. After booting, a client receives an ICMPv6 RA message with the M flag set to 0 and the O flag set to 1. What does this indicate?

   A. The client should request an IPv6 address directly from a DHCPv6 server.

   B. The client should automatically configure an IPv6 address without contacting a DHCPv6 server.

   C. The client should automatically configure an IPv6 address and then contact a DHCPv6 server for more information.

   D. The client should be statically configured with an IPv6 address because the local router does not support autoconfiguration.

4. List the four DHCP message types in order for the DHCPv6 process when a client first connects to an IPv6 network.

5. When a client is requesting an initial address lease from a DHCP server, why is the DHCPREQUEST message sent as a broadcast?

   A. The client does not yet know the IP address of the DHCP server that sent the offer.

   B. The DHCP server might be on a different subnet, so the request must be sent as a broadcast.

   C. The client does not have a MAC address assigned yet, so it cannot send a unicast message at Layer 2.

   D. The client might have received offers from multiple servers, and the broadcast serves to implicitly decline those other offers.

6. Which command will allow a network administrator to check the IP address that is assigned to a particular MAC address?

   A. Router# **show ip dhcp binding**

   B. Router# **show ip dhcp pool**

   C. Router# **show ip dhcp server statistics**

   D. Router# **show running-config I section_dhcp**

7. Fill in the blank. Do not abbreviate. An administrator is troubleshooting a DHCPv4 issue on a router. By issuing the **debug ip dhcp** _____ command, the administrator can watch, in real time, the IP address assignments that are performed by the router.

8. Which alternative to DHCPv6 dynamically assigns IPv6 addresses to hosts?

   A. ARP

   B. EUI-64

   C. ICMPv6

   D. SLAAC

9. Which command should be configured on a router interface to set the router as a stateful DHCPv6 client?

   A. **ipv6 enable**

   B. **ipv6 address dhcp**

   C. **ipv6 address autoconfigure**

   D. **ipv6 dhcp server stateful**

10. Which message does an IPv4 host use to reply when it receives a DHCPOFFER message from a DHCP server?

    A. DHCPACK

    B. DHCPDISCOVER

    C. DHCPOFFER

    D. DHCPREQUEST

CHAPTER 8

Wireless LANs

Objectives

Upon completion of this chapter, you will be able to answer the following questions:

- How do you describe wireless LAN technology and standards?

- How do you describe the components of a wireless LAN infrastructure?

- How do you describe wireless technologies?

- How do you describe the 802.11 frame structure?

- How do you describe the media access method used by wireless technology?

- How do you describe channel management in a WLAN?

- How do you describe threats to wireless LANs?

- How do you describe wireless LAN security mechanisms?

- How do you configure a wireless router to support a remote site?

- How do you configure wireless clients to connect to a wireless router?

- How do you troubleshoot common wireless configuration issues?

Key Terms

This chapter uses the following key terms. You can find the definitions in the Glossary.

Introduction (8.0.1.1)

Wireless networks can provide client mobility, the ability to connect from any location and at any time, and the ability to roam while staying connected. A *wireless LAN (WLAN)* is a classification of wireless network that is commonly used in homes, offices, and campus environments. Although it uses radio frequencies instead of cables, it is commonly implemented in a switched network environment and its frame format is similar to Ethernet.

This chapter covers WLAN technology, components, security, planning, implementation, and troubleshooting. The types of network attacks to which wireless networks are particularly susceptible are discussed.

Class Activity 8.0.1.2: Make Mine Wireless

As the network administrator for your small- to medium-sized business, you realize that your wireless network needs updating, both inside and outside of your building. Therefore, you decide to research how other businesses and educational and community groups set up their WLANs for better access to their employees and clients.

To research this topic, you visit the "Customer Case Studies and Research" website to see how other businesses use wireless technology. After viewing a few of the videos, or reading some of the case study PDFs, you decide to select two to show to your CEO to support upgrading to a more robust wireless solution for your company.

To complete this class modeling activity, open the accompanying PDF for further instructions on how to proceed.

Wireless Concepts (8.1)

In this section, you begin to learn about the world of wireless technologies, concepts, and devices. In particular, you will explore the components of a wireless LAN and wireless LAN topologies.

Introduction to Wireless (8.1.1)

This topic introduces the major considerations with wireless networks. Supporting mobility drives much of wireless network technology development. Specifically, you learn about radio frequencies, 802.11 standards, and Wi-Fi certification.

Supporting Mobility (8.1.1.1)

Business networks today are evolving to support people who are on the move. People are connected using multiple devices, including computers, laptops, tablets, and smart phones. This is the vision of mobility, where people can take their connection to the network along with them on the road.

There are many different infrastructures (wired LAN, service provider networks) that make this type of mobility possible, but in a business environment, the most important is the wireless LAN (WLAN).

Productivity is no longer restricted to a fixed work location or a defined time period. People now expect to be connected at any time and place, from the office to the airport or the home. Traveling employees used to be restricted to pay phones for checking messages and returning a few phone calls between flights. Now employees can check email, voice mail, and the status of projects on smart phones.

Users now expect to be able to roam wirelessly. Roaming enables a wireless device to maintain Internet access without losing connection.

Video

Video 8.1.1.1: Cisco Enterprise Mobility Solutions

Go to the online course and play the video in the graphic to view how wireless networks enable mobility.

Benefits of Wireless (8.1.1.2)

There are many benefits to supporting wireless networking, both in the business environment and at home. Some of the benefits include increased flexibility, increased productivity, reduced costs, and the ability to grow and adapt to changing requirements.

Most businesses rely on switch-based LANs for day-to-day operation within the office. However, employees are becoming more mobile and want to maintain access to their business LAN resources from locations other than their desks. Workers want to take their wireless devices to meetings, coworkers' offices, conference rooms, and even customer sites, all while maintaining access to office resources. Wireless networking provides this type of flexibility. Instead of spending a significant amount of time transporting necessary company material or locating wired connections to access network resources, using the wireless network, LAN resources can be easily made available to a variety of wireless devices.

Although hard to measure, wireless access can result in increased productivity and more relaxed employees. With wireless networking, employees have the flexibility to work when they want, where they want. They can respond to customer inquiries whether at the office, or out to dinner. They can access email and other work-related resources quickly and easily, providing better management, better and faster results for customers, and increased profits.

Wireless networking can also reduce costs. In businesses with a wireless infrastructure already in place, savings are realized anytime equipment changes or moves are required, such as when relocating an employee within a building, reorganizing equipment or a lab, or moving to temporary locations or project sites.

Another important benefit of wireless networking is the ability to adapt to changing needs and technologies. Adding new equipment to the network is fairly seamless with wireless networking. Consider the wireless connectivity of the home. Users can surf the web from their kitchen table, living rooms, or even outdoors. Home users connect new devices, such as smart phones and smart pads, laptops, and smart televisions.

A wireless home router allows the user to connect to these devices without the additional cost or inconvenience of running cables to different locations in the home.

Wireless Technologies (8.1.1.3)

Wireless communications are used in a variety of professions.

Although the mix of wireless technologies is continually expanding, the focus of this discussion is on wireless networks that allow users to be mobile. Wireless networks can be classified broadly as

- *Wireless Personal-Area Networks (WPAN)*: Operate in the range of a few feet. Bluetooth or Wi-Fi Direct–enabled devices are used in WPANs.

- **Wireless LANs (WLAN)**: Operate in the range of a few hundred feet, such as in a room, home, office, and even campus environment.

- *Wireless Wide-Area Networks (WWAN)*: Operate in the range of miles, such as a metropolitan area, cellular hierarchy, or even on intercity links through microwave relays.

There are various wireless technologies available to connect devices to the wireless network:

- *Bluetooth*: Originally an *IEEE 802.15* WPAN standard that uses a device-pairing process to communicate over distances up to 0.05 mile (100m). Newer Bluetooth versions are standardized by the Bluetooth Special Interest Group (www.bluetooth.org). Variations include Bluetooth v1 to Bluetooth v3. Bluetooth supports speeds up to 24 Mb/s (Bluetooth v3). Three power ranges are supported: 100 meters (long range), 10 meters (ordinary range), and 10 cm (short range).

- *Wireless fidelity (Wi-Fi)*: An IEEE 802.11 WLAN standard commonly deployed to provide network access to home and corporate users, to include data, voice, and video traffic to distances up to 300m (0.18 mile). Variations include 802.11a/b/g/n/ac/ad. Speeds vary based on the technology.

- *Worldwide Interoperability for Microwave Access (WiMAX)*: An *IEEE 802.16* WWAN standard that provides wireless cellular broadband access of up to 30 miles (50 km) in a point-to-multipoint topology. WiMAX is an alternative to cable and DSL broadband connections. Mobility was added to WiMAX in 2005 and can now be used by service providers to provide cellular broadband. WiMAX supports speeds up to 1 Gb/s.

- *Cellular/Mobile broadband*: Consists of various corporate, national, and international organizations using service provider cellular access to provide mobile broadband network connectivity. First available with second-generation cell phones in 1991 (*2G*: GSM, CDMA, or TDMA), with higher speeds becoming available in 2001 and 2006, respectively, as part of the third (*3G*: UMTS, CDMA2000, EDGE, or HSPA+) and fourth (*4G*: WiMAX or LTE) generations of mobile communication technology. Download speeds up to 12 Mb/s are supported.

- *Satellite broadband*: Provides network access to remote sites through the use of a directional satellite dish that is aligned with a specific *geostationary Earth orbit (GEO) satellite*. It is usually more expensive and requires a clear line of sight, but is ideal in remote areas where no other wireless access is available. Download speeds up to 1 Gb/s are available, depending on the satellite provider infrastructure.

There are many types of wireless technologies available. However, the focus of this chapter is on 802.11 WLANs.

Radio Frequencies (8.1.1.4)

All wireless devices operate in the radio waves range of the electromagnetic spectrum. It is the responsibility of the *International Telecommunication Union - Radiocommunication Sector (ITU-R)* to regulate the allocation of the *radio frequency (RF)* spectrum. Ranges of frequencies, called bands, are allocated for various purposes. Some bands in the electromagnetic spectrum are heavily regulated and are used for applications, such as air traffic control and emergency responder communications networks. Other bands are license free, such as the *Industrial, Scientific, and Medical (ISM)* and the *Unlicensed National Information Infrastructure (UNII)* frequency bands.

Note

WLAN networks operate in the ISM 2.4-GHz frequency band and the UNII 5-GHz band.

Wireless communication occurs in the radio waves range (that is, 3 Hz to 300 GHz) of the electromagnetic spectrum, as shown in Figure 8-1. The radio waves range is subdivided into a radio frequencies section and a microwave frequencies section. Notice that WLANs, Bluetooth, cellular, and satellite communication all operate in the microwave UHF, SHF, and EHF ranges. *Very Low Frequency (VLF)* is used for radio navigation, submarine communication, and wireless heart rate monitors.

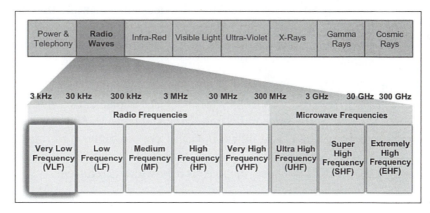

Figure 8-1   Radio Waves of the Electromagnetic Spectrum

Wireless LAN devices have transmitters and receivers tuned to specific frequencies of the radio waves range. Specifically, the following frequency bands are allocated to 802.11 wireless LANs:

- **2.4 GHz (*UHF*)**: 802.11b/g/n/ad

- **5 GHz (*SHF*)**: 802.11a/n/ac/ad

- **60 GHz (*EHF*)**: 802.11ad

802.11 Standards (8.1.1.5)

The IEEE 802.11 WLAN standard defines how RF in the unlicensed ISM frequency bands is used for the physical layer and the MAC sublayer of wireless links.

Various implementation of the IEEE 802.11 standard have been developed over the years. The following highlight these standards:

- *IEEE 802.11*: Released in 1997 and now obsolete, this is the original WLAN specification that operated in the 2.4-GHz band and offered speeds of up to 2 Mb/s. When it was released, wired LANs were operating at 10 Mb/s, so the new wireless technology was not enthusiastically adopted. Wireless devices have one antenna to transmit and receive wireless signals.

■ *IEEE 802.11a*: Released in 1999, it operates in the less crowded 5-GHz frequency band and offers speeds of up to 54 Mb/s. Because this standard operates at higher frequencies, it has a smaller coverage area and is less effective at penetrating building structures. Wireless devices have one antenna to transmit and receive wireless signals. Devices operating under this standard are not interoperable with the 802.11b and 802.11g standards.

■ *IEEE 802.11b*: Released in 1999, it operates in the 2.4-GHz frequency band and offers speeds of up to 11 Mb/s. Devices implementing this standard have a longer range and are better able to penetrate building structures than devices based on 802.11a. Wireless devices have one antenna to transmit and receive wireless signals.

■ *IEEE 802.11g*: Released in 2003, it operates in the 2.4-GHz frequency band and offers speeds of up to 54 Mb/s. Devices implementing this standard, therefore, operate at the same radio frequency and range as 802.11b, but with the bandwidth of 802.11a. Wireless devices have one antenna to transmit and receive wireless signals. It is backward compatible with 802.11b. However, when supporting an 802.11b client, the overall bandwidth is reduced.

■ *IEEE 802.11n*: Released in 2009, it operates in the 2.4-GHz and 5-GHz frequency bands and is referred to as a dual-band device. Typical data rates range from 150 Mb/s to 600 Mb/s with a distance range of up to 70 m (0.5 mile). However, to achieve the higher speeds, APs and wireless clients require multiple antennas using the *multiple-input and multiple-output (MIMO)* technology. MIMO uses multiple antennas as both the transmitter and receiver to improve communication performance. Up to four antennas can be supported. The 802.11n standard is backward compatible with 802.11a/b/g devices. However, supporting a mixed environment limits the expected data rates.

■ *IEEE 802.11ac*: Released in 2013, operates in the 5-GHz frequency band and provides data rates ranging from 450 Mb/s to 1.3 Gb/s (1300 Mb/s). It uses MIMO technology to improve communication performance. Up to eight antennas can be supported. The 802.11ac standard is backward compatible with 802.11a/n devices; however, supporting a mixed environment limits the expected data rates.

■ *IEEE 802.11ad*: Scheduled for release in 2014 and also known as "*WiGig*," it uses a tri-band Wi-Fi solution using 2.4 GHz, 5 GHz, and 60 GHz, and offers theoretical speeds of up to 7 Gb/s. However, the 60-GHz band is a line-of-sight technology and, therefore, cannot penetrate through walls. When a user is roaming, the device switches to the lower 2.4-GHz and 5-GHz bands. It is backward compatible with existing Wi-Fi devices. However, supporting a mixed environment limits the expected data rates.

Table 8-1 summarizes each 802.11 standard.

Table 8-1 Comparing 802.11 Standards

IEEE Standard	Maximum Speed	Frequency	Backward Compatible
802.11	2 Mb/s	2.4 GHz	—
802.11a	54 Mb/s	5 GHz	—
802.11b	11 Mb/s	2.4 GHz	—
802.11g	54 Mb/s	2.4 GHz	802.11b
802.11n	600 Mb/s	2.4 GHz and 5 GHz	802.11a/b/g
802.11ac	1.3 Gb/s	5 GHz	802.11a/n
802.11ad	7 Gb/s	2.4 GHz, 5 GHz, and 60 GHz	802.11a/b/g/n/ac

Wi-Fi Certification (8.1.1.6)

Standards ensure interoperability between devices made by different manufacturers. Internationally, the three organizations influencing WLAN standards are

- **ITU-R**: Regulates the allocation of the RF spectrum and satellite orbits.

- **IEEE**: Specifies how RF is modulated to carry information. It maintains the standards for local- and metropolitan-area networks (MAN) with the *IEEE 802* LAN/MAN family of standards. The dominant standards in the IEEE 802 family are 802.3 Ethernet and 802.11 WLAN. Although the IEEE has specified standards for RF modulation devices, it has not specified manufacturing standards; therefore, interpretations of the 802.11 standards by different vendors can cause interoperability problems between their devices.

- *Wi-Fi Alliance*: The Wi-Fi Alliance (www.wi-fi.org) is a global, nonprofit, industry trade association devoted to promoting the growth and acceptance of WLANs. It is an association of vendors whose objective is to improve the interoperability of products that are based on the 802.11 standard by certifying vendors for conformance to industry norms and adherence to standards.

The Wi-Fi Alliance certifies Wi-Fi and the following product compatibility:

- IEEE 802.11a/b/g/n/ac/ad compatible

- *IEEE 802.11i* secure using WPA2 and *Extensible Authentication Protocol (EAP)*

- *Wi-Fi Protected Setup (WPS)* to simplify device connections

- *Wi-Fi Direct* to share media between devices

- *Wi-Fi Passpoint* to simplify securely connecting to Wi-Fi hotspot networks

- *Wi-Fi Miracast* to seamlessly display video between devices

Note

Other Wi-Fi certification products are available, such as *Wi-Fi Multimedia (WMM)*, *Tunneled Direct Link Setup (TDLS)*, and *WMM-Power Save*.

Figure 8-2 displays the Wi-Fi Alliance logos identifying specific feature compatibility. Devices displaying specific logos support the identified feature. A device can display a combination of these logos.

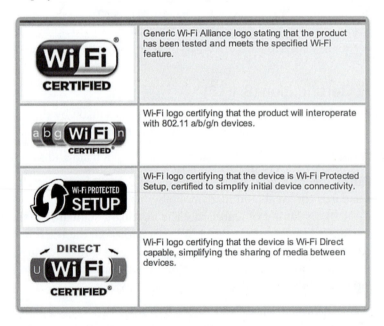

Figure 8-2   Common Wi-Fi Certified Logos

Video

Video 8.1.1.6: Common Wi-Fi Certified Logos

Go to the online course and view the playful videos of the Wi-Fi Direct, Wi-Fi Passpoint, and Wi-Fi Miracast features in the second, third, and fourth graphics.

Comparing WLANs to a LAN (8.1.1.7)

WLANs share a similar origin with Ethernet LANs. The IEEE has adopted the 802 LAN/MAN portfolio of computer network architecture standards. The two dominant 802 working groups are 802.3 Ethernet and 802.11 WLAN. However, there are important differences between the two.

WLANs use RF instead of cables at the physical layer and MAC sublayer of the data link layer. In comparison to cable, RF has the following characteristics:

- RF does not have boundaries, such as the limits of a wire in a sheath. This allows data frames traveling over the RF media to be available to anyone who can receive the RF signal.

- RF is unprotected from outside signals, whereas cable is in an insulating sheath. Radios operating independently in the same geographic area, but using the same or a similar RF, can interfere with each other.

- RF transmission is subject to the same challenges inherent in any wave-based technology, such as consumer radio. For example, as the radio travels farther away from the source, radio stations can start playing over each other and static noise increases. Eventually the signal is completely lost. Wired LANs have cables that are of an appropriate length to maintain signal strength.

- RF bands are regulated differently in various countries. The use of WLANs is subject to additional regulations and sets of standards that are not applied to wired LANs.

WLANs also differ from wired LANs as follows:

- WLANs connect clients to the network through a wireless *access point (AP)* or *wireless router*, instead of an Ethernet switch.

- WLANs connect mobile devices that are often battery powered, as opposed to plugged-in LAN devices. *Wireless network interface cards (NIC)* tend to reduce the battery life of a mobile device.

- WLANs support hosts that contend for access on the RF media (frequency bands). IEEE 802.11 prescribes *Carrier Sense Multiple Access with Collision Avoidance (CSMA/CA)* instead of collision detection (CSMA/CD) for media access to proactively avoid collisions within the media.

- WLANs use a different frame format than wired Ethernet LANs. WLANs require additional information in the Layer 2 header of the frame.

- WLANs raise more privacy issues because radio frequencies can reach outside the facility.

Interactive Graphic

Activity 8.1.1.8: Identify the Wireless Technology

Go to the online course to perform this practice activity.

Interactive Graphic

Activity 8.1.1.9: Compare Wireless Standards

Go to the online course to perform this practice activity.

Interactive Graphic

Activity 8.1.1.10: Compare WLAN and LAN Technologies

Go to the online course to perform this practice activity.

Components of WLANs (8.1.2)

In this topic, you learn about wireless NICs, wireless home routers, wireless access points, and wireless antennas.

Wireless NICs (8.1.2.1)

The simplest wireless network requires a minimum of two devices. Each device must have a radio transmitter and a radio receiver tuned to the same frequencies.

However most wireless deployments require

- End devices with wireless NICs

- An infrastructure device, such as a wireless router or wireless AP

To communicate wirelessly, end devices require a wireless NIC that incorporates a radio transmitter/receiver and the required software driver to make it operational. Laptops, tablets, and smart phones now all include integrated wireless NICs. However, if a device does not have an integrated wireless NIC, a USB wireless adapter can be used.

Figure 8-3 displays two USB wireless adapters:

- Linksys AE6000 Mini USB Wi-Fi Wireless-AC Dual-Band Adapter, supporting 2.4 or 5 GHz

- Linksys AE3000 High-Performance Dual-Band N USB Adapter

Figure 8-3   Wireless USB Adapters

Wireless Home Router (8.1.2.2)

The type of infrastructure device that an end device associates and authenticates with varies on the size and requirement of the WLAN.

For example, a home user typically interconnects wireless devices using a small, integrated wireless router. These smaller, integrated routers serve as

- **Access point:** Provides 802.11a/b/g/n/ac wireless access

- **Switch:** Provides a four-port, full-duplex, 10/100/1000 Ethernet switch to connect wired devices

- **Router:** Provides a default gateway for connecting to other network infrastructures

For example, the Cisco Linksys EA6500 router, shown in Figure 8-4, is commonly implemented as a small business or residential wireless access device, performing the role of access point, router, and Ethernet switch. The wireless router connects to the ISP DSL modem and advertises its services by sending beacons containing its shared *Service Set Identifier (SSID)*. Internal devices wirelessly *discover* the router SSID and attempt to associate and authenticate with it to access the Internet.

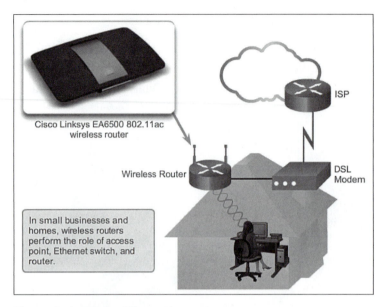

Figure 8-4   Typical Home Network

The expected load on the Linksys EA6500 router, in this environment, is low enough that it should be able to manage the provision of WLAN and 802.3 Ethernet and connect to an ISP. It also provides advanced features, such as having high-speed access, being optimized to support video streaming, being IPv6 enabled, providing QoS, providing easy setup using Wi-Fi WPS, and having USB ports to connect printers or portable drives.

Additionally, for home users who want to extend their network services, both wireless and wired *wireless powerline adapters* can be implemented. With these devices, a device can connect directly to the network through electrical outlets, which is ideal for HD video streaming and online gaming. They are easy to set up: Simply plug into a wall outlet or power strip and connect the device with a push of a button.

Video

Video 8.1.2.2: Linksys Powerline Adapters

Go to the online course and play the video in the second graphic to see an overview of the Linksys Powerline adapters.

Business Wireless Solutions (8.1.2.3)

Organizations providing wireless connectivity to their users require a WLAN infrastructure to provide additional connectivity options.

> **Note**
>
> IEEE 802.11 refers to a wireless client as a *station (STA)*. In this chapter, the term *wireless client* is used to describe any wireless-capable device.

The small business network shown in Figure 8-5 is an 802.3 Ethernet LAN. Each client (that is, PC1 and PC2) connects to a switch using a network cable. The switch is the point where the clients gain access to the network. Notice that the wireless AP also connects to the switch. In this example, either the Cisco WAP4410N AP or the WAP131 AP could be used to provide wireless network connectivity.

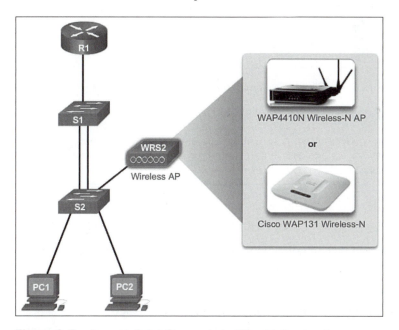

Figure 8-5   Access Point Connects to Wired Infrastructure

Wireless clients use their wireless NIC to discover nearby APs advertising their SSID. Clients then attempt to associate and authenticate with an AP, as shown in Figure 8-6. After being authenticated, wireless users have access to network resources.

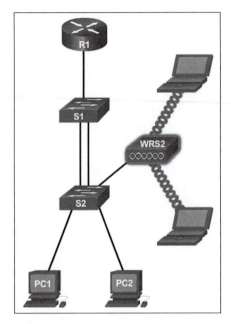

Figure 8-6 Clients Connect to AP

Wireless Access Points (8.1.2.4)

APs can be categorized as either *autonomous APs* or *controller-based APs*.

Autonomous APs

Autonomous APs, sometimes referred to as heavy APs, are standalone devices configured using the Cisco CLI or a GUI. Autonomous APs are useful in situations where only a couple of APs are required in the network. Optionally, multiple APs can be controlled using *Cisco Wireless Domain Services (WDS)* and managed using *CiscoWorks Wireless LAN Solution Engine (WLSE)*. Note that WLSE is end of life and is no longer being sold.

Note

A home router is an example of an autonomous AP because the entire AP configuration resides on the device.

Figure 8-7 displays an autonomous AP in a small network. If the wireless demands increase, more APs would be required. Each AP would operate independently of other APs and require manual configuration and management.

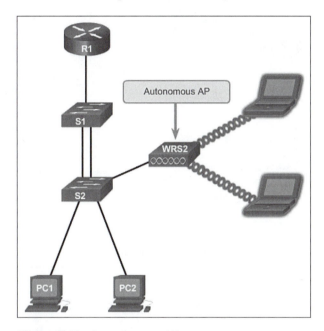

Figure 8-7   Autonomous AP

Controller-Based APs

Controller-based APs are server-dependent devices that require no initial configuration. Cisco offers two controller-based solutions. Controller-based APs are useful in situations where many APs are required in the network. As more APs are added, each AP is automatically configured and managed by a WLAN controller.

Figure 8-8 displays a controller-based AP in a small network. Notice how a WLAN controller is now required to manage the APs. The benefit of the controller is that it can be used to manage many APs.

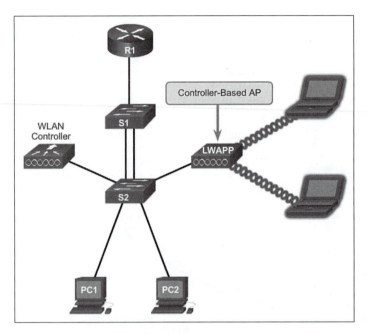

Figure 8-8   Controller-Based AP

Small Wireless Deployment Solutions (8.1.2.5)

For small wireless deployment requirements, Cisco offers the following wireless autonomous AP solutions:

- **Cisco WAP4410N AP:** This AP is ideal for small organizations requiring two APs and supporting a small group of users.

- **Cisco WAP121 and WAP321 APs:** These APs are ideal for small organizations that want to simplify their wireless deployment using several APs.

- **Cisco AP541N AP:** This AP is ideal for small- to mid-sized organizations that want a robust and an easily manageable cluster of APs.

Figure 8-9 displays and summarizes the Cisco small-business APs.

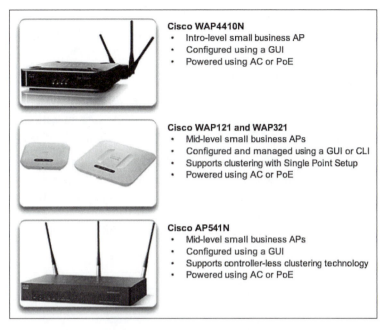

Figure 8-9   Cisco Small-Business Autonomous APs

Figure 8-10 displays a sample topology for a small-business network using the WAP4410N APs. Each AP is configured and managed individually. This can become a problem when several APs are required.

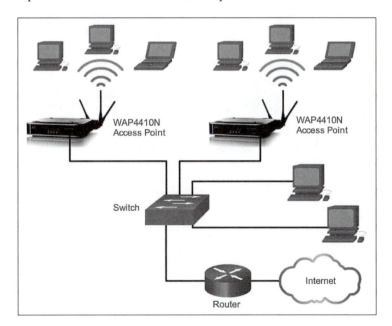

Figure 8-10   Simple WLAN Using WAP4410N APs

For this reason, the WAP121, WAP321, and AP541N APs support the clustering of APs without the use of a controller. The cluster provides a single point of administration and enables the administrator to view the deployment of APs as a single wireless network, rather than a series of separate wireless devices. The clustering capability makes it easy to set up, configure, and manage a growing wireless network. Multiple APs can be deployed and push a single configuration to all the devices within the cluster, managing the wireless network as a single system without worrying about interference between APs, and without configuring each AP as a separate device.

Specifically, the WAP121 and WAP321 support Single Point Setup (SPS), which makes AP deployment easier and faster, as shown in Figure 8-11. SPS helps to enable the wireless LAN to scale up to four WAP121 and up to eight WAP321 devices to provide broader coverage and support additional users as business needs change and grow. The Cisco AP541N AP can cluster up to ten APs together and can support multiple clusters.

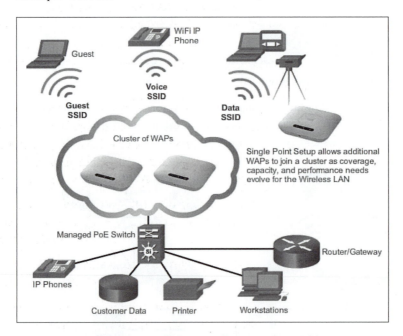

Figure 8-11   Simple WLAN Using a Cluster of WAP321 APs

A cluster can be formed between two APs if the following conditions are met:

- Clustering mode is enabled on the APs.
- The APs joining the cluster have the same Cluster Name.

- The APs are connected on the same network segment.

- The APs use the same radio mode (that is, both radios use 802.11n).

To see the configuration interface for an AP541N, go to www.cisco.com/assets/sol/ sb/AP541N_GUI/AP541N_1_9_2/Getting_Started.htm.

Large Wireless Deployment Solutions (8.1.2.6)

Organizations requiring the clustering of multiple APs require a more robust and scalable solution. For larger organizations with many APs, Cisco provides controller-based managed solutions, including the *Cisco Meraki Cloud Managed Architecture* and the *Cisco Unified Wireless Network Architecture*.

> **Note**
>
> There are other controller-based solutions, such as the controllers using Flex mode. Visit www.cisco.com for more information.

Cisco Meraki Cloud Managed Architecture

The Cisco Meraki cloud architecture is a management solution used to simplify the wireless deployment. Using this architecture, APs are managed centrally from a controller in the cloud, as shown in Figure 8-12. Cloud networking and management provide centralized management, visibility, and control without the cost and complexity of controller appliances or overlay management software.

Figure 8-12   Cloud-Managed Wireless AP

This process reduces costs and complexity. The controller pushes management settings, such as firmware updates, security settings, wireless network, and SSID settings, to the Meraki APs.

> **Note**
>
> Only management data flows through the Meraki cloud infrastructure. No user traffic passes through Meraki's data centers. Therefore, if the Cisco Meraki cannot access the cloud, the network continues to function normally. This means that users can still authenticate, firewall rules remain in place, and traffic flows at full line rate. Only management functions, such as reports and configuration tools, are interrupted.

The Cisco Meraki cloud managed architecture requires the following:

- **Cisco MR Cloud-Managed Wireless APs:** Various models exist to address a broad range of wireless deployment. MR12, MR16, and MR24 models work indoors and are self-configuring for a plug-and-play deployment. The units are self-healing with a zero configuration mesh. The MR12 is for teleworker environments, small branches, and low-density deployments. The MR16 is recommended for organizations that are mobility intensive. The MR24 is for large-enterprise deployments and is ideal for performance-critical wireless LANs and high-density environments. The MR62 and MR66 models work outdoors and are designed for harsh, rugged environments (IP-67 rated); these units provide enterprise-grade security with guest access and BYOD support, and the units support external antennas.

- *Meraki Cloud Controller (MCC)*: The MCC provides centralized management, optimization, and monitoring of a Meraki WLAN system. The MCC is not an appliance that must be purchased and installed to manage wireless APs. Rather, the MCC is a cloud-based service that constantly monitors, optimizes, and reports the behavior of the network. The two versions of MCC are the Meraki Enterprise Cloud Controller and the Meraki Pro Cloud Controller.

- **Web-based Dashboard:** Meraki's web-based Dashboard interface to the MCC provides remote network monitoring, configuration, diagnostics, and troubleshooting capabilities.

Figure 8-13 shows components of the Cisco Meraki architecture.

MR12, MR16, and MR24 Cloud Managed
Wireless APs

MR62 and MR66 Cloud
Managed Wireless APs

Meraki Cloud Controller (MCC)

Figure 8-13   MR Cloud-Managed Wireless Access Points

Large Wireless Deployment Solutions, Cont. (8.1.2.7)

The Cisco Unified Wireless Network Architecture solution, using a *split MAC* design, controls APs using a *WLAN controller (WLC)* and can be optionally managed using *Cisco Wireless Control Systems (WCS)*. The lightweight APs communicate with the WLAN controller using the *Lightweight Access Control Point Protocol (LWAPP)*. The controller has all the intelligence for communication, and the AP is a "*dumb terminal*" that simply processes packets.

The Cisco Unified Wireless Network Architecture requires the following devices:

- **Lightweight APs:** Cisco Aironet 1600, 2600, or 3600 wireless APs models provide robust, dependable wireless network access for hosts.

- **Controllers for small- and medium-sized businesses:** Cisco 2500 Series Wireless Controllers, Cisco Virtual Wireless Controller, or the Cisco Wireless Controller Module for Cisco ISR G2 provide small-branch or single-site enterprise WLAN deployments with entry-level wireless for data.

Other WLAN controllers of greater capacity are also available. For example, the Cisco 5760 Wireless Controller and the Cisco 8500 Series Controller are designed to cost-effectively manage, secure, and optimize the performance of sizeable wireless networks, such as service provider and large campus deployments.

Figure 8-14 summarizes the lightweight APs.

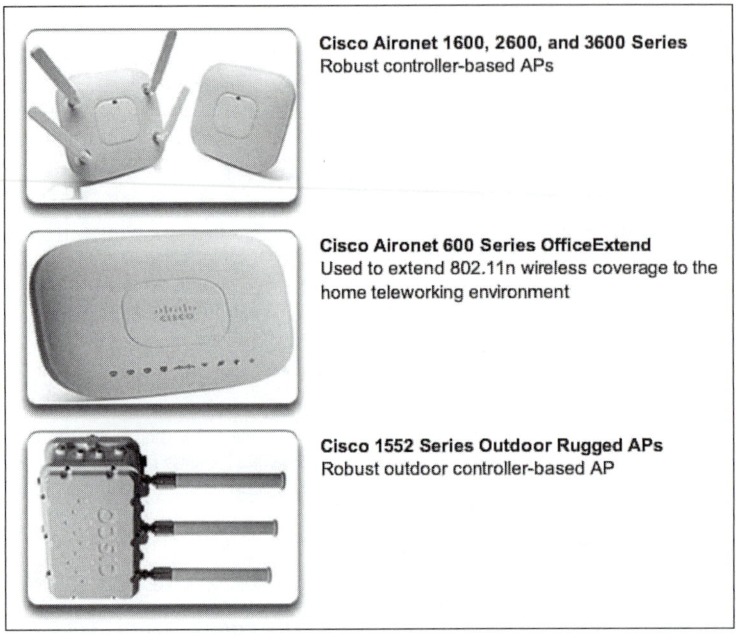

Cisco Aironet 1600, 2600, and 3600 Series
Robust controller-based APs

Cisco Aironet 600 Series OfficeExtend
Used to extend 802.11n wireless coverage to the home teleworking environment

Cisco 1552 Series Outdoor Rugged APs
Robust outdoor controller-based AP

Figure 8-14   Controller-Based Wireless APs

Figure 8-15 displays controllers for small- and medium-sized businesses:

- *Cisco Virtual Controller*: This controller is deployed on an x86 server that supports VMware ESXI 4.x or 5.x, one virtual CPU, 2 GB memory, 8 GB disk space, and two or more virtual network interface cards (vNIC). It is used to configure, manage, and troubleshoot up to 200 APs and 3000 clients.

- *Cisco Wireless Controller* on the *Cisco Services Ready Engine (SRE)*: These controllers include the Integrated Services Module 300 (ISM-300), which supports up to ten APs, and the SM-710 and SM-910 modules, which support up to 50 APs and 500 clients. All of these controllers have PCI functionality for scanner and kiosk support.

- Cisco 2500 Series: These are standalone, small-form-factor appliances. They have four Gigabit Ethernet ports, two of which are PoE. The units support up to 75 APs and 1000 clients. They also have PCI functionality for scanner and kiosk support.

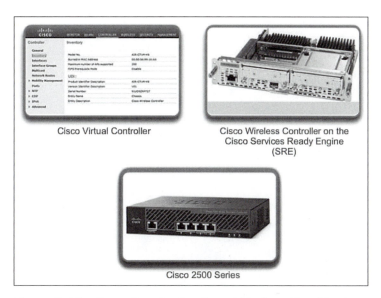

Figure 8-15   Controllers for Small- and Medium-Sized Businesses

Wireless Antennas (8.1.2.8)

Most business-class APs require the use of external antennas to make them fully-functioning units. Cisco has developed *Wi-Fi antennas* specifically designed for use with 802.11 APs while accommodating specific deployment conditions, including physical layout, distance, and aesthetics.

Cisco Aironet APs can use

- *Omnidirectional Wi-Fi Antennas*: Factory Wi-Fi gear often uses basic dipole antennas, also referred to as a "rubber duck" design, similar to those used on walkie-talkie radios. Omnidirectional antennas provide 360-degree coverage and are ideal in open office areas, hallways, conference rooms, and outside areas.

- *Directional Wi-Fi Antennas*: Directional antennas focus the radio signal in a given direction. This enhances the signal to and from the AP in the direction the antenna is pointing, providing stronger signal strength in one direction and less signal strength in all other directions.

- *Yagi Antennas*: A type of directional radio antenna that can be used for long-distance Wi-Fi networking. These antennas are typically used to extend the range of outdoor hotspots in a specific direction, or to reach an outbuilding.

Figure 8-16 displays various Cisco indoor and outdoor antennas.

Figure 8-16   Wireless Cisco Antennas

IEEE 802.11n/ac/ad use MIMO technology to increase available bandwidth. Specifically, MIMO uses multiple antennas to exchange more data than it would be possible to do using a single antenna. Up to four antennas can be used to increase throughput.

Note

Not all wireless routers are the same. For example, entry-level 802.11n routers support 150-Mb/s bandwidth using one *Wi-Fi radio* and one antenna attached to the unit. To support the higher data rates, an 802.11n router requires more radios and antennas to manage more channels of data in parallel. For example, two radios and two antennas on an 802.11n router support up to 300 Mb/s, while 450 and 600 Mb/s require three and four radios and antennas, respectively.

Interactive Graphic

Activity 8.1.2.9: Identify WLAN Component Technology

Go to the online course to perform this practice activity.

Lab 8.1.2.10: Investigating Wireless Implementations

In this lab, you will complete the following objectives:

- Part 1: Explore Integrated Wireless Routers
- Part 2: Explore Wireless Access Points

802.11 WLAN Topologies (8.1.3)

This topic introduces the *ad hoc mode* (IBSS) and the *infrastructure mode* (BSS and ESS).

802.11 Wireless Topology Modes (8.1.3.1)

Wireless LANs can accommodate various network topologies. The 802.11 standard identifies two main wireless topology modes:

- **Ad Hoc mode:** When two devices connect wirelessly without the aid of an infrastructure device, such as a wireless router or AP. Examples include Bluetooth and Wi-Fi Direct.
- **Infrastructure mode:** When wireless clients interconnect through a wireless router or AP, such as in WLANs. APs connect to the network infrastructure using the wired distribution system (DS), such as Ethernet.

Figure 8-17 displays an example of ad hoc mode.

Figure 8-17 Ad Hoc Mode

Figure 8-18 displays an example of infrastructure mode.

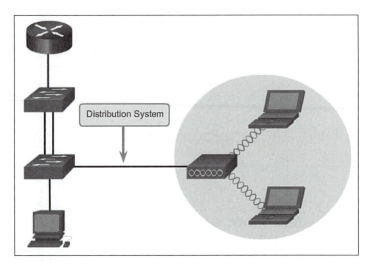

Figure 8-18   Infrastructure Mode

Ad Hoc Mode (8.1.3.2)

An ad hoc wireless network is when two wireless devices communicate in a peer-to-peer (P2P) manner without using APs or wireless routers. For example, a client workstation with wireless capability can be configured to operate in ad hoc mode, enabling another device to connect to it. Bluetooth and Wi-Fi Direct are examples of ad hoc mode.

> **Note**
>
> The IEEE 802.11 standard refers to an ad hoc network as an ***Independent Basic Service Set (IBSS)***.

Table 8-2 summarizes ad hoc mode.

Table 8-2   Ad Hoc Mode (IBSS) Summary

WLAN Topology Mode	Ad Hoc
802.11 Wireless Topology	Independent BSS
Number of APs	None
802.11 Coverage Area	Basis Service Area (BSA)

A variation of the ad hoc topology is when a smart phone or tablet with cellular data access is enabled to create a personal hotspot. This feature is sometimes referred to as tethering. A hotspot is usually a temporary quick solution that enables a smart phone to provide the wireless services of a Wi-Fi router. Other devices can associate and authenticate with the smart phone to use the Internet connection. The Apple iPhone refers to this as the *Personal Hotspot* feature, while Android devices refer to it as either *Tethering* or *Portable Hotspot*.

Infrastructure Mode (8.1.3.3)

The IEEE 802.11 architecture consists of several components that interact to provide a WLAN that supports clients. It defines two infrastructure mode topology building blocks: a *Basic Service Set (BSS)* and an *Extended Service Set (ESS)*.

Basic Service Set

A BSS consists of a single AP interconnecting all associated wireless clients. In Figure 8-19, two BSSs are displayed. The circles depict the coverage area within which the wireless clients of the BSS can remain in communication. This area is called the *Basic Service Area (BSA)*. If a wireless client moves out of its BSA, it can no longer directly communicate with other wireless clients within the BSA. The BSS is the topology building block, while the BSA is the actual coverage area (the terms BSA and BSS are often used interchangeably).

Figure 8-19   Basic Service Set

The Layer 2 MAC address of the AP is used to uniquely identify each BSS, which is called the *Basic Service Set Identifier (BSSID)*. Therefore, the BSSID is the formal name of the BSS and is always associated with only one AP.

Table 8-3 summarizes the Basic Service Set.

Table 8-3   Basic Service Set (BSS) Summary

WLAN Topology Mode	Infrastructure
802.11 Wireless Topology	Basic Service Set (BSS)
Number of APs	1
802.11 Coverage Area	Basis Service Area (BSA)

Extended Service Set

When a single BSS provides insufficient RF coverage, two or more BSSs can be joined through a common *Distribution System (DS)* into an ESS. As shown in Figure 8-20, an ESS is the union of two or more BSSs interconnected by a wired DS. Wireless clients in one BSA can now communicate with wireless clients in another BSA within the same ESS. Roaming mobile wireless clients can move from one BSA to another (within the same ESS) and seamlessly connect.

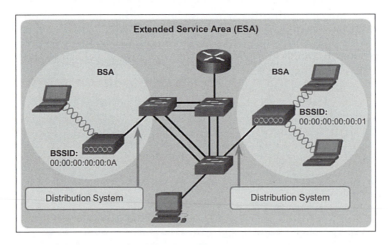

Figure 8-20   Extended Service Set

The rectangular area depicts the coverage area within which members of an ESS can communicate. This area is called the *Extended Service Area (ESA)*. An ESA typically involves several BSSs in overlapping and/or separated configurations.

Each ESS is identified by an SSID, and in an ESS, each BSS is identified by its BSSID. For security reasons, additional SSIDs can be propagated through the ESS to segregate the level of network access.

Table 8-4 summarizes the Extended Service Set.

Table 8-4   Extended Service Set (ESS) Summary

WLAN Topology Mode	Infrastructure
802.11 Wireless Topology	Extended Service Set (ESS)
Number of APs	2 or more
802.11 Coverage Area	Extended Service Area (ESA)

Note

The 802.11 standard refers to ad hoc mode as an IBSS.

Activity 8.1.3.4: Identify WLAN Topology Technology

Go to the online course to perform this practice activity.

Wireless LAN Operations (8.2)

This section focuses on wireless LAN operations, including 802.11 frame structure and channel management.

802.11 Frame Structure (8.2.1)

IEEE 802.11 frame structure differs from Ethernet frame structure, which is to be expected because they are distinct Layer 2 standards specified by the IEEE. This topic explores the frame control field, the wireless frame type, management frames, and control frames.

Wireless 802.11 Frame (8.2.1.1)

All Layer 2 frames consist of a header, payload, and FCS section, as shown in Figure 8-21. The 802.11 frame format is similar to the Ethernet frame format, with the exception that it contains more fields.

Figure 8-21   Generic Frame

As shown in Figure 8-22, all 802.11 wireless frames contain the following fields:

- **Frame Control:** Identifies the type of wireless frame and contains subfields for protocol version, frame type, address type, power management, and security settings.

- **Duration:** Typically used to indicate the remaining duration needed to receive the next frame transmission.

- **Address1:** Usually contains the MAC address of the receiving wireless device or AP.

- **Address2:** Usually contains the MAC address of the transmitting wireless device or AP.

- **Address3:** Sometimes contains the MAC address of the destination, such as the router interface (default gateway) to which the AP is attached.

- **Sequence Control:** Contains the Sequence Number and the Fragment Number subfields. The Sequence Number indicates the sequence number of each frame. The Fragment Number indicates the number of each fragment of a fragmented frame.

- **Address4:** Usually missing because it is used only in ad hoc mode.

- **Payload:** Contains the data for transmission.

- **FCS:** Frame Check Sequence; used for Layer 2 error control.

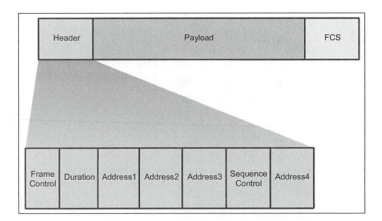

Figure 8-22   Content of a Wireless 802.11 Frame Header

Figure 8-23 displays a Wireshark capture of a WLAN beacon frame. Notice how the Frame Control field has also been expanded to display its subfields.

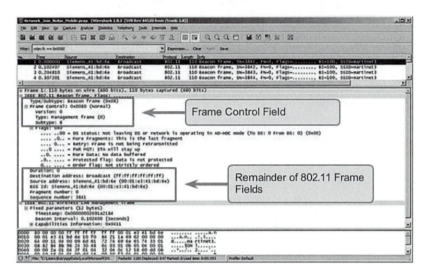

Figure 8-23   Wireshark Capture of an 802.11 Frame

The content of the Address fields varies depending on settings in the Frame Control field.

Frame Control Field (8.2.1.2)

The Frame Control field contains multiple subfields, as shown in Figure 8-24.

Specifically, the Frame Control field contains the following subfields:

- *Protocol Version*: Provides the current version of the 802.11 protocol used. Receiving devices use this value to determine whether the version of the protocol of the received frame is supported.

- *Frame Type* and *Frame Subtype*: Determine the function of the frame. A wireless frame can either be a *control frame*, a *data frame*, or a *management frame*. There are multiple subtype fields for each frame type. Each subtype determines the specific function to perform for its associated frame type.

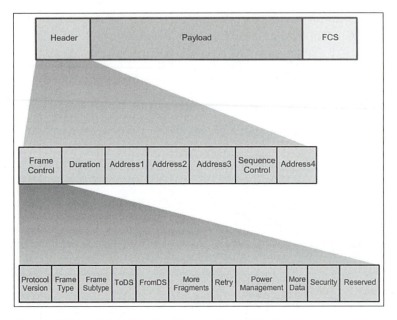

Figure 8-24   Content of the Frame Control Field

- *ToDS* (Distribution System) and *FromDS*: Indicate whether the frame is going to or exiting from the DS, and are only used in data frames of wireless clients associated with an AP.

- **More Fragments:** Indicates whether more fragments of the frame, either data or management type, are to follow.

- **Retry:** Indicates whether the frame, for either data or management frame types, is being retransmitted.

- *Power Management*: Indicates whether the sending device is in active mode or power-save mode.

- **More Data:** Indicates to a device in power-save mode that the AP has more frames to send. It is also used for APs to indicate that additional broadcast/multicast frames are to follow.

- **Security:** Indicates whether encryption and authentication are used in the frame. It can be set for all data frames and management frames, which have the subtype set to authentication.

- **Reserved:** Can indicate that all received data frames must be processed in order.

Figure 8-25 displays a Wireshark capture of a WLAN beacon frame. Notice that the Frame Type field and the Frame Subtype fields identify whether the frame is a management frame, a control frame, or a data frame. In the example, the Frame Type is 0x0, identifying it as a management frame. The subtype value 8 identifies this as a beacon frame. The frame is specifically identified as 0x08.

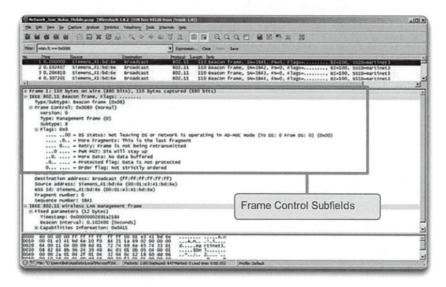

Figure 8-25   Wireshark Capture of an 802.11 Frame

Wireless Frame Type (8.2.1.3)

Note

The Frame Type and Frame Subtype fields are used to identify the type of wireless transmission. As shown in Figure 8-26, a wireless frame can be one of three frame types:

- **Management Frame:** Used in the maintenance of communication, such as finding, authenticating, and associating with an AP.
- **Control Frame:** Used to facilitate the exchange of data frames between wireless clients.
- **Data Frame:** Used to carry the payload information such as web pages and files.

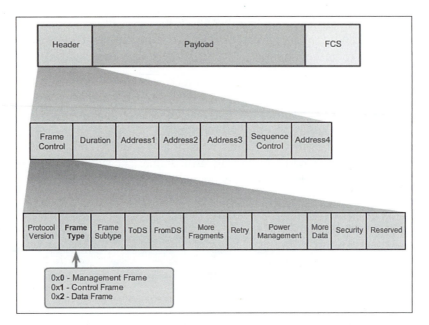

Figure 8-26   Content of the Frame Control Field

Management Frames (8.2.1.4)

Management frames are used exclusively to find, authenticate, and associate with an AP.

Figure 8-27 displays the field value of common management frames including

- *Association request frame*: (0x00) Sent from a wireless client, it enables the AP to allocate resources and synchronize. The frame carries information about the wireless connection including supported data rates and the SSID of the network to the wireless client that wants to associate. If the request is accepted, the AP reserves memory and establishes an association ID for the device.

- *Association response frame*: (0x01) Sent from an AP to a wireless client containing the acceptance or rejection to an association request. If it is an acceptance, the frame contains information, such as an association ID and supported data rates.

- *Reassociation request frame*: (0x02) A device sends a reassociation request when it drops from the range of the currently associated AP and finds another AP with a stronger signal. The new AP coordinates the forwarding of any information that might still be contained in the buffer of the previous AP.

- *Reassociation response frame*: (0x03) Sent from an AP containing the acceptance or rejection to a device reassociation request frame. The frame includes information required for association, such as the association ID and supported data rates.

- *Probe request frame*: (0x04) Sent from a wireless client when it requires information from another wireless client.

- *Probe response frame*: (0x05) Sent from an AP containing capability information, such as the supported data rates, after receiving a probe request frame.

- *Beacon frame*: (0x08) Sent periodically from an AP to announce its presence and provide the SSID and other preconfigured parameters.

- *Disassociation frame*: (0x0A) Sent from a device wanting to terminate a connection. Allows the AP to relinquish memory allocation and remove the device from the association table.

- *Authentication frame*: (0x0B) The sending device sends an authentication frame to the AP containing its identity.

- *Deauthentication frame*: (0x0C) Sent from a wireless client wanting to terminate the connection from another wireless client.

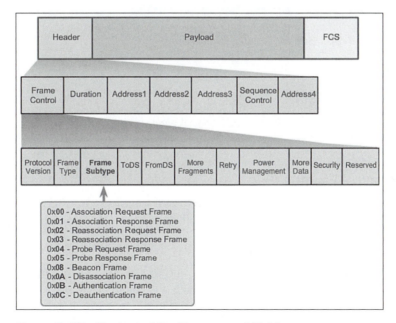

Figure 8-27   Content of the Management Fields

Beacons are the only management frame that can regularly be broadcast by an AP. All other probing, authentication, and association frames are used only during the association (or reassociation) process.

Figure 8-28 displays a sample Wireshark screen capture of a management frame. The field values change to reflect the purpose of the frame.

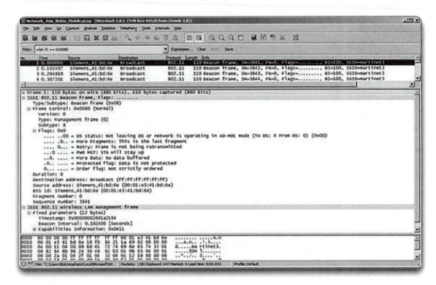

Figure 8-28 Beacon Management Frame

Note

The example provided was captured using Wireshark. However, Wireshark must be specifically configured to capture WLAN traffic. The ability to capture traffic varies between operating systems and might require a special wireless NIC.

Control Frames (8.2.1.5)

Control frames are used to manage the information exchange between a wireless client and an AP. They help prevent collisions from occurring on the wireless medium.

Figure 8-29 displays the field value of common control frames including

- *Request to Send (RTS) frame*: The RTS and CTS frames provide an optional collision reduction scheme for APs with hidden wireless clients. A wireless client sends an RTS frame as the first step in the two-way handshake, which is required before sending data frames.

- *Clear to Send (CTS) frame*: A wireless AP responds to an RTS frame with a CTS frame. It provides clearance for the requesting wireless client to send a data frame. The CTS contributes to collision control management by including a time value. This time delay minimizes the chance that other wireless clients will transmit while the requesting client transmits.

- *Acknowledgment (ACK) frame*: After receiving a data frame, the receiving wireless client sends an ACK frame to the sending client if no errors are found. If the sending client does not receive an ACK frame within a predetermined period of time, the sending client resends the frame.

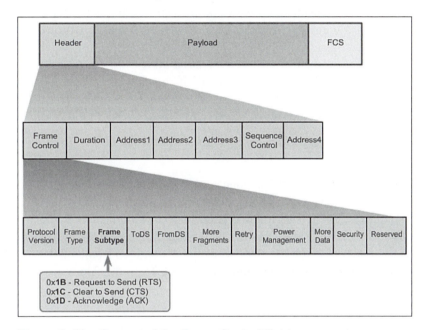

Figure 8-29   Content of the Frame Control Field

Control frames are integral to wireless transmission and play a significant role in the media contention method used by wireless, known as Carrier Sense Multiple Access with Collision Avoidance (CSMA/CA).

Activity 8.2.1.6: Identify the 802.11 Frame Control Fields

Go to the online course to perform this practice activity.

Wireless Operation (8.2.2)

In this topic, the detailed, behind-the-scenes operation of wireless LAN technology is explored.

Carrier Sense Multiple Access with Collision Avoidance (8.2.2.1)

Recall that the media contention method is the method in which devices determine how and when to access the media when traffic must be forwarded across the network. The IEEE 802.11 WLANs use the MAC protocol CSMA/CA. While the name is similar to the Ethernet CSMA/CD, the operating concept is completely different.

Wi-Fi systems are half-duplex, shared media configurations; therefore, wireless clients can transmit and receive on the same radio channel. This creates a problem because a wireless client cannot hear while it is sending, thus making it impossible to detect a collision. To address this problem, the IEEE developed an additional collision avoidance mechanism called the *Distributed Coordination Function (DCF)*. Using DCF, a wireless client transmits only if the channel is clear. All transmissions are acknowledged. Therefore, if a wireless client does not receive an acknowledgment, it assumes that a collision occurred and retries after a random waiting interval.

Wireless clients and APs use the RTS and CTS control frames to facilitate the actual data transfer.

As shown in Figure 8-30, when a wireless client sends data, it first senses the media to determine whether other devices are transmitting. If not, it then sends an RTS frame to the AP. This frame is used to request dedicated access to the RF medium for a specified duration. The AP receives the frame and, if available, grants the wireless client access to the RF medium by sending a CTS frame of the same time duration. All other wireless devices observing the CTS frame relinquish the media to the transmitting node for transmission.

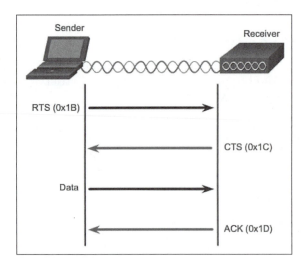

Figure 8-30   CSMA/CA Flowchart

The CTS control frame includes the time duration that the transmitting node is allowed to transmit. Other wireless clients withhold transmissions for at least the specified duration.

Figure 8-31 displays a flowchart detailing the CSMA/CA process.

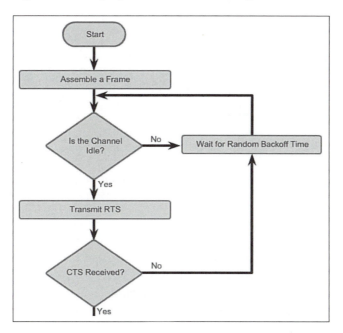

Figure 8-31   Using Control Frames for Data Transfer

Wireless Clients and Access Point Association (8.2.2.2)

For wireless devices to communicate over a network, they must first *associate* with an AP or wireless router. An important part of the 802.11 process is discovering a WLAN and subsequently connecting to it.

Management frames are used by wireless devices to complete the following three-stage process (see Figure 8-32):

- Discover new wireless AP.

- Authenticate with AP.

- Associate with AP.

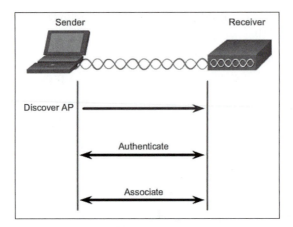

Figure 8-32   Three-Stage Process

To associate, a wireless client and an AP must agree on specific parameters. Parameters must be configured on the AP and subsequently on the client to enable the negotiation of these processes.

Association Parameters (8.2.2.3)

Figure 8-33 displays the wireless settings on a Linksys EA6500 wireless router. Common configurable wireless parameters include

- **SSID:** An SSID is a unique identifier that wireless clients use to distinguish between multiple wireless networks in the same vicinity. The SSID name appears in the list of available wireless network on a client. Depending on the network configuration, several APs on a network can share an SSID. Names are usually 2 to 32 characters long.

- **Password:** Required from the wireless client to authenticate to the AP. A password is sometimes called the security key. It prevents intruders and other unwanted users from accessing the wireless network.

- **Network mode:** Refers to the 802.11a/b/g/n/ac/ad WLAN standards. APs and wireless routers can operate in a *mixed mode*, meaning that they can simultaneously use multiple standards.

- *Security mode*: Refers to the security parameter settings, such as WEP, WPA, or WPA2. Always enable the highest security level supported.

- **Channel settings:** Refers to the frequency bands being used to transmit wireless data. Wireless routers and APs can choose the channel setting, or it can be set manually if there is interference with another AP or wireless device.

Figure 8-33   Wireless Settings Window

Notice that the Linksys EA6500 supports 2.4-GHz and 5-GHz radios.

Figure 8-34 displays the options for the 2.4-GHz radio Network mode. Notice that it can support Mixed, Wireless-N Only, or Wireless-G Only. The Mixed setting provides more flexibility, but it can also slow communication. For example, if all the wireless clients connecting to the router are using 802.11n, they all enjoy the better data rates provided. If 802.11g wireless clients associate with the AP, all the faster wireless clients contending for the channel must wait on 802.11g clients to clear the channel before transmitting. However, if all wireless clients support 802.11n, select Wireless-N Only for best performance.

Figure 8-34   2.4-GHz Radio Network Modes

Figure 8-35 displays the Network mode options for the 5-GHz radio. Notice that it also supports a Mixed setting, along with the Wireless-N Only and Wireless-AC Only settings.

Figure 8-35   5-GHz Radio Network Modes

Notice that the Linksys EA6500 does not support 802.11ad.

The Security options listed in Figure 8-36 are choices of security protocols available on the Linksys EA6500 wireless router. Home users should choose WPA2/WPA Mixed Personal, while business users would typically choose WPA2/WPA Mixed Enterprise. The 5-GHz radio offers the identical choices. The wireless end device must also support the selected security option to associate.

Figure 8-36   Security Settings

Note

All wireless routers and APs should be secured using the highest available settings. The None or WEP options should be avoided and only used in situations where security is of no concern.

Figure 8-37 displays the Channel settings for the 2.4-GHz radio. The preferred option to use is Auto. However, a specific channel could be selected if there were other APs or other devices nearby interfering with the channel selected by the router. Although the 5-GHz radio also has the Auto option, in the example, it lists a specific channel (153) and channel width.

Figure 8-37   Wireless Frequency Channels

Discovering APs (8.2.2.4)

Wireless devices must discover and connect to an AP or wireless router. Wireless clients connect to the AP using a scanning (probing) process. This process can be

- **Passive mode:** The AP openly advertises its service periodically, but continually sends broadcast beacon frames containing the SSID, supported standards, and security settings. The primary purpose of the beacon is to allow wireless clients to learn which networks and APs are available in a given area, thereby allowing them to choose which network and AP to use.

- **Active mode:** Wireless clients must know the name of the SSID. The wireless client initiates the process by broadcasting a probe request frame on multiple channels. The probe request includes the SSID name and standards supported. Active mode might be required if an AP or wireless router is configured to not broadcast beacon frames.

Figure 8-38 illustrates how passive mode works, with the AP broadcasting a beacon frame every so often.

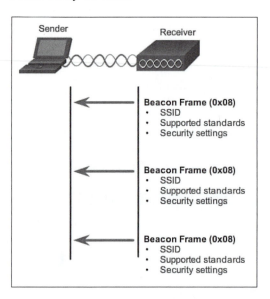

Figure 8-38   Client Devices Listen for an AP

Figure 8-39 illustrates how active mode works, with a wireless client broadcasting a probe request for a specific SSID. The AP with that SSID responds with a probe response frame.

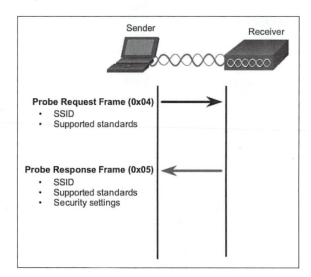

Figure 8-39   AP Broadcasts Periodic Beacon Frames

A wireless client could also send a probe request without an SSID name to discover nearby WLAN networks. APs configured to broadcast beacon frames would respond to the wireless client with a probe response and provide the SSID name. APs with the broadcast SSID feature disabled do not respond.

Authentication (8.2.2.5)

The 802.11 standard was originally developed with two authentication mechanisms:

- *Open authentication*: Fundamentally a NULL authentication where the wireless client says "authenticate me" and the AP responds with "yes." Open authentication provides wireless connectivity to any wireless device and should only be used in situations where security is of no concern.

- *Shared key authentication*: The technique is based on a key that is pre-shared between the client and the AP.

Figure 8-40 provides a simple overview of the authentication process.

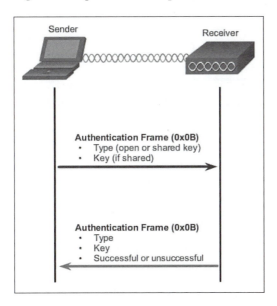

Figure 8-40   AP Client and AP Authenticate

However, in most shared key authentication installations, the exchange is as follows:

1. The wireless client sends an authentication frame to the AP.

2. The AP responds with a challenge text to the client.

3. The client encrypts the message using its shared key and returns the encrypted text to the AP.

4. The AP then decrypts the encrypted text using its shared key.

5. If the decrypted text matches the challenge text, the AP authenticates the client. If the messages do not match, the wireless client is not authenticated and wireless access is denied.

After a wireless client has been authenticated, the AP proceeds to the association stage. As shown in Figure 8-41, the association stage finalizes settings and establishes the data link between the wireless client and the AP.

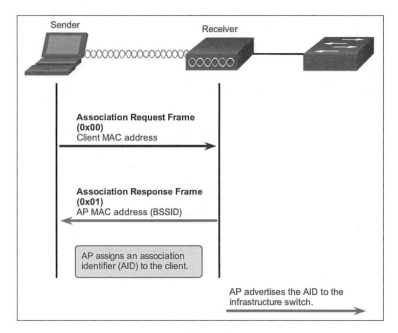

Figure 8-41 AP Client and AP Associate

As part of this stage

- The wireless client forwards an Association Request frame that includes its MAC address.

- The AP responds with an Association Response that includes the AP BSSID, which is the AP MAC address.

- The AP maps a logical port known as the *Association Identifier (AID)* to the wireless client. The AID is equivalent to a port on a switch and allows the infrastructure switch to keep track of frames destined for the wireless client to be forwarded.

After a wireless client has associated with an AP, traffic is now able to flow between the client and the AP.

Interactive Graphic

Activity 8.2.2.6: Order the Steps in the Client and AP Association Process

Go to the online course to perform this practice activity.

Channel Management (8.2.3)

This section describes the concepts of frequency channel saturation, as well as how to select channels and plan a wireless LAN deployment.

Frequency Channel Saturation (8.2.3.1)

As previously explained, wireless LAN devices have transmitters and receivers tuned to specific frequencies of radio waves to communicate. A common practice is for frequencies to be allocated as ranges. Such ranges are then split into smaller ranges called channels.

If the demand for a specific channel is too high, that channel is likely to become over-saturated. The saturation of the wireless medium degrades the quality of the communication. Over the years, a number of techniques have been created to improve wireless communication and alleviate saturation. The following techniques mitigate channel saturation by using the channels in a more efficient way:

- *Direct-sequence spread spectrum (DSSS)*: DSSS is a spread-spectrum modulation technique. Spread-spectrum is designed to spread a signal over a larger frequency band, making it more resistant to interference. With DSSS, the signal is multiplied by a "crafted noise" known as a spreading code. Because the receiver knows about the spreading code and when it was added, it can mathematically remove it and reconstruct the original signal. In effect, this creates redundancy in the transmitted signal in an effort to counter quality loss in the wireless medium. DSSS is used by 802.11b. Also used by cordless phones operating in the 900-MHz, 2.4-GHz, and 5.8-GHz bands; CDMA cellular; and GPS networks. See Figure 8-42.

- *Frequency-hopping spread spectrum (FHSS)*: FHSS also relies on spread-spectrum methods to communicate. It is similar to DSSS but transmits radio signals by rapidly switching a carrier signal among many frequency channels. With FHSS, sender and receiver must be synchronized to "know" which channel to jump. This channel-hopping process allows for a more efficient usage of the channels, decreasing channel congestion. Walkie-talkies and 900-MHz cordless phones also use FHSS, and Bluetooth uses a variation of FHSS. FHSS is also used by the original 802.11 standard. See Figure 8-43.

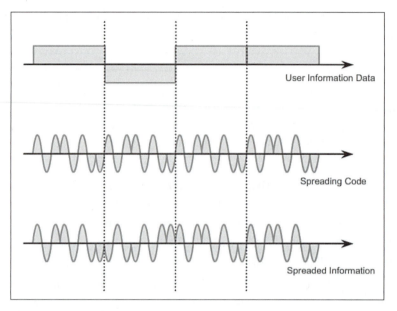

Figure 8-42   DSSS Example

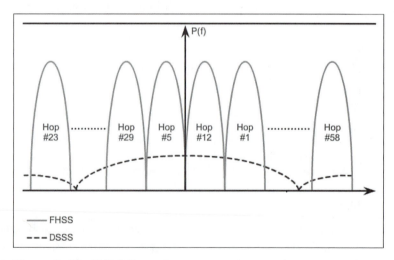

Figure 8-43   FHSS Example

■ *Orthogonal frequency-division multiplexing (OFDM)*: OFDM is a subset of frequency-division multiplexing in which a single channel utilizes multiple subchannels on adjacent frequencies. Subchannels in an OFDM system are precisely orthogonal (perpendicular) to one another, which allow the subchannels to overlap without interfering. As a result, OFDM systems are able to maximize spectral efficiency without causing adjacent channel interference. In effect, this makes it easier for a receiving station to "hear" the signal. Because OFDM uses subchannels, channel usage is very efficient. OFDM is used by a number of communication systems, including 802.11a/g/n/ac. See Figure 8-44.

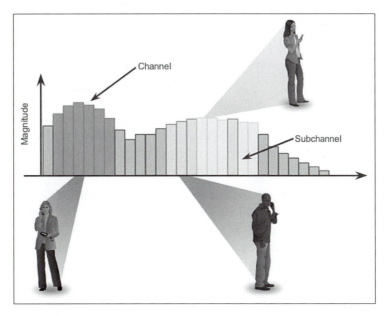

Figure 8-44   OFDM Example

Selecting Channels (8.2.3.2)

The IEEE 802.11b/g/n standards all operate in the microwaves frequencies of the radio spectrum. The IEEE 802.11b/g/n standards operate in the 2.4-GHz–to–2.5-GHz spectrum, while 802.11a/n/ac standards operate in the more heavily regulated 5-GHz band. Figure 8-45 highlights which 802.11 standard operates in the 2.4-GHz, 5-GHz, and 60-GHz bands. Each spectrum is subdivided into channels with a center frequency and bandwidth, analogous to the way that radio bands are subdivided.

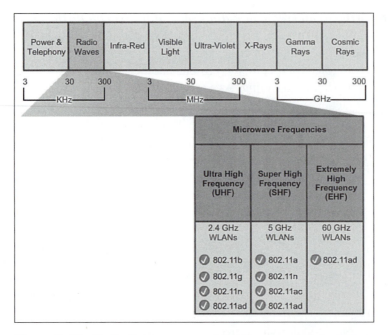

Figure 8-45   Radio Subspectrum of the Electromagnetic Spectrum

The 2.4-GHz band is subdivided into multiple channels. The overall, combined channel bandwidth is 22 MHz, with each channel separated by 5 MHz. The 802.11b standard identifies 11 channels for North America. The 22-MHz bandwidth, combined with the 5-MHz separation between frequencies, results in an overlap between successive channels, as shown in Figure 8-46.

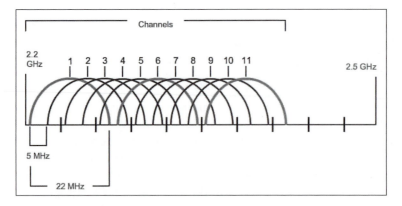

Figure 8-46   802.11b Channels

Note

In Europe, there are 13 802.11b channels.

Interference occurs when an undesired signal overlaps a channel reserved for a desired signal, causing possible distortion. The solution to interference is to use non-overlapping channels. Specifically, channels 1, 6, and 11 are nonoverlapping 802.11b channels, as shown in Figure 8-47.

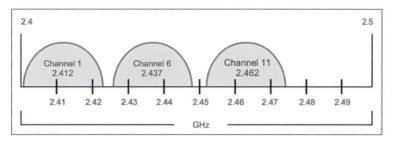

Figure 8-47   802.11b (DSSS) Channel Width 22 MHz

A best practice for WLANs requiring multiple APs is to use nonoverlapping channels. If there are three adjacent APs, use channels 1, 6, and 11. If there are just two, select any two that are five channels apart, such as channels 5 and 10. Most APs can automatically select a channel based on adjacent channels used. Some products continuously monitor the radio space to adjust the channel settings dynamically in response to environmental changes.

As enterprise WLANs migrate to 802.11n, they can use channels in the larger, less-crowded 5-GHz band, reducing "accidental denial of service (DoS)." For example, the 802.11n standard uses OFDM and can support four nonoverlapping channels, as shown in Figure 8-48.

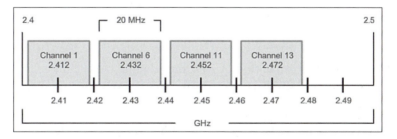

Figure 8-48   802.11g/n (OFDM) Channel Width 20 MHz

802.11n can also use channel bonding, which combines two 20-MHz channels into one 40-MHz channel, as shown in Figure 8-49. Channel bonding increases throughput by using two channels at one time to deliver data.

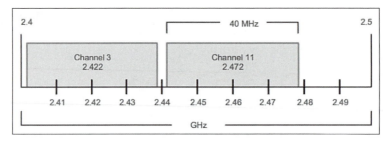

Figure 8-49 802.11n (OFDM) Channel Width 40 MHz

Most modern APs can auto-adjust channels to circumvent interference.

> **Note**
>
> IEEE 802.11ac uses OFDM with channel widths of 80, 160, and 80+80.

Planning a WLAN Deployment (8.2.3.3)

Implementing a WLAN that takes the best advantage of resources and delivers the best service can require careful planning. WLANs can range from relatively simple installations to very complex and intricate designs. There should be a well-documented plan before a wireless network can be implemented.

The number of users that a WLAN can support is not a straightforward calculation. The number of users depends on the geographical layout of the facility, including the number of bodies and devices that can fit in a space, the data rates that users expect, the use of nonoverlapping channels by multiple APs in an ESS, and transmit power settings.

Refer to the floor plan in Figure 8-50.

When planning the location of APs, the administrator cannot simply draw coverage area circles and drop them over a plan. The approximate circular coverage area is important, but there are some additional recommendations:

- If APs are to use existing wiring or if there are locations where APs cannot be placed, note these locations on the map.

- Position APs above obstructions.

- Position APs vertically near the ceiling in the center of each coverage area, if possible.

- Position APs in locations where users are expected to be. For example, conference rooms are typically a better location for APs than a hallway.

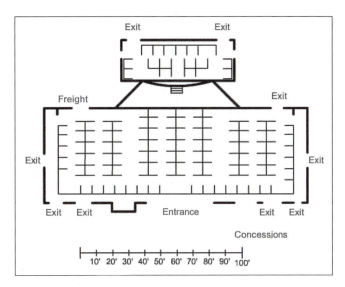

Figure 8-50   Sample Floor Plan

When these points have been addressed, estimate the expected coverage area of an AP. This value varies depending on the WLAN standard or mix of standards that are deployed, the nature of the facility, the transmit power that the AP is configured for, and so on. Always consult the specifications for the AP when planning for coverage areas.

BSAs represent the coverage area provided by a single channel. An ESS should have a 10 to 15 percent overlap between BSAs in an ESS. With a 15 percent overlap among BSAs, an SSID, and nonoverlapping channels (that is, one cell on channel 1 and the other on channel 6), roaming capability can be created.

Figure 8-51 provides a sample of how the BSAs could overlap.

Other factors include site surveys, which are detailed analyses of where to locate the various APs.

Interactive Graphic

Activity 8.2.3.4: Identify Channel Management Technology

Go to the online course to perform this practice activity.

Interactive Graphic

Activity 8.2.3.5: Cisco Wireless Explorer Game

Go to the online course to perform this practice activity.

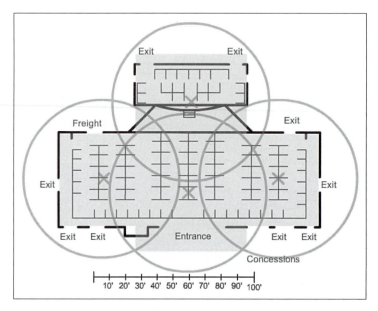

Figure 8-51   BSA Coverage

Wireless LAN Security (8.3)

Wireless LAN security is one of the most important aspects of security to an organization. There is so much to lose if the wrong people gain access to an organization's network by way of the wireless LAN. For this reason, experts in wireless technology are always inventing new mitigation techniques to thwart attacks associated with the wireless LAN.

WLAN Threats (8.3.1)

In this topic, you explore various WLAN threats. Some of these include DoS attacks, management frame attacks, rogue access points, and man-in-the-middle attacks.

Securing Wireless (8.3.1.1)

The difficulties in keeping a wired network secure are amplified with a wireless network. Security should be a priority for anyone who uses or administers networks.

A WLAN is open to anyone within range of an AP and with the appropriate credentials to associate to it. With a wireless NIC and knowledge of cracking techniques, an attacker might not have to physically enter the workplace to gain access to a WLAN.

Security concerns are even more significant when dealing with business networks, because the livelihood of the business relies on the protection of its information. Security breaches for a business can have major repercussions, especially if the business maintains financial information associated with its customers. Wireless networks are increasingly being deployed in enterprises and, in many cases, have evolved from a convenience to a mission-critical part of the network. Although WLANs have always been a target for attacks, with their rise in popularity increasing, they are now a major target.

Attacks can be generated by outsiders, disgruntled employees, and even unintentionally by employees. Wireless networks are specifically susceptible to several threats, including

- **Wireless intruders:** Unauthorized users attempting to access network resources. The solution is to deter intruders using authentication.

- **Rogue apps:** Unauthorized APs installed by a well-intentioned user or willingly for malicious purpose. Use wireless management software to detect rogue APs.

- **Interception of data:** Wireless data can easily be captured by eavesdroppers. Protect data exchanged between client and AP using encryption.

- **DoS attacks:** WLAN services can be compromised either accidentally or for malicious intent. Various solutions exist depending on the source of DoS.

Wireless threat types are summarized in Figure 8-52.

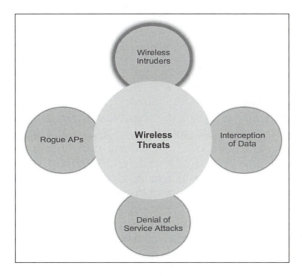

Figure 8-52   Common Wireless Threats

Note

Other threats, such as AP/wireless client MAC spoofing, cracking, and infrastructure attacks, are outside the scope of this chapter.

DoS Attack (8.3.1.2)

Wireless DoS attacks can be the result of

- **Improperly configured devices:** Configuration errors can disable the WLAN. For example, an administrator could accidentally alter a configuration and disable the network, or an intruder with administrator privileges could intentionally disable a WLAN.

- **A malicious user intentionally interfering with the wireless communication:** His goal is to disable the wireless network completely or to the point where no legitimate device can access the medium.

- **Accidental interference:** WLANs operate in the unlicensed frequency bands and, therefore, all wireless networks, regardless of security features, are prone to interference from other wireless devices. Accidental interference can occur from such devices as microwave ovens, cordless phones, baby monitors, and more. The 2.4-GHz band is more prone to interference than the 5-GHz band.

To minimize the risk of a DoS attack because of improperly configured devices and malicious attack, harden all devices, keep passwords secure, create backups, and ensure that all configuration changes are incorporated off-hours.

Accidental interference only happens when another wireless device is introduced. The best solution is to monitor the WLAN for any interference problems and address them as they appear. Because the 2.4-GHz band is more prone to interference, the 5-GHz band could be used in areas prone to interference. Some WLAN solutions enable APs to automatically adjust channels and use the 5-GHz band to compensate for interference. For example, some 802.11n/ac/ad solutions automatically adjust to counter interference.

Figure 8-53 illustrates how common consumer devices, such as a cordless phone, or even a microwave oven, can interfere with WLAN communication, effecting a denial of service.

The *Cisco CleanAir technology* enables devices to identify and locate non-802.11 interference sources. It creates a network that has the ability to adjust automatically to changes in its environment.

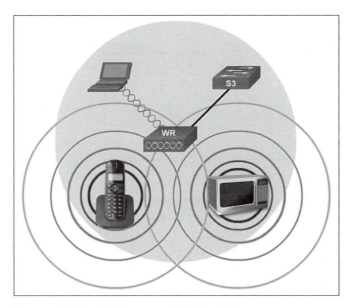

Figure 8-53   802.Common Wireless Threats

Management Frame DoS Attacks (8.3.1.3)

Although unlikely, a malicious user could intentionally initiate a DoS attack using *RF jamming* devices that produce accidental interference. It is more likely that the user will attempt to manipulate management frames to consume the AP resources and keep channels too busy to service legitimate user traffic.

Management frames can be manipulated to create various types of DoS attacks. Two common management frame attacks include

- *Spoofed disconnect attack*: This occurs when an attacker sends a series of "disassociate" commands to all wireless clients within a BSS. These commands cause all clients to disconnect. When disconnected, the wireless clients immediately try to reassociate, which creates a burst of traffic. The attacker continues sending disassociate frames and the cycle repeats itself.

- *CTS flood*: This occurs when an attacker takes advantage of the CSMA/CA contention method to monopolize the bandwidth and deny all other wireless clients access to the AP. To accomplish this, the attacker repeatedly floods the BSS with Clear to Send (CTS) frames to a bogus STA (station). All other wireless clients sharing the RF medium receive the CTS frames and withhold their transmissions until the attacker stops transmitting the frames.

Figure 8-54 displays how a wireless client and an AP normally use CSMA/CA to access the medium.

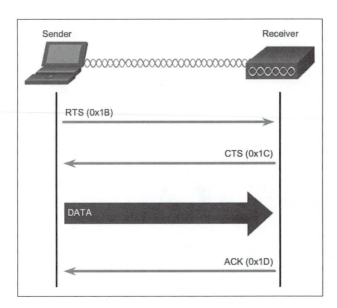

Figure 8-54   Normal Operation with CSMA/CA

Figure 8-55 illustrates how a CTS flood is created by an attacker sending out CTS frames to a bogus wireless client. All other clients must now wait the specified duration in the CTS frame. However, the attacker keeps sending CTS frames, thus making the other clients wait indefinitely. The attacker now has control of the medium.

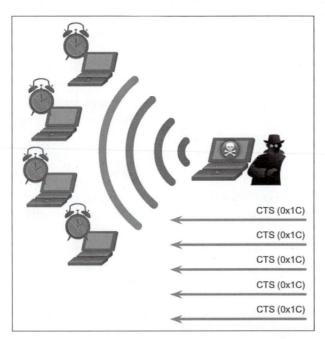

Figure 8-55   Attacker Creating a CTS Flood DoS Attack

Note

This is only one example of a management frame attack. Many others exist.

To mitigate many of these attacks, Cisco has developed a variety of solutions, including the *Cisco Management Frame Protection (MFP)* feature, which also provides complete proactive protection against frame and device spoofing. The Cisco Adaptive Wireless IPS contributes to this solution by an early detection system where the attack signatures are matched.

The IEEE 802.11 committee has also released two standards in regard to wireless security. The 802.11i standard, which is based on Cisco MFP, specifies security mechanisms for wireless networks, while the *IEEE 802.11w* management frame protection standard addresses the problem of manipulating management frames.

Rogue Access Points (8.3.1.4)

A *rogue AP* is an AP or wireless router that has either been

- Connected to a corporate network without explicit authorization and against corporate policy. Anyone with access to the premises can install (maliciously or nonmaliciously) an inexpensive wireless router that can potentially allow access to secure network resources.

- Connected or enabled by an attacker to capture client data such as the MAC addresses of clients (both wireless and wired), to capture and disguise data packets, to gain access to network resources, or to launch man-in-the-middle attacks.

Another consideration is how easy it is to create a personal network hotspot. For example, a user with secure network access enables his authorized Windows host to become a Wi-Fi AP. Doing so circumvents the security measures, and other unauthorized devices can now access network resources as a shared device.

To prevent the installation of rogue APs, organizations must use monitoring software to actively monitor the radio spectrum for unauthorized APs. For example, the sample Cisco Prime Infrastructure network management software screen shot in Figure 8-56 displays an RF map identifying the location of an intruder with a spoofed MAC address detected.

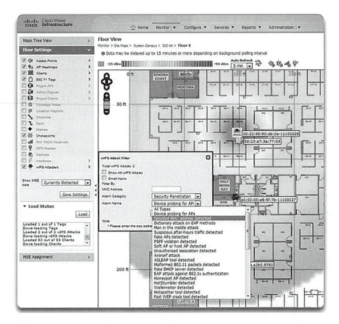

Figure 8-56   Rogue AP Detection

Note

Cisco Prime is network management software that works with other management software to provide a common look and central location for all network information. It is usually deployed in very large organizations.

Man-in-the-Middle Attack (8.3.1.5)

One of the more sophisticated attacks a malicious user can use is called a ***man-in-the-middle (MITM) attack***. There are many ways in which to create a MITM attack.

A popular wireless MITM attack is called the ***evil twin AP attack***, where an attacker introduces a rogue AP and configures it with the same SSID as a legitimate AP. Locations offering free Wi-Fi, such as airports, cafes, and restaurants, are hotbeds for this type of attack because of the open authentication.

Connecting wireless clients would see two APs offering wireless access. Those near the rogue AP find the stronger signal and most likely associate with the evil twin AP. User traffic is now sent to the rogue AP, which in turn captures the data and forwards it to the legitimate AP. Return traffic from the legitimate AP is sent to the rogue AP, captured, and then forwarded to the unsuspecting STA. The attacker can steal the user password, gather personal information, gain network access, and compromise the user system.

For example, in Figure 8-57, a malicious user is in Bob's Latte coffee shop and wants to capture traffic from unsuspecting wireless clients. The attacker launches software, which enables his laptop to become an evil twin AP, matching the same SSID and channel as the legitimate wireless router.

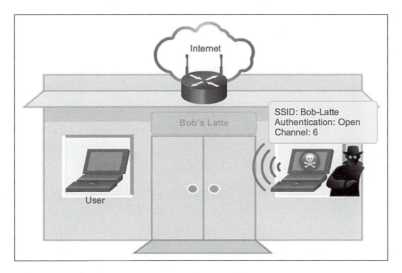

Figure 8-57   Malicious User Launches Evil Twin Attack

In Figure 8-58, a user sees two wireless connections available, but chooses and associates with the evil twin AP. The attacker captures the user data and forwards to the legitimate AP, which in turn directs the return traffic back to the evil twin AP. The evil twin AP captures the return traffic and forwards the information to the unsuspecting user.

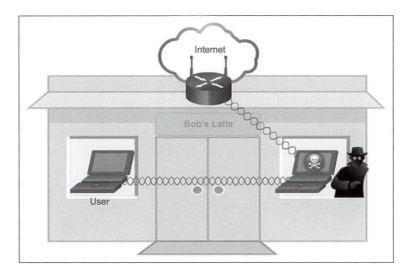

Figure 8-58   Evil Twin Attack Successful

Defeating an attack like an MITM attack depends on the sophistication of the WLAN infrastructure and the vigilance in monitoring activity on the network. The process begins with identifying legitimate devices on the WLAN. To do this, users must be authenticated. After all the legitimate devices are known, the network can be monitored for abnormal devices or traffic.

Enterprise WLANs that use state-of-the-art WLAN devices provide administrators with tools that work together as a wireless intrusion prevention system (IPS). These tools include scanners that identify rogue APs and ad hoc networks, and *Radio Resource Management (RRM)*, which monitors the RF band for activity and AP load. An AP that is busier than normal alerts the administrator of possible unauthorized traffic.

Securing WLANs (8.3.2)

Securing wireless LANs involves authentication and encryption. How this is implemented depends on the size of the organization.

Wireless Security Overview (8.3.2.1)

Security has always been a concern with Wi-Fi because the network boundary has moved. Wireless signals can travel through solid matter, such as ceilings, floors, and walls, and outside of the home or office space. Without stringent security measures in place, installing a WLAN can be the equivalent of putting Ethernet ports everywhere, even outside.

To address the threats of keeping wireless intruders out and protecting data, two early security features were used:

- *SSID cloaking*: APs and some wireless routers allow the SSID beacon frame to be disabled. Wireless clients must manually identify the SSID to connect to the network.

- *MAC addresses filtering*: An administrator can manually allow or deny clients wireless access based on their physical MAC hardware address.

Although these two features would deter most users, the reality is that neither SSID cloaking nor MAC address filtering would deter a crafty intruder. SSIDs are easily discovered even if APs do not broadcast them and MAC addresses can be spoofed. The best way to secure a wireless network is to use *authentication* and *encryption* systems, as shown in Figure 8-59.

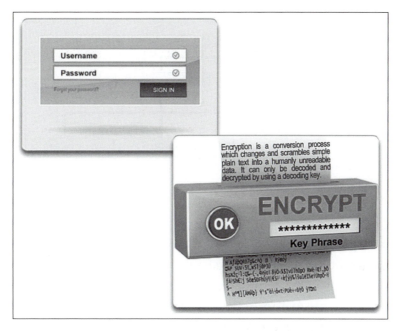

Figure 8-59   Authentication

Two types of authentication were introduced with the original 802.11 standard:

- **Open system authentication:** Any wireless client should easily be able to connect, and should only be used in situations where security is of no concern, such as in locations providing free Internet access like cafes, hotels, and in remote areas.

- **Shared key authentication:** Provides mechanisms, such as WEP, WPA, or WPA2 to authenticate and encrypt data between a wireless client and AP. However, the password must be pre-shared between both parties to connect.

The chart in Figure 8-60 summarizes the various types of authentication.

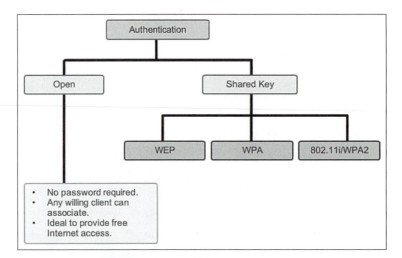

Figure 8-60   Authentication Methods

Shared Key Authentication Methods (8.3.2.2)

As shown in Figure 8-61, there are three shared key authentication techniques available:

- *Wired Equivalent Privacy (WEP)*: The original 802.11 specification designed to provide privacy similar to connecting to a network using a wired connection. The data is secured using the *RC4* encryption method with a static key. However, the key never changes when exchanging packets, making it easy to hack.

- *Wi-Fi Protected Access (WPA)*: A Wi-Fi Alliance standard that uses WEP, but secures the data with the much stronger *Temporal Key Integrity Protocol (TKIP)* encryption algorithm. TKIP changes the key for each packet, making it much more difficult to hack.

- IEEE 802.11i/*WPA2*: IEEE 802.11i is the industry standard for securing wireless networks. The Wi-Fi Alliance version is called WPA2. 802.11i and WPA2 both use the *Advanced Encryption Standard (AES)* for encryption. AES is currently considered the strongest encryption protocol.

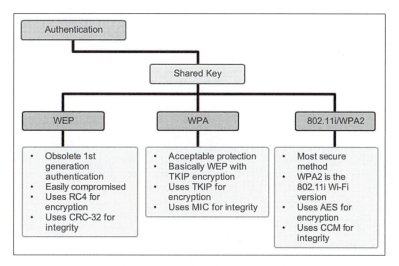

Figure 8-61   Shared Key Authentication Methods

WEP is no longer recommended. Its shared WEP keys have proven to be flawed and, therefore, should never be used. To counteract shared WEP key weakness, the very first approach by companies was to try techniques such as cloaking SSIDs and filtering MAC addresses. These techniques have also proven to be too weak.

Following the weakness of WEP-based security, there was a period of interim security measures. Vendors like Cisco, wanting to meet the demand for better security, developed their own systems while simultaneously helping to evolve the 802.11i standard. On the way to 802.11i, the TKIP encryption algorithm was created, which was linked to the Wi-Fi Alliance WPA security method.

Modern wireless networks should always use the 802.11i/WPA2 standard. WPA2 is the Wi-Fi version of 802.11i and, therefore, the terms WPA2 and 802.11i are often used interchangeably.

Since 2006, any device that bears the Wi-Fi Certified logo is WPA2 certified.

Note

Wireless-N networks should use the WPA2-*Personal security mode* for best performance.

Table 8-5 summarizes the three types of shared key authentication methods.

Table 8-5   Shared Key Authentication Methods Comparison

	WEP	WPA	802.11i/WPA2
Authentication Method	Pre-shared key	PSK or 802.1x	PSK or 802.1x
Encryption	RC4	TKIP	AES
Message Integrity	CRC-32	MIC	CCMP
Security	Weak	Strong	Stronger

Encryption Methods (8.3.2.3)

Encryption is used to protect data. If an intruder has captured encrypted data, he would not be able to decipher it in any reasonable amount of time.

The IEEE 802.11i and the Wi-Fi Alliance WPA and WPA2 standards use the following encryption protocols:

- **Temporal Key Integrity Protocol (TKIP):** TKIP is the encryption method used by WPA. It provides support for legacy WLAN equipment by addressing the original flaws associated with the 802.11 WEP encryption method. It makes use of WEP, but encrypts the Layer 2 payload using TKIP, and carries out a *Message Integrity Check (MIC)* in the encrypted packet to ensure that the message has not been tampered with.

- **Advanced Encryption Standard (AES):** AES is the encryption method used by WPA2. It is the preferred method because it aligns with the industry-standard IEEE 802.11i. AES performs the same functions as TKIP, but it is a far stronger method of encryption. It uses the *Counter Cipher Mode with Block Chaining Message Authentication Code Protocol (CCMP)*, which allows destination hosts to recognize whether the encrypted and nonencrypted bits have been tampered with.

Note

Always choose WPA2 with AES when possible.

Authenticating a Home User (8.3.2.4)

Figure 8-62 displays the security mode choices of the Linksys EA6500 wireless router. Notice how the Security mode for the 2.4-GHz network uses open authentication (that is, None) and no password is required, while the Security mode for the 5-GHz network uses WPA2/WPA Mixed Personal authentication and a password is required.

Figure 8-62   Open and WPA2/WPA Mixed Authentication

Note

Typically both 2.4-GHz and 5-GHz networks would be configured with the same security modes. The example in the figure is for demonstration purposes only.

The Security mode drop-down list of the 2.4-GHz network displays the security methods available on the Linksys EA6500 router. It lists the weakest (None) to the strongest (WPA2/WPA Mixed Enterprise). The 5-GHz network includes the same drop-down list.

WPA and WPA2 support two types of authentication:

■ **Personal:** Intended for home or small office networks, users authenticate using a *pre-shared key (PSK)*. Wireless clients authenticate with the AP using a pre-shared password. No special authentication server is required.

■ **Enterprise:** Intended for enterprise networks but requires a *Remote Authentication Dial-In User Service (RADIUS)* authentication server. Although more complicated to set up, it provides additional security. The device must be authenticated by the RADIUS server, and then users must authenticate using the *IEEE 802.1X* standard, which uses the Extensible Authentication Protocol (EAP) for authentication.

Authentication in the Enterprise (8.3.2.5)

In networks that have stricter security requirements, an additional authentication or login is required to grant wireless clients such access. The *Enterprise security mode* choices require an Authentication, Authorization, and Accounting (AAA) RADIUS server.

Refer to the example shown in Figure 8-63. Notice the new fields displayed when choosing an Enterprise version of WPA or WPA2. These fields are necessary to supply the AP with the required information to contact the AAA server:

- **RADIUS Server IP address:** This is the reachable address of the RADIUS server.

- **UDP port numbers:** Officially assigned UDP ports 1812 for RADIUS Authentication and 1813 for RADIUS Accounting, but could also operate using UDP ports 1645 and 1646.

- **Shared key:** Used to authenticate the AP with the RADIUS server.

Figure 8-63 Entering the RADIUS Server Parameters

The shared key is not a parameter that must be configured on an STA. It is only required on the AP to authenticate with the RADIUS server.

Note

There is no Password field listed, because the actual user authentication and authorization are handled by the 802.1X standard, which provides a centralized, server-based authentication of end users.

The 802.1X login process uses EAP to communicate with the AP and RADIUS server. EAP is a framework for authenticating network access. It can provide a secure authentication mechanism and negotiate a secure private key that can then be used for a wireless encryption session utilizing TKIP or AES encryption.

Interactive Graphic

Activity 8.3.2.6: Identify the WLAN Authentication Characteristics

Go to the online course to perform this practice activity.

Wireless LAN Configuration (8.4)

Wireless LAN configuration involves configuring the wireless LAN router and the wireless LAN clients. Troubleshooting is almost always necessary in a wireless LAN environment, so you will explore some troubleshooting scenarios as well in this section.

Configure a Wireless Router (8.4.1)

Configuring a wireless router is the most intricate part of implementing a wireless LAN. There are many parameters that require an understanding of wireless operation. It takes experience with setting up a few wireless LANs to master the ability to configure the parameters optimally for a given environment.

Configuring a Wireless Router (8.4.1.1)

Modern wireless routers offer a variety of features, and most are designed to be functional out of the box with the default settings. However, it is good practice to change initial, default configurations.

Home wireless routers are configured using a GUI web interface.

The basic approach to wireless implementation, as with any basic networking, is to configure and test incrementally. For example, before implementing any wireless devices, verify that the existing wired network is operational and that wired hosts can access Internet services.

After the wired network operation has been confirmed, the implementation plan consists of the following:

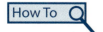

Step 1.   Start the WLAN implementation process with a single AP and a single wireless client, without enabling wireless security.

Step 2.   Verify that the client has received a DHCP IP address and can ping the local wired default router and then browse to the external Internet.

Step 3.   Configure wireless security using WPA2/WPA Mixed Personal. Never use WEP unless no other options exist.

Step 4.   Back up the configuration.

Before installing a wireless router, consider the following settings:

- **SSID Name:** Name of the WLAN network.

- **Network Password (if required):** If prompted, this is the password required to associate and access the SSID.

- **Router Password:** This is a management router password equivalent to the **enable secret** privileged EXEC mode password.

- **Guest Network SSID Name:** For security reasons, guests can be isolated to a different SSID.

- **Guest Network Password:** This is the password to access the guest SSID.

- **Linksys Smart Wi-Fi Username:** Internet account required to access the router remotely over the Internet.

- **Linksys Smart Wi-Fi Password:** Password to access the router remotely.

Table 8-6 outlines example settings used to configure the Linksys EA6500 wireless router.

Table 8-6   Management Parameters and Settings

Management Parameters	Settings
Network Name (SSID)	Home-Net
Network Password	cisco123
Router Password	cisco123
Guest Network Name (SSID)	Home-Net-Guest
Guest Network Password	cisco
Linksys Smart Wi-Fi Username	My-Name
Linksys Smart Wi-Fi Password	class12345

Setting Up and Installing Initial Linksys EA6500 (8.4.1.2)

The Linksys EA6500 wireless router is packaged with a Setup CD.

To set up and install the Linksys EA6500 router software, perform the following steps:

How To

Step 1.   Insert the CD into the CD or DVD drive and the Setup program should start automatically. If the Setup CD is not available, download the Setup program from http://Linksys.com/support. Figure 8-64 displays the initial Connect your Linksys EA6500 window with instructions to connect the router power and the Internet connection.

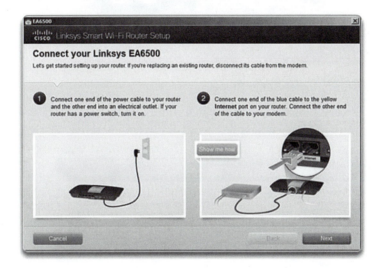

Figure 8-64   Initial Instructions

Note

In our example, the wireless router will not be connected to the Internet.

Step 2.   Click **Next** to begin the installation.

The Setup program begins the installation and displays a status window (Figure 8-65). During this time, the Setup program attempts to configure and enable the Internet connection. In the example, the Internet connection is unavailable, and after a few prompts to connect to the Internet, the option to skip this step displays.

Figure 8-65   Router Setup Status

The Linksys router settings window displays (Figure 8-66). This is where the SSID, wireless password, and administrative password are configured.

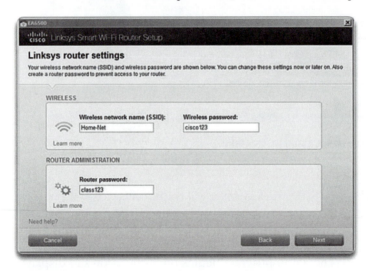

Figure 8-66   Enter the Linksys Router Settings

Step 3.   Click **Next** to display the summary router settings screen (Figure 8-67). Record these settings if the initial table was not previously completed.

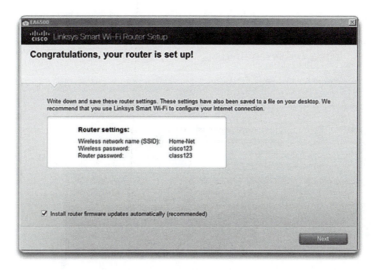

Figure 8-67   Summary of Router Settings

Step 4.   Click **Next** to display the option to create the *Linksys Smart Wi-Fi* account window (Figure 8-68).

Figure 8-68   Create the Linksys Smart Wi-Fi Account

This window enables you to manage the router remotely over the Internet. In this example, the Linksys Smart Wi-Fi account is not set up because there is no Internet access.

Step 5. Click **Continue** to display the Sign In window (Figure 8-69). Because the Internet connection has not been configured, the administrative router password is required.

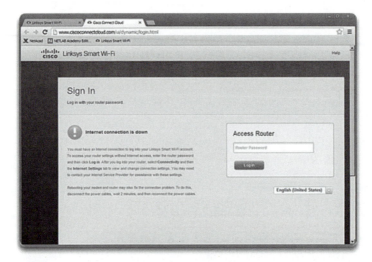

Figure 8-69 Log In to the Router

Step 6. When the password is entered, click **Log in** to display the Linksys Smart Wi-Fi home page (Figure 8-70).

Figure 8-70 EA6500 Web Dashboard

Configuring the Linksys Smart Wi-Fi Home Page (8.4.1.3)

The Linksys Smart-Wi-Fi home page is divided into the following three main sections:

- Smart Wi-Fi Router Settings

- Smart Wi-Fi Tools

- Smart Wi-Fi Widgets

Smart Wi-Fi Router Settings

Use this section to alter settings for connectivity, troubleshooting, wireless, and security. The Smart Wi-Fi Router Settings portion of the Smart Wi-Fi home page is shown in Figure 8-71.

Figure 8-71   Smart Wi-Fi Router Settings

Smart Wi-Fi Tools

Use this section to see who is currently connected to the network, create a separate network for guests, configure parental controls to keep kids safe, prioritize bandwidth to specific devices and applications, test the Internet connection speed, and control access to shared files. The Smart Wi-Fi Tools portion of the Smart Wi-Fi home page is shown in Figure 8-72.

Figure 8-72   Smart Wi-Fi Tools

Smart Wi-Fi Widgets

This window provides a quick summary of the Smart Wi-Fi Tools section. The Smart Wi-Fi Widgets portion of the Smart Wi-Fi home page is shown in Figure 8-73.

Figure 8-73   Smart Wi-Fi Widgets

Video

Video 8.4.1.3: Linksys Smart Wi-Fi

Go to the online course and play the video in the fourth graphic to see an overview of the Smart Wi-Fi interface.

Smart Wi-Fi Settings (8.4.1.4)

The Smart Wi-Fi settings enable you to

- Configure basic router settings
- Diagnose and troubleshoot connectivity issues
- Secure and personalize the wireless network
- Configure the security settings
- View connected devices on the network

Configure the Router's Basic Settings for the Local Network

This tool can be used to configure a DHCP reservation, change the router's administration password, change the IP address of the Linksys router, set up the Linksys routers with a static route, set up the router with cable Internet service, and configure the MTU settings of the Linksys router. Figure 8-74 shows the connectivity parameters in the GUI.

Figure 8-74   Connectivity Settings

Diagnose and Troubleshoot Connectivity Issues on the Network

The Troubleshooting page contains the current status of the router and connected devices. From this page ping tests and traceroute tests can be peformed, as well as the option to back up and restore the router's current settings, to check the WAN IP address, to reboot and reset the router to factory defaults, and to maintain the router's status. Figure 8-75 shows the screen for troubleshooting router settings.

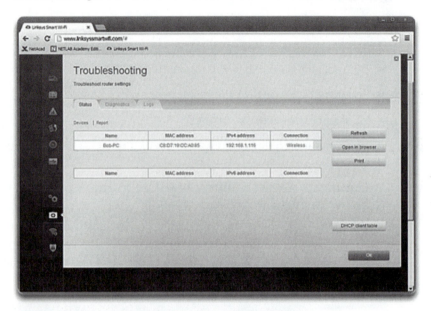

Figure 8-75   Troubleshooting the Wireless LAN

Secure and Personalize the Wireless Network

This feature enables the configuration of wireless MAC filters and the ability to connect devices easily using Wi-Fi Protected Setup (WPS). Figure 8-76 shows the tabs for configuring these wireless settings.

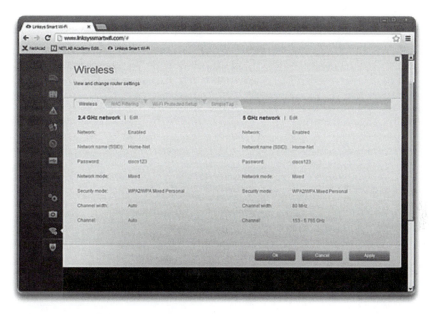

Figure 8-76   Wireless Settings

Configure the Security Settings

Keep the network safe from Internet threats by configuring the DMZ feature. Figure 8-77 shows the tabs available for configuring wireless network security features.

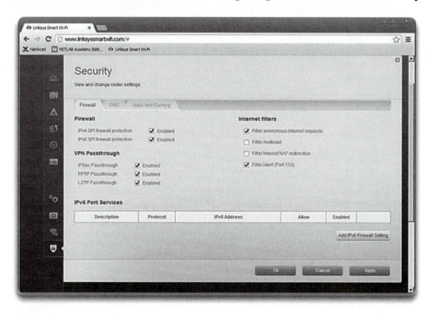

Figure 8-77   Security Settings

View Connected Devices on the Network

This feature enables you to view connected computers and devices on the network and provides the ability to set up port forwarding.

Smart Wi-Fi Tools (8.4.1.5)

The Smart Wi-Fi tools provide additional services including

- Device List
- Guest Access
- Parental Controls
- Media Prioritization
- Speed Test
- USB Storage

Device List

View to see who is connected to the WLAN. Device names and icons can be personalized. Devices can also be connected with this service. Figure 8-78 shows the device list window.

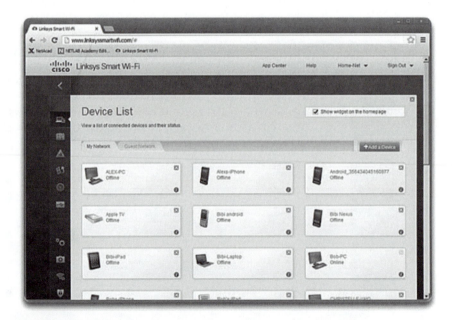

Figure 8-78   Device List

Guest Access

Create a separate network for up to 50 guests at home while keeping network files safe with the Guest Access tool. Figure 8-79 shows the guest access window.

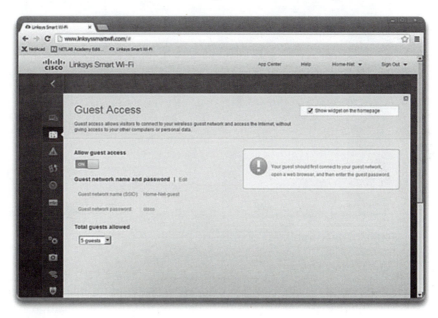

Figure 8-79   Guest Access

Parental Controls

Protect kids and family members by restricting access to potentially harmful websites. This tool is used to restrict Internet access on specific devices, control the time and days of specific devices that can access the Internet, block specific websites for certain devices, disable restrictions on Internet access, and disable the Parental Controls feature. Figure 8-80 shows the parental controls window.

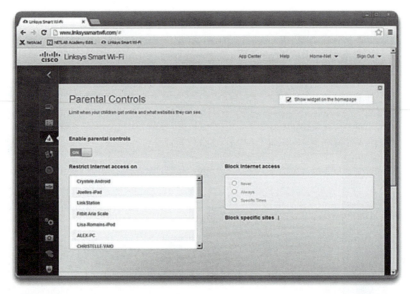

Figure 8-80   Parental Controls

Media Prioritization

Prioritize bandwidth to specific devices and applications. With this tool, optimize the online experience by prioritizing bandwidth on applications and devices that need it the most. This tool can use the Settings feature of the Media Prioritization tool, add more applications to be assigned with a specific bandwidth, and allocate higher bandwidth to an application, device, or online game by setting the bandwidth priority. Figure 8-81 shows the media prioritization window.

Figure 8-81   Media Prioritization

Speed Test

This tool is used to test the upload and download speed of the Internet link. It is useful for baselining. Figure 8-82 shows the speed test window.

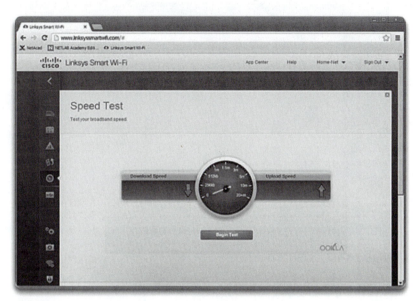

Figure 8-82 Speed Test

USB Storage

This tool controls access to shared files and configures how users can access shared files. With this tool, users can access USB storage in the local network, create shares on a USB storage device, configure the Folder Access settings, configure how devices and computers within the network can access the FTP server, and configure the access to a media server. Figure 8-83 shows the USB storage window.

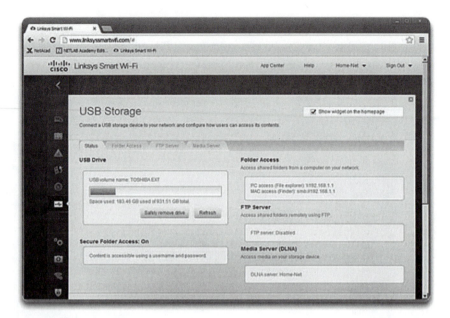

Figure 8-83   USB Storage

Backing Up a Configuration (8.4.1.6)

Just like the IOS of a Cisco router should be backed up in case of failure, so should the configuration of a home router. If a home router is left to its default configuration, backing up the configuration is not really warranted. However, if many of the Smart Wi-Fi tools have been customized, it can be advantageous to back up the configuration.

Backing up the configuration is easy to do with the Linksys EA6500 wireless router:

Step 1.   Log in to the Smart Wi-Fi home page. Click the **Troubleshooting** icon to display the Troubleshooting Status window (Figure 8-84).

Step 2.   Click the **Diagnostics** tab to open the Diagnostics Troubleshooting window (Figure 8-85).

Step 3.   Under the Router configuration title, click **Backup** and save the file to an appropriate folder.

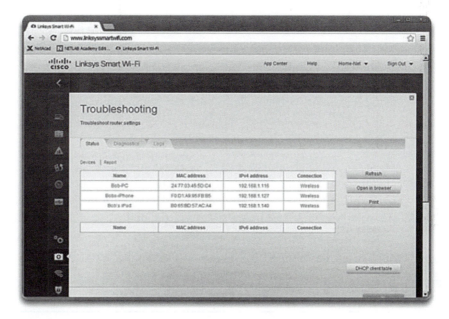

Figure 8-84   Open the Troubleshooting Window

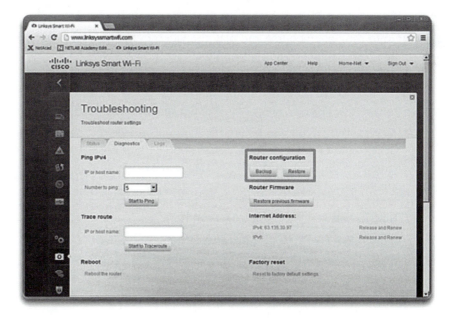

Figure 8-85   Open the Diagnostics Troubleshooting Window

To upload a previously saved backup, click **Restore**, locate the file, and start the restore process.

Configuring Wireless Clients (8.4.2)

Configuring wireless clients can involve quite a bit of troubleshooting in a mixed vendor environment. If the wireless router and the wireless clients are from the same vendor, establishing secure connectivity is usually quite easy. This topic describes the configuration of wireless clients with the more common operating systems.

Connecting Wireless Clients (8.4.2.1)

When the AP or wireless router has been configured, the wireless NIC on the client must be configured to allow it to connect to the WLAN. The user should also verify that the client has successfully connected to the correct wireless network, especially because there might be many WLANs available with which to connect.

Video 8.4.2.1-1: Connecting a Windows PC to the WLAN

Go to the online course and play the video in the first graphic to see a short video on how to connect a Windows computer to the WLAN.

Video 8.4.2.1-2: Connecting an Apple Device to the WLAN

Go to the online course and play the video in the first graphic to see a short video on connecting an iPod, iPhone, and iPad to the WLAN.

Packet Tracer Activity 8.4.2.2: Configuring Wireless LAN Access

In this activity, you will configure a Linksys wireless router, allowing for remote access from PCs, as well as wireless connectivity with WPA2 security. You will manually configure PC wireless connectivity by entering the Linksys router SSID and password.

Lab 8.4.2.3: Configuring a Wireless Router and Client

In this lab, you will complete the following objectives:

- Part 1: Configure Basic Settings on a Linksys EA Series Router
- Part 2: Secure the Wireless Network
- Part 3: Review Additional Features on a Linksys EA Series Router
- Part 4: Connect a Wireless Client

Troubleshoot WLAN Issues (8.4.3)

This final section explores the common issues in wireless LANs that require troubleshooting. The methodology of troubleshooting is also discussed.

Troubleshooting Approaches (8.4.3.1)

Troubleshooting any sort of network problem should follow a systematic approach. Logical networking models, such as the OSI and TCP/IP models, separate network functionality into modular layers.

When troubleshooting, these layered models can be applied to the physical network to isolate network problems. For example, if the symptoms suggest a physical connection problem, the network technician can focus on troubleshooting the circuit that operates at the physical layer. If that circuit functions properly, the technician looks at areas in another layer that could be causing the problem.

There are three main troubleshooting approaches used to resolve network problems:

- *Bottom-up*: Start at Layer 1 and work up. (Figure 8-86)

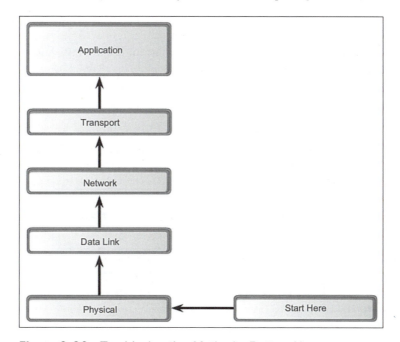

Figure 8-86   Troubleshooting Method – Bottom-Up

- *Top-down*: Start at the top layer and work down. (Figure 8-87)

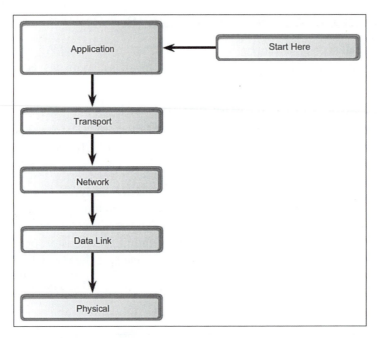

Figure 8-87   Top-Down Method

- *Divide-and-conquer*: Ping the destination. If the pings fail, verify the lower layers. If the pings are successful, verify the upper layers. (Figure 8-88)

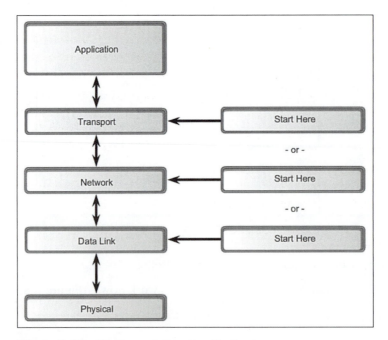

Figure 8-88   Divide-and-Conquer Method

Wireless Client Not Connecting (8.4.3.2)

When troubleshooting a WLAN, a process of elimination is recommended.

In Figure 8-89, a wireless client is not connecting to the WLAN. If there is no connectivity, check the following:

- Confirm the network configuration on the PC using the **ipconfig** command. Verify that the PC has received an IP address through DHCP or is configured with a static IP address.

- Confirm that the device can connect to the wired network. Connect the device to the wired LAN and ping a known IP address.

- If necessary, reload drivers as appropriate for the client. It might be necessary to try a different wireless NIC.

- If the wireless NIC of the client is working, check the security mode and encryption settings on the client. If the security settings do not match, the client cannot gain access to the WLAN.

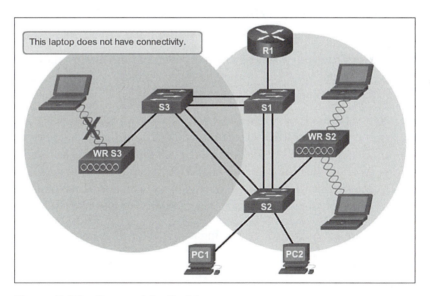

Figure 8-89   Connectivity Problem

If the PC is operational but the wireless connection is performing poorly, check the following:

- How far is the PC from an AP? Is the PC out of the planned coverage area (BSA)?

- Check the channel settings on the wireless client. The client software should detect the appropriate channel as long as the SSID is correct.

- Check for the presence of other devices in the area that might be interfering with the 2.4-GHz band. Examples of other devices are cordless phones, baby monitors, microwave ovens, wireless security systems, and potentially rogue APs. Data from these devices can cause interference in the WLAN and intermittent connection problems between a wireless client and AP.

Next, ensure that all the devices are actually in place. Consider a possible physical security issue. Is there power to all devices and are they powered on?

Finally, inspect links between cabled devices, looking for bad connectors or damaged or missing cables. If the physical plant is in place, verify the wired LAN by pinging devices, including the AP. If connectivity still fails at this point, perhaps something is wrong with the AP or its configuration.

When the user PC is eliminated as the source of the problem, and the physical status of devices is confirmed, begin investigating the performance of the AP. Check the power status of the AP.

Troubleshooting When the Network Is Slow (8.4.3.3)

To optimize and increase the bandwidth of 802.11n/ac dual-band routers, either

- **Upgrade your wireless clients:** Older 802.11b and even 802.11g devices can slow the entire WLAN. For the best performance, all wireless devices should support the same highest acceptable standard.

- **Split the traffic:** The easiest way to improve wireless performance is to split the wireless traffic between the 802.11n 2.4-GHz band and the 5-GHz band. Therefore, 802.11n (or better) can use the two bands as two separate wireless networks to help manage the traffic. For example, use the 2.4-GHz network for basic Internet tasks, such as web browsing, email, and downloads, and use the 5-GHz band for streaming multimedia, as shown in Figure 8-90.

There are several reasons for using a split-the-traffic approach:

- The 2.4-GHz band can be suitable for basic Internet traffic that is not time sensitive.

- The bandwidth can still be shared with other nearby WLANs.

- The 5-GHz band is much less crowded than the 2.4-GHz band and is ideal for streaming multimedia.

- The 5-GHz band has more channels; therefore, the channel chosen is likely interference-free.

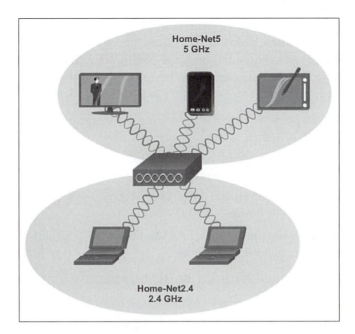

Figure 8-90   Split the Traffic

By default, dual-band routers use the same network name on both the 2.4-GHz band and the 5-GHz band. The simplest way to segment traffic is to rename one of the wireless networks, as shown in Figure 8-91. With a separate, descriptive name, it is easier to connect to the right network.

Figure 8-91   Name the Wireless Networks

To improve the range of a wireless network, ensure that the physical wireless router location is free of obstructions, such as furniture, fixtures, and tall appliances. These block the signal, which shortens the range of the WLAN. If this still does not solve the problem, using a Wi-Fi range extender or deploying the powerline wireless technology can be solutions.

Updating Firmware (8.4.3.4)

The IOS of the Linksys EA6500 router is called firmware. The firmware might need to be upgraded if there is a problem with the device or if there is a new feature included with a new firmware update. Regardless of the reason, most modern wireless home routers offer upgradeable firmware.

You can easily upgrade the Linksys EA6500 Smart Wi-Fi router firmware by performing the following steps:

Step 1.   Access the Linksys Smart Wi-Fi home page.

Step 2.   Click the **Connectivity** icon to open the Connectivity window (Figure 8-92).

Figure 8-92   Updating the Firmware

The router either responds with "No updates found" or it prompts to download and install the new firmware.

Note

Some routers require that the firmware file be downloaded ahead of time and then manually uploaded. To do so, select **Choose File.** If a firmware upgrade fails or makes the situation worse, the router can load the previous firmware by clicking **Troubleshooting, Diagnostics,** and then selecting **Restore previous firmware** (Figure 8-93).

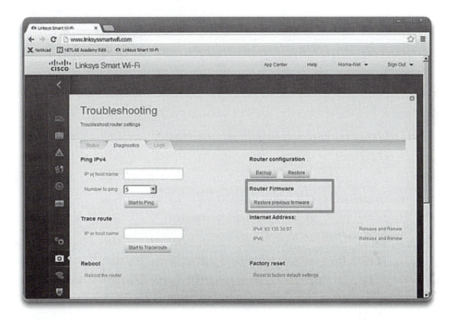

Figure 8-93   Restoring the Previous Firmware

Caution

Do not upgrade the firmware unless there are problems with the AP or the new firmware has a desired feature.

Activity 8.4.3.5: Identify the Troubleshooting Solution

Go to the online course to perform this practice activity.

Summary (8.5)

Class Activity 8.5.1.1: Inside and Outside Control

An assessment has been completed to validate the need for an upgrade to your small-to medium-sized wireless network. Approved for purchase are indoor and outdoor access points and one wireless controller. You must compare equipment models and their specifications before you purchase.

Therefore, you visit the "Wireless Compare Products and Services" website and see a features chart for indoor and outdoor wireless access points and controller devices. After reviewing the chart, you note there is some terminology with which you are unfamiliar:

- Federal Information Processing Standard (FIPS)
- MIMO
- Cisco CleanAir Technology
- Cisco FlexConnect
- Band Select

Research these terms. Prepare your own chart with your company's most important requirements listed for purchasing the indoor and outdoor wireless access points and wireless controller. This chart will assist in validating your purchase order to your accounting manager and CEO.

Packet Tracer Activity 8.5.1.2: Skills Integration Challenge

In this challenge activity, you will configure VLANs and inter-VLAN routing, DHCP, and Rapid PVST+. You will also be required to configure a Linksys router for wireless connectivity with wireless security. At the end of the activity, the PCs will not be able to ping each other but should be able to ping the outside host.

WLANs are often implemented in homes, offices, and campus environments. Only the 2.4-GHz, 5.0-GHz, and 60-GHz frequencies are used for 802.11 WLANs. The ITU-R regulates the allocation of the RF spectrum, while the IEEE provides the 802.11 standards to define how these frequencies are used for the physical and MAC sublayers of wireless networks. The Wi-Fi Alliance certifies that vendor products conform to industry standards and norms.

A wireless client uses a wireless NIC to connect to an infrastructure device, such as a wireless router or wireless AP. Wireless clients connect using an SSID. APs can be implemented as standalone devices, in small clusters, or in a larger controller-base network.

A Cisco Aironet AP can use an omnidirectional antenna, a directional antenna, or a Yagi antenna to direct signals. IEEE 802.11n/ac/ad standards specify the use of MIMO technology to improve throughput and support up to four antennas simultaneously.

In ad hoc mode or IBSS, two wireless devices connect to each other in a P2P manner.

In infrastructure mode, APs connect to network infrastructure using the wired DS. Each AP defines a BSS and is uniquely identified by its BSSID. Multiple BSSs can be joined into an ESS. Using a particular SSID in an ESS provides seamless roaming capabilities among the BSSs in the ESS. Additional SSIDs can be used to segregate the level of network access defined by which SSID is in use.

A wireless client first authenticates with an AP and then associates with that AP. The 802.11i/WPA2 authentication standard should be used. AES is the encryption method that should be used with WPA2.

When planning a wireless network, nonoverlapping channels should be used when deploying multiple APs to cover a particular area. There should be a 10–15 percent overlap between BSAs in an ESS. Cisco APs support PoE to simplify installation.

Wireless networks are specifically susceptible to threats, such as wireless intruders, rogue APs, data interception, and DoS attacks. Cisco has developed a range of solutions to mitigate these types of threats.

Practice

The following activities provide practice with the topics introduced in this chapter. The Labs and Class Activities are available in the companion *Switched Networks Lab Manual* (ISBN 978-1-58713-327-5). The Packet Tracer Activities PKA files are found in the online course.

Class Activities

- Class Activity 8.0.1.2: Make Mine Wireless
- Class Activity 8.5.1.1: Inside and Outside Control

Labs

- Lab 8.1.2.10: Investigating Wireless Implementations
- Lab 8.4.2.3: Configuring a Wireless Router and Client

Packet Tracer Activities

- Packet Tracer Activity 8.4.2.2: Configuring Wireless LAN Access

Check Your Understanding Questions

Complete all the review questions listed here to test your understanding of the topics and concepts in this chapter. The appendix "Answers to 'Check Your Understanding' Questions" lists the answers.

1. Which wireless RF band do IEEE 802.11b/g devices use?

    A. 900 MHz

    B. 2.4 GHz

    C. 5 GHz

    D. 60 GHz

2. What type of frames are used for advertising, authenticating, and associating with a wireless AP?

    A. Data

    B. Control

    C. Management

    D. Acknowledgment

3. Fill in the blank. A network administrator discovers a rogue AP in the network. The rogue AP is capturing traffic and then forwarding it on to the legitimate AP. This type of attack is known as a(n) _____ attack.

4. If an administrator is troubleshooting a WLAN using a bottom-up approach, which action would be taken first?

    A. Update the firmware on the AP.

    B. Make sure that all devices are powered on.

    C. Ping the AP.

    D. Verify that the GUI interface is accessible from a client.

5. What is a characteristic of a Yagi antenna that is used by Cisco Aironet access points?

   A. It provides 360-degree coverage.

   B. It can be used for long-distance Wi-Fi networking.

   C. It is also referred to as a "rubber duck" design.

   D. It has the same characteristics as an omnidirectional Wi-Fi antenna.

6. Fill in the blank. Known as "WiGig," the IEEE 802.11 _____ standard provides average speeds of up to 7 Gb/s, but will switch to a lower-GHz band when roaming is employed.

7. What Wi-Fi management frame is regularly broadcast by APs to announce their presence?

   A. Probe

   B. Beacon

   C. Association

   D. Authentication

8. To successfully connect to a wireless network, the Wi-Fi setting on an iPad must be switched on. Which icon should a user select to access the Wi-Fi menu?

   A. App Store

   B. Contacts

   C. Messages

   D. Settings

9. Which statement describes an ESS?

   A. An ESS consists of two or more BSSs that are interconnected wirelessly by a DS.

   B. Bluetooth is an example of ESS infrastructure mode.

   C. An ESS involves several BSSs that are joined through a common distribution system.

   D. An ESS is a connection of a BSS to an ad hoc wireless network.

10. An IEEE 802.11n network has been configured for mixed mode and has clients that are using 802.11n and 802.11g radios on the network. The 802.11n clients are complaining of slower-than-normal speeds. What is the problem?

   A. This is the normal behavior of a mixed-mode network.

   B. The access point is failing.

   C. The authentication is not allowing roaming.

   D. Roaming between access points is disabled.

11. The company handbook states that employees cannot have microwave ovens in their offices. Instead, all employees must use the microwave ovens located in the employee cafeteria. What wireless security risk is the company trying to avoid?

   A. Accidental interference

   B. Improperly configured devices

   C. Interception of data

   D. Rogue access points

12. Which of the following recommendations should an administrator follow when planning the location of multiple APs? (Choose two.)

   A. Position APs horizontally near the ceiling in the center of each coverage area, if possible.

   B. Position APs in locations where users are expected to be.

   C. An ESS should have 20 to 25 percent overlap between BSAs in an ESS.

   D. Overlap channels to provide roaming capability.

   E. Always consult the specifications for the AP when planning for coverage areas.

13. Which combination of WLAN authentication and encryption is recommended as a best practice for home users?

   A. WEP and TKIP

   B. WPA2 and AES

   C. EAP and AES

   D. WPA and PSK

   E. WEP and RC4

Answers to "Check Your Understanding" Questions

Chapter 1

1. A, C, F. Explanation: The access layer is the lowest layer, and it provides network access to users. The distribution layer has many functions, but it aggregates data from the access layer, provides filtering and policy control, and sets Layer 3 routing boundaries. The core layer provides high-speed connectivity.

2. A, C. Explanation: Converged networks have traditional user traffic as well as digitized voice and video traffic that once required separate networks. Now, instead of separate groups managing separate networks, one group of personnel can manage the network.

3. A. Explanation: Stackable switches provide fault tolerance and bandwidth availability by using special cables between switches and are less costly to implement than modular switches. A non-stackable switch does not provide these features. A fixed configuration switch is a single switch that does not support features beyond those that originally came with it. A modular switch usually provides fault tolerance and features for bandwidth availability but is rather costly to implement.

4. C. Explanation: For efficiency, scalability, and cost-effectiveness, building an extended star topology from a centralized site to all other campus sites is recommended. A mesh topology is much more expensive, and bus and dual-ring topologies are more difficult to troubleshoot and maintain.

5. D. Explanation: A modular switch provides fault tolerance and features for bandwidth availability and future expansion by using line cards but is rather costly to implement. Stackable switches provide fault tolerance and bandwidth availability by using special cables between the switches and are less costly to implement than modular switches. A nonstackable switch does not provide these features. A fixed configuration switch is a single switch that does not support features beyond those that originally came with it.

6. Power over Ethernet

7. B, E. Explanation: Each switch port corresponds to an independent collision domain. Ethernet frames are forwarded based on the destination MAC address.

8. A. Explanation: Forwarding rate is the overall amount of data that the switch can process each second. Wire speed is the data rate that each Ethernet port on a switch is capable of attaining. PoE is the technology that allows only directly connected devices to be powered through Ethernet. Port density is the number of ports available on a single switch and does not control the overall data rate on a switch.

9. D. Explanation: Store-and-forward switching performs an error check on an incoming frame after receiving the entire frame on the ingress port. Switches that use this method have the flexibility to support any mix of Ethernet speeds. The cut-through method begins the forwarding process after the destination MAC address of an incoming frame is looked up and the egress port has been determined.

10. B. Explanation: The automated attendant feature increases the speed of voice services by routing calls directly to individuals or departments. Point-to-point video and videoconferencing describe video services on a converged network. An IT management interface is part of a converged network solution that allows IT personnel to facilitate moves, adds, and changes through a centralized application.

11. B. Explanation: PoE allows IP phones to be added to the network and powered through a single Ethernet cable, thus increasing mobility and flexibility. PoE does not affect port density and as a hardware feature does not add Layer 3 functions to a switch.

12. B. Explanation: Store-and-forward switching performs an error check on an incoming frame after receiving the entire frame on the ingress port. Switches that use this method have the flexibility to support any mix of Ethernet speeds. The cut-through method begins the forwarding process after the destination MAC address of an incoming frame is looked up and the egress port has been determined.

Chapter 2

1. C, D, E. Explanation: The descriptions in A. and B. are permuted.

2. A. Explanation: Encryption makes it impossible to read captured traffic.

3. D. Explanation: Description in A. goes with DHCP starvation, in B. goes with CDP attack, and in C. goes with MAC address flooding.

4. C. Explanation: A Layer 2 switch is allotted at least one Layer 3 logical address in the form of a switch virtual interface (SVI), used for managing the switch.

5. D. Explanation: The default gateway provides a means for the administrator of the switch to access networks not directly connected to the switch.

6. A, C. Explanation: Autonegotiation sets duplex and speed.

7. C, B, E, D, A.

8. System, redundant power system (RPS), port status, port speed, Power over Ethernet.

9. Auto; note that 1-Gb/s ports can only operate in full-duplex mode.

10. Auto-MDIX.

11. 1518 bytes.

12. runt.

13. B. Explanation: SSH is very simple to configure after the domain name and local authentication are configured.

14. A. Explanation: This is a situation that is quite common with Cisco switches. Be sure to have a device active on a port in a VLAN in order for the VLAN to be fully functional, including SVI connectivity.

15. C. Explanation: Green is good! The port has transitioned into a forwarding state.

16. Numerous DHCP requests are sent to the DHCP server from spoofed hosts, thus exhausting the DHCP address pool. It is a form of a DoS attack.

17. Develop a written security policy for the organization. Shut down unused services and ports. Use strong passwords and change them often. Control physical access to devices. Avoid using standard insecure HTTP websites, especially for login screens; instead use the more secure HTTPS. Perform backups and test the backed-up files on a regular basis. Educate employees about social engineering attacks, and develop policies to validate identities over the phone, through email, and in person. Encrypt and password-protect sensitive data. Implement security hardware and software, such as firewalls. Keep software up to date by installing security patches weekly or daily, if possible.

18. C. Explanation: Because penetration tests can have adverse effects on the network, they are carried out under very controlled conditions, following documented procedures detailed in a comprehensive network security policy.

19. B. Explanation: If you want the sticky addresses to gain some permanence, copying the running configuration to the startup configuration will keep them viable upon reload.

20. C. Explanation: The default violation mode is shutdown. This causes the port to become error-disabled, turns off the port LED, sends an SNMP trap, logs a syslog message, and increments the violation counter. A **shutdown** followed by a **no shutdown** command will bring the port back up.

Chapter 3

1. A. Explanation: The **show interfaces trunk** command displays the ports that are trunk ports, the trunking mode, the encapsulation type, the trunk status, the native VLAN, and the allowed VLANs on the link.

2. C. Explanation: This command is used in conjunction with the **switchport mode access** command to ensure that hackers do not try to leverage DTP to gain access to other VLANs. VLAN 1 is the default native VLAN on Cisco switches.

3. C. Explanation: Before deleting an active VLAN, it is recommended that all ports currently assigned as a member of that VLAN be reassigned. Any port that is a member of a VLAN that is deleted will become unusable.

4. A. Explanation: An attacker can use switch spoofing or double-tagging to perform a VLAN hopping attack.

5. A, B. Explanation: Dynamic Trunking Protocol (DTP) manages trunk negotiation, and IEEE 802.1Q is the industry standard for trunking. DTP is found on Cisco devices. DTP can be disabled on a port by using the **switchport nonegotiate** command.

6. Assigns VLAN 10 for untagged traffic: C. Switch(config-if)# **switchport trunk native vlan 10**

   Activates the current interface as trunk: B. Switch(config-if)# **switchport mode trunk**

   Prohibits VLAN 10 on the trunk interface: A. Switch(config-if)# **switchport trunk allowed vlan remove 10**

7. A. Explanation: Turn trunking off on all ports that are used to connect to hosts and disable DTP negotiation on all trunking ports to prevent the VLAN hopping attack. This type of attack can be attempted through switch spoofing or double-tagging.

8. D. Explanation: As a best practice, the native VLAN should be something other than VLAN 1. It should be isolated with no other user traffic.

9. A. Explanation: Normal-range VLANs are stored in a file called vlan.dat and located in the flash memory.

10. D, E. Explanation: VLANs create smaller broadcast domains amongst the users connected to the switches, and in so doing help to limit the damage any particular user can have beyond their own broadcast domain. VLANs subdivide networks into smaller networks (subnets).

11. C. Explanation: DTP is a Cisco-proprietary protocol. Non-Cisco switches do not support DTP.

12. D. Explanation: A management VLAN is used to remotely access and configure a switch. Data VLANs are used to separate a network into groups of users or devices. The default VLAN is the initial VLAN that all switch ports are placed in when loading the default configuration on a switch. The 802.1Q trunk port places untagged traffic on the native VLAN.

Chapter 4

1. B. Explanation: After a Cisco switch boots, it will send out BPDUs containing its individual BID and the root ID for the network. By default, the initial root ID at bootup will be the ID of that individual switch. After a root bridge is elected, port states and paths are chosen.

2. A, E, F. Explanation: The Rapid PVST+ port states are discarding, learning, and forwarding.

3. D. Explanation: After the election of a root bridge has occurred, each switch will have to determine the best path to the root bridge from its location. The path is determined by summing the individual port costs along the path from each switch port to the root bridge.

4. A. B, C. Explanation: A port that is configured with PortFast will immediately transition from the blocking to the forwarding state. PortFast should only be configured on switch ports that support end devices, so no BPDUs should ever be received through a port that is configured with PortFast. Configuring a port with PortFast supports DHCP because PortFast will speed the transition from blocking to forwarding. Without PortFast, an end device can begin to issue DHCP requests before the port has transitioned to the forwarding state.

5. A. Explanation: Of all the commands that are listed, only the correct option, **show spanning-tree**, displays STP root bridge information.

6. B. Explanation: Ports in the blocking state are nondesignated ports and do not participate in frame forwarding. Ports in the listening state can participate in BPDU frame forwarding according to received BPDU frames, but do not forward data frames. Ports in the forwarding state forward data frames and send and receive BPDU frames. Ports in the disabled state are administratively disabled.

7. A, B, C. Explanation: They are in order! When a router in an FHRP implementation fails, multiple steps occur for the failover process to be complete.

8. A, C. Explanation: The First Hop Redundancy Protocols HSRP and GLBP are Cisco proprietary and will not function in a multivendor environment.

9. B, D. Explanation: During a broadcast storm, switches will forward broadcast traffic through every interface except the original ingress interface. New traffic arriving at the switch will be discarded by a switch in a broadcast storm because the switch will be unable to process the new traffic. During a broadcast storm, switches do not automatically adjust duplex settings. However, communication will often fail between end devices because of the heavy processing demands that are created by the broadcast traffic. Constant changes to the MAC address table during a broadcast storm can prevent a switch from forwarding frames.

10. D. Explanation: The first step that should be taken when there is a spanning tree failure in a Layer 2 network is to remove all redundant links in the failed segment of the network. This will eliminate the loops in the topology, allowing for a normalization of the traffic and CPU loads. The next step would be to investigate the failure of STP on the redundant links and fix these issues prior to restoring the links.

11. D. Explanation: Redundancy attempts to remove any single point of failure in a network by using multiple physically cabled paths between switches in the network.

12. A. Rapid PVST+, B. STP (the original 802.1D implementation), C. MSTP

13. B, E. Explanation: For a set of routers to present the illusion of being a single router, they must share both an IP address and MAC address. A static route, BID, or host name does not have to be shared in this context.

Chapter 5

1. B, C, F. Explanation: Most configuration tasks can be done on the EtherChannel interface, rather than on individual ports. Existing ports can be used, eliminating the need to upgrade ports to faster speeds. Spanning Tree Protocol runs on EtherChannel links in the same manner as it does on regular links, but it does not recalculate when an individual link within the channel goes down. EtherChannel also supports load balancing.

2. D. Explanation: Two protocols can be used to send negotiation frames that are used to try to establish an EtherChannel link: PAgP and LACP. PAgP is Cisco proprietary, and LACP adheres to the industry standard.

3. C. Explanation: An EtherChannel will be formed through PAgP when both switches are in on mode or when one of them is in auto or desirable mode and the other is in desirable mode.

4. A, C, F. Explanation: There are some EtherChannel modes that can be different and an EtherChannel will form, such as auto/desirable and active/passive. A port that is currently in the spanning tree blocking mode or has been configured for PortFast can still be used to form an EtherChannel.

5. E. Explanation: All ports in an EtherChannel bundle must either be trunk ports or be access ports in the same VLAN. If VLAN pruning is enabled on the trunk, the allowed VLANs must be the same on both sides of the EtherChannel.

6. C. Explanation: The **channel-group mode active** command enables LACP unconditionally, and the **channel-group mode passive** command enables LACP only if the port receives an LACP packet from another device. The **channel-group mode desirable** command enables PAgP unconditionally, and the **channel-group mode auto** command enables PAgP only if the port receives a PAgP packet from another device.

7. B. Explanation: Fast Ethernet and Gigabit Ethernet interfaces cannot be combined into a single EtherChannel interface. The interfaces must all be of the same type. EtherChannel links can be configured on Layer 2 and Layer 3 switches.

8. C, D. Explanation: Port Aggregation Protocol and Link Aggregation Control Protocol are used to implement EtherChannel. Spanning Tree Protocol and Rapid Spanning Tree Protocol are used to prevent switching loops. Cisco Discovery Protocol is Cisco proprietary and is used to discover information about adjacent Cisco devices such as model number and IP address.

9. **show etherchannel summary.** Explanation: When several port channel interfaces are configured on the same device, use the **show etherchannel summary** command to display a single line of information per port channel.

10. B. Explanation: EtherChannel relies on existing switch ports, so there is no need to upgrade the links. Configuration tasks are done on the EtherChannel interface, rather than individual ports. STP operates on EtherChannel in the same manner as it does on other links.

Chapter 6

1. B. Explanation: Layer 2 switches are able to perform static routing, but this method is inefficient with a large number of VLANs. Multilayer switching is more scalable than any other inter-VLAN routing implementation, with traffic being routed internally to the switch device. In router-on-a-stick inter-VLAN routing, where a single physical interface routes traffic among multiple VLANs on a network, there is no practical scalability. The legacy inter-VLAN routing is very inefficient and is no longer used in switched networks, because each VLAN requires a physical router interface that is connected to a different physical switch port.

2. **switchport.** Explanation: The output of the **show interfaces f0/1 switchport** command displays the administrative and operational mode as shown here:

```
Switch0# show interfaces f0/1 switchport
Name: Fa0/1
Switchport: Enabled
Administrative Mode: trunk
Operational Mode: trunk
Administrative Trunking Encapsulation: dot1q.
```

3. C. Explanation: To allow a router-on-a-stick configuration to function, a switch must be connected to the router through a trunk port to carry the VLANs to be routed. An SVI would be used on a multilayer switch where the switch is performing inter-VLAN routing.

4. B, D. Explanation: The errors in the configuration are: 1) The IP address and subnet mask for VLAN 20 are wrong. They have to be 172.17.20.1 and 255.255.255.0, respectively. 2) The VLAN that is assigned to subinterface Fa0/0.30 is incorrect. The **encapsulation dot1q 40** command should be **encapsulation dot1q 30**. There is not a single command to be issued on a router physical interface to configure trunking. The **no shutdown** command has to be issued on the physical interface, not on the subinterfaces. In this case, it was issued, because only the **shutdown** command is displayed in the **show running-config** command output.

5. B. Explanation: With router-on-a-stick, subinterfaces are used on one physical router interface. One subinterface per VLAN is used in this design. When multiple interfaces are used on a router, each physical interface, such as g0/0 and g0/1, is assigned one IP address. Each VLAN would require a physical interface. When routing through a multilayer switch, one SVI is assigned an IP address for each VLAN. Interdomain routing does not affect inter-VLAN communication.

6. B. Explanation: The FastEthernet0/2, FastEthernet0/3, and FastEthernet0/4 access interfaces are configured as trunk by the **switchport mode trunk** command. They should be configured as access interfaces. The administrator must issue the **switchport mode access** command.

7. 192.168.40.6. Explanation: The Fa0/2 port of Switch0 is assigned to VLAN40, so PC0 must be in the same subnet of the virtual interface VLAN40 of the Layer 3 switch Switch1. This means that VLAN40 has IP addresses in the range of 192.168.40.2 to 192.168.40.6. So the correct answer is 192.168.40.6.

8. D. Explanation: The steps to configure inter-VLAN routing must be completed in a specific order. Before configuring an IP address on a subinterface, the **encapsulation dot1q** *vlan-id* command must be specified first.

9. B. Explanation: A router-on-a-stick design is the same as having a trunked interface between the router and the switch. This design works but does not scale well, because all VLANs must traverse the one connection between the router and the switch. Multiple physical interfaces on the router would be faster than the router-on-a-stick design, but a router has a limited number of physical interfaces. Layer 3 switches with routing enabled have more Ethernet ports as well as the ability to route.

10. D. Explanation: The administrator can use the encapsulation command to specify the encapsulation type (IEEE 802.1Q or ISL), the VLAN ID, and optionally the native VLAN.

11. C. Explanation: The Cisco Switch Database Manager (SDM) provides multiple templates for the 2960 switch. The SDM lanbase-routing template can be enabled to allow the switch to route between VLANs and to support static routing. The other options provide templates for other roles that the 2960 switch can take.

12. B. Explanation: By default, the physical ports on a 3560 switch are Layer 2 interfaces. To make them routed ports, the interface command **no switchport** should be used. The other options do not describe the purpose of this command.

Chapter 7

1. C. Explanation: SOHO and home broadband routers are typically set to acquire an IPv4 address automatically from the ISP. The IP address that is assigned is typically a dynamic address to reduce the cost, but a static IP address is possible with more cost. However, if the router is assigned a dynamic IP address, DNS issues will result in the web server behind the router not being easily accessible to the public. Routers are typically also gateways for LANs, but this has no bearing on whether the router is configured as a DHCP client on its WAN link or not. Likewise, a router can be configured to be a DHCP client to obtain an IP address from the ISP, but at the same time, it can be configured as a DHCP server to serve the IP addressing for the devices on its LAN.

2. The broadcast DHCPDISCOVER message finds DHCPv4 servers on the network. When the DHCPv4 server receives a DHCPDISCOVER message, it reserves an available IPv4 address to lease to the client and sends the unicast DHCPOFFER message to the requesting client. When the client receives the DHCPOFFER from the server, it sends back a DHCPREQUEST. On receiving the DHCPREQUEST message, the server replies with a unicast DHCPACK message. DHCPREPLY and DHCPINFORMATION-REQUEST are DHCPv6 messages.

3. C. Explanation: The Managed Address Configuration (M) flag and the Other Configuration (O) flag in ICMPv6 RA messages are used to indicate to an IPv6 client how it should configure its IPv6 addresses. If the M flag is set to 0, it means that the host should automatically configure its own IPv6 interface address rather than asking for one from a DHCPv6 server. If the O flag is set to 1, it means that the client can find additional addressing information, such as a DNS server address, by contacting a DHCPv6 server after it has automatically configured its own address.

4. DHCPv6 SOLICIT, DHCPv6 ADVERTISE, DHCPv6 REQUEST, DHCP REPLY.

5. D. Explanation: During the initial DHCP exchange between a client and server, the client broadcasts a DHCPDISCOVER message looking for DHCP servers. Multiple servers can be configured to respond to this request with DHCPOFFER messages. The client will choose the lease from one of the servers by sending a DHCPREQUEST message. It sends this message as a broadcast so that the other DHCP servers that sent offers will know that their offers were declined and the corresponding address can go back into the pool.

6. A. Explanation: The **show ip dhcp binding** command will show the leases, including IP addresses, MAC addresses, lease expiration, type of lease, client ID, and username.

7. **server events.** Explanation: The **debug ip dhcp server events** command reports IP address assignments and database updates as they happen.

8. D. Explanation: Stateless Address Autoconfiguration (SLAAC) can be used as an alternative to DHCPv6 to dynamically assign IPv6 addresses to hosts. ARP is not used in IPv6. ICMPv6 messages are used by SLAAC to provide addressing and other configuration information. EUI-64 is a process that will create an Interface ID by using its 48-bit MAC address.

9. B. Explanation: When the **ipv6 address dhcp** command is configured on a router interface, it enables the router as a DHCPv6 client on this interface. The **ipv6 enable** command enables IPv6 on an interface and allows the router to configure its link-local address. The **ipv6 address autoconfigure** command tells the router to use either SLAAC or stateless DHCPv6 to configure its global unicast address. The **ipv6 dhcp server** command is used on a router that is running a DHCPv6 server to indicate what address information should be served to clients.

10. D. Explanation: When the client receives the DHCPOFFER from the server, it sends back a DHCPREQUEST broadcast message. On receiving the DHCPREQUEST message, the server replies with a unicast DHCPACK message.

Chapter 8

1. B. Explanation: 900 MHz is an FCC wireless technology that was used before the development of the 802.11 standards. 900-MHz devices have a larger coverage range than the higher frequencies have and do not require line of sight between devices. 802.11b/g/n/ad devices all operate at 2.4 GHz. 802.11a/n/ac/ad devices operate at 5 GHz, and 802.11ad devices operate at 60 GHz.

2. C. Explanation: Management frames include probes, association frames, and authentication frames and are used to facilitate connectivity between a client and an access point.

3. evil twin AP. Explanation: An evil twin AP attack involves the deployment of a rogue AP in a given network. User traffic is now sent to the rogue AP, which in turn captures the data and forwards it to the legitimate AP. Return traffic from the legitimate AP is sent to the rogue AP, captured, and then forwarded to the unsuspecting client. The attacker can steal the password and personal information of the user, gain network access, and compromise the system of the user.

4. B. Explanation: Bottom-up troubleshooting begins with the physical layer. Cables and power would be a logical place to begin the process. ICMP (ping) is a network layer utility. Channel settings are part of the client software. Firmware is the operating system software used by the AP.

5. B. Explanation: Yagi antennas are a type of directional radio antenna that can be used for long-distance Wi-Fi networking. They are typically used to extend the range of outdoor hotspots in a specific direction, owing to their high gain. Omnidirectional Wi-Fi antennas are referred to as a "rubber duck" design and provide 360-degree coverage.

6. ad

7. B. Explanation: Beacon frames are broadcast periodically by the AP to advertise its wireless networks to potential clients. Probing, association, and authentication frames are only sent when a client is associating to the AP.

8. D. Explanation: For an iPad to be configured to connect to a wireless router, the Wi-Fi setting on the iPad must be switched on. The Wi-Fi configuration submenu is located through the Settings icon, which is located on the iPad desktop. The App Store is an application that is used to buy games and applications for the iPad. The Contacts icon is used to keep a listing of family, friends, and business associates so that you can easily message them or have a videoconference with them. The Messages application allows you to send an instant message to anyone.

9. C. Explanation: An ESS consists of two or more BSSs that are interconnected by a wired DS. Bluetooth is an example of ad hoc mode.

10. A. Explanation: The mixed setting can slow communication. When all the clients that are connecting to the router are using 802.11n, they all enjoy the better data rates that are provided. If 802.11g clients associate with the AP, all the faster clients that are contending for the channel have to wait for 802.11g clients to clear the channel before those faster clients can transmit.

11. A. Explanation: Denial of service attacks can be the result of improperly configured devices, which can disable the WLAN. Accidental interference from devices such as microwave ovens and cordless phones can impact both the security and performance of a WLAN.

12. B, E. Explanation: Some recommendations are

- Position APs vertically near the ceiling in the center of each coverage area, if possible.

- Position APs in locations where users are expected to be. For example, conference rooms are typically a better location for APs than a hallway.

- Always consult the specifications for the AP when planning for coverage areas.

- A BSA represents the coverage area that is provided by a single channel. An ESS should have a 10 to 15 percent overlap in coverage area between BSAs in an ESS. With a 15 percent overlap between BSAs, an SSID, and nonoverlapping channels (that is, one cell on channel 1 and the other on channel 6), roaming capability can be created.

13. B. Explanation: WPA2 is the Wi-Fi Alliance version of 802.11i, the industry standard for authentication. Neither WEP nor WPA possesses the level of authentication provided by WPA2. AES aligns with WPA2 as an encryption standard, and is stronger than TKIP or RC4. PSK refers to pre-shared passwords, an authentication method that can be used by either WPA or WPA2. EAP is intended for use with enterprise networks that use a RADIUS server.

A

Access Layer The access layer is where end users connect to the network.

access point (AP) A device that connects wireless communication devices to form a wireless network, analogous to a hub connecting wired devices to form a LAN. The AP usually connects to a wired network and can relay data between wireless devices and wired devices. Several APs can link together to form a larger network that allows roaming.

Acknowledgment (ACK) frame An ACK frame is sent by receiving stations to confirm receipt of data.

Active mode When an AP is in active mode, wireless clients must know the name of the SSID. The wireless client initiates the process by broadcasting a probe request frame on multiple channels. The probe request includes the SSID name and standards supported. Active mode might be required if an AP or wireless router is configured to not broadcast beacon frames.

Active router An active router is a router running HSRP, that is actively forwarding packets for the HSRP group.

ad hoc A WLAN topology, also called independent basic service set, where mobile clients connect directly without an intermediate access point. Referred to as IBSS by the IEEE.

Advanced Encryption Standard (AES) AES replaced Wired Equivalent Privacy (WEP) as the most secure method of encrypting data. AES is an option for WPA2.

alternate port A switch port in an RSTP topology that offers an alternate path toward the root bridge. An alternate port assumes a discarding state in a stable, active topology. An alternate port will be present on nondesignated bridges and will make a transition to a designated port if the current path fails.

association The state achieved when a properly configured wireless client is able to wirelessly communicate with an access point.

association identifier (AID) An access point maps a logical port, known as the association identifier (AID), to the WLAN client. The AID is equivalent to a port on a switch.

Association request frame Frame sent from a wireless client that enables the AP to allocate resources and synchronize.

Association response frame   Frame sent from an AP to a wireless client containing the acceptance or rejection to an association request.

authentication   In network security, authentication is the verification of the identity of a person or process. Authentication is also used to describe the process a client device goes through before it can join a WLAN.

Authentication frame   Frame sent from a wireless client to the AP, communicating the identity of the client.

Auto mode   Mode on a switch port describing speed or duplex being configured to automatically detect the respective speed or duplex setting, depending on the attached device.

Automated attendant   Automated attendant allows callers to locate people in an organization without talking to a receptionist.

Automatic allocation   Automatic allocation describes the automatic allocation of a permanent IP address to a client device.

Autonomous AP   An autonomous AP is a stand-alone AP that does not require the support of a wireless LAN controller.

B

backup port   In a Rapid Spanning Tree Protocol (RSTP) topology, this is a switch port on a designated bridge with a redundant link to the segment for which the switch is designated. A backup port has a higher port ID than the designated port on the designated bridge. The backup port assumes the discarding state in a stable, active topology.

basic service area (BSA)   The area of radio frequency coverage provided by an access point. This area is also referred to as a microcell.

basic service set (BSS)   A WLAN infrastructure mode whereby mobile clients use a single access point for connectivity to each other or to wired network resources.

basic service set identifier (BSSID)   The MAC address of the access point serving the BSS.

beacon   A wireless LAN packet that signals the availability and presence of the wireless device. Beacon packets are sent by access points and base stations; however, client radio cards send beacons when operating in computer-to-computer (ad hoc) mode.

black hole VLAN   The black hole VLAN for a switch or switched infrastructure is defined by the switch administrator as a dummy VLAN distinct from all other VLANs. All unused switch ports are assigned to the black hole VLAN so that any device connecting to an unused switch port will be assigned to the black hole VLAN. Any traffic associated with the black hole VLAN is not allowed on trunk links, thus preventing any device associated with the black hole VLAN from communicating beyond the switch to which it is connected.

blocking state   With the Spanning Tree Protocol, a port is in the blocking state if it is a nondesignated port and does not participate in frame forwarding. The port continues to process received BPDU frames to determine the location and root ID of the root bridge and determine what port role the switch port should assume in the final active STP topology.

Bluetooth   Bluetooth is a type of wireless personal-area network. Bluetooth devices are often used for connecting devices, such as mice, keyboards, and computers. Bluetooth headsets are wireless devices frequently used to connect to smart phones and softphones.

Bottom-up troubleshooting   Bottom-up troubleshooting is troubleshooting where one starts with the physical components of the network (OSI Layer 1) and moves up through the layers of the OSI model until the cause of the problem is found. Bottom-up troubleshooting is a good approach to use when a physical problem is suspected.

BPDU guard   BPDU guard is a feature used in conjunction with spanning tree and PortFast that enforces spanning-tree domain borders and keeps the active topology predictable. The devices behind the ports that have PortFast enabled are not able to influence the spanning-tree topology. At the reception of BPDUs, the BPDU guard operation disables the port that has PortFast configured. The BPDU guard transitions the port into the errdisable state, and a message appears on the console.

bridge protocol data unit (BPDU)   A Spanning Tree Protocol Ethernet frame that is sent out at regular intervals to exchange information among bridges in the network relating to spanning-tree topology formation.

Broadcast domain   A broadcast domain is the set of all devices that will receive broadcast frames originating from any device from the set. Broadcast domains are defined by routers, multi-layer switches, and VLANs.

Broadcast storm   A broadcast storm is an event in which broadcasts are sent simultaneously across a series of network segments, and often monopolizes sufficient network bandwidth to affect network time-outs.

Brute force password attack   The first phase of a brute force password attack starts with the attacker using a list of common passwords and a program designed to try to establish a remote connection using each word in the dictionary list. In the second phase of a brute force attack, the attacker uses a program that creates sequential character combinations in an attempt to "guess" the password. Given enough time, a brute force password attack can crack almost all passwords used.

C

Call control   Call control allows users to initiate calls easily, usually by integration with an LDAP system. Call control provides access to media resources such as audio conferencing, and enables features such as music on hold.

Carrier Sense Multiple Access with Collision Avoidance (CSMA/CA)   This media access method requires WLAN devices to sense the medium for energy levels and wait until the medium is free before sending.

Cellular/mobile broadband   Cellular broadband is often referred to as mobile broadband, and it refers to various corporate, national, and international organizations using service provider cellular access to provide mobile broadband network connectivity. Examples include 2G, 3G, and 4G (WiMAX or LTE).

CHADDR   CHADDR is an abbreviation for client hardware address.

channel   A channel consists of a range of frequencies. Channels are used by wireless devices to hone in on a particular signal to differentiate it from wireless communications taking place at other frequencies. For example, the 2.4-GHz band is broken down into 11 channels in North America and 13 channels in Europe.

CIADDR   CIADDR is an abbreviation for client IP address.

Cisco Borderless Network   The Cisco Borderless Network is a network architecture combining innovation and design that allows organizations to support a borderless network that can connect anyone, anywhere, anytime, on any device—securely, reliably, and seamlessly. This architecture is designed to address IT and business challenges, such as supporting the converged network and changing work patterns.

Cisco CleanAir technology   Cisco CleanAir technology uses silicon-level intelligence to create a spectrum-aware, self-healing, and self-optimizing wireless network that mitigates the impact of wireless interference and offers performance protection for 802.11n networks.

Cisco Discovery Protocol (CDP)   A media- and protocol-independent device-discovery protocol that runs on all Cisco-manufactured equipment, including routers, access servers, bridges, and switches. Using CDP, a device can advertise its existence to other devices and receive information about other devices on the same LAN or on the remote side of a WAN.

Cisco Management Frame Protection (MFP)   MFP is a variety of Cisco technologies created to mitigate spoofed disconnect attacks and CTS floods, which are wireless network attacks involving management frames.

Cisco Meraki Cloud Managed Architecture   The Cisco Meraki cloud architecture is a management solution used to simplify wireless deployment. Using this architecture, APs are managed centrally from a controller in the cloud. Cloud networking and management provide centralized management, visibility, and control without the cost and complexity of controller appliances or overlay management software.

Cisco Prime   Cisco Prime is network management software that works with other management software to provide a common look and central location for all network information. It is usually deployed in very large organizations.

Cisco Services Ready Engine (SRE)   Cisco SRE modules are router blades for ISR G2 that provide the capability to host third-party and custom applications.

Cisco Unified Wireless Network Architecture   The Cisco Unified Wireless Network Architecture solution, using a split MAC design, controls APs using a WLC and can be optionally managed using Cisco WCS. The lightweight APs communicate with the WLAN controller using LWAPP. The controller has all the intelligence for communication, and the AP is a "dumb terminal" that simply processes packets.

Cisco Virtual Controller   Cisco Virtual Controller is deployed on an x86 server that supports VMware ESXI 4.x or 5.x, one virtual CPU, 2 GB memory, 8 GB disk space, and two or more virtual NICs. It is used to configure, manage, and troubleshoot up to 200 APs and 3000 clients.

Cisco Wireless Control System (WCS)   Cisco WCS is the comprehensive life cycle management platform for the Cisco Unified Wireless Network.

Cisco Wireless Controller   Cisco Wireless Controllers include the Integrated Services Module 300 (ISM-300), which supports up to ten APs, and the SM-710 and SM-910 modules, which support up to 50 APs and 500 clients. All of these controllers have PCI functionality for scanner and kiosk support.

Cisco Wireless Domain Services (WDS)   WDS is a collection of Cisco IOS features that enhance WLAN client mobility and simplify WLAN deployment and management. WDS enables fast secure roaming, WLSE interaction, and radio management.

CiscoWorks Wireless LAN Solution Engine (WLSE)   WLSE is a centralized, systems-level application for managing and controlling an entire autonomous Cisco WLAN infrastructure.

clear-to-send (CTS)   A mechanism used in wireless technology to indicate that a wireless device is ready to accept data. RTS/CTS is used to resolve device access to avoid the hidden node problem.

Collision domain   A collision domain is the network area within which frames that have collided are propagated. Repeaters and hubs propagate collisions; LAN switches, bridges, and routers do not propagate collisions.

Common Spanning Tree (CST)   Common Spanning Tree is a single instance of spanning tree for an entire bridged network. In the original implementations of spanning tree, CST was the only option.

Control Frame   A control frame is used to facilitate the exchange of data frames between wireless clients.

Controller-Based AP   A controller-based AP is an access point that requires the intervention of a wireless LAN controller to function.

Converged network   A converged network is one that combines voice and video communications with data communication.

Core   The core layer of a network is the portion of an enterprise campus network providing fast transport between distribution switches.

Counter Cipher Mode with Block Chaining Message Authentication Code Protocol (CCMP)   CCMP is the protocol used by destination hosts employing AES to recognize whether the encrypted and nonencrypted bits have been tampered with.

CTS flood   A CTS flood occurs when an attacker takes advantage of the CSMA/CA contention method to monopolize the bandwidth and deny all other wireless clients access to the AP. To accomplish this, the attacker repeatedly floods the BSS with CTS frames to a bogus end station. All other wireless clients sharing the RF medium receive the CTS and withhold their transmissions until the attacker stops transmitting the CTS frames.

cut-through switching   An Ethernet frame-switching approach that streams data through a switch so that the leading edge of a packet exits the switch at the egress port before the packet finishes entering the ingress port. A device using cut-through packet switching reads, processes, and forwards packets as soon as the destination address is read and the egress port determined.

D

Data frame   A data frame is one that carries payload information between clients.

data VLAN   A VLAN that is configured to carry only user-generated traffic. In particular, a data VLAN does not carry voice-based traffic or traffic used to manage a switch.

Deauthentication frame   A deauthentication frame is sent from a wireless client wanting to terminate a connection with another wireless client.

default template   The Switch Database Manager (SDM) provides multiple templates on the Cisco 2960 switch. The templates can be enabled to support specific roles depending on how the switch is used in the network. The default template is the one that is loaded by default.

default VLAN   The VLAN that all the ports on a switch are members of when a switch is reset to factory defaults. All switch ports are members of the default VLAN after the initial boot of the switch. On a Catalyst switch, VLAN 1 is the default VLAN.

Denial of service attack   A denial of service attack is an attempt by a single person or a group of people to cause a site or a node to deny service to its customers.

designated port   In spanning tree, a nonroot switch port that is permitted to forward traffic on the network. For a trunk link connecting two switches, one end connects to the designated bridge through the designated port. One and only one end of every trunk link in a switched LAN (with spanning tree enabled) connects to a designated port. The selection of designated ports is the last step in the spanning-tree algorithm.

DHCP Acknowledgment   Upon receiving a DHCP Request message, the DHCP server verifies the lease information by returning a DHCP Acknowledgment.

DHCP binding   DHCP binding refers to the mapping between MAC addresses and IP addresses assigned by a DHCP server.

DHCP client   A DHCP client is a network node that receives its IP address information from a DHCP server.

DHCP Discover   A DHCP Discover message is sent by DHCP clients to discover DHCP servers on the network.

DHCP lease   The DHCP lease refers to the duration that allocated IP address information remains viable for a DHCP client.

DHCP Offer   A DHCP server sends a binding unicast DHCP Offer message to a requesting client.

DHCP pool   A DHCP pool is a set of IP addresses allocatable by a DHCP server.

DHCP relay agent   A DHCP relay agent is a network device that forwards DHCP messages between DHCP servers and DHCP clients on distinct networks.

DHCP Request   A DHCP client sends a DHCP Request message for both lease origination and lease renewal.

DHCP server   A DHCP server is a network device that allocates IP address information to DHCP clients.

DHCP snooping   DHCP snooping is a DHCP security feature that provides network security by filtering untrusted DHCP messages and by building and maintaining a DHCP snooping binding database, also referred to as a DHCP snooping binding table.

DHCP starvation attack   A DHCP starvation attack works by the broadcast of DHCP requests with spoofed MAC addresses. If enough requests are sent, the network attacker can exhaust the address space available to the DHCP servers for a period of time. The network attacker can then set up a rogue DHCP server on his or her system and respond to new DHCP requests from clients on the network.

DHCPv4   DHCPv4 is version 4 of the Dynamic Host Configuration Protocol. It is used with IPv4.

DHCPv6   DHCPv6 is version 6 of the Dynamic Host Configuration Protocol. It is used with IPv6.

DHCPv6 ADVERTISE   A DHCPv6 ADVERTISE message informs a DHCPv6 client that the server is available for DHCPv6 service.

DHCPv6 INFORMATION-REQUEST   A DHCPv6 INFORMATION-REQUEST message is sent to a DHCPv6 server by a stateless DHCPv6 client only requesting configuration parameters, such as DNS server addresses.

DHCPv6 REPLY   A DHCPv6 REPLY message is sent to a DHCPv6 client and contains the information requested in the REQUEST or INFORMATION-REQUEST message.

DHCPv6 REQUEST   A DHCPv6 REQUEST message is sent to a DHCPv6 server by a stateful DHCP client to obtain an IPv6 address and all other configuration parameters.

DHCPv6 SOLICIT   A DHCPv6 client sends a DHCPv6 SOLICIT multicast message to locate a DHCPv6 server.

direct-sequence spread spectrum (DSSS)   One of the modulation techniques set forth in IEEE 802.11 and the one chosen by the 802.11 Working Group for IEEE 802.11b devices.

Directional Wi-Fi antenna   Directional antennas focus the radio signal in a given direction. This enhances the signal to and from the AP in the direction that the antenna is pointing, providing stronger signal strength in one direction and less signal strength in all other directions.

disabled   A disabled port is a switch port that is shut down.

disassociation frame   A disassociation frame is sent from a device wanting to terminate a connection. It allows the AP to relinquish memory allocation and remove the device from the association table.

discarding   Discarding refers to an RSTP port state that encompasses the traditional disabled, blocking, and listening spanning-tree states. A port in this state prevents the forwarding of data frames.

distributed coordination function (DCF)   All wireless devices in a WLAN use CSMA/CA—the function of coordinating access to the medium is distributed. If an access point receives data from a client station, it sends an acknowledgment to the client that the data has been received. This acknowledgment keeps the client from assuming that a collision occurred and prevents data retransmission by the client. Access to the network is a coordinated process with an access control function that uses assigned wait times to distribute access to the network, thus limiting collisions.

Distribution Layer   The distribution layer of a network is where policy-based connectivity is applied, such as access control lists and QoS. The distribution layer includes routers and multilayer switches.

distribution system (DS)   A distribution system is a system of network devices and the wires connecting them, in reference to servicing APs and wireless clients.

Divide-and-conquer troubleshooting   One starts by collecting users' experiences with the problem and documenting the symptoms. Then, using that information, an informed guess is made about the OSI layer at which to start the investigation. After verifying that a layer is functioning properly, it is safe to assume that the layers below it are functioning, and to continue working upward through the OSI layers. If an OSI layer is not functioning properly, one works downward through OSI layers

Double-Tagging Attack   A double-tagging (or double-encapsulated) VLAN hopping attack takes advantage of the way that hardware on most switches operates. Most switches perform only one level of 802.1Q deencapsulation, which allows an attacker to embed a hidden 802.1Q tag inside the frame. This tag allows the frame to be forwarded to a VLAN that the original 802.1Q tag did not specify.

Dumb terminal   A dumb terminal is an end station in a network that relies on other computers on the network to do any processing.

Duplicate Address Detection (DAD)   DAD is part of ICMPv6 Neighbor Discovery and is recommended by RFC 4861.

Dynamic allocation   Dynamic allocation refers to a DHCPv4 address allocation method whereby the DHCPv4 server dynamically assigns or leases an IPv4 address from a pool of addresses for a limited period of time.

dynamic desirable mode   DTP mode on a switch port where the interface actively attempts to convert the link to a trunk link. The interface becomes a trunk link if the neighboring interface is set to trunk, desirable, or auto mode.

Dynamic Host Configuration Protocol (DHCP)   DHCP is a technology used to automate the configuration of IP addresses on network nodes configured as DHCP clients.

Dynamic secure MAC address   Dynamic secure MAC addresses are MAC addresses that are dynamically learned and stored only in the address table. MAC addresses configured in this way are removed when the switch restarts.

Dynamic Trunking Protocol (DTP)   A Cisco-proprietary protocol that negotiates both the status and encapsulation of trunk ports.

E

edge port   An RSTP edge port is a switch port that is never intended to be connected to another switch device. It immediately transitions to the forwarding state when enabled. Edge ports are conceptually similar to PortFast-enabled ports in the Cisco implementation of IEEE 802.1D.

egress port   An egress port on a networking device describes a port that traffic is exiting. Egress is used in reference to a flow of traffic: If the flow of traffic involves the exiting of a port on a device, that port is an egress port for that traffic flow.

encryption   The application of a specific algorithm to data so as to alter the appearance of the data, making it incomprehensible to those who are not authorized to see the information.

enterprise security mode   Enterprise security mode is a wireless security mode that requires an independent RADIUS server to authenticate wireless clients.

Error disabled   Error disabled describes the state of a port on a Cisco switch. The port is disabled due to an event triggered by a feature or technology running on the switch, such as port security.

EtherChannel   EtherChannel is now used to describe the logical bundling of switch ports on a Cisco switch using either LACP or PAgP.

Evil twin AP attack   An evil twin AP attack is a popular wireless MITM attack where an attacker introduces a rogue AP and configures it with the same SSID as a legitimate AP. Locations offering free Wi-Fi, such as airports, cafes, and restaurants, are hotbeds for this type of attack due to the open authentication.

extended service area (ESA)   The coverage area of an ESS.

extended service set (ESS)   A WLAN infrastructure mode whereby two or more basic service sets are connected by a common distribution system. An ESS generally includes a common SSID to allow roaming from access point to access point without requiring client configuration.

Extensible Authentication Protocol (EAP)   A universal authentication framework frequently used in wireless networks defined by RFC 3748. Although the EAP protocol is not limited to WLANs and can be used for wired LAN authentication, it is most often used in WLANs. The WPA and WPA2 standards have adopted five EAP types as their official authentication mechanism.

Extremely High Frequency (EHF)   60 GHz. EHF pertains to IEEE 802.11ad.

F

FHRP (First Hop Redundancy Protocol)   FHRPs are protocols used for redundancy at the portion of the network where access layer switches connect to routers or multilayer switches.

Fixed configuration switch   A fixed configuration switch is one that does not permit the addition or insertion of modules to enhance functionality.

Flexibility   In networking, flexibility refers to the ability to allow intelligent traffic load sharing by using all network resources.

Form factor   Form factor is a characterization of switch type. The basic form factors are modular, fixed, and stackable.

Forwarding   A port in the spanning-tree forwarding state is considered part of the active topology. It forwards data frames and sends and receives BPDU frames.

Forwarding rate   Forwarding rates define the processing capabilities of a switch by rating how much data the switch can process per second.

Fourth Generation (4G)   The fourth generation of cellular/mobile broadband technology, which includes WiMAX and LTE.

Fragment free switching   Fragment free switching is a modified form of cut-through switching in which the switch waits for the collision window (64 bytes) to pass before forwarding the frame.

Frame forwarding   Frame forwarding is a process that results in a frame exiting one interface after entering another interface.

Frame subtype   A wireless frame subtype determines the specific function to perform for its associated frame type.

Frame type   The wireless frame type determines the function of a frame. The frame type can be a control frame, a data frame, or a management frame.

Frequency-Hopping Spread Spectrum (FHSS)   FHSS relies on spread-spectrum methods to communicate. It is similar to DSSS but transmits radio signals by rapidly switching a carrier signal among many frequency channels. With FHSS, the sender and receiver must be synchronized to "know" which channel to jump. This channel-hopping process allows for a more efficient usage of the channels, decreasing channel congestion.

FromDS   FromDS indicates that a wireless frame is exiting the DS.

G

Geostationary Earth Orbit (GEO) satellite   A GEO satellite is fixed above a certain point on the Earth.

GIADDR   GIADDR is an abbreviation for gateway IP address.

GLBP (Gateway Load Balancing Protocol)   GLBP is a Cisco-proprietary First Hop Redundancy Protocol (FHRP) that protects data traffic from a failed router or circuit, like HSRP and VRRP, while also allowing load balancing (also called load sharing) between a group of redundant routers.

H

HSRP (Hot Standby Router Protocol)   HSRP is a Cisco-proprietary FHRP designed to allow for transparent failover of a first-hop IPv4 device. HSRP provides high network availability by providing first-hop routing redundancy for IPv4 hosts on networks configured with an IPv4 default gateway address. HSRP is used in a group of routers for selecting an active device and a standby device.

I

ICMPv6 Neighbor Discovery   ICMPv6 Neighbor Discovery is a mechanism used in IPv6 networks to identify information about neighbor devices.

IEEE 802   IEEE 802 is a family of standards used to describe technologies and protocols in LANs and MANs.

IEEE 802.1AX-2008 IEEE 802.1AX-2008 is a standard for local- and metropolitan-area networks that defines LACP (originally defined in 802.3ad).

IEEE 802.1D-1998 IEEE 802.1D-1998 is the original IEEE 802.1D version that provides a loop-free topology in a network with redundant links. This specification assumes a Common Spanning Tree (CST), with one spanning-tree instance for the entire bridged network, regardless of the number of VLANs.

IEEE 802.1D-2004 IEEE 802.1D-2004 is an updated version of the spanning-tree standard, incorporating IEEE 802.1w. IEEE 802.1D-2004 includes the RSTP specification.

IEEE 802.1Q A project in the IEEE 802 standards process to develop a mechanism to allow multiple bridged networks to transparently share the same physical network link without leaking information between networks. IEEE 802.1Q is also the name of the encapsulation protocol used to implement this mechanism over Ethernet networks.

IEEE 802.1w IEEE 802.1w is an evolution of spanning tree that provides faster convergence than the original 802.1D implementation. This version addresses many convergence issues, but because it still provides a single instance of spanning tree, it does not address the suboptimal traffic flow issues. To support that faster convergence, the CPU usage and memory requirements of this version are slightly higher than those of Common Spanning Tree (CST), but less than those of RSTP+.

IEEE 802.1x A standard for port-based network access control. It provides authentication to devices attached to a LAN port, establishing a point-to-point connection or preventing access

from that port if authentication fails. It is used for wireless access points and is based on EAP.

IEEE 802.11 A standard that defines how radio frequency in the ISM frequency bands is used for the physical layer and the MAC sublayer of wireless links.

IEEE 802.11a A standard specifying wireless data communication at up to 54 Mbps at the 5-GHz range using OFDM.

IEEE 802.11ac IEEE 802.11ac refers to wireless operation in the 5-GHz frequency band and provides data rates ranging from 450 Mb/s to 1.3 Gb/s (1300 Mb/s). It uses multiple input/multiple output (MIMO) technology to improve communication performance. Up to eight antennas can be supported. The 802.11ac standard is backward compatible with 802.11a/n devices; however, supporting a mixed environment limits the expected data rates.

IEEE 802.11ad IEEE 802.11ad is also known as WiGig. It uses 2.4 GHz, 5 GHz, and 60 GHz, and offers theoretical speeds of up to 7 Gb/s. However, the 60-GHz band is a line-of-sight technology and therefore cannot penetrate through walls. When a user is roaming, the device switches to the lower 2.4-GHz and 5-GHz bands. It is backward compatible with existing Wi-Fi devices.

IEEE 802.11b A standard specifying wireless data communication at up to 11 Mbps at the 2.4-GHz range using DSSS.

IEEE 802.11g A standard specifying wireless data communication at up to 54 Mbps at the 2.4-GHz range using DSSS and OFDM.

IEEE 802.11i A standard specifying security mechanisms for wireless networks.

IEEE 802.11n   IEEE 802.11n operates in the 2.4-GHz and 5-GHz frequency bands. Typical data rates range from 150 Mb/s to 600 Mb/s, with a distance range of up to 70m (0.5 mile). However, to achieve the higher speeds, APs and wireless clients require multiple antennas using the multiple-input and multiple-output (MIMO) technology. MIMO uses multiple antennas as both the transmitter and receiver to improve communication performance. Up to four antennas can be supported. The 802.11n standard is backward compatible with 802.11a/b/g devices.

IEEE 802.11n (draft)   A draft standard specifying wireless data communication at up to 248 Mbps at an unspecified frequency range and using MIMO.

IEEE 802.15   IEEE 802.15 is a wireless personal-area network standard that originally included Bluetooth.

IEEE 802.16   IEEE 802.16 is a wireless wide-area network standard that includes WiMAX.

independent BSS (IBSS)   The IEEE terminology for an ad hoc topology.

industrial, scientific, and medical (ISM)   The ISM radio bands were originally reserved internationally for the use of RF electromagnetic fields for industrial, scientific, and medical purposes other than communications. Communications equipment must accept any interference generated by ISM equipment.

Infrastructure mode   Infrastructure mode refers to when wireless clients interconnect through a wireless router or AP, such as in WLANs. APs connect to the network infrastructure using the wired distribution system.

Ingress port   An ingress port on a networking device describes a port that traffic is entering. Ingress is used in reference to a flow of traffic: If the flow of traffic involves entering a port on a device, that port is an ingress port for that traffic flow.

Inter-VLAN Routing   Inter-VLAN routing simply means routing between VLANs!

Interface ID (IID)   The 64-bit end station ID used in IPv6 networking.

International Telecommunication Union – Radiocommunication Sector (ITU-R)   The ITU-R regulates the allocation of the RF spectrum.

Internet Control Message Protocol version 6 (ICMPv6)   ICMPv6 is similar to ICMPv4 but includes additional functionality and is a much more robust protocol. SLAAC uses ICMPv6.

IRDP (ICMP Router Discovery Protocol)   IRDP is specified in RFC 1256 and is a legacy FHRP solution. IRDP allows IPv4 hosts to locate routers that provide IPv4 connectivity to other (nonlocal) IP networks.

L

lanbase-routing template   The Switch Database Manager (SDM) provides multiple templates on the Cisco 2960 switch. The templates can be enabled to support specific roles depending on how the switch is used in the network. The lanbase-routing template can be enabled to allow the switch to route between VLANs and to support static routing.

Layer 2 EtherChannel   A Layer 2 EtherChannel is one where the individual participating ports are configured as access ports or trunk ports.

Layer 3 EtherChannel   A Layer 3 EtherChannel is one where the individual participating ports are configured as routed ports.

Learning   Learning describes a spanning-tree port state in which the port learns the MAC addresses. The port prepares to participate in frame forwarding and begins to populate the MAC address table.

Lease origination   Lease origination is the origination of a DHCP lease.

Lease renewal   Lease renewal is the renewal of a DHCP lease.

Legacy Inter-VLAN Routing   Legacy inter-VLAN routing refers to inter-VLAN routing where multiple physical router interfaces are required.

Lightweight Access Point Protocol (LWAPP)   Lightweight APs communicate with the WLAN controller using the Lightweight Access Control Point Protocol.

Link aggregation   Link aggregation is the logical bundling of physical ports to create higher-bandwidth links between switches.

Link Aggregation Protocol (LACP)   LACP is an IEEE 802.3ad–defined protocol used for link aggregation.

Link type   The link type provides a categorization for each port participating in RSTP by using the duplex mode on the port. Depending on what is attached to each port, two different link types can be identified: point-to-point and shared.

Linksys Smart Wi-Fi   Linksys Smart Wi-Fi is the GUI used to configure a Linksys router.

listening   In the original implementation of spanning tree, a port can be classified as being in the listening state. In this state, the port listens for the path to the root. Spanning tree has determined that the port can participate in frame forwarding according to the BPDU frames that the switch has received thus far. At this point, the switch port not only receives BPDU frames, but it also transmits its own BPDU frames and informs adjacent switches that the switch port is preparing to participate in the active topology.

M

M flag   The Managed Address Configuration flag in IPv6 RA messages.

MAC address filtering   MAC address filtering permits or denies association with an AP based on the MAC address of the host.

MAC address flooding   As frames arrive on switch ports, the source MAC addresses are recorded in the MAC address table. If an entry exists for the MAC address, the switch forwards the frame to the correct port. If the MAC address does not exist in the MAC address table, the switch floods the frame out of every port on the switch, except the port where the frame was received.

MAC address table   The MAC address table on a Cisco switch contains the port–to–MAC address mappings for devices connected to the switch.

man-in-the-middle (MITM)   An attack in which the attacker is able to read, insert, and modify at will messages between two endpoints without either party being aware that the data path has been compromised.

Management Frame   Management frames are wireless frames used in the maintenance of communication, such as finding, authenticating, and associating with an AP.

Management VLAN   The management VLAN is the VLAN that contains the IP address of the switch used for remote access.

manual allocation   In DHCPv4, manual allocation occurs when the administrator assigns a preallocated IPv4 address to the client, and DHCPv4 communicates only the IPv4 address to the device.

Meraki Cloud Controller (MCC)   The MCC provides centralized management, optimization, and monitoring of a Meraki WLAN system. The MCC is not an appliance that must be purchased and installed to manage wireless APs; rather, the MCC is a cloud-based service that constantly monitors, optimizes, and reports the behavior of the network.

message integrity check (MIC)   Part of the IEEE 802.11i standard. MIC is an 8-byte field placed between the data portion of an IEEE 802.11 frame and the 4-byte ICV (Integrity Check Value). The algorithm that implements MIC is known as *Michael*; Michael also implements a frame counter, which discourages replay attacks.

Mixed mode   Mixed mode is a configuration setting on an AP that allows multiple standards to be implemented for client wireless access.

Mobility   Mobility is the ability to connect from any location and at any time, and the ability to roam while staying connected.

Modular switch   Modular configuration switches come with chassis that allow for the installation of different numbers of modular line cards.

Modularity   Modularity refers to the ability to allow seamless network expansion and integrated service enablement on an on-demand basis.

multilayer switch   A multilayer switch filters and forwards packets based on OSI Layer 2 through Layer 7 information at wire speed by utilizing dedicated hardware that stores data structures mirroring routing table, ARP table, and ACL information.

Multilayer switching (inter-VLAN Routing) Multilayer switching is a generic term referring to the high-speed forwarding of data traffic between distinct VLANs. Multilayer switching requires a combination of dedicated software and hardware technologies to be implemented on the switch.

multiple input/multiple output (MIMO) MIMO technology, used in IEEE 802.11n wireless devices, splits a high-data-rate stream into multiple lower-rate streams and broadcasts them simultaneously over the available radios and antennas. This allows for a theoretical maximum data rate of 248 Mbps.

Multiple Instance Spanning Tree Protocol (MISTP)   A prestandard version of MSTP used on Catalyst 6000 family switches running CatOS.

Multiple Spanning Tree (MST) Multiple Spanning Tree (MST) is an IEEE standard, specified by IEEE 802.1s. MST is distinguished by the flexibility to choose which VLANs participate in a given instance of spanning tree.

Multiple Spanning Tree Protocol (MSTP) MSTP, introduced as IEEE 802.1s, is an evolution of IEEE 802.1D STP and IEEE 802.1w (RSTP). MSTP enables multiple VLANs to be mapped to the same spanning-tree instance, reducing the number of instances needed to support a large number of VLANs.

N

native VLAN A native VLAN is assigned to an IEEE 802.1Q trunk port. An IEEE 802.1Q trunk port supports tagged and untagged traffic coming from many VLANs. The 802.1Q trunk port places untagged traffic on the native VLAN. Native VLANs are set out in the IEEE 802.1Q specification to maintain backward compatibility with untagged traffic common to legacy LAN scenarios. A native VLAN serves as a common identifier on opposing ends of a trunk link. It is a security best practice to define a native VLAN to be a dummy VLAN distinct from all other VLANs defined in the switched LAN. The native VLAN is not used for any traffic in the switched network.

Network Time Protocol (NTP) Network Time Protocol (NTP) is a protocol that is used to synchronize the clocks of computer systems over packet-switched, variable-latency data networks. NTP allows network devices to synchronize their time settings with an NTP server. A group of NTP clients that obtain time and date information from a single source will have more consistent time settings.

O

O flag The Other Configuration flag in IPv6 RA messages.

Omnidirectional Wi-Fi antenna Factory Wi-Fi gear often uses basic dipole antennas, also referred to as "rubber duck" designs, similar to those used on walkie-talkie radios. Omnidirectional antennas provide 360-degree coverage and are ideal in open office areas, hallways, conference rooms, and outside areas.

On mode (LACP) This On mode forces an interface to channel without LACP. Interfaces configured in the On mode do not exchange LACP packets.

On mode (PAgP) This On mode forces an interface to channel without PAgP. Interfaces configured in the On mode do not exchange PAgP packets.

Open authentication Fundamentally, open authentication is NULL authentication, where the wireless client says "authenticate me" and the AP responds with "yes." Open authentication provides wireless connectivity to any wireless device and should only be used in situations where security is of no concern.

orthogonal frequency division multiplexing (OFDM) A modulation technique used with IEEE 802.11g and IEEE 802.11a.

P

passive mode   In passive mode, an AP openly advertises its service periodically, but continually sends broadcast beacon frames containing the SSID, supported standards, and security settings. The primary purpose of the beacon is to allow wireless clients to learn which networks and APs are available in a given area, thereby allowing them to choose which network and AP to use.

path cost   The cumulative STP cost from a device to the root bridge; it is a function of the bandwidths of the individual links connecting the device to the root bridge.

Penetration testing   Penetration testing is a simulated attack against the network to determine how vulnerable it would be in a real attack. This allows a network administrator to identify weaknesses within the configuration of networking devices and make changes to make the devices more resilient to attacks.

Personal Hotspot   Personal Hotspot is an iPhone feature that enables other devices to authenticate and associate with the smart phone.

Personal security mode   WPA2-Personal security mode is recommended with wireless-N networks for best performance.

point-to-point link type   In an RSTP topology, nonedge ports are categorized into two link types: point-to-point and shared. The link type is automatically determined but can be overwritten with an explicit port configuration. Point-to-point link types are used except on links connected to a shared multiaccess half-duplex environment.

Port-channel interface   A port-channel interface is a logical interface on a Cisco switch representing an EtherChannel bundle.

Port Aggregation Protocol (PAgP)   PAgP is a Cisco-proprietary protocol used for link aggregation.

port cost   The spanning-tree port cost is a measure assigned on a per-link basis in a switched LAN; it is determined by the link bandwidth, with a higher bandwidth giving a lower port cost.

Port density   Port density refers to the capacity of a network switch to connect a given number of devices.

Port role   In spanning tree, port role describes the port's relation in the network to the root bridge. Possible roles are root, designated, alternate, backup, and disabled.

Port security   Port security limits the number of valid MAC addresses allowed on a port. The MAC addresses of legitimate devices are allowed access, while other MAC addresses are denied. Port security can be configured to allow one or more MAC addresses.

Port state   In spanning tree, the port state determines the functionality of the port with regard to forwarding BPDU frames, forwarding data frames, and learning MAC addresses.

Portable Hotspot   Portable Hotspot is an Android smart phone feature that enables other devices to authenticate and associate with the smart phone.

PortFast   A Cisco Catalyst switch technology. When a switch port configured as an access port is configured with PortFast, the port transitions from the blocking to the forwarding state immediately, bypassing the usual STP listening and learning states. PortFast is used on ports that are connected to end devices, such as workstations, servers, and printers. If an interface configured with PortFast receives a BPDU frame, spanning tree can put the port into the blocking state using a feature called BPDU guard.

Power management   Power management is a subfield in the Frame Control field of a wireless frame that indicates whether the sending device is in active mode or power-save mode.

Power over Ethernet (PoE)   The powering of network devices over Ethernet cable. IEEE 802.3af and Cisco specify two different PoE methods. Cisco power sourcing equipment (PSE) and powered devices (PD) support both PoE methods.

pre-shared key (PSK)   A key used in various encryption schemes whereby the opposing ends of a connection share the knowledge of a secret key used to encrypt and decrypt the data. PSK is also an alternative method for authentication in a network that does not have a RADIUS server.

Private VLAN (PVLAN) Edge   The PVLAN Edge feature, also known as protected ports, ensures that there is no exchange of unicast, broadcast, or multicast traffic between the ports on the switch configured with this feature.

Probe request frame   A probe request frame is sent from a wireless client when it requires information from another wireless client.

Probe response frame   A probe response frame is sent from an AP containing capability information, such as the supported data rates, after receiving a probe request frame.

Protect   With port security configured on a port with the protect violation mode, when the number of secure MAC addresses reaches the limit allowed on the port, packets with unknown source addresses are dropped until a sufficient number of secure MAC addresses are removed, or the number of maximum allowable addresses is increased. There is no notification that a security violation has occurred.

Protected Port   A protected port is a port configured with the Private VLAN (PVLAN) Edge feature.

Protocol Version   The Protocol Version of a wireless Frame Control field provides the current version of the 802.11 protocol used. Receiving devices use this value to determine whether the version of the protocol of the received frame is supported.

PVST+ (Per-VLAN Spanning Tree+)   This is a Cisco enhancement of the original 802.1D standard that provides a separate 802.1D spanning-tree instance for each VLAN configured in the network.

R

radio frequency (RF)   A generic term referring to frequencies that correspond to radio transmissions. Cable TV, WLANs, and broadband networks use RF technology.

radio resource management (RRM)   RRM monitors the RF band for activity and access point load. An access point that is busier than normal alerts the administrator of possible unauthorized traffic.

Rapid Per-VLAN Spanning Tree Plus (Rapid PVST+)   A Cisco implementation of the Rapid Spanning Tree Protocol (RSTP). It supports one instance of RSTP for each VLAN.

Rapid Spanning Tree Protocol (RSTP)   RSTP, specified by IEEE 802.1w, is a dramatic improvement to IEEE 802.1D, providing very fast spanning-tree convergence on a link-by-link basis using a proposal-and-agreement process independent of timers.

RC4   RC4 is a legacy encryption method employing a static key.

Reassociation request frame   A wireless client sends a reassociation request when it drops from range of the currently associated AP and finds another AP with a stronger signal. The new AP coordinates the forwarding of any information that might still be contained in the buffer of the previous AP.

Reassociation response frame   An AP sends a reassociation response frame containing the acceptance or rejection to a device reassociation request frame. The frame includes information required for association, such as the association ID and supported data rates.

Remote Authentication Dial-In User Service (RADIUS)   An authentication protocol for controlling access to network resources within an IEEE 802.1x framework. RADIUS is commonly used by ISPs, enterprise networks, and corporations managing access to Internet or internal networks across an array of access technologies, including modems, DSL, wireless, and VPNs.

request to send/clear to send (RTS/CTS)   A feature used in the CSMA/CA media access method of WLANs to allow a negotiation between a client and an access point without collisions.

Resiliency   Resiliency is a networking principle that describes to what extent a network is "always on."

Restrict   With port security, when the number of secure MAC addresses reaches the limit allowed on the port, packets with unknown source addresses are dropped until a sufficient number of secure MAC addresses are removed, or the number of maximum allowable addresses is increased. In this mode, there is a notification that a security violation has occurred.

RF jamming   RF jamming describes accidental interference on a wireless network. A DoS attack using RF jamming can be purposely initiated.

rogue access point/rogue AP   An access point, placed on a WLAN, that is used to interfere with normal network operation, capture client data, or gain access to servers. A rogue access point is an unauthorized AP accessing the WLAN.

root bridge   The root of a spanning-tree topology. A root bridge exchanges topology information with other bridges in a spanning-tree topology to notify all other bridges in the network when topology changes are required; this prevents loops and provides a measure of defense against link failure.

root port   The unique port on a nonroot bridge that has the lowest path cost to the root bridge. Every nonroot bridge in an STP topology must elect a root port. The root port on a switch is used for communication between the switch and the root bridge.

Routed port   A routed port is a physical Layer 3 interface on a switch similar to a physical interface on a Cisco IOS router.

router-on-a-stick (inter-VLAN Routing)   A term used to describe the topology of a Layer 2 switch trunked to an interface on a router for the purposes of inter-VLAN routing. In this topology, the router interface is configured with one logical subinterface for each VLAN.

Router Advertisement (RA)   RA messages are sent by routers to provide addressing information to clients configured to obtain their IPv6 addresses automatically. The RA message includes the prefix and prefix length of the local segment. A client uses this information to create its own IPv6 global unicast address. A router sends an RA message periodically, or in response to an RS message. By default, Cisco routers send RA messages every 200 seconds. RA messages are always sent to the IPv6 all-nodes multicast address FF02::1.

Router Solicitation (RS)   When a client is configured to obtain its addressing information automatically using Stateless Address Autoconfiguration (SLAAC), the client sends an RS message to the router. The RS message is sent to the IPv6 all-routers multicast address.

S

Satellite broadband   Satellite broadband is a type of wireless broadband that provides network access to remote sites through the use of a directional satellite dish that is aligned with a specific geostationary Earth orbit satellite.

SDM template   The Cisco Switch Database Manager (SDM) provides multiple templates for the 2960 switch. The templates can be enabled to support specific roles depending on how the switch is used in the network.

Second Generation (2G)   2G is the second generation of cellular/mobile broadband, first available in 1991. 2G includes GSM, CDMA, and TDMA.

Secure MAC address   A secure MAC address is a MAC address that has been secured with port security. There are static, dynamic, and sticky secure MAC addresses.

Secure Shell (SSH)   Secure Shell (SSH) is a protocol that provides a secure (encrypted) management connection to a remote device. SSH should replace Telnet for management connections.

Security audit   A security audit reveals the type of information an attacker can gather simply by monitoring network traffic.

Security mode   Refers to the wireless security parameter settings, such as WEP, WPA, or WPA2. Normally the best practice is to enable the highest security level supported.

service set identifier (SSID)   A code attached to all packets on a wireless network to identify each packet as part of that network. The code is a case-sensitive text string that consists of a maximum of 32 alphanumeric characters. All wireless devices attempting to communicate with each other must share the same SSID. Apart from identifying each packet, the SSID also serves to uniquely identify a group of wireless network devices used in a given service set.

Shared key authentication   Shared key authentication is a technique based on a key that is pre-shared between the client and the AP.

shared link type   Nonedge ports are categorized into two link types: point-to-point and shared. The link type is automatically determined but can be overwritten with an explicit port configuration. The shared link type is associated with ports connecting to a shared multiaccess half-duplex environment.

Shutdown   In this (default) violation mode, a port security violation causes the interface to immediately become error-disabled and turns off the port LED. It increments the violation counter. When a secure port is in the error-disabled state, it can be brought out of this state by entering the **shutdown** and **no shutdown** interface configuration mode commands.

Small form-factor pluggable (SFP)   Fixed-configuration switches typically have options for up to four additional ports for small form-factor pluggable (SFP) devices. SFP devices enable connections that are often higher bandwidth than the fixed ports on the same switch.

Small Office/Home Office (SOHO)   SOHO is an acronym for small office/home office.

spanning-tree algorithm (STA)   Spanning-tree algorithm describes the algorithm used by the original implementation of spanning tree created by Radia Perlman.

Spanning-tree load balancing   Spanning-tree load balancing leverages multiple root bridges to handle traffic for distinct groups of VLANs.

Split MAC   Split MAC is used with LWAPP. The APs making up an ESS are split into two component types: the LWAPP AP and the WLC. These are linked through the LWAPP protocol across a network to provide the same functionality of radio services, as well as bridging of client traffic, in a package that is simpler to deploy and manage than individual APs connected to a common network.

Spoofed disconnect attack   A spoofed disconnect attack occurs when an attacker sends a series of "disassociate" commands to all wireless clients within a BSS. These commands cause all clients to disconnect. When disconnected, the wireless clients immediately try to reassociate, which creates a burst of traffic. The attacker continues sending disassociate frames and the cycle repeats itself.

SSID cloaking   APs and some wireless routers allow the SSID beacon frame to be disabled. Wireless clients must manually identify the SSID to connect to the network.

Stackable switch   Stackable configuration switches can be interconnected using a special cable that provides high-bandwidth throughput between the switches. Cisco StackWise technology allows the interconnection of up to nine switches. Switches can be stacked one on top of the other with cables connecting the switches in a daisy-chain fashion. The stacked switches effectively operate as a single larger switch.

Standby router   Hot Standby Router Protocol (HSRP) is used in a group of routers for selecting an active device and a standby device. In a group of device interfaces, the active device is the device that is used for routing packets; the standby device is the device that takes over when the active device fails, or when preset conditions are met. The function of the HSRP standby router is to monitor the operational status of the HSRP group and to quickly assume packet-forwarding responsibility if the active router fails.

Stateful DHCPv6   Stateful DHCPv6 (DHCPv6 only) is very similar to DHCPv4. With stateful DHCPv6, an RA message informs the client not to use the information in the RA message. All addressing information and configuration information must be obtained from a stateful DHCPv6 server. This is known as stateful DHCPv6 because the DHCPv6 server maintains IPv6 state information.

Stateless Address Autoconfiguration (SLAAC)   SLAAC is a method in which a device can obtain an IPv6 global unicast address without the services of a DHCPv6 server. At the core of SLAAC is ICMPv6. ICMPv6 is similar to ICMPv4 but includes additional functionality and is a much more robust protocol. SLAAC uses ICMPv6 Router Solicitation and Router Advertisement messages to provide addressing and other configuration information that would normally be provided by a DHCP server.

Stateless DHCPv6   Stateless DHCPv6 leverages both RAs and DHCPv6. The client is informed to use the information in the RA message for addressing, but additional configuration parameters are available from a DHCPv6 server. Using the prefix and prefix length in the RA message, along with EUI-64 or a randomly generated IID, the client creates its IPv6 global unicast address.

Static secure MAC address   Static secure MAC addresses are manually configured on a port by using the **switchport port-security mac-address** *mac-address* interface configuration mode command. MAC addresses configured in this way are stored in the address table and are added to the running configuration on the switch.

Station (STA)   STA is an abbreviation for station or end station. It is also an abbreviation for spanning-tree algorithm.

Sticky secure MAC address   Sticky secure MAC addresses can be dynamically learned or manually configured. They are stored in the address table and added to the running configuration.

store-and-forward switching   A technique in which frames are completely processed before being forwarded out the appropriate port. This processing includes calculating the CRC and checking the destination address. In addition, frames must be temporarily stored until network resources are available to forward the message.

subinterface   A virtual interface associated with a single physical interface on a router.

Super high frequency (SHF)   5 GHz. SHF pertains to IEEE 802.11a/n/ac/ad.

Switch database manager (SDM)   Cisco SDM provides multiple templates for the 2960 switch. The templates can be enabled to support specific roles depending on how the switch is used in the network.

Switch spoofing attack   Switch spoofing is a type of VLAN hopping attack that works by taking advantage of an incorrectly configured trunk port. By default, trunk ports have access to all VLANs and pass traffic for multiple VLANs across the same physical link, generally between switches. In a switch spoofing attack, the attacker takes advantage of the fact that the default configuration of the switch port is dynamic auto. The network attacker configures a system to spoof itself as a switch. By tricking a switch into thinking that another switch is attempting to form a trunk, an attacker can gain access to all the VLANs allowed on the trunk port.

switch virtual interface (SVI)   A Layer 3 logical interface associated with a specific virtual LAN (VLAN). You need to configure an SVI for a VLAN if you want to route between VLANs or to provide IP host connectivity to the switch. By default, an SVI is created for VLAN 1 on a Catalyst switch.

T

Temporal Key Integrity Protocol (TKIP)   Also referred to as Temporary Key Integrity Protocol, TKIP was designed by the IEEE 802.11i task group and the Wi-Fi Alliance as a solution to replace WEP without requiring the replacement of legacy hardware. This was necessary because the breaking of WEP had left Wi-Fi networks without viable link-layer security, and a solution was required for already deployed hardware. The Wi-Fi Alliance endorsed TKIP under the name Wi-Fi Protected Access (WPA). The IEEE also endorsed TKIP.

Tethering   Tethering refers to when a smart phone or tablet with cellular data access is enabled to create a personal hotspot.

Third Generation (3G)   3G is the third generation of cellular/mobile broadband and includes UMTS, CDMA2000, EDGE, and HSPA+.

ToDS   ToDS indicates that a frame is going to the distribution system (DS) and is only used in data frames of wireless clients associated with an AP.

Top-down troubleshooting   With top-down troubleshooting, one starts with end-user applications and moves down through the layers of the OSI model until finding the cause of the problem. One tests end-user applications of an end system before tackling the more specific networking pieces. Use this approach for simpler problems or when the problem is likely with a piece of software.

Traffic flow analysis   Traffic flow analysis is the process of measuring the bandwidth usage on a network and then analyzing the data for performance tuning, capacity planning, and making hardware improvement decisions. Analyzing the various traffic sources and their impact on the network allows you to more accurately tune and upgrade the network to achieve the best possible performance.

Tunneled Direct Link Setup (TDLS)   TDLS is a type of Wi-Fi certification for automatic creation of secure direct links between devices after they access a Wi-Fi network.

U

Ultra High Frequency (UHF)   2.4 GHz. UHF pertains to IEEE 802.11b/g/n/ad.

Unlicensed National Information Infrastructure (UNII)   UNII is a regulatory body governing the allocation and use of frequency bands in wireless networking.

User VLAN   A user VLAN is a data VLAN that is dedicated to carrying user traffic.

V

Very Low Frequency (VLF)   3 kHz to 30 kHz. VLF is used for radio navigation, submarine communication, and wireless heart rate monitors.

Violation mode   Port security has three violation modes: protect, restrict, and shutdown.

Virtual IP address   A virtual IP address is an IP address configured in an FHRP design that serves as a default gateway for the hosts on the network.

virtual LAN (VLAN)   A group of hosts with a common set of requirements that communicate as if they were attached to the same wire, regardless of their physical location. A VLAN has the same attributes as a physical LAN, but it allows for end stations to be grouped together even if they are not located on the same LAN segment. Network reconfiguration can be done through software instead of physically relocating devices.

Virtual MAC address   A virtual MAC address is a MAC address used in an FHRP design that serves as the MAC address associated with the virtual IP address of the virtual default gateway.

Virtual Redundancy Router Protocol (VRRP)   VRRP is a nonproprietary election protocol that dynamically assigns responsibility for one or more virtual routers to the VRRP routers on an IPv4 LAN. A VRRP router is configured to run the VRRP protocol in conjunction with one or more other routers attached to a LAN. In a VRRP configuration, one router is elected as the virtual router master, with the other routers acting as backups, in case the virtual router master fails.

Virtual router   A virtual router is a generic term describing a virtual device referenced in an FHRP implementation, serving as a default gateway for the hosts on the network.

VLAN trunk   An Ethernet point-to-point link between an Ethernet switch interface and an Ethernet interface on another networking device, such as a router or a switch, carrying the traffic of multiple VLANs over the singular link. A VLAN trunk allows you to extend the VLANs across an entire switched LAN.

Voice messaging   Voice messaging refers to voicemail.

voice VLAN   Specialized Catalyst switch VLANs with an accompanying Catalyst CLI command set. Voice VLANs are designed for and dedicated to the transmission of voice traffic involving Cisco IP Phones or Cisco softphones. QoS configurations are applied to voice VLANs to prioritize voice traffic.

W

Wi-Fi Alliance   The Wi-Fi Alliance owns the trademark to Wi-Fi. The Wi-Fi Alliance is a global, nonprofit, industry trade association devoted to promoting the growth and acceptance of wireless technology.

Wi-Fi Antenna   Wi-Fi uses omnidirectional, directional, and Yagi antennas.

Wi-Fi Direct   Wi-Fi Direct is a technology used for devices to communicate wirelessly in ad hoc mode.

Wi-Fi Miracast   Wi-Fi Miracast is a technology used to seamlessly display video between devices wirelessly.

Wi-Fi Multimedia (WMM)   Wi-Fi Multimedia is comprised of wireless devices that are Wi-Fi certified.

Wi-Fi Passpoint   Wi-Fi Passpoint is used to simplify securely connecting to Wi-Fi hotspot networks.

Wi-Fi Protected Access (WPA and WPA2)   A class of systems to secure wireless LANs. It was created in response to several serious weaknesses that researchers had found in the previous system, Wired Equivalent Privacy (WEP). WPA implements the majority of the IEEE 802.11i standard and was intended as an intermediate measure to take the place of WEP while IEEE 802.11i was prepared. WPA is specifically designed to also work with pre-WPA wireless network interface cards (through firmware upgrades), but not necessarily with first-generation wireless access points. WPA2 implements the full standard and supports AES encryption (WPA does not support AES).

Wi-Fi Protected Setup (WPS)   WPS is used to simplify wireless connections for devices.

Wi-Fi radio   A Wi-Fi radio is a Wi-Fi antenna (transmitter and receiver).

WiGig   WiGig is another name for IEEE 802.1ad, which offers theoretical speeds up to 7 Gb/s.

Wired Equivalent Privacy (WEP)   An algorithm to secure IEEE 802.11 wireless networks. Wireless networks broadcast messages using radio frequencies and are more susceptible to eavesdropping than wired networks. WEP, introduced in 1999, was intended to provide confidentiality comparable to that of a traditional wired network.

Wireless Fidelity (Wi-Fi)   Wi-Fi refers to devices and technologies certified by the Wi-Fi Alliance.

Wireless LAN (WLAN)   A LAN with wireless access points, together with the devices supporting them and supported by them.

Wireless LAN Controller (WLC)   A wireless LAN controller is used with lightweight APs to seamlessly provide roaming wireless access by clients in the range of the APs bound to the WLC. In this topology, the APs act somewhat like dumb terminals.

Wireless network interface card (NIC)   The device that makes a client station capable of sending and receiving RF signals is a wireless NIC. Some access points also have removable wireless NICs.

Wireless Personal-Area Network (WPAN)   A WPAN operates in the range of a few feet. Bluetooth and Wi-Fi Direct–enabled devices are used in WPANs.

Wireless powerline adapter   Wireless powerline adapters enable devices to connect directly to the network through electrical outlets.

Wireless router   A wireless router is a router with AP functionality.

Wireless Wide-Area Network (WWAN)   WWANs operate in the range of miles, such as a metropolitan area, cellular hierarchy, or even intercity links through microwave relays.

WMM-Power Save   WMM-Power Save uses IEEE-based mechanisms to save power.

Worldwide Interoperability for Microwave Access (WiMAX)   WiMAX is an IEEE 802.16 WWAN standard that provides wireless cellular broadband access of up to 30 miles (50 km) in a point-to-multipoint topology. WiMAX is an alternative to cable and DSL broadband connections. Mobility was added to WiMAX in 2005 and can now be used by service providers to provide cellular broadband. WiMAX supports speeds up to 1 Gb.

Y

Yagi antenna   A Yagi antenna is a type of directional radio antenna that can be used for long-distance Wi-Fi networking. These antennas are typically used to extend the range of outdoor hotspots in a specific direction, or to reach an outbuilding.

Index

C

D

U-V

X-Y-Z